Foul Means

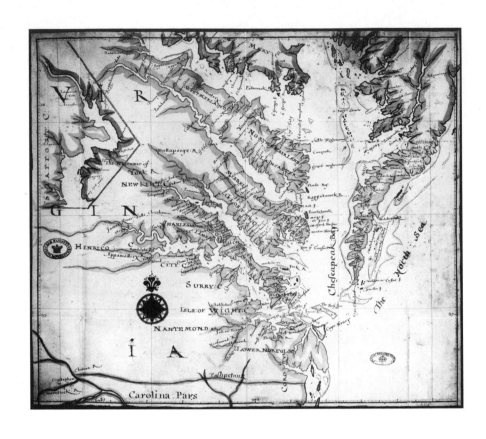

Plate 1. Map of Virginia and Maryland. 1681. MPG 1/375.
Courtesy, The National Archives, Public Record Office,
Kew, Richmond, Surrey

Foul Means

*The Formation of a Slave Society
in Virginia, 1660-1740*

Anthony S. Parent, Jr.

Published for the Omohundro Institute of Early
American History and Culture, Williamsburg, Virginia,
by the University of North Carolina Press,
Chapel Hill and London

The Omohundro Institute of Early American History
and Culture is sponsored jointly by the
College of William and Mary and the Colonial Williamsburg Foundation.
On November 15, 1996, the Institute adopted the present name
in honor of a bequest from Malvern H. Omohundro, Jr.

Manufactured in the United States of America

Library of Congress Cataloging-in-Publication Data
Parent, Anthony S.
Foul means : the formation of a slave society in Virginia, 1660–1740 /
Anthony S. Parent, Jr.
p. cm.
Includes bibliographical references (p.) and index.
ISBN 0-8078-2813-0 (cloth : alk. paper) —
ISBN 0-8078-5486-7 (pbk. : alk. paper)
1. Slavery—Virginia—History—17th century.   2. Slavery—Virginia—
History—18th century.   3. Plantation life—Virginia—History.   4. Plantation
owners—Virginia—Social conditions.   5. Slaves—Virginia—Social conditions.
6. Elite (Social sciences)—Virginia—History.   7. Social conflict—Virginia—
History.   8. Virginia—Race relations.   9. Virginia—Social conditions—
17th century.   10. Virginia—Social conditions—18th century.   I. Omohundro
Institute of Early American History & Culture.   II. Title.
E445.V8 P37   2003
326'.09755'09032—dc21
2002155801

The paper in this book meets the guidelines for permanence
and durability of the Committee on Production Guidelines for
Book Longevity of the Council on Library Resources.

This volume received indirect support from an unrestricted
book publication grant awarded to the Institute by the L. J. Skaggs
and Mary C. Skaggs Foundation of Oakland, California.

cloth   07   06   05   04   03   5   4   3   2   1
paper   07   06   05   04   03   5   4   3   2   1

For Gigi

Acknowledgments

This book is a long time coming. I owe a host of friends, scholars, institutions, and family.

I thank my colleagues in the Department of History and deans Thomas Mullen, Paul D. Escott, and Gordon A. Melson at Wake Forest University for their patience and support. My research, writing, and travel were supported by university funds: Archie Fund Grant (1990), Junior Faculty Leave (1992), and a Research and Publication Fund Grant (1990, 1998). Janice Walker typed an early draft of the manuscript, and, using her vast technical skills, Jamila Ferguson Griffey entered quantitative data; the departmental Griffin Fund paid both Walker and Griffey.

I have been blessed with the tandem effort of two excellent editors, Fredrika J. Teute (Editor of Publications) and Virginia L. Montijo (Senior Editor of Publications) at the Omohundro Institute of Early American History and Culture. I owe my first debt to Teute for selecting my manuscript, which began a ten-year journey of renewal and affirmation that has become this book. Teute's and Montijo's comments, queries, and suggestions have forced me to rethink every word and thought in this book. It would be a much poorer book without their assistance.

Three historians have read various drafts of the manuscript. Gerald Horne read this manuscript with a critical eye, pointing out areas that needed elaboration. Peter Wood, sensitive to the wider literature, encouraged me to broaden my approach. David Ammerman gave the manuscript an incisive reading at a critical juncture in its history.

I have benefited from presenting chapters of this book to the Early American Thesis Seminar, hosted by Gary B. Nash, who directed my dissertation at the University of California at Los Angeles (UCLA), the Triangle Early American History Seminar at the National Humanities Center, and the Poteat Humanities Club and the Social Science Research Seminar at Wake Forest University. Reginald Butler of the Carter G. Woodson Institute at the University of Virginia and Sally Gant of the Museum of

Early Southern Decorative Arts (MESDA), Old Salem, each invited me three times to present work at their Chesapeake summer seminars.

I have used the collections, images, and the expertise of the staffs at the Colonial Williamsburg Foundation, the Huntington Library, Art Collections, and Botanical Gardens, the Manuscript Division of the Library of Congress, the Earl Gregg Swem Library at the College of William and Mary, the Charles E. Young Research Library at UCLA, MESDA, the Virginia Historical Society, the Library of Virginia, the Alderman Library at the University of Virginia, the Z. Smith Reynolds Library at Wake Forest University, the Granger Collection, the Public Record Office, United Kingdom, the Cushing Memorial Library at Texas A&M University, the Reeves Center at Washington and Lee University, Archives and Special Collections at the University of California at Riverside, and the Mashantucket Pequot Museum and Research Center. Acknowledgment is made to these institutions and to Dell Upton of the University of Virginia for permission to quote material or to use images from their collections at a discounted academic rate.

I owe my greatest debt to my family. My parents Anthony S. Parent (deceased) and Marian Parent gave me unconditional love and the necessary foundation to build a life. My sons Anthony and Frederick have grown up with this book. I thank them for accepting without complaint this rival sibling competing for their father's time. Gigi Parent, my wife, has sustained me through this work and helped me more than anyone else. At no time did she falter in her belief that I would finish this book, and her faith, more than anything else, enabled me to press forward. This book is dedicated with love to Gigi.

Contents

Illustrations

TABLES

Abbreviations

BL   William Blathwayt Collection, Colonial Williamsburg
      Foundation, Williamsburg, Va.
BR   Brock Collection, Huntington Library, San Marino, Calif.
BT   Board of Trade
CO   Colonial Office, Public Record Office, London
CP   Nell Marion Nugent, ed., *Cavaliers and Pioneers: Abstracts of
      Virginia Land Patents and Grants, 1623–1800,* 7 vols.
      (Richmond, Va., 1934–1980)
CWCJS Philip L. Barbour, ed., *The Complete Works of Captain John
      Smith (1580–1631),* 3 vols. (Chapel Hill, N.C., 1986)
CWF   Colonial Williamsburg Foundation, Williamsburg, Va.
EJCCV H. R. McIlwaine, ed., *Executive Journals of the Council of
      Colonial Virginia,* 6 vols. (Richmond, Va., 1925–1966)
FPP   Fulham Palace Papers, Lambeth Palace Library, London
HL   Huntington Library, San Marino, Calif.
JHB   John Pendleton Kennedy and H. R. McIlwaine, eds., *Journals
      of the House of Burgesses of Virginia, 1619–1776* (Richmond,
      Va., 1905–1915)
LC   Library of Congress, Washington, D.C.
LJCCV H. R. McIlwaine, ed., *Legislative Journals of the Council of
      Colonial Virginia,* 3 vols. (Richmond, Va., 1918–1919)
MCGC H. R. McIlwaine, ed., *Minutes of the Council and General
      Court of Colonial Virginia, 1622–1632, 1670–1676* (Richmond,
      Va., 1924)
PC   Privy Council Office, Public Record Office, London
PRO   Public Record Office, London
SAL   William Waller Hening, *The Statutes at Large; Being a
      Collection of All the Laws of Virginia, from the First Session of
      the Legislature, in the Year 1619,* 13 vols. (Richmond, Va.,
      1809–1823)

SPG   Society for the Propagation of the Gospel in Foreign Parts
ST   Stowe Collection, Huntington Library, San Marino, Calif.
T   Treasury, Public Record Office, London
UCLA   University of California at Los Angeles
UVA   University of Virginia, Charlottesville
VCRP   Virginia Colonial Records Project (CWF, UVA, VHS, VSL)
VHS   Virginia Historical Society, Richmond
VMHB *Virginia Magazine of History and Biography*
VSL   The Library of Virginia, Richmond
WMQ   *William and Mary Quarterly*

Foul Means

[An] unhappy Effect of Many Negroes, is the necessity of being severe. Numbers make them insolent, and then foul Means must do, what fair will not. We have however nothing like this Inhumanity here, that is practiced in the Islands, and God forbid we ever should. But these base Tempers require to be rid with a taut rein, or they will be apt to throw their Riders. Yet even this is terrible to a good natur'd Man, who must submit to be either a Fool or a Fury. And this will be more our unhappy case, the more the Negroes are increast amongst us.

—William Byrd II to John Perceval, earl of Egmont, July 12, 1736

Introduction

Virginia has meant so much to our national romance of adventurers, first families, and freedom that its reality of slavery jars our historical sensibility. Yet our national narrative cannot breathe freely until slavery and its persistent legacy in racism confront freedom's romance. For this reason, American historians of our generation admire Edmund Morgan's *American Slavery, American Freedom* more than any other monograph. Morgan resuscitated American history by placing black slavery and white freedom as its central paradox. He located its genesis in 1676, with Bacon's Rebellion, when ambitious white men, hungry for land, fanned racism against the Indians into a rebellion against the crown. The recruitment of servants into the rebel ranks frightened the elite. After the rebellion, this fear led the authorities to turn toward racial slavery. By elevating the status of servants and making whites equal, at least racially, white elites had a more docile laboring force in enslaved blacks producing tobacco. Herein lies the rub: enslaved blacks produced the wealth that made possible white freedom in 1776. It is all here—an explanation for American nationalism, Indian removal, white solidarity and racism, the relative absence of class politics, and black exclusion. But is it? In making his prognostication, Morgan leapfrogged a century of history from 1676 to 1776. These questions must be asked: What about this lapse of time? What more can we learn from the pre-Revolutionary generations?[1]

1. Edmund S. Morgan, *American Slavery, American Freedom: The Ordeal of Colonial Virginia* (New York, 1975); Kenneth Cmiel, "History against Itself," *Journal of American History*, LXXXI (1994–1995), 1206; Nathan Irvin Huggins, *Black Odyssey: The African-American Ordeal in Slavery*, 2d rev. ed. (New York, 1990), xi–lxx; Huggins, "The Deforming Mirror of Truth: Slavery and the Master Narrative of American History," and Peter H. Wood, Peter Dimock, and Barbara Clark Smith, "Three Responses," *Radical History*,

This book attempts to fill in part of that historical gap by analyzing the role of slavery in Virginia's social formation from 1660 to 1740, when the Old Dominion assumed its distinctive character. The analysis challenges the generally accepted belief that the shift to racial slavery was an "unthinking decision" on the part of a wide variety of aspiring planters who were responding to market and labor forces. Rather, it contends that a small emerging class of great planters with large landholdings and political connections brought racial slavery to Virginia. To preserve their investment in enslaved laborers, they had to contend with domestic distress, class conflict, and black revolt. Reactions to these tensions led them to buttress their hegemony by articulating an ideology of partriarchism and a strategy of slave proselytism. In other words, during a brief period in the late seventeenth and early eighteenth century, a small but powerful planter class, acting in their short-term interest, gave America its racial dilemma.[2]

This study investigates what Antonio Gramsci calls the dialectics of events and the "inexorable logic of their development" during Virginia's formative years, when it became a highly oppressive and antagonistic slave society. It employs a methodology of class to comprehend slavery's role in the formation of Virginia. Class analysis is a heuristic method that not only unearths the relationship between the slaveholders and the enslaved but also illuminates the totality of the colonized society. The enslaved, forced out of the internal, often intergenerational, conflicts of Africa's history, struggled against the conflicts generated by mercantilism, colonialism, and slavery.[3]

---

no. 49 (Winter 1991), 25–48, 49–59; Theodore W. Allen, *Class Struggle and the Origins of Racial Slavery: The Invention of the White Race* (Hoboken, N.J., 1975); Thomas C. Holt, "Marking: Race, Race-Making, and the Writing of History," *American Historical Review,* C (1995), 1–20; Dorothy Ross, "Grand Narrative in American Historical Writing: From Romance to Uncertainty," ibid., 651–677.

2. Winthrop D. Jordan, *White over Black: American Attitudes toward the Negro, 1550–1812* (Chapel Hill, N.C., 1968), 44–98.

3. Antonio Gramsci, "Real Dialectics" (1921), *Selections from Political Writings, 1921–1926,* ed. and trans. Quintin Hoare (New York, 1978), 15–16. Frederick Douglass saw this dialectic of events in May 1861: "Any attempt now to separate the freedom of the slave from the victory of the Government . . . will be labor lost. The American people and the Government at Washington may refuse to recognize it for a time; but the *'inexorable logic of events'* will force it upon them in the end; that the war now being waged in this land is a war for and against slavery; and that it can never be effectually put down till one or the other of these vital forces is completely destroyed" (Douglass, quoted in James M. McPherson, *The Negro's Civil War: How American Negroes Felt and Acted during the War for the Union* [New York, 1965], 17–18 [emphasis is mine]).

A historical category of social and economic relationships, class and its cultural derivative class consciousness assist analysis of the distribution of power in a society. As determined by the relations of production, a group's status, cultural attributes, and interests flow from economic conditions. The chief classes in society are the owners of the means of production and the actual producers. The friction among classes, as Karl Marx has written, "reveals the innermost secret, the hidden foundation, of the entire social edifice." Class status, amorphous and fluid, can be observed as it changes over time in dialectical tension with productive forces. A class becomes conscious of itself in relation to society as a whole by perceiving its interests based on its particular role in production. Class consciousness is thus constructed from daily experiences; those experiences are then expressed in a variety of political principles and cultivated into strategies for interacting with other classes in society.[4]

* * *

THIS STUDY examines the origins, behavior, and ideology of Virginia's great-planter class, yielding insights into the formation of Virginia's slave society. The gentry's origins are explored in Part I. Their behavior, though assessed throughout the book, comes under scrutiny in Part II, along with black behavior that precipitated white response and conflict. Ideology is the topic of Part III.

Toward the end of the seventeenth century, an elite evolved, consolidated its power, and fixed itself as an extensive land- and slaveholding class. The great-planter class gained power by organizing land, labor, and trade to serve their interests. They engrossed the land seized from the Powhatans, switched from white servants to enslaved blacks in the labor base, and positioned themselves at the control point in the tobacco and slave trades. Initially, the English eyed cultivated Indian land. They cov-

4. Tom Bottomore, ed., *A Dictionary of Marxist Thought* (Cambridge, Mass., 1983), s.v., "class," "class consciousness." E. P. Thompson has written that class is "an historical phenomenon, unifying a number of disparate and seemingly unconnected events, both in the raw material of experience and in consciousness." "If we stop history at a given point, then there are no classes but simply a multitude of individuals with a multitude of experiences. But if we watch these men over an adequate period of social change, we observe patterns in their relationships, their ideas, and their institutions. Class is defined by men as they live their own history, and, in the end, this is its only definition" (Thompson, *The Making of the English Working Class* [1963; reprint, New York, 1966], 9–11 [quotations on 9, 11]). See also Georg Lukács, *History and Class Consciousness: Studies in Marxist Dialectics,* trans. Rodney Livingstone (Cambridge, Mass., 1971), 50–51.

eted it for the production of their newfound staple tobacco. Indentured labor proved adequate at first, but increasingly the emerging gentry looked toward slavery as a solution to their labor woes. By the turn of the eighteenth century, the English had effectively removed the Indians from the land east of the mountains and had shifted from indentured to enslaved labor. In doing so, mere tobacco planters had turned themselves into great planters. Slavery proved no solution to the troubled economy, for the great planters, saddled with the debt of the slave trade, struggled with low tobacco prices.[5]

Slavery engendered legal, racial, and class conflicts. These topics are presented in Part II by analyzing the tensions generated by petitioners, fugitives, mass assemblies, tobacco rioters, debtors, interlopers, and insurrectionists. Virginia at the turn of the eighteenth century was a fluid place where social prerogative and economic position were not yet locked into place. In seizing Indian land and enslaving blacks, the great planters began to accentuate the racial differences between themselves and darker people. They wrote racial slavery into law. Yet the turn toward slavery generated competition and anxiety. The status of common whites improved in the law as the great planters pressed them into policing blacks. The blacks continued to push for freedom, which was most dramatically demonstrated in the Chesapeake rebellion of 1730. Massive black resistance threatened white control. If whites were generally anxious, owners of large numbers of blacks had even more to lose. At the same time, the great planters perceived a loss of status resulting from a crown indifferent to their objections to maritime regulation, royal appointments, and mercantile intrusion in the tobacco and slave trades. Friction and conflict in white society made the planters fearful of the enslaved, the class they exploited the most. Class status was not a vulgar determination of economic interest; it was spawned by the social and cultural expectations of a burgeoning planter class.

The great planters' cultural ethos of rising expectations was fraught with threats from subalterns at home and mercantile interests abroad. Virginia's elite began in the late 1720s and the 1730s to look for cultural distinctiveness as they became weaker in their dealings with the crown, more dependent on English merchants, challenged by parvenu planters,

---

5. John J. McCusker and Russell R. Menard write: "Close study of the origins, behavior, and ideology of the Chesapeake gentry promises a deepened understanding of the political economy of the tobacco coast" (*The Economy of British America, 1607–1789* [Chapel Hill, N.C., 1985], 139).

anxious in their relations with women, and threatened by blacks. These concerns informed the ideology of patriarchism, discussed in Part III. In strained conditions largely out of their control, the Virginia planters sought to assert their authority and bolster their legitimacy. The great planters invoked an ideal of hierarchical responsibility and obedience to deal with the contradictions ever present in slavery and enslaved blacks' relationship to civil society. The great planters came to see Christianity as a support for patriarchal authority, rather than a marker of English liberty. They began baptizing American-born blacks in the late 1720s and 1730s as a method of controlling them. The enslaved, however, continued to see Christianity as a precursor to their freedom, which they dramatically demonstrated during the Chesapeake rebellion in 1730 when blacks raised the banner of liberty for Christians.[6]

I offer this book as a contribution to a new narrative of American history, rooted in Nathan Irvin Huggins's counsel that "slavery and freedom, white and black, are joined at the hip." The paradox of slavery and freedom, then, was, not that whites were becoming free in the face of black enslavement, but that they began to learn of liberty from the black struggle for freedom. (Perhaps, Samuel Johnson, that is why we hear the loudest yelps for liberty from the drivers of the enslaved.) Rather than project republican reasoning forward and extend liberty to blacks, the great planters retreated to an older ideology—patriarchism—to suppress the strivings of the enslaved. Slave resistance to subordination forced the great planters to defend their own freedom as the antithesis of slavery.[7]

6. As Peter Lake said about participants in the English Civil War who had earlier turned toward patriarchalism, this response was "evidence of a desperate search for ideological and historical bearings in an utterly unfamiliar and deeply menacing set of circumstances." See Lake, review of *The Causes of the English Civil War; The Fall of the British Monarchies; Unrevolutionary England*, by C. S. R. Russell, *Huntington Library Quarterly*, LVII (1994), 193.

7. Huggins, *Black Odyssey*, xliv. As Kenneth A. Lockridge writes, "The Virginia gentry labored constantly at their control of their slaves, a control so total that it became to them the necessary definitional antithesis of their passionate conception of their own freedom"; see Lockridge, *On the Sources of Patriarchal Rage: The Commonplace Books of William Byrd and Thomas Jefferson and the Gendering of Power in the Eighteenth Century* (New York, 1992), 96.

I

Origins

Land, Labor, and Trade

CHAPTER 1

The Landgrab

Three conditions are necessary for the emergence of a slave society, wrote Moses I. Finley: private, concentrated landownership, sufficient development of commodity production and markets, and unavailability of an internal labor supply. "As always," he insisted, "the starting-point is the land." Concentrated land holdings require labor beyond its owners' productive capacity. Yet, before there is a demand for enslaved laborers, the society must develop an exportable commodity; then the internal labor supply must be insufficient to produce that commodity. The English met all three conditions in seventeenth- and eighteenth-century Virginia: they engrossed the land, developed the tobacco trade, and turned to slavery when the internal servant trade proved inadequate.[1]

Possessing the Fruits of Others' Labors

Queen Elizabeth I, delighted with Walter Raleigh's Roanoke expedition in 1584, knighted him and named the land Virginia for herself, the Virgin Queen. This was an odd appellation for the fertile country where the English later made landfall in 1607. Virginia called by this or any other name at the time of European contact was already both fruitful and husbanded. The new settlers soon learned of the intricacy of its estuaries, the fecundity of its soils, the diversity of its flora and fauna, and the activity of its people. They found Virginia well watered by four great rivers and their branches, her life's blood, bearing the names of the people who resided there: the Powhatan (James), the Pamunkey (York), the Patawomeck (Potomac), and the Rappahannock. These rivers flowed from the

---

1. M. I. Finley, *Ancient Slavery and Modern Ideology* (New York, 1980), 86, 132 (quotation).

banks and valleys of the Appalachians, "the Great Mountains," especially the Blue Ridge, in a southeasterly, parallel direction into the Chesapeake *(k'tchisipik),* the "great water." The Algonquian word *rappahannock*— meaning "rise and fall of water"—described all these rivers of the tide-water basin, where, at times in the spring, their flow was so heavy that fresh water could be found up to one hundred miles below the tidal breaks. At other times in July and August, their flow diminished, and the tidewaters backed into the rivers, making the water both salty and brackish.[2]

Virginia then as now could be divided into the tidewater, the piedmont, and the headwaters. The four great rivers up to the fall line and smaller rivers and creeks that flow from marshes and swamps watered the tide-water basin. The soil is "generally of a low, moist and fat Mould," observed Robert Beverley II. Here and there are strips of "cold, hungry, sandy" wet-lands, where huckleberries, cranberries, and chinquapins flourish. Else-where in the tidewater, poplars, pines, cedars, cypresses, sweet gums, and a wide assortment of evergreens, hollies, sweet myrtles, and live oaks crowd together. The contour of the land in the piedmont rising from the fall line to the foothills is flat with slight breaks and bends, but its soil is diverse: its topsoil is either "black, fat, and thick laid" or "looser, lighter, and thin," its foundation gravel, clay, or marl. The ground in the ridges between the rivers and in the middle of the necks is either poor wispy sand or red or white clay. It sustains chestnuts, chinquapins, acorns, and scrub oaks and during the summer months sprouts reedy grasses. Rich soil hugs the rivers, where large oak, walnut, hickory, ash, beech, and poplar trees penetrate its banks. More contrast in the terrain and greater soil variety can be found in the headwaters region. Hills, valleys, and plains jostle with one another; fruit and timber trees mix it up. Low-lying rich ground and marshes, savannalike meadows, and swamplike thickets with towering trees combine to make a majestic, motley landscape.[3]

2. John Smith, *The Generall History of Virginia, the Somer Iles, and New England, with the Names of the Adventurers and Their Adventures* . . . (1623), *CWCJS,* II, 67–68; Smith, *A Map of Virginia; with a Description of the Countrey, the Commodities, People, Government and Religion* (1612), *CWCJS,* I, 145–156; Helen C. Rountree, *The Powhatan Indians of Virginia: Their Traditional Culture* (Norman, Okla., 1989), 18–23, 45; James Hagemann, *The Heritage of Virginia: The Story of Place Names in the Old Dominion,* 2d ed. (Chester, Pa., 1988), 47, 126, 206, 276; Carville V. Earle, "Environment, Disease, and Mortality in Early Virginia," in Thad W. Tate and David L. Ammerman, eds., *The Chesapeake in the Seventeenth Century: Essays on Anglo-American Society* (Chapel Hill, N.C., 1979), 102–103.

3. Robert Beverley, *The History and Present State of Virginia* (1705, 1722), ed. Louis B. Wright (Chapel Hill, N.C., 1947), 117–142 (quotations on 123, 124).

Plate 2. *John Smith,* A Map of Virginia; with a Description of the
Countrey, the Commodities, People, Government and Religion . . . , *1612.*
Courtesy, Virginia Historical Society, Richmond

On this land, about fourteen thousand Algonquian-speakers were organized into thirty self-governing communities, composing the Powhatan
paramount chiefdom, when the English arrived in 1607. Although Captain
John Smith's 1612 *Map of Virginia* impresses one with a natural terrain of
forests, rivers, and hills, Smith was aware of the Powhatans' husbandry
and society. He identified their chiefs' houses and towns, which were their
district capitals—centers of tribute-paying regional chiefdoms governed
by a *werowance* (male) or a *werowansqua* (female). Clearly, in the English
mind the Indians loomed large over the landscape. In one corner of the
map is the *mamanatowick,* or paramount chief, Wahunsenacawh (Powhatan) in council. In another corner is the larger-than-life "picture of the
greatest specimen" that Smith had encountered of the Susquehannock, an
Iroquoian people living above the falls of the Susquehanna River, returning from the hunt armed with bow and mattock.[4]

4. Smith, *Map of Virginia, CWCJS,* I, 140-142, 149-150, 185-190; Rountree, *Powhatan Indians,* 7-15, 46, 114-115.

Plate 3. Algonquian Man, Twenty-Three Years of Age. By Wencelaus Hollar. *1645. Courtesy, Mashantucket Pequot Museum and Research Center, Archives and Special Collections, Mss 12, Mashantucket, Conn.*

The Powhatans were farmers. They divided their land into garden plots near a river or a fresh spring. Most plots ranged from twenty to forty acres, but some were as large as one hundred or two hundred acres. Each household furnished its own female labor to cultivate a plot, retained as community property. The Powhatans communally farmed their largest garden for the werowance. They cultivated vine-born fruit, including muskmelons, watermelons, pumpkins, crooknecks, macocks, and gourds; four varieties of Indian corn, or maize, which ripened at different times of the year; "Kidney-Shaped" peas, beans, red and white potatoes, and tobacco. The Powhatans venerated corn and tobacco. They used corn as their "Staff of Food," celebrating it at their most important harvest festival each year. Unlike the other plants, only the men cultivated the tobacco plants, which they called *uppowoc*. "Great Smoakers," the Indians used tobacco leaves in their sacred rituals, burning it as incense and smoking it in pipes.[5]

When the English arrived in Virginia on Sunday, April 26, 1607, "certaine" Indians, probably the Chickahominys, fired at them that evening with arrows and "Pistoll shot," a remnant of a previous European encounter. They returned fire, foreshadowing the hostility between them. The English settlers, an eclectic assortment of adventurers, gentlemen, and ne'er-do-wells, had come to find gold and a passage to the Indies; they found neither. The London Company of Adventurers had instructed them not to offend the "naturals," yet their very presence proved offensive. Instead of planting gardens to supply their needs, as directed, they idly passed their time bowling in the streets and drinking. As a result, they needed the Indians' corn to keep from starving.[6]

5. Smith, *Generall History, CWCJS*, II, 116; Beverley, *History and Present State of Virginia*, ed. Wright, 143–145; Timothy Silver, *A New Face on the Countryside: Indians, Colonists, and Slaves in South Atlantic Forests, 1500–1800* (Cambridge, 1990), 44; Rountree, *Powhatan Indians*, 46; Kevin J. Hayes, "Defining the Ideal Colonist: Captain John Smith's Revisions from *A True Relation* to the *Proceedings* to the Third Book of the *Generall Historie*," *VMHB*, XCIX (1991), 123–144; John Brickell, *The Natural History of North-Carolina; with an Account of the Trade, Manners, and Customs of the Christian and Indian Inhabitants* (Dublin, 1737), 287.

6. George Percy, "Discourse" (1608?), in Philip L. Barbour, ed., *The Jamestown Voyages under the First Charter, 1606–1609* . . . , 2 vols., Hakluyt Society, 2d Ser., nos. 136–137 (London, 1969), I, 133–135; John Smith, *A True Relation of Such Occurrences and Accidents of Noate as Hath Hapned in Virginia* . . . (1608), *CWCJS*, I, 17, 27; David Freeman Hawke, ed., *Captain John Smith's History of Virginia: A Selection* (Indianapolis, Ind., 1970), xiii; James Axtell, *The Invasion Within: The Contest of Cultures in Colonial North America* (Oxford, 1985), 10–11; Edmund S. Morgan, *American Slavery, American Freedom: The Ordeal of Colonial Virginia* (New York, 1975), 83–84.

Plate 4. Secota. Drawing by John White, engraved by Theodore De Bry. 1588.
Courtesy, Virginia Historical Society, Richmond

Plate 5. Indians Working in Tobacco Fields. *From Johann Neander,*
Tobacologia Medico-Cheirvico-Pharmacevtica *(Leyden, 1622). Courtesy, Earl*
Gregg Swem Library, College of William and Mary, Williamsburg, Va.

Indeed, corn figured significantly in the conflict between the Powhatans and the English. The Powhatans warily traded their corn with the English until Smith precipitated conflict by organizing marauders to intimidate them into giving it to him early in 1609. In one escapade, Smith held a pistol to the head of Opechancanough, werowance of the Pamunkeys, until the Indians paid a ransom of corn for his release. In response, Opechancanough's brother Wahunsenacawh contributed to the "starving time" of the English on Jamestown Island from October 1609 to June 1610 by blocking their boats, thus cutting off their supply of corn. Because of this blockade and the warfare that ensued, the English continued to have great difficulty securing Indian corn.[7]

With this shortage in mind, early in 1614 the London Company sent Captain Samuel Argall—who had already distinguished himself by finding a direct route from England to Virginia—on the *Treasurer* to the upper

7. Smith, *Generall History, CWCJS,* II, 192–203, 231–233; J. Frederick Fausz, "An 'Abundance of Blood Shed on Both Sides': England's First Indian War, 1609–1614," *VMHB,* XCVIII (1990), 20–21, 26–27.

Potomac River. In March, he spied Pocahontas, whom Smith had credited with his reprieve from the order of death given by her father Wahunsenacawh in 1607. Argall made her his hostage (which he would call his "gift" to Virginia) to coerce a peace with Wahunsenacawh. Three months later, the English offered Pocahontas for ransom on the condition that Wahunsenacawh give them "five hundred bushels of Corne, and for ever be friends with us." Yet, not until after a brief skirmish when the English went on the shore of the Pamunkey River, where they "burned all their houses, and spoiled all they . . . could finde," was a peace concluded. It was sealed with the marriage of John Rolfe and Pocahontas on April 5, 1614.[8]

After his marriage, Rolfe turned his attention to the commercial potential of tobacco. He had begun experimenting with Caribbean tobacco (varina) as early as 1611, undoubtedly impressed with Indian production of the crop. By 1617, he had discovered tobacco's marketability, which set off a mania for planting. When Argall returned to Jamestown from England in May of that year, he found not only "the market-place, and streets, and all other spare places planted with Tobacco" but also, to his anxiety, "the Colonie Dispersed all about, planting Tobacco."[9]

This frenzied planting made land a premium concern in the fledgling colony. The English, restricted to the Jamestown peninsula, turned covetous eyes on the Indians' land. John Smith asked rhetorically: Why heed commotion's clamor over land at "such great rents and rates" when there is "good, or rather better" land available? With visions of empire and without scruples, Smith projected that the Indians' land was underused, justifying English seizure of it and the establishment of plantations there. The Indians, he wrote, had "more land than all the people in Christendom can manure, and yet more to spare than all the natives of those Countries can use and culturate [cultivate]."[10]

With land pressure and the conflict over corn, the relationship soured

8. Smith, *Generall History*, *CWCJS*, II, 243-247 (quotations on 244, 245); Fausz, "England's First Indian War," *VMHB*, XCVIII (1990), 43-49; David R. Ransome, "Pocahontas and the Mission to the Indians," *VMHB*, XCIX (1991), 85-86; Nicholas Canny, " 'To Establish a Common Wealthe': Captain John Smith as New World Colonist," *VMHB*, XCVI (1988), 219-220; David D. Smits, " 'Abominable Mixture': Toward the Repudiation of Anglo-Indian Intermarriage in Seventeenth-Century Virginia," *VMHB*, XCV (1987), 157-192.

9. Smith, *Generall History*, *CWCJS*, II, 262.

10. John Smith, *Advertisements for the Unexperienced Planters of New England, or Any Where* (1631), *CWCJS*, III, 276.

between the Indians and the colonists. Because they planted their land in tobacco, the colonists continued to depend on the Indians for their corn supply; they forced the trade of corn by threat of arms for beads, copper, and "other trucking Stuffe." Opechancanough complained to the colony in 1619, demanding the end of this coercion. The newly installed House of Burgesses chastised the offenders and passed an act forbidding trade with the Indians, unless traders were licensed and bonded. To relieve land pressure and to lessen the demand for Indian corn, the General Assembly, as late as January 1622, moved to restrict the "excessive" planting of tobacco by stinting its output to one hundred plants per head and encouraged the planting of corn instead.[11]

This land-use policy was too little, too late. Opechancanough led the Pamunkeys against the colonists on March 22, 1622, to stop their encroachment on farms, game, and wild food preserves. The murder of the mystic and war hero Nemattanew two weeks earlier had precipitated the attack. Despite its timing, the uprising was fundamentally about land. The enthusiasm for tobacco had weakened the colonial defense, for it encouraged the Indian presence within Jamestown and dispersed the settlement outside it. The attack, which badly crippled the settlement by killing 330 settlers (about one-fourth of the total), provided the English with the pretext for their first move toward engrossing Indian land: conquest "by right of Warre, and law of Nations." The Pamunkeys had restricted the English to wastelands that the Indians did not want and had maintained their advantage in trade relations. The righteous English stood their ground and recruited more settlers. Still frustrated with their disadvantages, they now contended that an invasion of Pamunkey country was much easier and more glorious than "civilizing them by faire meanes." They anticipated "possessing the fruits of others labours." "Now their cleared grounds in all their villages (which are situate[d] in the fruitfullest places of the land) shall be inhabited by us, whereas heretofore the grubbing of woods was the greatest labour."[12]

11. *JHB, 1619–1658/59,* 5 (quotations), 14, 17.

12. Edward Waterhouse, "A Declaration of the State of the Colony . . . a Relation of the Barbarous Massacre . . ." (1622), in W. Stitt Robinson, ed., *Virginia Treaties, 1607–1722,* vol. IV of Alden T. Vaughan, gen. ed., *Early American Indian Documents: Treaties and Laws, 1607–1789* (Frederick, Md., 1983), 37–38; Smith, *Generall History, CWCJS,* II, 262; Vaughan, "'Expulsion of the Salvages': English Policy and the Virginia Massacre of 1622," *WMQ,* 3d Ser., XXXV (1978), 73–74; John Frederick Fausz, "The Powhatan Uprising of 1622: A Historical Study of Ethnocentrism and Cultural Conflict" (Ph.D. diss., College of William and Mary, 1977), 312–313, 343–349, 358–359, 399, 472, 510–512.

Unable to destroy the Powhatans at once, the settlers pursued a policy of "perpetual enmity." Expeditions annually went out to destroy Indian cornfields and villages. The English counterattacked in the summer and fall of 1622, after which Governor Francis Wyatt reported that the English had killed more Indians during that time than they had since first contact with them. The English attained a further measure of retribution for the massacre when the colonists, led by Captain William Tucker, met with Indian leaders on May 12, 1623, in Patawomeck under the pretense of a peace negotiation. After offering the Indians tainted drink that incapacitated them, the English fired upon them, killing two hundred. Afterward, they scalped some. In the autumn of 1624, Wyatt, who as wartime governor had distinguished himself in previous raids, led sixty Englishmen against eight hundred Pamunkeys. While losing only sixteen, the English dealt the Indians—who suffered "many casualties"—a severe defeat by seizing their cornfields, the granary of the Powhatans, taking away their ability to feed four thousand warriors that season.[13]

For defense, the English built a palisade, extending from the James River to the Pamunkey River, across from Opechancanough's capital. To bolster their offensive on the Pamunkey River, the Council of State issued an order on January 13, 1626, that the English establish a "sufficient party" at Chischiak "to annoy the Indians, and [be] of a good retreat in case wee may have beene overpowered by too powerfull a forreine enemy." Using the lure of Indian land to further dispossess the Indians, the court, on October 8, 1630, offered a considerable incentive to colonists who would secure themselves and settle in "the forrest bordering upon the cheife residence of the Pamunky King the most dangerous head of the Indian Enemie." Fifty acres, with an additional twenty-five acres if the settler lived out the year, would be the reward. By the early 1630s, these efforts resulted in an outpost and a settlement at Chischiak. Drought during the summer of 1632 encouraged the settlers to sue for peace with the Chickahominys and the Pamunkeys so that they could "trade with the Indians for corn," even though they still did not trust them. The peace officially ended the war, but the council would record that the colonists were still at odds with their "irreconcilable enemies."[14]

13. *SAL*, I, 153; *MCGC*, 479; Wesley Frank Craven, *White, Red, and Black: The Seventeenth-Century Virginian* (Charlottesville, Va., 1971), 51, 55; Morgan, *American Slavery, American Freedom*, 98–100; Hagemann, *Heritage of Virginia*, 50; Fausz, "Powhatan Uprising," 510–512; Vaughan, "'Expulsion of the Salvages,'" *WMQ*, 3d Ser., XXXV (1978), 77.

14. *MCGC*, 136, 480, 484; *CP*, I, 44; *SAL*, I, 139–141.

The colonists cornered the Pamunkeys during the dozen years after the 1632 treaty, leaving them without enough land to maintain their cultural integrity. English expansion and depredations precipitated Opechanca-nough's second campaign in 1644, during which five hundred settlers were killed, or about one-twelfth of the colonists. This second attack not only vindicated the settlers' earlier rationale for engrossing the Indians' land but also gave them the opportunity for removing the Pamunkeys from their ancestral territory. After this attack, the General Assembly declared: "Wee will for ever abandon all formes of peace and familiarity with the whole Nation and will to the uttmost of our power pursue and root out those which have any way had theire hands in the shedding of our blood and Massacring of our People." This time the English defeated the Pamunkeys, and Opechancanough was killed when an English soldier "basely" shot the reputedly one-hundred-year-old chief in the back after he had been captured and caged. The treaty of 1646 made with the new "King of the Indians," Necotowance, removed the Pamunkeys from the James-York peninsula, leaving "free that tract of land . . . to the English to inhabitt on." The Pamunkeys lost their reserved land on the north side of the York in 1649, when Governor William Berkeley opened its lower reaches to settlers. Settlers patented the peninsula between the York and the Rappahannock Rivers over the next two decades, reducing the Pamunkeys to five thousand acres in the Pamunkey Neck and across the Mattaponi River.[15]

The Indians were vanquished. Their demise can be measured by the rapidity of English settlement after the peace of 1646, despite waning immigration because of the English Civil War. Settlers usurped reserved Indian land by chicanery, delusion, and intimidation, checked only by the restraint of the assembly. Cheating caused Indian distrust during the Commonwealth era from 1652 to 1659, when Governor Berkeley was politically incapacitated. Opportunists habitually swindled the Indians of their land and spoiled neighboring cornfields by letting loose their cattle and hogs. Indians, in turn, killed the livestock. The threat of renewed hostilities with the Indians and "a continuall necessity of allotting them new lands and possessions" moved legislators in 1654 to protect the tributary tribes in their reserve, frustrating covetous backcountry speculators. The

15. "Acts, Orders, and Resolutions of the General Assembly of Virginia, 1643–1646" (June 1, 1644), "Treaty of Peace with Necotowance, King of the Indians," both in Robinson, ed., *Virginia Treaties,* 63, 68–69; Beverley, *History and Present State of Virginia,* ed. Wright, 62; Fausz, "Powhatan's Uprising," 582; Helen C. Rountree, *Pocahontas's People: The Powhatan Indians of Virginia through Four Centuries* (Norman, Okla., 1990), 84.

assembly in March 1658 restricted patents in the Pamunkey Neck, affirming the reserve for the Pamunkeys and Chickahominys.[16]

Encroachment on Indian land on the Eastern Shore from 1650 to 1652 led Berkeley to caution restraint and the assembly in turn to restrict sales to Quarterly Court sessions. Yet, contrary to this 1652 statute, the Indians began to sell land directly to the English, who reneged on payment. For example, Andrianon, werowance of the Occochannocks and the Curratucks, accused the Reverend Thomas Teackle and two others of taking their land without paying for it in 1654. The assembly responded in that year by distinguishing between the Eastern Shore tribes who had remained neutral during the wars and other tributary Indians. It limited land sales to Eastern Shore Indian towns where the majority had agreed to it and stopped them altogether everywhere else. Ostensibly because of the Assateagues' "acts of rapine and violence," the colonists then began to press them, who already felt "straightened for want of land," in their reserve on the northern Eastern Shore peninsula. The English ended Indian opposition to expansion there after forays led by Edmund Scarburg and Philip Taylor in 1659.[17]

To stop further intrusions, the assembly in 1662 affirmed the prohibition against land sales (extending it to the Eastern Shore), abrogated earlier purchases, and called for the destruction of houses and barns built in Indian territory. In a special bill it ordered Colonel Moore off the Rappahannocks' land and fined him fifteen matchcoats in damages payable to the werowance. (A matchcoat, from the Powhatan *matshcore*, was a loose-fitting mantle made of fur and feathers.) The tributary Indians needed the government's protection. By 1669, when the warriors of the nineteen tributary tribes numbered just 725, the western frontier running roughly along the fall line had been cleared of any serious Indian opposition to expansion in that direction.[18]

16. *SAL,* I, 396, 467.

17. *SAL,* I, 391; James R. Perry, *The Formation of a Society on Virginia's Eastern Shore, 1615–1655* (Chapel Hill, N.C., 1990), 39, 210–211; Joseph Douglas Deal III, "Race and Class in Colonial Virginia: Indians, Englishmen, and Africans on the Eastern Shore during the Seventeenth Century" (Ph.D. diss., University of Rochester, 1981), 20–21.

18. *SAL,* I, 328–329, 353–354, 455–457, II, 139, 152; *MCGC,* 510; Warren M. Billings, ed., *The Old Dominion in the Seventeenth Century: A Documentary History of Virginia, 1606–1689* (Chapel Hill, N.C., 1975), 229; Craven, *White, Red, and Black,* 56, 58; Susie M. Ames, *Studies of the Virginia Eastern Shore in the Seventeenth Century* (Richmond, Va., 1940), 6; Sarah S. Hughes, *Surveyors and Statesmen: Land Measuring in Colonial Virginia* (Richmond, Va., 1979), 13, 58; Morgan, *American Slavery, American Freedom,* 149; Nancy

Governor Berkeley (reinstalled in 1660 at the end of the English Civil War), his councillor clique (known as the Green Spring faction after his estate on the James River), and an acquiescent assembly (which did not have to face an election from 1662 to 1676) continued to check expansion into Indian territory. Thomas Ludwell, a prominent member of the clique, as secretary of the colony approved all land patents, limiting the access of parvenu planters. Elite immigrants, who had attained transcounty economic power, resented the hold that Berkeley and his faction held on land and political offices. These speculators in backcountry acreage were frustrated by their inability to annex adjacent Indian lands. Ordinary planters, too, hungered for new land, their prospects limited by its engrossment by the wealthy and well connected. They had difficulty expanding their estates or securing enough acreage to pass on to their children. Without the prospect of proprietorship, they had to work as either tenants or wage laborers or move as squatters to the frontier, where they were exposed to Indian attacks.[19]

By 1676, the lure of Indian land led to Bacon's Rebellion. Some of the newcomers, such as Giles Bland and the younger Nathaniel Bacon, "whose lost and desperate fortunes had thrown him into that remote part of the world," felt excluded from the landgrab. Representative of new elite immigrants, both Bland and Bacon, although recently appointed to the Council of State, resented Berkeley's authority, especially his Indian policy. This policy was tested in July 1675 when a Doeg trading party from the northern Chesapeake disputed a transaction with Thomas Matthews, a prominent planter in Stafford County. The subsequent skirmish left several Doegs and Matthews's overseer dead. The overseer's death provided the spark for the rebellion. Berkeley's hesitancy in dealing with the event inflamed the combustible undergrowth of backcountry frustration, providing speculators in frontier tracts a ruse to seize Indian land. In northern Virginia, dominant planters George Mason, George Brent, John Washington, and Isaac Allerton called out the militias on their own initiative and attacked the Susquehannocks in the Potomac and Rappahannock region. Bacon struck a chord among backcountry residents and speculators alike

---

Oestreich Lurie, "Indian Cultural Adjustment to European Civilization," in James Morton Smith, ed., *Seventeenth-Century America: Essays in Colonial History* (Chapel Hill, N.C., 1959), 33–60.

19. Wilcomb E. Washburn, *The Governor and the Rebel: A History of Bacon's Rebellion in Virginia* (Chapel Hill, N.C., 1957), 160–167, 237.

when he agreed to lead the war against the Indians, including the tributary tribes.[20]

The colonists coveted the land reserved for the Pamunkeys, the chief target of the settlers' wrath. The focus of the rebellion in and around New Kent County gives evidence of poor white settlers' anxiety on the frontier and resentment toward the Pamunkeys occupying adjacent territory. The Council of State had only two years before the rebellion voided all sales with the Pamunkeys and the Chickahominys and declared that the Indians did not have the authority to "sell or alienate" land. During the attack, the Pamunkeys abandoned their homes for the Dragon Swamp and hid there from Bacon's men. Werowansqua Cockacoeske hid in the woods for fourteen days with a ten-year-old child as her only companion and the leg of a terrapin as her only sustenance. The rebels pursued the Pamunkeys and, after weeks of futile searching, finally found them and dealt them a severe defeat. Governor Berkeley and the loyalists later crushed the rebellion, rehabilitated Cockacoeske, and restored the Pamunkeys to their land.[21]

The rebellion ended the necessity for the Middle Plantation (later Williamsburg), a name derived from the planting of a defensive settlement in the middle section of the palisade that was constructed following the 1622 massacre. By the terms of the Middle Plantation's treaties (1677–1680), the Indians held their reservation by patent, subject to an annual quitrent each March of three arrows to the crown and a gift of twenty beaver pelts to the governor. The colonists were forbidden to settle within three miles of the Indians. The shortsighted Pamunkeys, contrary to the statutes of 1654, 1656, and 1662, began selling off acreage, believing they still retained enough to support their diminished population. Despite their willingness to sell some of their land, they were able to collect only partial payment for it. After their appeal for the remainder in October 1677, the assembly voided the deal. Almost nine years later, the new werowance, along with

20. Ibid., 18–30, 54, 69; Morgan, *American Slavery, American Freedom,* 370.

21. *MCGC,* 370; Royal Commissioners, "A True Narrative of the Late Rebellion in Virginia" (1677), in Robinson, ed., *Virginia Treaties,* 75; Philip Ludwell to Mr. Sec. Henry Coventry, Apr. 14, 1677, BR, box 766, 69–70, HL; Warren M. Billings, John E. Selby, and Thad W. Tate, *Colonial Virginia: A History* (New York, 1986), 93–94; James H. Merrell, "Some Thoughts on Colonial Historians and American Indians," *WMQ,* 3d Ser., XLVI (1989), 101; "Virginia Colonial Records; Commissions, Bacon's Rebellion, etc. . . . ," *VMHB,* XIV (1906–1907), 289–296; Martha W. McCartney, "Cockacoeske, Queen of Pamunkey: Diplomat and Suzeraine," in Peter H. Wood, Gregory A. Waselkov, and Thomas M. Hatley, eds., *Powhatan's Mantle: Indians in the Colonial Southeast* (Lincoln, Nebr., 1989), 177–180; Washburn, *Governor and the Rebel,* 348.

Indians south of the James River, unsuccessfully petitioned the assembly to allow them to sell land that was officially closed to settlers.[22]

By the 1690s, planters were aggressively acquiring Indian land by fraud, petition, and leasehold. Indians began to sell land to the English but also complained of English theft and treachery in land dealings, which the government continued to attempt to check. Late in the 1680s, ten planters exchanged with the Chickahominys 130 yards of duffels, or coarse woolens, 120 pounds of shot, hogs, a bridle, and a saddle for 5,730 acres in the Pamunkey Neck. The Chickahominys were hustled away to the Dragon Swamp. The council on October 24, 1690, voided the transaction, ordered the removal of the settlers, and repatriated the Chickahominys. Still, the English were quick to secure Indian land. The Pamunkeys had shown Sarah Bland, the mother of Giles, the location of a silver mine on their reserve, which prompted Colonel William Byrd I and Colonel William Randolph to survey the land for a patent in March 1690. Byrd and Colonel Edward Hill agreed to split shares of the "pretended" mine, but Governor Francis Nicholson refused to sign the patent unless they could show "unusual limitations." Elsewhere, the Indians continued to accuse the English of fraudulent land dealings.[23]

Contemporaries observed unceasing encroachment upon reserves. Speculators insisted that they should have access to the land because of the Indians' demise. At first the crown refused to accept their requests but later relented after their persistent incursion. The council in May 1688 unsuccessfully petitioned the crown to settle the Pamunkey Neck and the Blackwater Swamp because the Indians were now "wasted and dwindled away." Only two years later, William Byrd I made reference to complaints being made against surveyors of Indian lands in the Pamunkey Neck and

22. Rountree, *Pocahontas's People*, 101, 112–114; Hagemann, *Heritage of Virginia*, 158.

23. *EJCCV*, I, 94, 135; William Byrd I to Philip Ludwell, Oct. 29, 1690, in Marion Tinling, ed., *The Correspondence of the Three William Byrds of Westover, Virginia, 1684–1776*, 2 vols. (Charlottesville, Va., 1977), I, 139 (hereafter cited as *Byrd Correspondence*). The profit from these land deals and his eleven enslaved blacks placed Thomas Teackle's estate within the top 15 percent of those probated in the 1690s. See *SAL*, I, 396, II, 139, 152; "An Account of the Severall Grants of Lands in Pomonky Neck by the Chickahomony Indians and to Whome" (ca. 1689), BR, box 227, folder 2, HL; Jon Butler, "Thomas Teackle's 333 Books: A Great Library on Virginia's Eastern Shore, 1697," *WMQ*, 3d Ser., XLIX (1992), 452–453; Perry, *The Formation of a Society on Virginia's Eastern Shore*, 187n; "Petition to Nathaniel Bacon, President of H. M.'s Council, from Edward Hill, Charles Goodrich, Edward Chilton, John Taylor, Jr.," Mar. 10, 1689/90, Sarah Bland to William Blathwayt, Mar. 16, 1689/90, William Blathwayt Papers, XVII, folder 8, reel 2, CWF.

beyond the Blackwater Swamp. As a result, William Cole suggested to William Blathwayt in October 1690 that the Lords of Trade move to lay aside sufficient land for the Indians, but to no avail. "In some parts of the Country where the Indians Inhabited (as Pamunkey Neck and the Southside of James River) those lands were severall years forbidden, to be taken up," Edward Randolph, commissioner of customs, wrote in 1696. But having nearly eliminated the Indians in those areas, members of the General Assembly could successfully petition Governor Edmund Andros to grant away those lands.[24]

After a century of contact, the English had effectively removed the Indians from eastern Virginia. The Indians that remained in the region were weak, isolated, and miserable prey to the acquisitive English. They suffered from European diseases, especially smallpox, engaged in internecine violence, and were debilitated by alcohol. Governor Andros, near the end of his term in 1697, questioned whether the tributary Indians had the capacity to muster more than 362 bowmen, including 100 from the nine small nations on the Eastern Shore. By the turn of the century, the Indian population in eastern Virginia had declined to about 1,900, a decrease of almost 85 percent from when the Indians first made contact with the English. When the assembly took away half of all remaining Indian reserves in 1705, Colonel Robert Beverley II assessed the conditions of the Indian towns in eastern Virginia as "almost wasted." The other half was made available to the "highest bidder" in 1735, ostensibly to pay Indians' debts owed to settlers. One year later, William Byrd II observed that the Nottoways, composed of only 200 men, women, and children, were "the only Indians of any consequence now remaining within the Limits of Virginia." "The rest are either removed, or dwindled to a very inconsiderable Number, either by destroying one another, or else by the Small-Pox and other Diseases. Tho' nothing has been so fatal to them as their ungovernable Passion for Rum, with which, I am sorry to say it, they have been but too liberally supply'd by the English that live near them." With this diminution of Indians in the tidewater, the English could now impose their scheme of land tenure on the seized land.[25]

24. [William] Cole to William Blathwayt, Oct. 30, 1690, Blathwayt Papers, XVII, folder 5, reel 4; Edward Randolph to BT, Oct. 6, 1696, CO 5/1359, 22, transcript, LC.

25. Hughes, *Surveyors and Statesmen,* 58; Craven, *White, Red, and Black,* 64; Peter H. Wood, "The Changing Population of the Colonial South: An Overview by Race and Region, 1685-1790," in Wood, Waselkov, and Hatley, eds., *Powhatan's Mantle,* 38; Axtell, *The Invasion Within,* 195; Beverley, *History and Present State of Virginia,* ed. Wright, 61-63;

Misery and Mischief

The amount of land seized after the Indian war of 1644–1646 and the increasing immigration to Virginia led to a land boom. But the increase in speculation can also be attributed to the changing attitudes of the emerging elite, who had begun treating land as a commodity. At first, during the company period (1612–1624), English adventurers had viewed land as an endowment rather than a commercial concern. It was a permanent entitled estate, such as Berkeley Hundred or Martin Brandon Hundred, a mark of station in the tradition of the manor in the English feudal past. Indeed, these hundreds were established under the quitrent system, a manorial relic in which the grantee paid a tribute or fee to the grantor. Then in the 1630s, well-connected planters, assisted by their English merchant associates organized in syndicates, acquired these hundreds. The acquisition of this land proved to be a worthwhile investment, securing the landed elite in the Council of State.[26]

The men who invested in Virginia plantations were looking for a way to break into the English commercial world. The established London merchants, including the older merchant adventurers and the newer Levant and East India traders, ignored America. The adventurers exported cloth to northern Europe, and the traders imported the spices, silks, and porcelains of Asia. The unwillingness of these merchants to risk investment in the Americas left an opening for an amorphous class to venture into Virginia. These men were from ports other than London or from the countryside, and they were from middling backgrounds, either younger sons of gentry or prosperous sons of yeoman families. Many were shopkeepers, an occupation compatible with colonization. With the demise of the Virginia Company in 1624, these men gained control over Virginia's booming to-

---

SAL, III, 466; William Byrd, *Histories of the Dividing Line betwixt Virginia and North Carolina* (ca. 1728–1736), ed. William K. Boyd (1929; reprint, New York, 1967), 116, 118.

26. Wesley Frank Craven, letter, *VMHB*, LXXX (1972), 371 (concerning Edmund S. Morgan's review of *White, Red, and Black*); Clarence L. Ver Steeg, *The Formative Years, 1607–1763* (New York, 1964), 56; Robert Brenner, "Merchants, Planters, and Politics in Virginia" (paper presented at the annual meeting of the Organization of American Historians, Boston, Apr. 18, 1975), 40–46; Brenner, *Merchants and Revolution: Commercial Change, Political Conflict, and London's Overseas Traders, 1550–1653* (Princeton, N.J., 1993), 141–145, 147–148; J. Mills Thornton, "The Thrusting Out of Governor Harvey . . . ," *VMHB*, LXXVI (1968), 24–25; Aubrey C. Land, "Economic Behavior in a Planting Society: The Eighteenth-Century Chesapeake," *Journal of Southern History*, XXXIII (1967), 480–481.

bacco trade, a burgeoning but frenetic field. Some of these men returned to England, setting themselves up as London merchants. Others operated their own plantations, marketing the tobacco themselves. A network of merchant-planters and London merchants developed that promoted their own commercial interests and organized syndicates for the patenting of land.[27]

The elite, who controlled the Council of State, stood to gain the most from the financing of immigration. In the initial landgrab, the merchant-planter-councillors, such as William Claiborne, Samuel Matthews, and William Tucker, used headrights to secure title to land. The headright system devised by the Virginia Company in 1617 became the chief method of patenting land and encouraging immigration to Virginia. An importer of labor received a headright patent for fifty acres for paying an immigrant's fare to the colony. The patent recipient, in turn, was required to pay a one-shilling quitrent annually for each fifty-acre grant. The system provided that immigrants should serve seven years as indentured servants and then have the opportunity to serve themselves. The labor recruiters realized the benefit of the patents immediately in their concentrated landholdings.[28]

During the 1630s, Governor John Harvey, wary of the Pamunkeys and Chickahominys despite a treaty with them in 1632, refused to issue headright patents for imported servants, inhibiting the expansionist dreams of tobacco planters. Harvey also believed that the elite already held title to more acreage than they intended to cultivate, as much as 300 to 400 acres each. The councillors feared that Harvey's policy signaled the crown's intention to revoke their title and return it to absentee stockholders of the defunct Virginia Company, as it had to English and Scottish landlords in Ulster in 1609. The councillors claimed that the Great Charter of 1618 entitled the person paying the passage fare to a 50-acre headright. In the first move toward colonial administration, Charles I in 1634 appointed William Laud (1573–1645), archbishop of Canterbury, head of a commission of twelve, formally the Lords Commissioners of Foreign Plantations,

27. Robert Brenner, "The Social Basis of English Commerical Expansion, 1550–1650," *Journal of Economic History*, XXXII (1972), 380.

28. Susan Myra Kingsbury, ed., *The Records of the Virginia Company of London*, 4 vols. (Washington, D.C., 1906–1935), III, 98–109, 153–177; Manning C. Voorhis, "Crown versus Council in the Virginia Land Policy," *WMQ*, 3d Ser., III (1946), 499; Brenner, "Merchants, Planters, and Politics," 40; Brenner, *Merchants and Revolution*, 104, 118–120, 144; Wesley Frank Craven, *The Southern Colonies in the Seventeenth Century, 1607–1689* (Baton Rouge, La., 1949), 50, 121, 127, 128, 175–177.

to oversee the colonies and approve patents and charters. The Laud Commission's first order of business was to deal with land disputes between Governor Harvey and the Council of State. After review, the commission approved the headright system. Harvey's obstinacy over approving claims, despite the crown's endorsement of the headright system, was the most grievous offense of despotism alleged by the council, resulting in his eventual expulsion from Virginia in 1635. Within months of Harvey's departure, the new governor, John West, formerly a member of the council, issued under the council's authority 377 headright patents for 18,850 acres to councillors and merchant-planters. West himself received a grant for 2,000 acres from the council "in the right of his son being the first born Christian at Chischiak."[29]

After eight years of haggling beginning with an audit in 1627, the councillors began breaking up the former Virginia Company land grants, opening the way for themselves and their associates to patent the land. By then, with Harvey removed, the charter owners of the defunct Virginia Company were resigned to their loss. The merchant-planters and their London associates seized these hundreds, taking title to tens of thousands of acres. The boundaries of the 200,000-acre Southhampton Hundred, the object of the audit, had withered away by 1635, opening the way to avaricious speculation. In that year, syndicates patented the 8,000-acre Barclay Hundred and the 80,000-acre Martin's Hundred; in 1637, they patented the 4,500-acre Martin's Brandon Hundred and the 8,000-acre Berkeley Hundred.[30]

After midcentury, the elite secured their economic interests through the headright system. They amassed acres, at first hundreds of thousands and then tens of thousands, for both speculative and productive purposes. The

29. Brenner, *Merchants and Revolution*, 140–148; Brenner, "Merchants, Planters, and Politics," 40–42; Thornton, "The Thrusting Out of Governor Harvey," *VMHB*, LXXVI (1968), 17–19, 24–25; Craven, *The Southern Colonies*, 121, 127, 128, 175–177; Kingsbury, ed., *Records of the Virginia Company*, III, 98–109, 153–177; Voorhis, "Crown versus Council," *WMQ*, 3d Ser., III (1946), 499; *CP*, I, 44; Hageman, *Heritage of Virginia*, 50; Philip Alexander Bruce, *Institutional History of Virginia in the Seventeenth Century: An Inquiry into the Religious, Moral, Educational, Legal, Military, and Political Condition of the People . . .* , 2 vols. (New York, 1910), II, 269, 318; Charles M. Andrews, *The Colonial Period of American History* (New Haven, Conn., 1934–1938), IV, 369.

30. Philip Alexander Bruce, *Economic History of Virginia in the Seventeenth Century: An Inquiry into the Material Condition of the People, Based upon Original and Contemporaneous Records*, 2 vols. (New York, 1896), I, 507–509; Brenner, *Merchants and Revolution*, 145–148.

watershed of Bacon's Rebellion shaped the course of this landgrab. The rebellion exposed ridges of discontent among the English poor, reversing the flow of their immigration to Virginia. The poor were responding to the constrained economic opportunity in Virginia, especially their access to land. The decline in immigration drained both the number of headrights issued and the potential market of new land buyers.

Before the rebellion in 1676, speculators claimed 47,000 headright patents, primarily acquired by a few dozen speculators on each of the major rivers. These patents included not only headrights on new immigrants but also dormant headrights from the pre-1650 immigration, used after the Indian wars once the land became available. During the fifteen-year period beginning in 1650, when the 1,924 headrights patented signaled the landgrab, through 1664, when the land titles secured by headrights peaked for the century at 3,243, almost a million acres were acquired. During the next ten years, speculators secured another million acres by taking patents on more than 2,000 headright certificates per year.[31]

Speculators cheaply engrossed land before 1665, platting it for rent or sale to small planters, including freed servants. They bought the land at a penny an acre and received a highly inflated profit, as much as fifty to one hundred times. As lessors of unimproved land, they insisted upon long-term contracts, twenty-one years or life, specifying that the tenants not only pay rents in tobacco but also clear the land, plant fruit trees, and build barns, houses, and fences. As sellers of improved land, they found buyers willing to pay from five shillings to a pound per acre by accepting mortgages for plantation-size parcels of 250 acres or less.[32]

Speculative activity peaked after 1665. In Surry County, for example, the 1650 price of land at twenty-one pounds of tobacco per acre had more than doubled by 1666 and more than doubled again by 1674. These sales were concentrated in the James River basin. Land subsequently became less expensive in Surry County, cresting at ninety pounds of tobacco per acre in 1678 before dropping to fifty-one in 1690, when lands were being sold in the Blackwater Swamp region. It became increasingly more difficult for laborers (who could produce about fifteen hundred pounds of

31. Edmund S. Morgan, "Headrights and Headcounts," review of *White, Red, and Black: The Seventeenth-Century Virginian,* by Wesley Frank Craven, *VMHB,* LXXX (1972), 366–369.

32. Aubrey C. Land, "Economic Base and Social Structure: The Northern Chesapeake in the Eighteenth Century," *Jour. Econ. Hist.,* XXV (1965), 648–649; Land, "Economic Behavior in a Planting Society," *Jour. So. Hist.,* XXXIII (1967), 481–482.

tobacco per year at ten shillings per hundredweight) to save enough from their wages or tenancy (about six pounds to fifteen pounds in disposable income) to become landholders. They either remained tenants or wage earners or moved to the frontier where they were at risk of Indian attack, their frustration readying them to answer Bacon's call to arms.[33]

After Bacon's Rebellion, a new pattern of land acquisition emerged. Fewer headrights were issued, in part because of a decline in the servant trade, even though more headrights were distributed for enslaved laborers. Nevertheless, speculators still claimed more than one and a quarter million acres on 25,233 immigrants from 1675 to 1699. Land prices fluctuated after the rebellion but remained too high for freed servants to become landowners. The collapse of the tobacco economy, the poorer quality of land now being sold, and the decline in potential buyers had depressed overall prices. Yet the artificial scarcity because of engrossment still made land difficult for poor planters to purchase. Owing to the wane in potential buyers, the elite began to amass great estates.[34]

The immigration from England begun in the 1640s and continuing for the next thirty years fed the emerging gentry. These immigrants often inherited family claims to land in the colony. Along with others carrying purses with them from England, they participated in the early landgrab before Bacon's Rebellion in 1676. Newcomers, such as Nicholas Spencer, William Fitzhugh, and William Byrd I, were, for the most part, absorbed into the older elite, forming the gentry. Securing favorable marriages to wealthy widows facilitated this class formation in Virginia.[35]

The men of this emerging elite had common characteristics as estranged younger sons with both metropolitan and mercantile experience. They were in part driven by the psychological need to liberate themselves by

33. Deal, "Race and Class in Colonial Virginia," 161–162; Kevin P. Kelly, "'In Dispers'd Country Plantations': Settlement Patterns in Seventeenth-Century Surry County, Virginia," in Tate and Ammerman, eds., *The Chesapeake in the Seventeenth Century*, 195–198; Kevin Peter Kelly, "Economic and Social Development of Seventeenth-Century Surry County, Virginia" (Ph.D. diss., University of Washington, 1972), 136–138.

34. Morgan, "Headrights and Headcounts," review of *White, Red, and Black*, by Craven, *VMHB*, LXXX (1972), 366–369.

35. [William Berkeley], *A Discourse and View of Virginia* (London, 1662), 4; Daniel Blake Smith, *Inside the Great House: Planter Family Life in Eighteenth-Century Chesapeake Society* (Ithaca, N.Y., 1980), 79–81; Allan Kulikoff, *Tobacco and Slaves: The Development of Southern Cultures in the Chesapeake, 1680–1800* (Chapel Hill, N.C., 1986), 167–173; Morgan, *American Slavery, American Freedom*, 162–168; Perry, *Formation of a Society*, 80.

work and material success from the rejection inherent in primogeniture. The anonymity of the city and the impersonality of the market had freed them from a feudal tradition that might have inhibited them. They were innovative, independent, enterprising, acquisitive, and competitive. Escaping the encumbrances of primogeniture in England, they freely speculated in land and willingly exploited the labor of others.[36]

A portrait of the great planter began to emerge by the 1680s. Indeed, contemporaries used the term "great planter" to describe this new elite. They were a class of men who had diversified their wealth beyond land and labor to include business activities and plural officeholding. They maintained accounts with English merchants and contacts with smaller planters within a fifteen- to twenty-five-mile radius of their homes, which were advantageously positioned on rivers. Their colonywide offices and transatlantic contacts distinguished them from middling planters. They had attained wealth and power by the 1680s but had not yet developed the accoutrements of class hegemony. On average, they had accumulated two thousand or more acres and had personal estates worth more than two thousand pounds. Only about 125 men could count themselves as great planters in 1700.[37]

The biographies of the emerging gentry are remarkably similar, as the lives of William Fitzhugh and William Byrd I demonstrate. Both Fitzhugh

36. Martin H. Quitt, "Immigrant Origins of the Virginia Gentry: A Study of Cultural Transmission and Innovation," *WMQ*, 3d Ser., XLV (1988), 629, 635; Bernard Bailyn, "Politics and Social Structure in Virginia," in Smith, ed., *Seventeenth-Century America*, 98–99, 104; David Hackett Fischer, *"Albion* and the Critics: Further Evidence and Reflection," *WMQ*, 3d Ser., XLVIII (1991), 278, 287; Fischer, *Historians' Fallacies: Toward a Logic of Historical Thought* (New York, 1970), 189; Peter Gay, *Freud for Historians* (New York, 1985), 11; Land, "Economic Behavior in a Planting Society," *Jour. So. Hist.*, XXXIII (1967), 482.

37. John C. Rainbolt, "The Alteration in the Relationship between Leadership and Constituents in Virginia, 1660 to 1720," *WMQ*, 3d Ser., XXVII (1970), 412–414; Hughes, *Surveyors and Statesmen*, 12; Warren M. Billings, *Virginia's Viceroy: Their Majesties' Governor General: Francis Howard, Baron Howard of Effingham* (Fairfax, Va., 1991), 20–21; Jacob M. Price, *Perry of London: A Family and a Firm on the Seaborne Frontier, 1615–1753* (Cambridge, 1992), 29, 37, 66; Paul G. E. Clemens, *The Atlantic Economy and Colonial Maryland's Eastern Shore: From Tobacco to Grain* (Ithaca, N.Y., 1980); Lorena S. Walsh, "Staying Put or Getting Out: Findings for Charles County Maryland, 1650–1720," *WMQ*, 3d Ser., XLIV (1987), 89–103; Darrett B. Rutman and Anita H. Rutman, *A Place in Time: Middlesex County, Virginia, 1650–1750* (New York, 1984), 128–163; Alan Gallay, "Jonathan Bryan's Plantation Empire: Land, Politics, and the Formation of a Ruling Class in Colonial Georgia," *WMQ*, 3d Ser., XLV (1988), 257.

and Byrd, whose families belonged to England's middling gentry, immigrated to Virginia to seek their fortune and married into established families. Like their class contemporaries, they were educated men who held a plurality of offices, speculated extensively in land, and eventually engaged in the system of slavery.[38]

William Fitzhugh, the youngest son of a substantial family of Bedford, was born in 1651 and immigrated to Virginia in 1670 or 1671. Carrying a purse with him from England, he acquired land early in the Northern Neck. He married into the Tucker family in 1674, one of Virginia's first families, choosing eleven-year-old Sarah, daughter of twice-widowed Rose Tucker, ensuring his status in the colony. He made a name for himself as a lawyer, especially in land suits, and in 1676 secured a seat in the House of Burgesses from Stafford County. Using his position, he obtained plantations, which he described in 1686: "One of them contains 21996 Acres another 500 acres, and one other 1000 Acres, all good convenient and commodious Seats, and wch. in a few years will yield a considerable annual Income." His most significant official post, however, was, not as county representative, but as agent of Culpepper's Northern Neck proprietary, which involved him in the land system beginning in 1693. From this estate, estimated at one million acres, Fitzhugh could "give, grant, or by other means sell or alienate" acreage—an activity with which he and the other agent George Brent busied themselves by disbursing large tracts to each other and to friends. By this means, Fitzhugh and Brent, and later proprietary agent Robert "King" Carter, amassed vast stretches of land in the Northern Neck. At his death in 1701, Fitzhugh had accumulated 52,260 acres in dozens of tracts across several counties.[39]

William Byrd I, born in London in 1652, came to Virginia in the early 1670s to learn the deerskin trade from his uncle Thomas Stegge, the auditor general, who carried on extensive trade with the Indians at the falls of the James River. Byrd married into one of Virginia's established fami-

38. Land, "Economic Behavior in a Planting Society," *Jour. So. Hist.*, XXXIII (1967), 482; Quitt, "Immigrant Origins of the Virginia Gentry," *WMQ*, 3d Ser., XLV (1988), 642; Pierre Marambaud, "William Byrd I: A Young Virginia Planter in the 1670s," *VMHB*, LXXXI (1973), 131–150.

39. Richard Beale Davis, ed., *William Fitzhugh and His Chesapeake World, 1676–1701: The Fitzhugh Letters and Other Documents* (Chapel Hill, N.C., 1963), 7–48 (quotation on 39), 175–176 (quotation); Beverley, *History and Present State of Virginia*, ed. Wright, 94; "The Northern Neck of Virginia," *WMQ*, 1st Ser., VI (1897–1898), 222–226; Fairfax Harrison, "The Proprietors of the Northern Neck: Chapters of Culpeper Genealogy," *VMHB*, XXXIV (1926), 19–64.

lies, wedding Mary Filmer, widow of Samuel Filmer. Byrd enjoyed a virtual monopoly in the deerskin trade until March 1676, when the General Assembly passed a bill excluding regular traders from the traffic and authorizing commissions issued by the county courts for that purpose. Unable to regain his monopoly, Byrd turned to politics and land speculation. He secured his interest in 1676 by taking a seat as a burgess from Henrico, where he patented 7,351 acres. In 1679, Byrd and Lawrence Smith, burgess from Gloucester County, tried to use their influence in the General Assembly to protect their extensive landholdings in the upper reaches of the James and the Rappahannock Rivers by building two fortified towns. The crown authorities prevented the scheme, but Byrd's ambition was undeterred. The governor appointed him to the Council of State in 1683 and deputy auditor and receiver general of revenues in 1687. In that year, Byrd claimed 2,776 acres in Henrico with forty-one headrights. He expanded his holdings in Henrico County in 1696 by patenting 5,644 more acres on Falling Creek. And he encroached on the Pamunkey Reserve during the 1690s, purchasing 3,805 acres on the Pamunkey River in 1701. Byrd paid quitrents on 19,500 acres in Henrico County in 1704.[40]

Fitzhugh and Byrd were thus representative of those men who used their offices as leverage to appropriate land and become the ruling oligarchy in Virginia. The elite could carry out their agenda because the landgrab was accomplished with both the knowledge and connivance of the government. Indeed, land acquisition was a direct consequence of holding political office. Officeholders secured 39 percent of the land patented from 1660 to 1705 in seven counties: Charles City, Henrico, Isle of Wight, Lancaster, Northumberland, Accomack, and Northampton. During the final quarter of the seventeenth century, officeholders patented from one-third to three-quarters of the land in twenty counties. By the century's end, 60 percent of all estates with more than two thousand acres belonged to families with political connections.[41]

Contemporaries made the connection between officeholding and landholding. Commissioner of Customs Edward Randolph described the great-planter class as "the Members of the Council and others, who make

40. *Byrd Correspondence*, I, 1–7; Hughes, *Surveyors and Statesmen*, 43, 52, 54, 68–69; Morgan, *American Slavery, American Freedom*, 279–280; *CP*, III, 11.

41. Billings, Selby, and Tate, *Colonial Virginia*, 122–123; Martin H. Quitt, *Virginia House of Burgesses, 1660–1706: The Social, Educational, and Economic Bases of Political Power* (New York, 1989), 133–140; Morgan, *American Slavery, American Freedom*, 204–209; Rutman and Rutman, *A Place in Time*, 145–152.

an Interest in the Government, [and] have from time to time procured grants of very large Tracts of Land." Contemporary historian John Oldmixon made the same connection but believed officeholders were chosen primarily because they were men of property. Reversing the sequence, Oldmixon claimed, "Out of this Number [the owners of great estates] are chosen her Majesty's Council, the Assembly, the Justices and Officers of the Government." Undoubtedly influenced by his informants, such as William Byrd II, Oldmixon rendered the colonial elite's status as a natural result of their "trade and industry," rather than as an outcome of fraudulence and rapacity.[42]

At first, the emerging gentry used the Council of State and later the House of Burgesses as their bastion to engross estates, but they also used their other offices of profit and power. The governor appointed the most powerful planters to the council. Like their brethren in the house, the councillors could count on plural offices, but also on more prestigious and profitable positions befitting their status: secretary, escheator, naval officer, collector of customs, and deputy surveyor general. The deputy surveyor general was most important because he appointed all the county surveyors in the colony. The most shameless instance of land fraud involved surveyor general Philip Ludwell I, a member of the council. In 1673, Ludwell cooked the accounts, concocting twenty thousand acres from a patent of two thousand acres of land for forty headrights simply by adding a goose egg to each figure.[43]

Although the rising gentry was elected to the House of Burgesses by the smaller planters as well as the great, they, more often than not, represented their own interests and only residually the electorate at large. While serving as a burgess, a politico might hold a combination of minor offices such as petit juror, appraiser, constable, undersheriff, or surveyor of the highway. That same representative might hold a number of major offices: justice of the peace, grand juror, vestryman, churchwarden, coroner, sheriff, surveyor, notary public, militia commander, clerk of the court, or magistrate of the court. These offices were tied to the issue of land, for the official could exclusively control the patenting process. The county surveyor

42. Randolph to BT, Oct. 6, 1696, CO 5/1359, 20–22, transcript, LC; John Oldmixon, *The British Empire in America* . . . , 2 vols. (1708; reprint, London, 1741), I, x–xi, 322–323, 453–456.

43. *CP*, II, 130; Thomas Jefferson Wertenbaker, *The Old South: The Founding of American Civilization* (New York, 1942), 313; Morgan, *American Slavery, American Freedom,* 207–208.

was an especially influential man because he was in the unique position of knowing where the best land lay and having first access to it.[44]

The emerging elite secured hundreds of thousands of acres by using their official posts to bend the rules. False claims and malfeasance combined to form an enormity of abuse. Boundaries were exaggerated; false certificates were submitted; office clerks were bribed. Quitrents were delinquent, underestimated, or not paid. Henry Hartwell, a councillor, James Blair, the commissary, and Edward Chilton, the attorney general, identified this corruption in 1697, responding to the queries of the newly established Lords Commissioners of Trade and Plantations.[45] They reported that surveyors through "Ignorance and Knavery" exaggerated boundaries "so [that] the Persons for whom they survey'd might enjoy larger Tracts of Land, than they were to pay quit Rent for." Court justices were "lavish" in honoring headright certificates based upon uncorroborated oaths of ship captains, who sold them for a "small Matter." The purchasers would then present the certificates at a different court, duplicating the headrights. County clerks and "especially" clerks in the secretary's office, "which was and is still a constant Mint of these Rights," exercised "great Liberty" in distributing certificates "at very easy Rates" of one to five shillings for each headright.[46]

Edward Randolph, commissioner of customs, would confirm this pattern of malfeasance in 1696. He observed that the simplest method of securing land had been to bribe land-office clerks into selling fifty-acre headrights for as little as half a crown. The most serious violation of the claims was the underestimation of acreage actually secured with patents. "In many patents there is double the quantity of Land their patent expresses, whereby some hundred thousand Acres of Land are taken up, but not patented." By obtaining false certificates, the great-planter class procured large tracts of land, many as large as "20,000 to 30,000 acres very largely surveyed, without paying 1 penny quitrent."[47]

44. Hughes, *Surveyors and Statesmen,* 15–16, 17; Rutman and Rutman, *A Place in Time,* 143–146; Berkeley, *A Discourse and View of Virginia,* 3–4; Morgan, *American Slavery, American Freedom,* 205, 208–210.

45. The Lords of Trade (established in 1675) was replaced by the Lords Commissioners of Trade and Plantations, or Board of Trade, in May 1696. This body will hereafter be referred to in the text as the Board of Trade when discussing events after May 1696.

46. Henry Hartwell, James Blair, and Edward Chilton, *The Present State of Virginia, and the College* (1697; orig. pub. 1727), ed. Hunter Dickinson Farish (Williamsburg, Va., 1940), xviii, 16–20.

47. Randolph to BT, Oct. 6, 1696, CO 5/1359, 20–22, VCRP.

Holders of patents did not do the legal minimum to maintain these large tracts of land. An importer of labor received a headright in fee simple for each immigrant with the stipulation that he make improvements to the land and provide it with the proper military defense. A holder of a headright was required by law "to seat such land" within three years by building a house, by stocking his land with servants and hogs, and by planting the land with tobacco or some other crop. The General Assembly had in 1666 modified this rule by interpreting "seating" and "cleering" to mean building a house and keeping stock there for one year and "planting" to mean cultivating one acre of land. Randolph observed that the planters patent so much land that they desert it within three years. They abuse the intent of the law by cutting down twenty or thirty trees, by building a bark-covered hut, by turning two or three hogs into the woods, and by clearing an acre of ground where they plant corn. Perhaps, he wrote, they will begin to build a fence, "but [they] take no care of their Crop, nor make any further use of their Land." If this land was on the frontier, which was most often the case, four able-bodied and well-armed men were to guard it, but this condition, too, was ignored. The recipients, in turn, were to pay the crown a yearly quitrent of one shilling for every fifty acres, but "they never pay one penny Quit Rent for it."[48]

Class ties and the sheer size of estates inhibited enforcement of land-use laws. Bound by common interests to their fellow planters, sheriffs were slow to enforce payment of quitrents on patented land, even though they were governors' appointees. More often than not, they had previous experience in the House of Burgesses, where they returned after their one-year term of service expired. Indeed, eighteen of the sheriffs in twenty-two counties before 1705 had served as burgesses. They understood that both the acquisition and retention of even their own family estates resulted from the use, or, better, the abuse, of their offices. Moreover, the immensity of the holdings restrained sheriffs willing to enforce the law. When the sheriff of King and Queen County tried to collect payment on thirty-eight thousand acres in 1692, he was thwarted: there was "nothing on the lands" to seize because the owners of the patents lived in other counties. Hartwell observed: "There is a great concealments of quitrents, cheifly by the granting vast quantities of Land to the Richer sort of Inhabitants, some holding

48. *SAL,* II, 244; Hartwell, Blair, and Chilton, *Present State of Virginia,* ed. Farish, 19–20; Randolph to BT, Oct. 6, 1696, CO 5/1359, 20–22 (quotations on 21), transcript, LC; Beverley, *History and Present State of Virginia,* ed. Wright, 278–279, 355n.

forty fifty or sixty thousand acres, by whom the sheriffs are so overawed, that they take their accounts as they themselves would have it."[49]

The effect of the land fraud was land monopoly. The speculative activity of the great planters resulted in a pyramidal pattern in the 1704 quitrent roll: 400 estates had one thousand or more acres, 121 had more than two thousand, 17 had five thousand or more, but only 4 had ten thousand or more acres. One-quarter of the landowners in 1700 owned one-half of the land. In the five "best" tobacco-growing counties (James City, Henrico, Charles City, Middlesex, and King and Queen), the top quarter owned 70 percent of the land. Taken alone, land tenure in King and Queen County was even more skewed in favor of engrossment: 10 percent held the title on more than one-half of the land.[50]

The great planters' encroachment on land would check the expansion of the small-planter class after the 1660s, by which time landownership for poor whites had become a dubious possibility. The land system, initiated when indentured servants made up most of the labor force, permitted imported persons freedom to work for themselves once they had completed their indenture, and, if thrifty, eventually to buy land and claim headrights upon persons transported into the colony. The freed person's opportunity had been the linchpin in the cycle of laboring for wages, renting and owning land, and recruiting new servant labor.

Before 1660, most indentured servants who lived out their terms became small planters and worked the land themselves with their families, acquiring a hardscrabble success. Custom called for a master to provide his servants at the end of their indenture with corn and clothes, but not to the rights to fifty acres of land, as it did in Maryland until 1681. Virginia had no policy for giving freed servants the rights to land in the seventeenth century. If they wanted land, they had to buy or rent it from great or middling planters. The key to landownership for former servants was the savings that they accumulated from wage labor, sharecropping, and leaseholding. At midcentury, wages were high and used to escape tenancy. With the savings acquired from their labor and their produce, freed servants often bought land of their own during the 1640s and 1650s.[51]

49. Henry Hartwell to BT, CO 5/1359, 91–92 (quotation on 92), transcript, LC. See also Hartwell, Blair, and Chilton, *Present State of Virginia,* ed. Farish, 16–20; Quitt, *Virginia House of Burgesses,* 188–189.

50. Land, "Economic Behavior in a Planting Society," *Jour. So. Hist.,* XXXIII (1967), 469–481; Billings, Selby, and Tate, *Colonial Virginia,* 122.

51. Aubrey C. Land, "Economic Base and Social Structure: The Northern Chesapeake in the Eighteenth Century," *Jour. Econ. Hist.,* XXV (1965), 639–654; Hartwell, Blair,

Opportunity for landownership declined after the 1660s. Wages decreased as tobacco prices continued their downward spiral because of overproduction, Stuart mercantilist policies, and a poorly developed marketing system, which skimmed off the top the slight profit that planters received for their crop. More important, land prices were rising with the landgrab, increasing 135 percent between 1663 and 1700. The decline of European servants in the 1670s, becoming acute in the 1680s and 1690s, decreased small planters' prospects for augmenting landholdings because they required an exploitable class to realize their investment. Not only had the servant trade declined, but small planters could not afford slave labor, since an enslaved laborer was two to three times the cost of an indentured servant. The monopolization of land had made folly of the belief that Virginia was the land of opportunity for English servants who had paid their passage to Virginia with their labor. Secretary Thomas Ludwell, whose disbursement of patents contributed in no small way to the plight of poorer whites, believed in 1673 that one-quarter of all Virginia's freed servants owned no land, a phenomenon that augured their status as propertyless free laborers.[52]

With the decline in servitude, the great planters had to shift their land strategy. At first, they engrossed land, not to hoard it, but to resell it. But the use value of land could not be realized without an adequate supply of labor, and servants were now hard to come by. The great planters thus

and Chilton, *Present State of Virginia,* ed. Farish, 16; Voorhis, "Crown versus Council," *WMQ,* 3d Ser., III (1946), 504; Craven, *The Southern Colonies,* 191–192; Russell R. Menard, "From Servant to Freeholder: Status Mobility and Property Accumulation in Seventeenth-Century Maryland," *WMQ,* 3d Ser., XXX (1973), 49; Warren M. Billings, "The Law of Servants and Slaves in Seventeenth-Century Virginia," *VMHB,* XCIX (1991), 52 n. 24.

52. Rutman and Rutman, *A Place in Time,* 73–75; Morgan, "Headrights and Headcounts," *VMHB,* LXXX (1972), 369; David W. Galenson, "White Servitude and the Growth of Black Slavery in Colonial America," *Jour. Econ. Hist.,* XLI (1981), 40; Lois Green Carr and Russell R. Menard, "Immigration and Opportunity: The Freedman in Early Colonial Maryland," in Tate and Ammerman, eds., *The Chesapeake in the Seventeenth Century,* 206–242; Menard, "From Servant to Freeholder," *WMQ,* 3d Ser., XXX (1973), 5, 37–64; Lorena S. Walsh, "Servitude and Opportunity in Charles County, Maryland, 1658–1705," in Aubrey C. Land, Lois Green Carr, and Edward C. Papenfuse, eds., *Law, Society, and Politics in Early Maryland* (Baltimore, 1977), 111–133; Russell R. Menard, P. M. G. Harris, and Lois Green Carr, "Opportunity and Inequality: The Distribution of Wealth on the Lower Western Shore of Maryland, 1638–1705," *Maryland Historical Magazine,* LXIX (1974), 169–184; Land, "Economic Base and Social Structure," *Jour. Econ. Hist.,* XXV (1965), 639–654; Kulikoff, *Tobacco and Slaves,* 30–36.

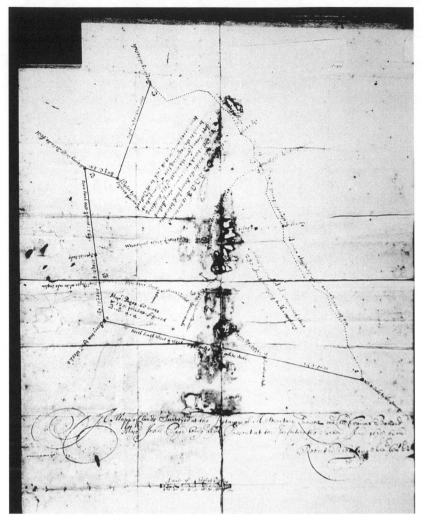

Plate 6. 1678 Mapp of Lands for Mr. Secretary Ludwell Done by
R. B., June 1678. . . . *Courtesy, the University Archives, Earl Gregg Swem
Library, College of William and Mary, Williamsburg, Va.*

moved from selling and leasing land to freed servants to the building of
great estates. These estates were either parceled out to tenants, or they
were manned by an increasing supply of blacks.

To retain their estates in perpetuity, the great planters erased their origins as the odd-man-out in primogeniture and began entailing their land.
Before 1680, lands entailed amounted to only 1 percent for each score of

years following 1620. With the landgrab, a shift in land tenure began from 1680 to 1700, when one-quarter of the wills probated contained provisions entailing 24 percent of the land. Testators entailed thousands of acres to their heirs, with some properties ranging from five thousand to fourteen thousand acres. These entailed estates removed permanently the amount of available acreage, making land prices even more dear.[53]

The great planters forced out a generation of impoverished planters from the soil. Laborers, unable to purchase land because of both its engrossment and the persistence of stagnant tobacco prices, left Virginia for the proprietary colonies. The crown sent roving commissioners to the colonies to report on the decline in revenues. If the reports of the commissioners were compromised by their charge to tighten reins on revenues and their ambition to work within the new Board of Trade, they were straight in pointing out the abuses of malfeasance and monopoly. They were also frank in discerning the collateral damage to the laboring poor. Colonial agent George Larkin, for example, had come to Virginia to investigate the tobacco revenue, but Governor Nicholson was in Maryland, and other officials were reticent in either talking or sharing public documents with him. Yet he did probe, even interviewing indentured servants. Larkin learned that an employer would abuse his servant "barbarously" during the final three months of his contract so that, in exchange for his freedom one month earlier, he would gladly forfeit his customary allowance of corn and clothes, a value slightly less than six pounds. This abuse and the absence of prospects drove many freed servants to Maryland, the Albemarle Sound region in Carolina, or Pennsylvania. The Council of State opined in 1708 that the "Cheif cause" for emigration from Virginia is the want of "Land to plant and cultivate."[54]

The freed servants became lumpen planters unable to find land of their own. The royal commissioners investigating the causes of Bacon's Rebellion charged in 1677 that the consolidation of landownership is "one of the most apparent causes of misery and mischief that attend this colony." It necessitates "the Planters to straggle to such remote distances when they

53. Holly Brewer, "Entailing Aristocracy in Colonial Virginia: 'Ancient Feudal Restraints' and Revolutionary Reform," *WMQ*, 3d Ser., LIV (1997), 321, 333; Quitt, *Virginia House of Burgesses*, 153–154.

54. George Larkin to BT, Dec. 22, 1701, CO 5/1360, 203–207, VCRP; *EJCCV*, III, 193; Larkin to BT, Dec. 22, 1701, in Great Britain, Public Record Office, *Calendar of State Papers*, Colonial Series, *America and West Indies*, ed. W. Noel Sainsbury et al. (London, 1860–), XIX, 692–693 (hereafter cited as *CSP*); Michael G. Hall, *Edward Randolph and the American Colonies, 1676–1703* (Chapel Hill, N.C., 1960), 136–138.

cannot find land nearer to seat themselves in a Continent they think hard."
Twenty years later, the commissioner of customs, Edward Randolph, observed that they were either forced to "hyer and pay a yearly Rent for some
of those lands" "or goe to the utmost bounds of the colony for Land exposed to danger and often times proves the Occasion of Warr with the
Indians."[55]

The engrossment of land contributed to the diminished supply of servants by discouraging emigration from England. With the increasing price
of land, potential servants without the prospect of landownership either
stayed home or chose more promising destinations. "The cheif and only
reason" potential English servants are unwilling to go to Virginia, Edward
Randolph reported to the Board of Trade in 1696, is that since the landgrab "there has not for many years been any vast Land to be taken up."
English immigration into Virginia has declined, concurred Larkin in his
report to the Board of Trade in 1701, because "all or greatest part of the
lands that lye any thing convenient, being taken up Some persons having
tracts of Land of twenty thirty or forty thousand acres and great part of it
unimployed." The development of other American settlements, especially
the proprietary colonies of Carolina, New York, Pennsylvania, and New
Jersey, offered English immigrants an alternative to Virginia, which they
increasingly chose in the last quarter of the century.[56]

With the amassment of landed estates by century's end, the formation
of an interconnected great-planter gentry concomitantly eclipsed the cycle
of servant into freeholder that replenished the ranks of the small planters.
To replace a dwindling supply of indentured servants, great planters began to manage plantations with enslaved labor. By controlling the source
of their labor and the descent of their estates through entail, they established themselves as a permanent ruling class.

A Very Great Cheat

By the turn of the century, the crown and the great planters struggled
over land allocation and its revenues in Virginia. The crown wanted to
put more land into production because the great planters' engrossment

55. "Instructions to Sir [William] Berkeley, Knight—Our Governor, Whitehall, London, [1662]," Commissioners Report, 1677, 27, BR 766, HL; Randolph to BT, Oct. 6,
1696, CO 5/1359, 20–22, transcript, LC.

56. Randolph to BT, Oct. 6, 1696, CO 5/1359, 20–22, transcript, LC; Larkin to BT,
Dec. 22, 1701, CO 5/1360, 203–207 (quotation on 206), VCRP.

left thousands of acres lying fallow. After evaluating twenty years of reports (1677–1697) from royal commissioners, royal governors, and royal
officers, the crown charged that the great planters had abused the intent
of the headright law. The crown thus began trying to regulate land tenure
by focusing on abuses in the headright, patent, and quitrent systems. The
great planters resisted each royal maneuver for land reform, insisting that
it would lead to the ruin of their families.

After a generation of commercial prosperity, the realm suffered a reversal of fortune following the Glorious Revolution in 1688. Reduced revenues resulting from price inflation, severe losses to the mercantile fleet
during the war with France (1689–1692), when tobacco ships had to be defended by convoy, and the diminution of tobacco customs precipitated a
colonial crisis. Deflation could be achieved by recycling old coins with silver, and war losses could be recouped by building new ships; however, the
decline in customs was systemic and could be rectified only by restructur-
ing the colonial office. After a three-year tour of the American Continental
Colonies (1692–1695), Edward Randolph, commissioner of customs, signaled the change of policy in his 1695 report of fraud in the tobacco trades
in Virginia, Maryland, and Pennsylvania. He attributed the great planters'
avarice, pluralism in officeholding, and duplicity in landholdings in the
royal colony of Virginia as the chief problem with tobacco revenues. Administrators of the House of Orange instituted the Board of Trade in 1696,
a departure from William Blathwayt's Lords of Trade, and installed John
Locke at its head to deal with these problems and to implement a new
colonial policy.[57]

Following Randolph's lead, Locke set as his first order of business the
land system in Virginia. He elicited from Commissary James Blair, who
was in London at the time, a report of the problems and solutions for Virginia. Blair, perhaps with Locke's collaboration, submitted a thirty-nine-
page brief, "Some of the Chief Grievances of the Present Constitution
of Virginia with an Essay towards the Remedies Thereof," which dealt
with land monopoly, tobacco production, and revenues. He described the
perversion of a land system that parceled out fifty-acre tracts for either
headrights or kickbacks. Since cultivation was in neither case given consideration in awarding great tracts of acreage, the peopling of Virginia

57. Hall, *Edward Randolph*, 138, 155–156, 166; Peter Laslett, "John Locke, the Great
Recoinage, and the Origins of the Board of Trade: 1695–1698," *WMQ*, 3d Ser., XIV
(1957), 371–373, 382, 398; [Charles Davenant], *Discourses on the Publick Revenues, and on
the Trade of England* . . . (London, 1698), pt. 2, 233–234, 236–237.

was retarded. The resultant poverty of population left Virginia without a proper defense, without economic diversification, and without an adequate labor force to produce tobacco revenues. The amassing of titles complicated fixing the land system; he nevertheless proposed elimination of the headright system, enforcement of the land-use laws, and regular collection of the quitrents, with delinquent landholdings returning to the crown. He also recommended a new law to assist cultivation of land: each five-hundred-acre tract must become a working plantation within three years of its patent anniversary; otherwise, this lapsed land would revert to the crown.[58]

Before acting on these recommendations, Locke queried Randolph and Blair further, using their earlier reports as a foundation. Randolph's October 6, 1696, letter and Blair's "Present State of Virginia and the College" (1697), coauthored by Edward Chilton and Henry Hartwell, affirmed the contention that land fraud and monopoly had limited the cultivation of tobacco. They reiterated the charge that the great planters had perverted the system by seizing land that they had no intention of cultivating. Locke concluded that he had to eliminate land hoarding, reinvigorate the governor's office, and affirm the integrity of colonial officials while stripping them of their plural offices, a source of malfeasance. Locke lobbied for Francis Nicholson's return as governor in 1698 to carry out land reform in Virginia.[59]

The Board of Trade in 1698 instructed Governor Francis Nicholson to curb engrossment by substituting homesteads, or family farms, for the more speculative headright tracts. The board, keeping in mind its mercantile interest, wanted to increase revenue by cultivating more land. It stipulated that "none shall acquire a Right by meerly importing, or buying of servants" and proposed that whoever occupies a "vacant peice of land" would receive one hundred acres for him and each laborer that he employs within three years of the patent anniversary. Any lands not paying quitrents would revert to royal domain. These instructions began a slow process by which royal governors tried to wrest control over the land from the great-planter class.[60]

The use of headrights for enslaved blacks became an issue in the

58. Laslett, "John Locke," *WMQ*, 3d Ser., XIV (1957), 400–401; Michael G. Kammen, ed., "Virginia at the Close of the Seventeenth Century: An Appraisal by James Blair and John Locke," *VMHB*, LXXIV (1966), 141–143.

59. Kammen, ed., "Virginia at the Close of the Seventeenth Century," *VMHB*, LXXIV (1966), 148–150, 153, 155; Hall, *Edward Randolph*, 148.

60. Instructions to Francis Nicholson, Sept. 13, 1698, Colonial Entry Book, CO 5/1359,

struggle over land. Speculators had claimed headrights on black immigrants after 1634, when the Laud Commission approved the headright system. The status of the charter generation of blacks, many from the Iberian colonies, remains ambiguous. In 1619, the same year that John Rolfe reported that a Dutch shipmaster had sold "20. And odd" blacks to Virginia planters, the House of Burgesses convened for the first time but would wait more than forty years to write legislation enslaving blacks. Little more than a score were listed in the censuses during the first half of the decade; these persons were delineated as "Negroes" without the benefit of surnames: twenty-two in 1624 and twenty-three in 1625. Some, such as Antonio (Anthony Johnson), were later able to escape enslavement, eke out an existence on the Eastern Shore, and claim acreage on enslaved labor. Their number undoubtedly increased during the 1630s, when the new merchants who captured the African trade from the English Guinea Company became the major suppliers of Africans, even though the most important market in the English system was Barbados. Without either a contract spelling out their term of service or custom, which protected English laborers, most blacks shipped to Virginia were likely enslaved. For example, husband and wife Congo and Cossongo were enslaved for life, passing their status on to their children.[61]

Headrights on enslaved blacks were accepted in violation of the "great Charter," which stipulated that servants could serve for only seven years and then be entitled to the fruits of their labor. Enslaved workers never completed their term of service, however, for their condition became perpetual. With the diminished supply of white servants, especially during the 1690s, blacks were important for the acquisition of land. Planters had been discouraged from taking up headrights for blacks during Lord Howard Effingham's tenure as governor from 1684 to 1689. Effingham, under instructions from James II, sought to enforce the Royal African Company's monopoly on the slave trade by cutting off the interloper trade from the West Indies. Hence, the planters who smuggled enslaved blacks were slow to reveal their acquisitions by applying for headrights. With the removal of Effingham in 1689, great planters again began to claim headrights on enslaved blacks imported into the colony. They claimed ninety-five

---

280–289, transcript, LC; Voorhis, "Crown versus Council," *WMQ*, 3d Ser., III (1946), 506–507.

61. Deal, "Race and Class in Colonial Virginia," 198; Alden T. Vaughan, "Blacks in Virginia: A Note on the First Decade," *WMQ*, 3d Ser., XXIX (1972), 469–478; Ira Berlin, *Many Thousands Gone: The First Two Centuries of Slavery in North America* (Cambridge, Mass., 1998), 29–34.

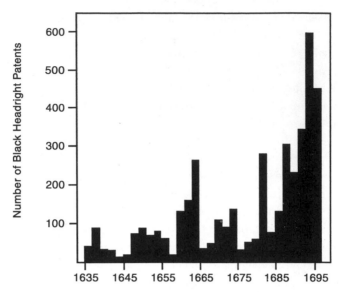

Figure 1. Black Headright Patents, 1635–1695. CP, *I–III.*
Drawn by Peter Schweighofer

thousand acres on nineteen hundred black headrights during the 1690s. In two of the largest applications, William Byrd I and Ralph Wormeley, both members of the Council of State, each used one hundred black headrights in patenting land in 1696.[62]

The use of black headrights was a coup for the great-planter class. Without question, indentured servants had secured capital in land; their time-limited labor had also generated wealth for their owners. At the end of their terms, they had provided a market for the sale of excess acres. Now, although the servant trade was in decline, the productive and specu-lative value of the land could still be realized: land and enslaved blacks could be entailed as great estates or leased to lesser planters. With one stroke, the great planters had ensured both a permanent, self-perpetuating labor force and capital in land.

62. Beverley, *History and Present State of Virginia,* ed. Wright, xxv–xxix; Craven, *White, Red, and Black,* 89–90; Sir Edmund Andros to BT, July 1, 1697, CO 5/1359, 113, VCRP; Kingsbury, ed., *Records of the Virginia Company,* III, 98–109, 153–177; *SAL,* I, 232; Voorhis, "Crown versus Council," *WMQ,* 3d Ser., III (1946), 499; Brenner, "Mer-chants, Planters, and Politics," 40; Craven, *The Southern Colonies,* 50, 121, 127, 128, 175–177; *CP,* III, 3, 11. Byrd's and Wormeley's applications accounted for 44.2 percent of the black headrights used in patenting land from 1635 to 1699.

Nicholson acted to stop the use of black headrights in April 1699, when several petitions to take up deserted lands based on black immigrants were placed before the General Court. The patentees produced headrights for blacks, asserting both "custom" and "inherit[ed] privilege confirmed" by the Great Charter of 1618. The General Court had been unable to conduct business because only three of the requisite five councillors were present — not enough to form a quorum. Nevertheless, Edward Hill, Edmund Jenings, and William Byrd I refused the petitions and issued an opinion that headrights should not be issued for "any others then His Xian [white] Subjects comeing to reside here."[63]

Why did the major beneficiaries of black headrights now so easily disallow their use? There are two explanations: the pressure that the crown exerted on the councillors and class competition in Virginia. The councillors, co-opted because their appointments were now being made in London, were sensitive to the crown's concern about engrossment. But they were more worried about holding onto their vast estates than adding to them by using black headrights. The crown's policy threatened to eliminate fraud in land transactions and constrict holdings to land that could be cultivated until the colony's population increased. Moreover, the imposition of inheritance taxes and quitrents would likely lead to the breakup of many massive estates. Returning this acreage to the crown for redistribution was, not an act of leveling, but an attempt to open land to industrious farmers, which would increase customs. The great planters believed that conceding on the issue of enslaved headrights would stall this drastic strategy. At the same time, they no doubt recognized the immediate advantage of restricting competition among the expanding numbers of tobacco planters. By removing the incentive of headrights for imported blacks, the great planters hoped to retard the expansion of slaveholding and, hence, the production of tobacco and to check the parvenus among them. Men who served on the council before 1700 had taken the lion's share of black headrights in the first phase of the landgrab from 1644 to 1676. By the 1690s, middling planters from the House of Burgesses were also patenting black headrights. Curtailing black headrights when the slave trade was increasing offered the great planters a way to arrest the expansion of these lesser planters.[64]

63. "At a Councill Held at James Citty the Fifteenth Day of Aprill 1699," *EJCCV*, I, 420; Nicholson to BT, July 1, 1699, CO 5/1359, 338–356, VCRP; Bruce, *Economic History of Virginia*, II, 85.
64. *CP*, I–III and supplement.

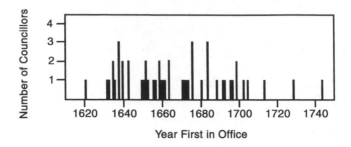

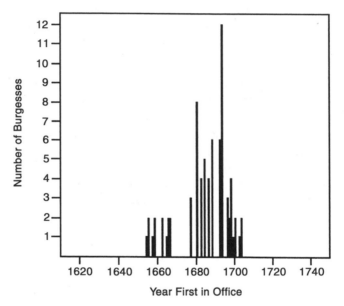

Figure 2. The Year First in Office for Men Who Secured Black
Headright Patents. CP, *I–III; Martin H. Quitt,* Virginia House
of Burgesses, 1660–1706: The Social, Educational, and
Economic Bases of Political Power *(New York, 1989), 304–364;
Cynthia Miller Leonard,* The General Assembly of Virginia,
July 30, 1619–January 11, 1978: A Bicentennial Register of
Members *(Richmond, Va., 1978). Drawn by Peter Schweighofer*

Nicholson realized that he could not effect redistribution in Virginia; he did aim, though, to bring the landed elite under control by making land hoarding unprofitable. He seized the opportunity to deny black head-rights in the interests of British mercantilism, decrying the practice as a "very Great cheat" and contrary to the intentions of Charles II. By the authority of the Privy Council, he issued an order against anyone's patent-ing lands for the importation of blacks, arguing that the practice sub-verted the system's design to encourage immigrants who could become freeholders. Manipulation of the slave trade was precluding that possi-bility. But Nicholson's real interest was in disciplining the great planters. Their massive landholdings, which deprived free white servants of realiz-ing the intentions of the headright system, menaced British mercantilism by restricting the planting of tobacco.[65]

Although the use of black headrights was now invalidated, the great planters still sought to secure their control over Virginia. They at first gave lip service to the crown's concern about engrossment, which should not be seen as a surrender to the royal land policy's restrictions. If the coun-cillors had bowed to the crown's authority on black headrights, they had not yielded on principle. To remedy the revocation of black headrights and the diminished supply of white servants, the councillors in June 1699 simply devised a new system of patenting land through treasury rights. With the payment of an immigrant's transportation and five shillings to the auditor for a treasury right, a speculator had the "same liberty" to sur-vey and patent fifty-acre tracts as he had with a headright. This arrange-ment appeared to be a nod to the crown's position to eliminate fraud in the clerk's office and increase revenue, but it really ensconced the great planters' advantage in landholding. Those with sufficient funds in Virginia could purchase rights to land for a pittance. Despite the crown's efforts to reform the land system, the great planters were still able to maintain large tracts of land and to dodge paying quitrents. Nicholson's remarks to the Board of Trade had become a familiar refrain by 1703. "Severall of [the great planters] might have contained as many thousand acres as they pleased, and I suppose that some of them should be ten or twenty thou-sand, and so to have [engrossed] all the good Land in these parts, by which means they would have kept other people from seasing of it, or else have made them pay for it."[66]

65. Nicholson to BT, Apr. 15, 1699, CO 5/1310, 47–48, transcript, LC.
66. *EJCCV,* I, 457; *CP,* III, vii–viii; Nicholson to BT, Oct. 22, 1703, CO 5/1360, 441, VCRP.

Nicholson tried a more efficient accounting of Virginia landholders by rewarding sheriffs for bringing in delinquents. This strategy resulted in the comprehensive quitrent rolls of 1704 and legal procedures against Colonel Lawrence Smith of Gloucester, who had ten thousand acres in several counties in arrears with the quitrent. Although the 1704 quitrent rolls were an important reckoning of Virginia landholdings, they did not solve the problem of land monopoly, for the sheriffs could seize only goods, not land. Nicholson was recalled to England when legal proceedings against Smith had only just begun. In the end, Smith was slapped on the wrist with a small fine. Nicholson had been able to invalidate the use of black headrights in land patents, but his continued assault on land monopoly made him a reprehensible character to the great planters, curtailing his effectiveness. Great planters Robert "King" Carter, Benjamin Harrison, John Lightfoot, Philip Ludwell, and Matthew Page joined Commissary Blair, a former ally of Nicholson who was now angered by his church policies, in petitioning the crown for Nicholson's removal in May 1703. They were successful partly because all six were councillors and partly because they attacked the governor's character rather than the crown's land policy. Further attempts at land reform would have to wait until after Nicholson had been forced to leave Virginia.[67]

The strained relationship between the Board of Trade and Virginia's elite continued with the appointment of the new royal governor, Colonel Edward Nott, in 1705. The land issue played no small part. The Board of Trade instructed Nott to continue its policy of land reform in Virginia, indicting the great planters for owning land that "they never intended to, or in truth could, occupy or cultivate." The board directed him to restrain unreasonable claims on land and with the council's advice to make a general survey of Virginia's landownership, giving an exact account of planters who owned more than twenty thousand acres. Nott was to discourage the headright system in favor of land distribution based on production and to collect quitrents within three years of the patent anniversary.[68]

The crown and the colony contested the turf in a tug-of-war in 1705.

67. "Virginia's Complaint against the Plaintiffs," 1705, Frank J. Klingberg Collection, Charles E. Young Research Library, UCLA; Richard L. Morton, *Colonial Virginia*, 2 vols. (Chapel Hill, N.C., 1960), I, 363; Voorhis, "Crown versus Council," *WMQ*, 3d Ser., III (1946), 506; Billings, Selby, and Tate, *Colonial Virginia*, 168.

68. "Instructions to Governor Nott," in *CSP*, XXII, 489–498 (quotation on 493); Voorhis, "Crown versus Council," *WMQ*, 3d Ser., III (1946), 505.

The great planters claimed the prerogative of their class for expanding their estates; the crown reclaimed Indian land for the royal domain. In response to the royal instructions, the General Assembly revised the law in 1705, producing some improvements in the administration of the land system and the regulation of surveyors but making no effort to adjust the inequity in landholding. Rather, the statute allowed owners of "at least" five taxable enslaved or indentured workers not only to claim more than five hundred acres in a single tract but also to take two hundred acres for each additional taxable worker up to four thousand acres. With these stipulations, the great planters limited the land access of smaller planters by tying existing labor holdings to land acquisition. The Board of Trade, in turn, stopped until further notice all patents for Nottoway land opened in 1699 in the region south of the Blackwater Swamp.[69]

With Nott's death in 1706 and the absence of a royal governor until 1710, the Council of State obstructed land reform, prolonging the struggle with the crown. One contested issue on which the council remained adamant concerned the confirmation of unsigned and double patents. Unsigned patents were those that had been issued or granted by the governor but were either lost, not recorded, or not properly entered in the secretary's ledger. Double patents referred to the practice of adding surplus or adjacent land to an original patent and then including both tracts in a new patent. The councillors wanted these faulty titles confirmed. The Board of Trade had instructed Nott to find the "true bounds" of estates in Virginia and to open to homesteading land secured with unsigned and double patents. After an investigation of the records of the secretary's office in April 1706, the council had found only the "usual and always expressed" practice of claiming headrights for land patents. The council, claiming both the charter of Charles II and the "constant custom of granting Land," proposed in 1708 that "free Liberty be given to all persons to take up Lands any where within the bounds of Virginia."[70]

Edmund Jenings, president of the council and interim governor, com-

69. *SAL*, III, 306; Councillors to BT, Oct. 19, 1709, CO 5/1362, 374–382, VCRP; *JHB, 1702/3–1705, 1705–1706, 1710–1712*, 127–136; Voorhis, "Crown versus Council," *WMQ*, 3d Ser., III (1946), 506; Morton, *Colonial Virginia*, I, 363; Helen C. Rountree, "The Termination and Dispersal of the Nottoway Indians of Virginia," *VMHB*, XCV (1987), 196.

70. "Instructions to Governor Nott," *CSP*, XXII, 489–498; *EJCCV*, III, 107, 117, 125, 193; Voorhis, "Crown versus Council," *WMQ*, 3d Ser., III (1946), 506–507; *SAL*, III, 308, 313–314.

plained to the Board of Trade that these unsigned patents were secured long before the board's alterations were proposed. He presented other arguments against the mercantile regulation of unsigned and double patents. The new, more stringent tenure arrangements, he believed, are a "very great prejudice" to both the crown and the colony, and he requested that the crown reconsider its actions and allow the customary land grants, which would increase both planting and revenues collected on quitrents. Jenings forewarned that the committee must suspend these requirements until like restrictions were placed on the proprietary colonies or face the council's ire. Since the proprietary colonies were not under such regulations, the "people will (as they do) now flock thither where they can take up land on much easier terms."[71]

The councillors also criticized the clauses concerning inheritance and the size of land patents. They contended that the royal instructions jeopardized the succession of land from father to son. Specifications dictated that land that could not be reasonably cultivated by the planter's family or that was in arrears with the quitrents should be returned to the public domain. They also contended that, since the "valuable and convenient" land had already been patented according to the old methods, leaving mostly waste, restricting patents to fewer than five hundred acres would proportionately reduce the amount of choice land available per title. These regulations foreboded disaster. The council petitioned the Board of Trade to repeal them, for they were contrary to "ancient constitutions" and could only cause the "greatest Confusion." Failure to pay the quitrent because of the owner's death, or loss of the "Servants or Slaves for w[hi]ch his Land was granted to him," or "any other Casualty" would result in his family's losing the land. "One Misfortune would so unavoidably introduce another till at last perhaps after all his Toil, his Land will be taken away by a Stranger who hath better fortune and his Children hurried out to seek for new Settlem[en]ts."[72]

Soon after Alexander Spotswood arrived in Virginia in 1710 to assume his post as governor, he continued imperial efforts to reform land use. His instructions were designed to make landholders prove that they wanted land for agriculture rather than speculation. Each holder of a patent had to cultivate three acres in each fifty-acre tract within three years after re-

71. Edmund Jenings to BT, Jan. 11, 1709, CO 5/1316, 133–135, VCRP.
72. Councillors to BT, Oct. 19, 1709, CO 5/1362, 374–382 (quotations on 379, 380), VCRP.

ceiving the grant. Spotswood arbitrarily inserted the three-acre cultivation clause in all new grants as royal prerogative rather than local law.[73]

Spotswood thought that he had found his opening to turn the land-reform measures into law when the great planters' pretensions offended smaller farmers. The General Assembly had extended the 1705 statute, permitting the owners of six enslaved laborers or more to pursue game that had traveled from their land onto adjacent property, essentially granting them the "liberty" to hunt on their neighbors' land. This law-of-the-chase clause extended hunting prerogatives to the gentry, not unlike the class-inspired English game act of 1670. Complaints from several counties were first made to the House of Burgesses, causing the members to delete the offensive clause; Spotswood then persuaded them to prepare a new bill. In the new act, anyone, regardless of slaveownership or class status, caught hunting on a neighbor's land without permission forfeited five hundred pounds of tobacco to him. Using the occasion of the hunting controversy, Spotswood attempted in this land act of 1710 to deal with the fraud and abuse identified earlier: neglected quitrents, faulty patents, and false certificates.[74]

Spotswood asserted crown authority, acting contrary to the interests "of some of the most considerable men in the Country and a Great part of the Assembly." To improve the collection of quitrents, the law provided that nonpayment forfeited the land involved. To correct old grants containing more acreage than specified in the patent, the new act required the owner of the patent to pay quitrents for the surplus. Failure to pay resulted in forfeiture after notice had been given by anyone who had surveyed the land and taken out a patent for the surplus. Finally, to maintain control, the act removed the General Court's authority over "Lapsed Land," making the governor's office the "last resort."[75]

Although Spotswood got these reforms enacted, they in no way jeopardized the extensive holdings of the great-planter class. The 1710 land act legitimized all existing grants, no matter how the patents had been

73. Morgan, *American Slavery, American Freedom*, 359; Voorhis, "Crown versus Council," *WMQ*, 3d Ser., III (1946), 507.

74. *SAL*, III, 328–329, 343, 534–535; Colonel Alexander Spotswood to BT, Mar. 6, 1710/1, CO 5/1365, 284–301, VCRP; E. P. Thompson, *Whigs and Hunters: The Origin of the Black Act* (New York, 1975), 21; Douglas Hay, "Poaching and Game Laws on Cannock Chase," in Hay et al., *Albion's Fatal Tree: Crime and Society in Eighteenth-Century England* (New York, 1975), 189–192.

75. Spotswood to BT, Mar. 6, 1710/1, CO 5/1365, 284–301, VCRP.

obtained and regardless of the fabrications made during surveying. It thwarted the crown's efforts for homesteading in Virginia by allowing the required three acres to be used for grazing cattle rather than cultivation. Although the act stipulated that applications for new patents be approved by the governor and the council before surveying, this procedure was finally left to the council.[76]

Trying to rectify the omissions of the 1710 act, Spotswood once again persuaded the General Assembly to reform the land system in 1713. The Council of State, prompted by Spotswood's proclamation of December 9, 1712, which included instructions for disallowing claims, examined rights from several counties where William Byrd II and Philip Ludwell II were active. Supporting the governor, the council rejected the following applications: rights proved before 1706, unless granted to the person imported, and rights for indentured workers who had received certificates for their own immigration, for "the Custom" then was for the "Merchant or Master to prove rights for Servants." The assembly in the act of 1713 followed suit, allowing for the forfeiture of land if the quitrent had not been paid during the previous three years. But the council sitting as the General Court countered, promptly issuing the opinion that the forfeiture clause did not apply to grants issued before 1710. Thus, the 1713 act had the effect of locking the henhouse door behind the fox. In his defense, Spotswood reported that his regulations had accounted for "£2,000 in [the] Bank" during the four years since their inception—more than that collected during the seventeen previous years under the administrations of the two William Byrds as receiver general of His Majesty's revenues.[77]

Spotswood realized that the great planters had the better end of the deal. He joined the landgrab. He actively acquired land, beginning in 1714, when he established forty German immigrants in the headwaters of the Rappahannock River, until 1722, when he gobbled up 85,000 acres there. Spotswood had made a 180-degree turn on the land issue by the time he was removed as governor in 1722. Spotswood's reversal pivoted on Germanna, a 3,429-acre tract that he granted to himself in trust of another.

76. *SAL*, III, 517–535; Morgan, *American Slavery, American Freedom*, 359–360.

77. *EJCCV*, III, 336; Spotswood to BT, Feb. 1, 1720, in R. A. Brock, ed., *The Official Letters of Alexander Spotswood, Lieutenant-Governor of the Colony of Virginia, 1710–1722*, 2 vols. (Richmond, Va., 1882–1885), II, 335; Rhys Isaac, *The Transformation of Virginia, 1740–1790* (Chapel Hill, N.C., 1982), 134; Voorhis, "Crown versus Council," *WMQ*, 3d Ser., III (1946), 509.

When queried by the crown about this acquisition and the exploitation of the German immigrants, Spotswood responded that his was but customary behavior. He knew of no regulation that kept a governor from obtaining "land to his own use." He conceded that using a "borrowed Name May Carry with it the colour of Fraud," but he had only engaged in the "constant practice of former Governors whenever they had a mind to take up Land for themselves." He excused his lease of land to the immigrants, for he had not only paid £150 for their transportation but was still indebted for their subsistence for two years. "If," he wrote, "I had pursued the common methods of the Country and taken advantage of the Law here—instead of being Tenants, they might have been my Servants for five years." When the German tenancy failed to work out, Spotswood invested in enslaved labor. He tried to join the great-planter class in one fell swoop when he contracted for four hundred enslaved blacks to be delivered from the Gambia on the *Dove* in 1723, hoping to realize the value on the 20,000 acres he had grabbed in his namesake Spotsylvania County.[78]

Spotswood and his successors did little to control the aggressive speculation in Virginia's backcountry. After 1720, the governors allowed the council autonomy in dispensing land grants of more than 400 acres. Without royal restraint after 1720 and without Indian resistance, the great planters grabbed acreage in the piedmont and what remained in the Southside and the Northern Neck all the way to the Blue Ridge Mountains. They reached westward across the Blue Ridge into the Shenandoah Valley and, before 1740, would stride across the Allegheny Mountains into what would become Augusta and Frederick Counties. After 1720, the great planters had a land-office business in the council chambers, routinely granting to themselves or their associates tens of thousands of acres. Although there were time restrictions on these grants, the council habitually issued extensions or exemptions. The council awarded tracts of 100,000 acres or more to great planters through petitions that promised to settle one family for each 1,000-acre plantation granted on a tract—a far cry from the modest aims of the headright system. William Byrd II, for example, had by 1739 accumulated 179,000 acres, of which more than 100,000 acres lay in the area of the Dan River, extending to the North Carolina line. By the beginning of the eighteenth century, Byrd and the other great planters who sat

78. Voorhis, "Crown versus Colony," *WMQ*, 3d Ser., III (1946), 507–514; Walter Minchinton, Celia King, and Peter Waite, eds., *Virginia Slave-Trade Statistics, 1698–1775* (Richmond, Va., 1984), 48; Brock, ed., *The Official Letters of Spotswood*, II, 217–218.

in the council chambers in Williamsburg stood in the countryside on legs
of land monopoly and slavery.[79]

*   *   *

OVER THE COURSE of the seventeenth century, lax colonial administration and the headright system allowed the great planters to achieve two
ends, the accumulation of large landed estates and the importation of a
permanent enslaved labor force. An added incentive to importing Africans
was the fraudulent practice of claiming headrights on them. Other factors, however, were at work in encouraging the shift to an enslaved black
workforce.

79. *EJCCV*, III, 553; Hughes, *Surveyors and Statesmen*, 74.

CHAPTER 2

The Labor Switch

More often than not, the literature on Virginia explains the colony's transition from indentured servants to enslaved laborers as a rational economic response by planters to supply and demand. Prices for servants rose as their supply waned, beginning about 1665. Given the shortage of labor and the abundance of land, planters had to consider a new source. By the 1680s, the higher cost of servants because of declining rates of immigration and the lower cost of enslaved workers in a less morbid environment made the slave trade economically viable. But other economic considerations flesh out the transition to slavery: adverse conditions in Virginia and England's changing economic circumstances, which contributed to the eventual collapse of the indentured servant trade; Africans' agricultural experience and enslaved laborers' potential for exploitation; and the opening of the slave trade. The role of independent slave traders then completes the transition to a slave society, or a society in which slavery is the primary source of income for the elite.[1]

1. This classical market interpretation is proved in John J. McCusker and Russell R. Menard's price series of servants and enslaved (McCusker and Menard, *The Economy of British America, 1607–1789* [Chapel Hill, N.C., 1985], 134–135, 137–138). See also Menard, "From Servants to Slaves: The Transformation of the Chesapeake Labor System," *Southern Studies,* XVI (1977), 355–390, where he writes: "Black slavery was more a consequence than a cause of the decline of white servitude" (371); and Allan Kulikoff, *Tobacco and Slaves: The Development of Southern Cultures in the Chesapeake, 1680–1800* (Chapel Hill, N.C., 1986), 41. For a definition of a slave society, see M. I. Finley, *Ancient Slavery and Modern Ideology* (New York, 1980), 82.

Englishmen Had Better Be Hanged: 1660–1680

The servant trade began to dry up during the 1660s, when the material conditions of servants made Virginia unattractive to the English poor. Former servants complained of poor diet and long hours in the field. They also objected to laboring and suffering alongside blacks, an indictment against how degraded their life had become. "By the early 1660's white men were loudly protesting against being made 'slaves,'" writes Winthrop D. Jordan, "in terms which strongly suggest that they considered slavery not as wrong but as inapplicable to themselves."[2]

Witnesses in Virginia addressed the comparable status of servants and the enslaved in popular tracts, travel literature, and official reports. The memorials of former servants focused on the material conditions of bound labor. They remembered that blacks and whites suffered miserably together, were both alienated from kith and kin, worked together long hours in the field, and ate only hominy and what they produced in their own plots after work. James Revel, a transported felon, issued an ominous warning to his countrymen when he returned to England after fourteen years in Virginia:

> Forc'd from your friends and country for to go,
> Among the Negroes to work at the hoe;
> In distant countries void of all relief,
> Sold for a slave because you prov'd a thief.
>
> . . . .
>
> We and the Negroes both alike did fare,
> Of work and food we had an equal share.

George Larkin, in buttressing the contention of the Lords of Trade that the repulsion of English laborers because of planter abuses contributed to the waning in tobacco revenues, concurred with Revel's notion that servant food and slave food were indistinguishable. Former servants told him: "Most of his [servant's] food [is] . . . hominie and Water, which is good for Negroes, but very disagreeable to English Constitutions. I have been told by some of them that they have not tasted flesh made once in three months." Larkin opined that the poor Englishman "had really better be hanged then come a Servant into the Plantations."[3]

2. Winthrop D. Jordan, *White over Black: American Attitudes toward the Negro, 1550–1812* (Chapel Hill, N.C., 1968), 80–81.

3. James Revel, "The Poor Unhappy Transported Felon's Sorrowful Account of His

Plate 7. Transportation. Ca. 1770–1785. Handkerchief, detail.
Courtesy, Colonial Williamsburg Foundation, Williamsburg, Va.

Virginia's promoters tried to dispel notions of the colony as a hellhole for the poor. They countered the debasing analogy of servants to enslaved by comparing the laboring conditions of blacks and whites to those of English husbandry, equating a settler's work with a yeoman's gardening in England. The labor of servants and the labor of the enslaved were not only similar, asserted Robert Beverley, but also differed little from that of free people, comparing favorably with the work of the common English laborer. His analogy appears to be more an effort to promote immigration than to depict social reality.[4]

By the end of the 1660s, white laborers began showing their discontent by running away. New servants plotted their escapes en route to the plantations or shortly before their arrival there. Runaways found underground assistance from planters who were not far removed in time or in material condition from them. Some planters in the proprietary colonies, covetous of their neighbors' labor, enticed servants away from their masters, deliberately leading them into crime. "North Carolina is and always was," wrote Thomas Culpeper, "the sink of America, the refuge of renegades." The escapes deprived planters of labor, for they lacked the means to pursue

Fourteen Years Transportation at Virginia in America" (ca. 1680), in Warren M. Billings, ed., *The Old Dominion in the Seventeenth Century: A Documentary History of Virginia, 1606–1689* (Chapel Hill, N.C., 1975), 140, 142. See also Thomas Heiller and Paul Williams, *The Vain Prodigal Life, and Tragical Penitent Death of Thomas Heiller . . .* (London, 1680); T. H. Breen, James H. Lewis, and Keith Schlesinger, "Motive for Murder: A Servant's Life in Virginia, 1678," *WMQ*, 3d Ser., XL (1983), 106–120; George Larkin to BT, Dec. 22, 1701, CO 5/1360, 203–207 (quotation on 207), VCRP.

4. Robert Beverley, *The History and Present State of Virginia* (1705, 1722), ed. Louis B. Wright (Chapel Hill, N.C., 1947), 271–272. The Reverend Hugh Jones used similar imagery, but Jones opposed slavery, believing it more prudent and charitable to employ England's poor in Virginia. See Jones, *The Present State of Virginia: From Whence Is Inferred a Short View of Maryland and North Carolina* (1724), ed. Richard L. Morton (Chapel Hill, N.C., 1956), 74–77, 120–131.

the fugitives, and masters became suspicious of those left behind. The bad example set for those servants remaining undermined discipline and often led to a planter's financial ruin.[5]

The social problems associated with transported felons clogged a channel of the labor supply. Their flight and criminality caused some great planters to promote slavery as a substitute for convict labor. Thomas Ludwell offered in 1665 to return servant runaways to New York for like assistance and suggested to Lord Arlington in 1670 that the West Indies might be a better place for English convicts than Virginia. That Ludwell owned "three pairs of new slaves" surely colored his remarks. James Revel recalled in verse the growing preference for blacks instead of felons during his sojourn in Virginia. After his owner's death, an attorney purchased the plantation and the blacks from his widow but refused to buy the servant convicts: "He bought the Negroes who for life were slaves, / But no transported Fellons would he have."[6]

The changed needs of the English economy aggravated the employment problem in Virginia by keeping the poor at home. By the 1660s, the English birthrate had decreased dramatically, which, coupled with the outbreak of plague, led to a decline in the number of young people entering the workforce. In 1661, the fifteen-to-twenty-four-year-old cohort, or those most likely to immigrate to Virginia as servants, reached its high point in the English population at 960,000 before dropping by 17 percent over the next twenty years. This decline reduced the pressure on the population, which had previously forced poor Englishmen to seek a new life in Virginia. At the same time, England experienced prosperity, resulting in a rise in real wages. The Great Fire of London in 1666 set off a boom

5. Thomas Ludwell to Richard Nicholls, June 12, 1665, BL 82, HL; see also "Representations of Mr. Byrd concerning Proprietary Governments, anno 1700," BR 744, HL; Thomas Culpeper, "The Present State of Virginia" (1681), in Great Britain, Public Record Office, *Calendar of State Papers*, Colonial Series, *America and West Indies*, ed. W. Noel Sainsbury et al. (London, 1860–), XI, 755 (hereafter cited as *CSP*).

6. Ludwell to Nicholls, June 12, 1665, BL 82, HL; Ludwell to [Lord Arlington], Apr. 29, 1670, CO 1/25, fol. 62, transcript, LC; [Lyon G. Tyler], "Temple Farm," *WMQ*, 1st Ser., II (1893–1894), 4–5; Edmund S. Morgan, *American Slavery, American Freedom: The Ordeal of Colonial Virginia* (New York, 1975), 236; Morgan, "Headrights and Headcounts," review of *White, Red, and Black: The Seventeenth-Century Virginian*, by Wesley Frank Craven, *VMHB*, LXXX (1972), 369; "1678 Mapp of Lands for Mr Secretry Ludwell Done by R. B., June 1678, Shewing the Land Sold to Page and Ballard by Secretary Ludwell," *WMQ*, 1st Ser., X (1901–1902), facing 90; Revel, "The Poor Unhappy Transported Felon's Sorrowful Account," in Billings, ed., *Old Dominion*, 141.

in the public and private building trades for the next twenty years, feeding ancillary industries. The laboring poor also increasingly found employment in industries linked to the colonial and cloth trades. This demand for material and labor was unprecedented in English history.[7]

Authorities began to see the poor, not as a national problem, but as a natural resource. Rather than shipping laborers and consumers to Virginia, they began encouraging domestic industries. Restoration-period writings recognized the laboring poor as integral to the new vision of a productive and wealthy nation. Since the country needed workers, it became a maxim of the period that only the poor could produce wealth, even though their massive unemployment was well known. Economists envisioned that with rationalized planning those uprooted as a result of the enclosures and demise of the manors could work in the new wage economy. Educating them in the habits of thrift, sobriety, and industry could reform their idleness. Economists not only promoted population increase but criticized the employment of Englishmen abroad as disastrous to the development of national wealth. William Petty captured the new Stuart attitude in a line in 1662: "Fewness of people is real poverty." With the new philosophy on the English poor in mind, Chief Justice Francis Pemberton began in the 1680s to prosecute merchants for spiriting Englishmen to Virginia plantations. The principal merchants complained to the Lords of Trade in 1681 that ship captains were unwilling to transport servants "for feare of being informed against."[8]

7. Russell R. Menard, "British Migration to the Chesapeake Colonies in the Seventeenth Century," in Lois Green Carr, Philip D. Morgan, and Jean B. Russo, eds., *Colonial Chesapeake Society* (Chapel Hill, N.C., 1988), 110; E. A. Wrigley and R. S. Schofield, *The Population History of England, 1541–1871: A Reconstruction* (Cambridge, Mass., 1981); J. D. Chambers, *Population, Economy, and Society in Pre-Industrial England* (London, 1972), 22–30, 86; Richard S. Dunn, "Servants and Slaves: The Recruitment and Employment of Labor," in Jack P. Greene and J. R. Pole, eds., *Colonial British America: Essays in the New History of the Early Modern Era* (Baltimore, 1984), 163–164; E. A. Wrigley, "A Simple Model of London's Importance in Changing English Society and Economy, 1650–1750," *Past and Present*, no. 37 (July 1967), 62; B. A. Holderness, *Pre-Industrial England: Economy and Society, 1500–1750* (London, 1976), 216; K. G. Davies, *The Royal African Company* (1957; reprint, New York, 1970), 55; Morgan, *American Slavery, American Freedom*, 295–315; Wesley Frank Craven, *White, Red, and Black: The Seventeenth-Century Virginian* (Charlottesville, Va., 1971), 58, 61; Maurice Dobb, *Studies in the Development of Capitalism*, rev. ed. (London, 1963), 197–198; David W. Galenson, *White Servitude in Colonial America: An Economic Analysis* (Cambridge, 1981), 153.

8. "Observations on Two Petitions of the Principal English Merchants Trading to the Plantations Who Are Liable to Prosecution for Landing Servants to Those Plantations"

The crown thus began to promote the slave trade in lieu of the servant trade to the colonies. Indeed, Jean Barbour, the slave trader, believed that Charles II promoted the slave trade to preserve English labor for England. English plantations needed a greater supply of labor "than could be well spared from hence, without the danger of depopulating his majesty's native dominions." Instead, "for the supplying of those plantations with Blacks," he would "invite all of his subjects to subscribe to a new joint stock," the Royal African Company. As far as the African was concerned, Charles II was to the English laborer what missionary Bartolomé de Las Casas was to the Indian. By protecting one labor group from exploitation, he promoted the enslavement of Africans.[9]

Blacks Can Make Tobacco Cheaper than Whites

The waning of the servant trade encouraged the great planters to reexamine the slave trade. They expected that slavery would offset both the initial purchase price of blacks and the cost of rearing enslaved children, making blacks a better investment than whites, who worked for only a limited number of years. Colonel Nicholas Spencer, secretary of the colony, welcomed the importation of blacks in 1683 because the "low price of Tobacco requires it should bee made as cheap as possible, and that Blacks can make it cheaper than Whites." Indeed, a plethora of conditions combined to make slave labor more profitable than servant labor.[10]

One such factor was the seasonal emigration to Virginia. Whites and blacks arrived at different times during the cycle of tobacco production. Merchants delivered white servants late in the fall, after tobacco had been packed in casks for the return voyage to England. They believed that meet-

---

(ca. 1681), Owen Wynne Collection, 211, 75r–76r, Codrington Library, All Souls College, Oxford University; William Petty, *A Treatise of Taxes and Contributions,* in Charles Henry Hull, ed., *Economic Writings of Sir William Petty* (Cambridge, 1899), 34; Christopher Hill, *The Century of Revolution, 1603–1714* (New York, 1961), 206; Joyce Oldham Appleby, *Economic Thought and Ideology in Seventeenth-Century England* (Princeton, N.J., 1978), 129–157; Abbot Emerson Smith, *Colonists in Bondage: White Servitude and Convict Labor in America, 1607–1776* (Chapel Hill, N.C., 1947), 76–77; Susan Alice Westbury, "Colonial Virginia and the Atlantic Slave Trade" (Ph.D. diss., University of Illinois at Urbana-Champaign, 1981), 29.

9. [Jean Barbour], *An Account of the Rise and Progress of Our Trade to Africa; Preceding the Year 1697,* in [Awnsham Churchill, ed.], *A Collection of Voyages and Travels . . . ,* V (London, 1732), 666.

10. Colonel [Nicholas] Spencer to BT, [Sept. 20, 1683], CO 5/1356, 138, VCRP.

ing the demand of the two-way carrying trade in the fall was more important than spring arrivals, even though white mortality was greater in autumn and little effort needed to be expended in tobacco production at this time of year. They were more concerned, however, with exploiting black labor than with the return cargo of tobacco. Traders thus arrived with blacks in the late spring and early summer, at the time of tobacco cultivation, when they could be put to work immediately in the fields.[11]

These seasonal patterns contributed to the instant use of enslaved labor and increased the profitability of slavery. The great planters could produce more with the same number of hands per acre because they worked blacks longer than servants during the week and granted them fewer holidays. They also could benefit from the labor of African women, who, unlike white women, routinely worked in the fields. This racial shift began as early as 1643 when the Virginia assembly differentiated women by race, taxing blacks as drudges and exempting whites as domestics. The assembly reconfirmed this discrimination in 1658, adding the caveat in 1662 of taxing white females commonly used as field laborers. By the turn of the century, a white woman, observed Robert Beverley, was "rarely or never put to work in the Ground, if she be good for any thing else." On the other hand, it was a "common thing" to find black women working "out of Doors."[12]

Africans' agricultural experience also made slave labor more profitable than servant labor. Africans were more familiar with tobacco cultivation than the English, which meant they spent less time learning and began producing profits sooner. Most Africans arrived with extensive knowledge of hoe agriculture, mound cultivation, replanting techniques, fallow or rotational planting, crop processing, and tobacco culture. The English, on the other hand, had no background in tobacco or forest husbandry. Nevertheless, they both had to adapt to a "Chesapeake system of hus-

11. Kulikoff, *Tobacco and Slaves*, 326–327; Galenson, *White Servitude in Colonial America*, 89; James Horn, "Servant Emigration to the Chesapeake in the Seventeenth Century," in Thad W. Tate and David L. Ammerman, eds., *The Chesapeake in the Seventeenth Century: Essays on Anglo-American Society* (Chapel Hill, N.C., 1979), 91.

12. Beverley, *History and Present State of Virginia*, ed. Wright, 271–272; Lois Green Carr and Russell R. Menard, "Land, Labor, and Economies of Scale in Early Maryland: Some Limits to Growth in the Chesapeake System of Husbandry," *Journal of Economic History*, XLIX (1989), 407, 415; Lorena S. Walsh, "Plantation Management in the Chesapeake, 1620–1820," ibid., 393; Kathleen M. Brown, *Good Wives, Nasty Wenches, and Anxious Patriarchs: Gender, Race, and Power in Colonial Virginia* (Chapel Hill, N.C., 1996), 115–120.

bandry," which combined Indian techniques—girdling trees or slash and burn, long fallow, and hoe cultivation—with European metal tools and draft animals. Workers planted tobacco in mounds rather than furrows as in England because planters had yet to realize the production benefits of plow cultivation. An Iron Age people, West Africans had for millennia engaged in husbandry using metal hoes and techniques remarkably similar to those used by native Americans. As late as 1732, William Hugh Grove observed that blacks "dont generally Plow the Land but manage it w[i]th the Broad Hough tho I have seen some Ox plough."[13]

Tobacco and corn, introduced in West Africa early in the sixteenth century, had become staple crops by the end of the seventeenth century. As early as 1623, Richard Jobson of the English Guinea Company observed Africans using tobacco in isolated coastal regions. Jean Barbot found that tobacco was traded in the Senegambia, the Gold Coast, and the islands of Principe and Fernando Póo. The Gold Coast tobacco, he wrote, was "country tobacco in untreated leaves," whereas the tobacco of Fernando Póo was "good tobacco (better than that of Brazil)." He even noted that to keep the captives "happy" during the Middle Passage slavers provided them with tobacco, pipes, and corn in between meals, indicating that Europeans understood these products as part of Africans' cultural repertoire. Francis Moore observed in 1723 that the Fulas in the Gambia River region bred cattle and horses, but they did not use their livestock as draft animals. They used hoes and planted their green gardens, cotton, corn, and tobacco near their houses for local use.[14]

Archaeological excavations support the documentary record of West African use of tobacco. Even before Columbus's voyages, West Africans

13. William Hugh Grove Diary, April 1732, microfilm, CWF; James Horn, *Adapting to a New World: English Society in the Seventeenth-Century Chesapeake* (Chapel Hill, N.C., 1994), 276; Ralph Gray and Betty Wood, "The Transition from Indentured to Involuntary Servitude in Colonial Georgia," *Explorations in Economic History,* XIII (1976), 353–370; Carr and Menard, "Land, Labor, and Economies of Scale in Early Maryland," *Jour. Econ. Hist.,* XLIX (1989), 407, 415; Menard, "From Servants to Slaves," *So. Stud.,* XVI (1977), 355–390; Galenson, *White Servitude in Colonial America,* 153–155.

14. P. E. H. Hair, Adam Jones, and Robin Law, eds., *Barbot on Guinea: The Writings of Jean Barbot on West Africa, 1678–1712,* 2 vols., Hakluyt Society, 2d Ser., nos. 175, 176 (London, 1992), I, 102, II, 547, 554 n. 4, 722, 727, 775; [George Story?], "Commonplace Book" (including travels in various parts of Africa, ca. 1680–1700), HM 31307, HL; Francis Moore, *Travels into the Inland Parts of Africa . . .* (London, 1738), 31–33; Matthew C. Emerson, "Decorated Clay Tobacco Pipes from the Chesapeake: An African Connection," in Paul A. Shackel and Barbara J. Little, eds., *Historical Archaeology of the Chesapeake* (Washington, D.C., 1994), 38.

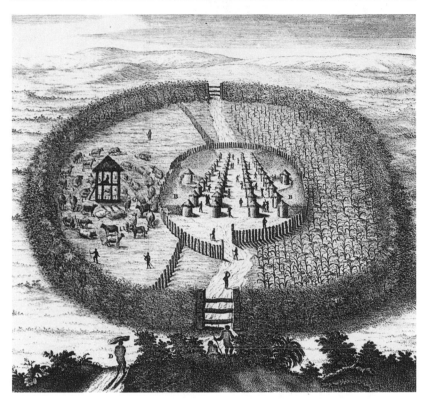

Plate 8. Draught of a Pholey [Fula] Town and Plantations about It. *From Francis Moore,* Travels into the Inland Parts of Africa . . . *(London, 1734). Courtesy, Cushing Memorial Library, Texas A & M University, College Station*

grew and smoked a species of tobacco, *Nicotiana rustica* (Barbot's "country tobacco"), which they called by the Afro-Asiatic name *tubbaq.* They quickly adapted the Virginia variety, *Nicotiana tobacum,* to their culture. Tobacco gardens have been found in each of four excavated Tiv compounds in Nigeria, which are believed to be at least four hundred years old. The size of one plot led archaeologists to characterize it as a farm. Among the Tiv, both men and women were involved in farming, clearing the land and harvesting grains. Men were responsible for planting and weeding the garden, and women maintained a kitchen garden.[15] More-

15. Ivan Van Sertima, *They Came before Columbus* (New York, 1976), 214–217, 220–221; C. A. Folorunso and S. O. Ogundele, "Agriculture and Settlement among the Tiv of Nigeria: Some Ethnoarchaeological Observations," in Thurstan Shaw et al., *The Archaeology of Africa: Food, Metals, and Towns* (New York, 1993), 276–284.

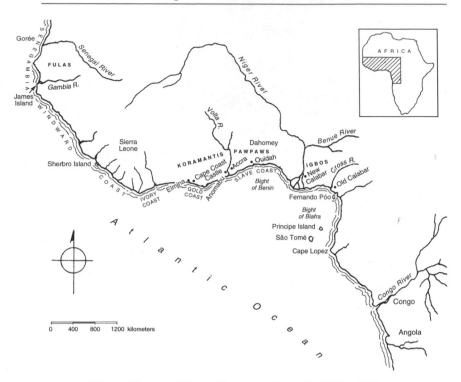

Map 1. Western Africa, 1660-1740. *Drawn by Richard Stinely*

over, clay smoking pipes have been found in excavations of Great Accra in Ghana, Mali, and the Gambia, which are similar in decoration, technique, and style to seventeenth-century pipes found in excavations in the Chesapeake. Stylistic patterns of the Akans in Ghana and the Tivs, Igbos, and Ejaghams in Nigeria have been identified on these utensils. Olaudah Equiano recalled that, "according to some" of his Igbo people, "the Creator . . . smokes a pipe, which is our favorite luxury." A smoking pipe is not a smoking gun, but it is evidence of a long familiarity with tobacco culture.[16]

Africans' experience in the production of tobacco explains, in part, why Virginia planters later favored enslaved laborers from the forest regions

16. Paul Edwards, ed., *Equiano's Travels: His Autobiography: The Interesting Narrative of the Life of Olaudah Equiano, or Gustavus Vassa, the African; Written by Himself,* 2 vols. (London, 1969), I, 28–29; Vincent Carretta, ed., *Olaudah Equiano: The Interesting Narrative and Other Writings* (New York, 1995), 241 n. 38; Emerson, "Decorated Clay Tobacco Pipes," in Shackel and Little, eds., *Historical Archaeology,* 38–46; Van Sertima, *They Came before Columbus,* 223–227.

of the Bight of Biafra and the Congo. In these regions, techniques used for yam cultivation were not unlike those employed for tobacco. Both included growing plants in forest clearings, using a hoe to prepare the soil, planting the seeds in mounds through the rainy season, and replanting. Conversely, planters from South Carolina and Barbados had a marked aversion to captives from the Bight of Biafra, especially the Igbos. South Carolina planters preferred instead rice growers from the Rice Coast and the Gambia, who were skilled in hydraulic techniques.[17] In Barbados, John Ashley, an agent for James Brydges, first duke of Chandos, believed that Africans' husbandry and concomitant diets played a role in planters' ethnic preferences. He found that Barbadian planters opted for forced migrants from Ouidah (Bight of Benin) and the Gold Coast "because they are in their own Country used to Labour and such dyet as can be afforded in Barbadoes." On the other hand, people from Congo, Bight of Biafra, Gambia, and Sierra Leone who are "used to plentifull Dyet and eat Flesh[,] are fittest for the Northern Colonys because they are better fed there than in the sugar plantations where land for Negroes is Scarce." Moreover, Ashley determined that profit on blacks from Ouidah and the Gold Coast resulted in a 35 percent net gain for Barbados, but only 19 percent for Virginia. On the other hand, the differential in the Congo trade was dramatic. The markup on each captive in Barbados averaged only 14 percent over the cost of procurement and delivery, whereas in Virginia it averaged 43 percent.[18]

17. Daniel C. Littlefield, *Rice and Slaves: Ethnicity and the Slave Trade in Colonial South Carolina* (Baton Rouge, La., 1981), 10; Kulikoff, *Tobacco and Slaves,* 321–322, 325; Philip D. Curtin, *The Atlantic Slave Trade: A Census* (Madison, Wis., 1969), 156–157; Michael A. Gomez, *Exchanging Our Country Marks: The Transformation of African Identities in the Colonial and Antebellum South* (Chapel Hill, N.C., 1998), 114–134, 144; Bassey W. Andah, "Identifying Early Farming Traditions of West Africa," in Shaw et al., *Archaeology of Africa,* 244, 247; Jones, *Present State of Virginia,* ed. Morton, 37–38, 77; Robert Rose, "Diary, 1746–1751," Aug. 27, 1750, HL.

18. John Ashley, "Calculate of Four Voyages from Angola and Gold Coast to Barbados and Virginia" (ca. 1721–1741), 46–47, James Brydges Papers Relating to African Affairs, ST 9, HL. Unfortunately, the entries by Ashley are undated and were probably copied into this book relating to African affairs for Brydges. Letters from Brydges to Ashley indicate that their correspondence lasted from 1721 to 1741 (personal communication from Mary L. Robertson, curator of manuscripts, HL, June 25, 1994). Cf. Littlefield, *Rice and Slaves,* 16–17; Darold D. Wax, "Preferences for Slaves in Colonial America," *Journal of Negro History,* LVIII (1973), 371, 401; Walter Rodney, "Upper Guinea and the Significance of the Origins of Africans Enslaved in the New World," ibid., LIV (1969), 327–345; Davies, *Royal African Company,* 332–333.

But such profits were yet to be realized by Virginia planters. Owing to the mercantilist policies of Restoration England under Charles II, the colony would remain for some time a marginal market in the English slave-trading system.

The Debt Crisis Has Opened the Negro Market: 1660–1697

As noted above, after losing the internal stream of servants, planters had to find a new source for tobacco workers. They thus began supporting legislation in favor of importing Africans. They offered exemption from local duties to Dutch ships carrying blacks to Virginia, for these taxes had proved "the greatest impediment to the advance of the estimation and value of our present only commodity tobacco." But the Navigation Act of 1660 cut off the Dutch traffic. In an effort to promote and encourage imperial trade, the crown restricted trade to ships owned by, commanded by, and three-fourths manned by English subjects.[19]

The English royal trading companies could not meet the Virginia demand for enslaved laborers. The crown offered little relief when Charles II issued to the Royal Adventurers into Africa a charter in December 1660 to trade, not for blacks, but for Guinea's gold. Although the company reorganized in 1663 as the English Company of Royal Adventurers Trading to Africa and was chartered to provide 3,000 Africans a year to the British colonies—a virtual monopoly on slave trading—it still supplied Virginia with few blacks. In 1663, the adventurers brought to Barbados 3,075 Africans and had contracted with an agent of the *Asiento* for 3,500 more to the Spanish colonies, but they imported only a few hundred blacks into Virginia. Sir William Berkeley noted in 1670 that not more than "two or three ships with negroes" had arrived in Virginia in the previous seven years.[20]

The crown made it even more difficult for Virginia to receive blacks during the 1670s. The rechartering of the Royal Adventurers in 1672 as a joint-stock company, renamed the Royal African Company, did not make a difference. The new charter not only excluded foreign vessels but also reinforced the Royal African Company's monopoly in 1674, forbidding

19. *SAL,* I, 540; Craven, *White, Red, and Black,* 89, 92; John R. Pagan, "Dutch Maritime and Commercial Activity in Mid-Seventeenth-Century Virginia," *VMHB,* XC (1982), 485–501.

20. Davies, *Royal African Company,* 42–44, 62–63; Elizabeth Donnan, ed., *Documents Illustrative of the History of the Slave Trade to America,* 4 vols. (Washington, D.C., 1930–1935), IV, 6. See *SAL,* II, 511–517; *CP,* I, II; Craven, *White, Red, and Black,* 86.

English-owned ships that were not part of the company from trading with African nations. The Royal African Company did not begin licensing ships to sell blacks in Virginia until 1678.[21]

To meet the demand for labor in Virginia, the great planters began to import blacks through the established intercolonial trade routes from the British West Indies, especially Barbados. As "some ancient Inhabitants conversant in [the slave] Trade" told Colonel Edmund Jenings, before 1680 most blacks came from Barbados, "for it was very rare to have a Negro ship come to this Country directly from Africa." The 1676 affidavit of Hugh Welburne of York revealed the typical procedure; he testified that George Pattison had "sailed from the Canary Islands to Barbados, and he there took into his Ship severall Blacks or Negroes and some Sugar which he then brought to Anamart (in Virginia) . . . and Sold 40 [of] the Negroes upon his owne account."[22]

Some of the enslaved came into Virginia with their owners from Barbados. Middling planters there, responding to economic consolidation in the last quarter of the century, sold out to great planters and moved elsewhere. John Sandford, owner of seventy-five acres of land, one manservant, and thirty-three blacks in Saint Andrew's Parish, Barbados, left the island for Virginia in the ship *Barbadoes* on October 1, 1679. A year later, Sandford patented 1,680 acres on Corretuck Bay in Lower Norfolk County with rights received for transporting thirty-four persons. Four blacks were identified in the patent application.[23]

21. See Donnan, ed., *History of the Slave Trade,* I, 194–196, and Thomas, Lord Culpeper to BT [instructions of Dec. 6, 1679, with marginal comments for each article], Dec. 12, 1681, IV, 56 n. 2; *MCGC,* 518; Evarts B. Greene and Virginia D. Harrington, eds., *American Population before the Federal Census of 1790* (New York, 1932), 137; Craven, *White, Red, and Black,* 86; Sarah S. Hughes, *Surveyors and Statesmen: Land Measuring in Colonial Virginia* (Richmond, Va., 1979), 14.

22. Colonel Edmund Jenings to BT, Nov. 27, 1708, CO 5/1362, 365–368, transcript, LC; "Case of Thomas Cox v. George Pattison—Testimony of Hugh Welburne, of York, a Worker Age 27," Nov. 10, 1676, York, R.As. 19/10, Borthwick Institute of Historical Research, York, VCRP. Captain James Knowles sold to John Berwick seven women and three men from Barbados; see "A Bill of Lading and an Invoice of Goods Bound for Virginia, 1661," Oct. 1, 1661, Lancaster County Inventories and Deeds, 1666–1682, 31–32, in Billings, ed., *Old Dominion,* 190. George Bennett of Bermuda wrote to the Board of Trade that, when the ships arrived in his colony from Africa in 1672 and 1683, they were sent to Virginia; see Colonel Bennett to BT, Aug. 4, 1708, CO 37/8, 319r–320v, transcript, LC; Bennett to BT, Aug. 4. 1708, CO 38/6, 441–443, transcript, LC.

23. The number of blacks brought into Virginia by Barbadian planters is not clear, but the offer of fifty acres for every black brought into the colony would have served as a con-

With the royal monopoly restraining slave traffic into Virginia and the supply of enslaved laborers from the West Indies remaining haphazard, many planters turned to the black market. Governor Culpeper estimated that before 1681 between 500 and 600 blacks were carried into Virginia each year, but the lack of supporting documentation makes it difficult to evaluate the source of these blacks. The 403 headrights that were claimed on enslaved workers from 1671 to 1680 call into question that estimation, even if that number should not be equated with total forced immigrants. Although there are numerous references to negotiations for the delivery of enslaved blacks on contract in the minutes of the Courts of Assistants, the number of the enslaved actually delivered to Virginia cannot be established from the Royal African Company records between 1672 and 1689. Some Royal African Company ships were likely evading regulations and supplying Virginia planters. It is also likely that other ship captains were picking up and smuggling in blacks. The number of the enslaved smuggled into Virginia, finding ready buyers, is impossible to calculate, but the General Court brought proceedings against licensees of the Royal African Company because more blacks were delivered than "ought to have been brought under contract." Indeed, Thomas Culpeper reported to the crown in 1681 that " 'tis impossible in those great bays and waters to hinder Interlopers."[24]

Compounding the labor-supply problem for Virginia planters, the price of tobacco dropped in 1681, affecting the slave trade to Virginia. "Our poverty this last year has quite spoiled that Trade," Culpeper wrote to the Lords of Trade, and "deters Every one from dealing with us." The crown advised Culpeper that it would encourage "Merchantable Negroes" at reasonable rates and terms in light of the bad market conditions. The Royal African Company consigned enslaved blacks designated for the West Indies to Virginia as a favor to London merchants Jeffrey Jeffrys and Micajah Perry II, who were anxious to supply their correspondents with blacks in place of the dwindling supply of servants.[25]

---

siderable incentive. Edward James, "Libraries in Colonial Virginia—Continued: Selections from the Records of Princess Anne County," *WMQ*, 1st Ser., IV (1895–1896), 16–17 n. 1; *CP*, II, 213; Peter H. Wood, *Black Majority: Negroes in Colonial South Carolina from 1670 through the Stono Rebellion* (New York, 1974), 13–34.

24. Susan Westbury, "Slaves of Colonial Virginia: Where They Came From," *WMQ*, 3d Ser., XLII (1985), 229–230; *MCGC*, 494, 519 (quotation); Donnan, ed., *History of the Slave Trade*, IV, 56 n. 2; Davies, *Royal African Company*, 45, 295.

25. *MCGC*, 519; Culpeper to BT [instructions of Dec. 6, 1679], Dec. 12, 1681, in Donnan, ed., *History of the Slave Trade*, IV, 56 n. 2.

The tobacco market improved dramatically in the summer of 1683, when a hurricane destroyed half of the tobacco crop. The great planters increased production to meet demand, but with both the diminishing supply of English servants and the irregular supply of enslaved laborers from the West Indies, they began to seek a new, cheaper, and more reliable labor supply. They found it in the direct trade from Africa. Nicholas Spencer encouraged the importation of blacks to Virginia at low prices as a long-term solution, not surprisingly because of his success in using them in Westmoreland County. Spencer estimated the profit from black labor in Virginia to be "far beyond any other plantation," about six pounds in customs for each arrival. He concluded: "I conceive it is for his Ma[jes]ty's Interest full as much as the Countrys, or rather much more to have Blacks as cheap as possible in Virginia." But it was economic crisis in Barbados that opened the Virginia market to a steady and, eventually, permanent supply of enslaved laborers.[26]

In Barbados, depressed sugar prices, soil exhaustion (a widespread condition by 1689), the monopoly of the Royal African Company, and the overinvestment in enslaved labor combined to create a debt crisis during the 1680s. The capital and interest extended to planters for the purchase of Africans (an estimated £271,000 in 1681 for the British West Indies) exceeded their capacity to repay. They began defaulting on bills of exchange —the "life of the trade"—and, from necessity, shipping their "refuse" blacks to Virginia. The Royal African Company, in turn, began to consider Virginia as an alternative market to Barbados. The company appears to have been more concerned about debt than price, about planters' defaulting on payments rather than the promise of future profits. For example, the company complained to its agent Colonel Hender Molesworth,

26. Nicholas Spencer to William Blathwayt, Aug. 14, 1683, William Blathwayt Papers, XVI, folder 2, reel 4, CWF; Hilary McD. Beckles and Andrew Downes, "The Economics of Transition to the Black Labor System in Barbados, 1630–1680," *Journal of Interdisciplinary History*, XVIII (1987–1988), 237; Spencer to BT, [Sept. 20, 1683], CO 5/1356, 138 (quotation), VCRP. Donnan, relying on transcripts and published accounts, identified this source as Lord Culpeper to BT, Sept. 20, 1683, in Donnan, ed., *History of the Slave Trade*, IV, 58. See Martin H. Quitt, *Virginia House of Burgesses, 1660–1706: The Social, Educational, and Economic Bases of Political Power* (New York, 1989), 77; "Letters of Wm. Fitzhugh," *VMHB*, I (1893–1894), 274; "Genealogy," ibid., VII (1899–1900), 73; "Slave Owners in Princess Anne County, Virginia," *WMQ*, 1st Ser., III (1894–1895), 55. Sir Jonathan Atkins made a similar observation in 1680 Barbados about the "convenience and cheapness" of black labor. Peter H. Wood cites Atkins and writes that Carolina planters were probably aware of the low cost of black labor, which helps to explain their predisposition to black labor; see Wood, *Black Majority*, 46.

former governor of Jamaica, that "our capitall stocke is now all amongst [the Barbadian planters] and we cannot see a likelihood of saveing our stocke from ruine." The protested bills of exchange, the "broken voyages being sett against the Proffitt," and the "extra-ordinary freight and insurance wee pay" in Barbados encouraged the company directors to look to Virginia. As a consequence, the company ships and those under its license combined to make shipments of blacks to Virginia "more and more frequent."[27]

Thus, encouraged by the favorable market conditions, the great planters began in the 1680s to shift from recruiting servants to buying enslaved blacks. They saw in the slave trade a solution to the recurring problem of replacing labor, and their wealth positioned them to absorb the possible losses of slave mortality and reap the long-term benefits of slave labor. Not only did they have workers for life, but they owned their progeny as well. No longer dependent on the cycle of freed servants starting tobacco farms, the great planters began expanding and developing their estates with a perpetual enslaved labor force shipped directly from Africa. William Fitzhugh and William Byrd I were typical of those planters making the transition to slavery. Their letters indicate a change of mind regarding slavery, their sensitivity to the Barbados market, and their interest in finding a direct supply from Africa.[28]

William Fitzhugh settled in Stafford County in the early 1670s, when few farmers there used enslaved labor. Stafford's labor system resembled its parent county, Westmoreland, where indentured servants toiled in the tobacco fields. Fitzhugh developed one of the first plantations using an en-

27. Royal African Company to Colonel Hender Molesworth, Feb. 26, 1689, T 70/57, VCRP; Royal African Company to Colonel Elwyn and Mr. Benjamin Skrutt, [Oct. 1, 1689; sent December 1689], T 70/57, 42v–43r, VCRP; "Address of the Council and Assembly of Jamaica to King James II," July 26, 1689, *CSP*, XIII, 106–107; Jenings to BT, Nov. 27, 1708, CO 5/1362, 365–367, transcript, LC; *EJCCV*, I, 196, 219, 235, 236, 252–253; Galenson, *White Servitude in Colonial America*, 153–154; Eric Williams, *Capitalism and Slavery* (1944; reprint, Chapel Hill, N.C., 1994), 31, 218 n. 9; Westbury, "Slaves of Colonial Virginia," *WMQ*, 3d Ser., XLII (1985), 230; Westbury, "Colonial Virginia and the Atlantic Slave Trade," 24; Menard, "From Servants to Slaves," *So. Stud.*, XVI (1977), 358–371.

28. On Fitzhugh, see Martin H. Quitt, "Immigrant Origins of the Virginia Gentry: A Study of Cultural Transmission and Innovation," *WMQ*, 3d Ser., XLV (1988), 642; on Byrd, see Pierre Marambaud, "William Byrd I: A Young Virginia Planter in the 1670s," *VMHB*, LXXXI (1973), 131–150; Marion Tinling, ed., *The Correspondence of the Three William Byrds of Westover, Virginia, 1684–1776*, 2 vols. (Charlottesville, Va., 1977), II, 825–827 (hereafter cited as *Byrd Correspondence*); Donald M. Sweig, "The Importation of African Slaves to the Potomac River, 1732–1772," *WMQ*, 3d Ser., XLII (1985), 507–508.

slaved workforce in the county. He not only wrote to fellow great planters and agents of the Royal African Company about his desire to purchase blacks; he also tried to manipulate the market in human flesh. Upon hearing that slave ships would arrive in the York River, he requested in June 1681 that Ralph Wormeley buy five or six blacks for him, fearing that his remoteness would cause all to be sold "but the refuse." By December, Fitzhugh was asking legal advice "upon the Report the protested Bills [in Barbados] has opened the Negro market," for, if an advantage could be made, "I will also myself buy six or eight, if the market be slow as is here reported." He sought to pass bills of exchange to his advantage, instructing his agent in June 1682 to buy one to six blacks, preferably men or boys. That same month, he wrote to William Leigh in New Kent County that a "friend" "in these parts has about £100 sterling" to lay out for "Negroes if any good ones are to be purchased and reasonable in your Parts."[29]

Early in 1683, Fitzhugh proposed a more sophisticated method of exchange, recognizing the economic inefficiency of piecemeal purchasing. He suggested to New Hampshire merchants Eleanor Cutt and George Jefferies that the practice of sending goods to planters' landings could be supplanted by maintaining a factor system in Virginia. This proposal to establish stores satisfied a prerequisite of John Jackson, another New Hampshire merchant licensed by the Royal African Company to bring the slave trade to Virginia. Although Fitzhugh encouraged New England merchants like Jackson to sell blacks to him directly from Africa, he primarily ordered them from London merchants who were agents of the Royal African Company.[30]

Fitzhugh was unable to secure a direct trade from Africa, but he did hit upon the economic advantage of natural increase. By the 1680s, he began

29. William Fitzhugh to Ralph Wormeley, June 19, July 14, 1681, to John Buckner, Dec. 3, 1681, to John Withers, June 5, 1682, to William Leigh, June 27, 1682, all in Richard Beale Davis, ed., *William Fitzhugh and His Chesapeake World, 1676–1701: The Fitzhugh Letters and Other Documents* (Chapel Hill, N.C., 1963), 92–93, 104, 106, 119, 122; Philip Alexander Bruce, *Economic History of Virginia in the Seventeenth Century: An Inquiry into the Material Condition of the People, Based upon Original and Contemporaneous Records*, 2 vols. (New York, 1907), II, 83.

30. Fitzhugh to [John Jackson], Feb. 11, 1682/3, to Eleanor Cutt and Mr. George Jefferies, Feb. 25, 1682/3, to Oliver Luke, Aug. 15, 1690, all in Davis, ed., *Fitzhugh and His Chesapeake World*, 127–129, 279–280. Fitzhugh had commercial dealings with William Dains of Bristol, who as early as 1690 had petitioned Parliament to allow the Bristol merchants a share of the Royal African Company's monopoly (356 n. 1). See also Bruce, *Economic History of Colonial Virginia*, II, 77–84.

to realize that he did not have to purchase laborers; he could grow his own. He thought of his blacks as stock, not unlike cattle, that could be bred indefinitely. He boasted in 1686 that most of his twenty-nine enslaved workers were Virginia-born, and the Africa-born were as "likely as most in Virginia." He anticipated that their children, "being all young, and a considerable parcel of breeders," would "keep that Stock good for ever."[31]

While Fitzhugh was attempting to become a trading agent in the Northern Neck in 1683, William Byrd I had yet to make a commitment to slavery. Indeed, in 1683 and during the first half of 1684 Byrd was more concerned with the harmful effects of the debt incurred on enslaved blacks than with their use in producing tobacco. He had a preference for white servants and was willing to "pay somewhat extraordinary" for a carpenter, bricklayer, or mason. He also requested that his London correspondents Perry and Lane secure for him by the first ship six, eight, or ten white "men or lusty boys" to work in the tobacco fields, if their prices were not too dear. But English servants were dear.[32]

Byrd lamented the plight of the planters to Perry and Lane. He complained that not only were the prices of servants too high, but the increasingly unfavorable balance of trade hurt the tobacco market, for planters were indebted to merchants, perhaps as much as two to three times the value of their crops. The slave trade would throw their accounts even further out of kilter. When a ship arrived earlier that year in June, probably from Barbados, carrying thirty-four blacks, muscovado (raw sugar obtained from the juice of sugar cane), a considerable quantity of dry goods, and seven or eight tons of rum, Byrd worried about the deleterious effect that the debt incurred on the cargo might have on planters' earnings. The cost of blacks, especially their provisions, he believed, had already disposed of the next year's crop.[33]

Shifting economic circumstances led Byrd to begin appreciating the advantage of a perpetual labor force. In April 1684, Byrd wrote to Perry and Lane that he "shall say no more about [English servants], for Negro's (if

31. Fitzhugh to Doctor Ralph Smith, Apr. 22, 1686, in Davis, ed., *Fitzhugh and His Chesapeake World,* 175–176. The increase of Fitzhugh's enslaved to fifty-one in 1703 made good that prediction ("An Inventory of the Estate of Collnl. Fitzhugh, Deceased," ibid., 382); Philip D. Morgan, *Slave Counterpoint: Black Culture in the Eighteenth-Century Chesapeake and Lowcountry* (Chapel Hill, N.C., 1998), 80.

32. William Byrd I to Perry and Lane, Feb. 25, 1683/4, *Byrd Correspondence,* I, 10.

33. Byrd to Perry and Lane, Feb. 25, 1683/4, Apr. 29, Dec. 30, 1684, to Thomas Grendon, June 21, 1684, all in *Byrd Correspondence,* I, 10, 14–15, 22–23, 27–29.

they come) I shall take some if they prove well." In June 1684, he requested that his correspondents send their ship to Barbados on his account for five or six blacks between twelve and twenty-four years old, one hundred gallons of rum, three thousand to four thousand pounds of muscovado, and two hundred pounds of ginger. By spring 1685, Byrd's attitude toward blacks had undergone a sea change, and he was now concerned only with their availability. It is fairly clear from his correspondence that, after 1686, he believed blacks were essential to producing tobacco. Thereafter, Byrd mentioned only one purchase of an English servant, an apprentice boy from Christ Hospital, a charity school in London that was a source for trained indentured servants "such as are very capable of our buisinesse."[34]

Byrd, like Fitzhugh, would attempt to secure direct trade to Africa. Byrd's actions and Fitzhugh's overtures to the New England merchants demonstrate that they were not content to sit on the sidelines and tolerate the uncertainty of the Barbados reexport trade. In 1698, one year after Parliament opened the slave trade, Byrd even made an aggressive foray into the slave trade, going one step further than Fitzhugh. Byrd sent the *William and Jane* to the Gambia to purchase Africans. The English not only had Fort James there, but the captives were cheaper and "proved well." French privateers captured the *William and Jane* in 1699, ending Byrd's flirtation with the African market.[35]

Despite the activity of the 1680s, the Royal African Company refused to alter its overall policy toward Virginia and allowed only ships operating under its license to deliver Africans to Virginia. For example, Captain Bramble of the *Coaster* delivered 177 enslaved laborers under company contract for Micajah Perry II and others in 1687. At the same time, the company fretted at its inability to stop interlopers—such as the *Society of Bristol*, which delivered 120 Africans to Virginia—from violating its monopoly. The company virtually ignored Virginia during the 1690s. The *Jeffery*, which sailed in 1693 from the Calabars with 330 Africans and ar-

34. "Royal African Company Instructions to Capt. Thomas James," Mar. 18, 1685, T 70/6, VCRP; Byrd to Perry and Lane, June 21, 1684, Mar. 29, 1685, Mar. 8, 1685/6, Nov. 10, 1686, to Sadler and Thomas, Feb. 10, Oct. 18, 1685/6, to ———, May 10, 1686, to Arthur North, Nov. 29, 1686, all in *Byrd Correspondence*, I, 22–23, 30–31, 50, 58, 59, 64–66; Fitzhugh to John Cooper, Aug. 20, 1690, in Davis, ed., *Fitzhugh and His Chesapeake World*, 283; David W. Galenson, "White Servitude and the Growth of Black Slavery in Colonial America," *Jour. Econ. Hist.*, XLI (1981), 40–41.

35. Louis B. Wright, ed., "William Byrd I and the Slave Trade," *Huntington Library Quarterly*, VIII (1945), 379, 381–382.

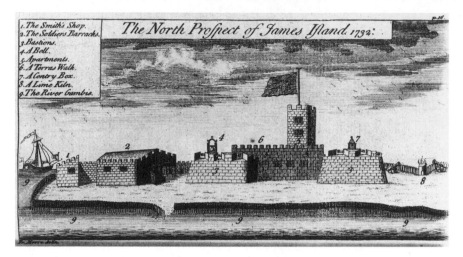

1. The Smiths Shop.
2. The Soldiers Barracks.
3. Bastions.
4. A Bell.
5. Apartments.
6. A Terras Walk.
7. A Centry Box.
8. A Lime Kiln.
9. The River Gambia.

The North Prospect of James Island. 1732:

Plate 9. The North Prospect of James Island, 1732. *From Francis Moore,* Travels
into the Inland Parts of Africa . . . *(London, 1734). Courtesy, Cushing Memorial
Library, Texas & M University, College Station*

rived in Virginia with 265 survivors, was the only ship of fifty-four dispatched by the company from 1693 to 1697.[36]

Reckoning the number of the enslaved before 1698 is hardly definitive.
The planters had bought about twelve hundred to thirteen hundred blacks
from 1670 to 1698. Their population numbered two thousand in 1670,
less than 5 percent of Virginia's population but 25 percent of its bound
labor force. It increased to five thousand in 1698, with blacks composing
about 9 percent of the population but more than one-half of the bound
labor force. In the older sweet-scented tobacco-growing areas, blacks were
more than 40 percent of the population and were the predominant tobacco
workers. In any event, blacks became increasingly important to Virginia
after 1697, when the Board of Trade took notice of its plantations and encouraged the slave trade as a cheap source of labor.[37]

36. "Table of Royal African Company Ships," 1691, T 70/61, 164v–166r, Royal African
Company to William Sherwood, Jan. 14, 1695, T 70/57, 120v–121r, VCRP.

37. *SAL,* II, 515; Greene and Harrington, *American Population,* 136. Darrett B. Rutman
and Anita H. Rutman count blacks as 20 percent of the bound labor force in Middlesex
County in 1668 and a majority in 1699 (*A Place in Time: Middlesex County, Virginia, 1650–
1750* [New York, 1984], 72, 166); Representation of the BT to the House of Commons,
Dec. 23, 1697, in Leo Francis Stock, ed., *Proceedings and Debates of the British Parlia-
ments respecting North America,* 2 vols. (Washington, D.C., 1927), II, 265–266n; Elizabeth
Louise Suttell, "The British Slave Trade to Virginia, 1698–1728" (master's thesis, College

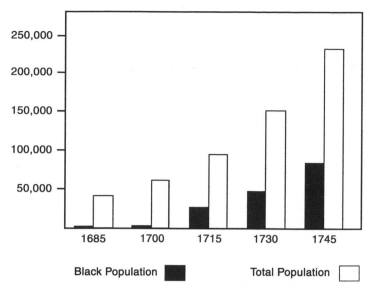

Figure 3. The Population of Virginia, 1685–1745. *Compiled from Peter H. Wood, "The Changing Population of the Colonial South: An Overview by Race and Region, 1685–1790," in Peter H. Wood, Gregory A. Waselkov, and Thomas Hatley, eds.,* Powhatan's Mantle: Indians in the Colonial Southeast *(Lincoln, Nebr., 1989), 38. Drawn by Peter Schweighofer*

The Prevailing Humor: 1698–1710

The relative inactivity of the Royal African Company in the Chesapeake in the face of the growing demand for blacks prompted independent merchants in Virginia to press Parliament to break the company's monopoly on the slave trade. The company had quadrupled its capital stock during 1671–1690, arousing the merchants' ire. They decried the company's charter "as a Monopoly inconsistent with the Liberty of thee Subject, And

of William and Mary, 1965), 17–18; Westbury, "Slaves of Colonial Virginia," *WMQ*, 3d Ser., XLII (1985), 230; Peter H. Wood, "The Changing Population of the Colonial South," in Wood, Gregory A. Waselkov, and Thomas M. Hatley, eds., *Powhatan's Mantle: Indians in the Colonial Southeast* (Lincoln, Nebr., 1989), 38; Robert V. Wells, *The Population of the British Colonies in America before 1776: A Survey of Census Data* (Princeton, N.J., 1975), 161–162; Craven, *White, Red, and Black,* 88–90; Jenings to BT, Nov. 27, 1708, CO 5/1362, 365–368, transcript, LC; Beverley, *History and Present State of Virginia,* ed. Wright, xxviii–xxix; Morgan, *American Slavery, American Freedom,* 306–307.

not established by act of parliament and that therefore they would exercise their natural Right of Trading to Africa as well as the Company." They petitioned in 1696 that the Royal African Company's sphere not be extended beyond the Gambia southeasterly to Accra, opening the region from Accra to Angola to free trade. They promulgated the principle that profitable and advantageous colonies must be "well supplied with Negroes." Interlopers flouted the Royal African Company monopoly and supplied as many blacks to Virginia planters as merchants licensed by the Royal African Company, which contributed to the breakup of the company monopoly in 1698. In that year, Parliament opened the slave trade to independent merchants, who were called the separate traders to Africa. They were also called 10 percent men after the duty they paid on slave exports, which helped defray the company's cost of maintaining forts on the African coast.[38]

In 1700, the Royal African Company was more concerned with collecting the 10 percent duty on enslaved blacks delivered by separate traders than with direct trade to Virginia. The company evaluated the market anew in 1701 in light of Virginia's seasonal demand. As mentioned above, timing was critical for the selling of Africans. The best time for slave ships to arrive in Barbados was between mid-November and mid-May, when corn and breadfruit were plentiful, little rain fell, and sugar was in the making. The late spring and early summer, on the other hand, was the best time in Virginia, when "New Negroes" could be put to work cultivating tobacco. Jenings observed that the separate traders sent their ships in the beginning of summer, when "the planters are abundantly more fond of them [blacks], and will give greater prices for them, because they are sure of the advantage of their labor in that years Crop." The weather was warmer than the damp, chilly fall and winter months, which could cause respiratory sickness and death to people accustomed to the heat of the tropics. To compete with the separate traders, the company instructed its captains after 1701 to deliver Africans before the end of August to Virginia, "the best market for the sale of your Negroes."[39]

38. Davies, *Royal African Company*, 46; "Petition to Open African Slave Trade," March 1695/6, BL 299, HL. John K. Thornton has suggested that the provenance of captives from "Angola" in the English record was really a reference to the Kongo or the region of modern Angola, not the Portuguese colony of Angola; see Thornton, "African Dimensions of the Stono Rebellion," *American Historical Review*, XCVI (1991), 1103–1104.

39. Jenings to BT, Jan. 11, 1710, CO 5/1316, 133, 135, transcript, LC ("A List of All Ships from Africa, June 1699–October 1708," CO 5/1316, 52, transcript, LC, demonstrates the

Virginia's poor credit ultimately discouraged the company's business. Nine protested bills of exchange for £269 were returned in 1705 and 1706. The company sent fifty-one protested bills of exchange to its agent Richard Corbin in 1707, worth £1,686.13.5. The company wrote to Corbin in February 1706: "We have nothing to induce us to encrease our Consignations to Virginia, but that extraordinary Character we had of you from your brother, and Mr. Micajah Perry and severall others of your friends in London." Of the 101 vessels dispatched by the Royal African Company between 1698 and 1707, only 6, carrying 679 Africans, arrived in Virginia.[40] Blacks were still imported from Barbados, and, to a lesser extent, Jamaica, but not in the quantity of the earlier trade. Jenings estimated that only 236 blacks were imported from Barbados between 1699 and 1708. At least one ship, perhaps the sloop *Elizabeth*, left the port of Carlisle, Barbados, in 1703, bound for the James River with rum, sugar, molasses, and a "fraught of 18 Negroes and one White boy."[41]

The great planters, exasperated by both the company's inattentiveness and their difficulty in procuring English servants, petitioned Parliament in 1708 to instruct the company to maintain a constant supply of Africans

---

truth of Jenings's statement); Royal African Company to James Howell, Apr. 23, 1700, T 70/50, 157v, to John Prowdre, Oct. 23, 1701, T 70/58, 18, to Messrs. Thomas Horne and Darbadees Willy, Oct. 23, 1701, T 70/58, 16–18, to Edward Hill, Dec. 2, 1701, T 70/58, 29, to Mr. Paul Sorel, Dec. 16, 1701, T 70/62, 106–109, to Captain Thomas Arnall, July 21, 28, 1702, T 70/62, 121–126, 129, "Instruction to Captain Joseph Bemister," Nov. 3, 1702, T 70/62, 162–166, Royal African Company to Captain Joseph Bemister, Dec. 23, 1702, T 70/62, 173, all in VCRP. The *Evans* might have been the ship described by Francis Louis Michel (Oct. 26, 1701–December 1702) that arrived with 230 Africans; about 100 had died en route; see Wm. J. Hinke, ed., "Report of the Journey of Francis Louis Michel from Berne, Switzerland, to Virginia, October 2, (1), 1701–December 1, 1702," *VMHB*, XXIV (1916), 116; Kulikoff, *Tobacco and Slaves*, 326–327.

40. The company, reacting to Virginia's poor credit and more stable markets in the sugar islands and in the Spanish colonies, ignored Virginia after 1707 (until 1718, when a duty on blacks expired, prices improved, and bills of exchange expected their yield). See Royal African Company to Richard Corbin, Feb. 20, 1705/6, T 70/58, 217, "Copies of Instructions from the Royal African Company . . . to the Captains of Ships in Their Service," 1705–1709, T 70/63, [1v, 2v, 4v], Royal African Company to William Cooke, Apr. 9, 1706, T 70/63, 80–83, to Captain Thomas Mackly, Jan. 28, 1706/7, T 70/63, 111–113, to Garwin Corbin, Mar. 27, Sept. 20, 1707, T 70/58, 277–279, 304, all in VCRP; Walter Minchinton, Celia King, and Peter Waite, eds., *Virginia Slave-Trade Statistics, 1698–1755* (Richmond, Va., 1984), 14n, 15, 16n, 18n, 19.

41. Jenings to BT, Nov. 27, 1708, CO 5/1362, 365–368, VCRP; Minchinton, King, and Waite, eds., *Virginia Slave-Trade Statistics*, 10; Westbury, "Slaves of Colonial Virginia," *WMQ*, 3d Ser., XLII (1985), 231.

at moderate prices in Virginia, for "white servants were not to be had." An anonymous writer captured the planters' indignation and asserted their right to laborers, whether black, Indian, or Scot, in light of the dwindling supply of English servants:

> Henceforth Shall None Rule with content one hour
> Each Jack Shall Check and dare his Governour
> The Englishman be gon,
> That we may ride a Native of our own
> Or Scot, who may our Purpose prov' wishes crown.[42]

Independent merchants met this demand by taking better advantage of the "prevailing humour" of the Virginia planters to buy blacks than did the Royal African Company. The traders supplied more blacks and at higher prices to Virginia planters than did the company, shipping them directly from Africa.[43] A representative of the independent merchants calculated in 1707 that they were annually supplying Virginia with 800 blacks, whereas the Royal African Company had carried in naught for seven years. (This figure is clearly hyperbole, for the company had brought in 679 enslaved blacks.) The company supplied more blacks than the traders did only to Barbados in 1707—674 to 130. In the largest market, Jamaica, the traders imported 6,041 blacks to the company's 4,288. The Leeward Islands, the smallest market, received 260 from the traders, yet none from the company. The discrepancy in the supply was most dramatic in the Chesapeake, where the company was absent when the traders sold 1,425 blacks to tobacco planters. Richard Beaumont, an accountant for the Royal African Company, concurred with the traders' representative. Not only was Virginia the smallest of the company's markets, but the prices received there were less.[44]

42. "Virginia's Complaint against the Plaintiffs," 1705, Frank J. Klingberg Collection, University Research Library, UCLA; Thomas Pindar, Royal African Company, to Richard Corbin, Apr. 20, 1708, T 70/58, 332, VCRP. Lorena S. Walsh has noted that a second shift in the procurement of white servants occurred in the eighteenth century; see "Discussion" (of David W. Galenson, "White Servitude and the Growth of Black Slavery in Colonial America"), *Jour. Econ. Hist.*, XLI (1981), 48. Craven notes that English Virginians were prejudiced against Scottish immigrants in the seventeenth century; see *White, Red, and Black*, 1-2. See also Clifford Lewis III, "Some Recently Discovered Extracts from the Lost Minutes of the Virginia Council and General Court, 1642-1645," *WMQ*, 2d Ser., XX (1940), 69.

43. Minutes of BT, Nov. 28, 1707, CO 391/19, 386, VCRP.

44. "Table of Slave Trade to Virginia, 29 September 1707 to July 1708," [1708], CO

The separate traders thus carried 6,835 blacks into Virginia from 1699 to 1710, more than tenfold the 679 blacks carried in by the Royal African Company. A representative of the traders threw down the gauntlet on this issue in 1710, defying "the African Company to prove that they have imported so many as two thousand into that particular Province since they have been a Joint Body." Unwilling or unable to take up the glove, the company responded that their ability to supply the colonies had been weakened by the "insupportable insolence of the Natives encouraged by the Dutch and Contending Interests by the Separate Traders." Its position would become untenable without a change in policy. Threatening to make the African slave traders "more depending on the Company's settlements both for trade and protection" and to exclude the separate traders, they warned that the English could lose the slave trade to the Dutch, especially on the Gold Coast. The company whined that thirteen years of experiment in free trade had led to the devaluation of the Royal African Company's capital stock.[45]

The success of the independent slave traders after 1698 greatly increased the number of blacks in Virginia. A report of the separate traders estimated the number of enslaved at "upwards 15,000" in 1710, a threefold increase over twelve years. Blacks were about 20 percent of the population and had become the mass of bound laborers. Virginia had become a slave society.[46]

390/12, 225–226, VCRP. For the number of ships sent by the Royal African Compnay from Sept. 29, 1707, to Sept. 29, 1708, see Statement of Richard Beaumont, accountant of the Royal African Company, [ca. 1708], CO 390/12, 247, VCRP.

45. Royal African Company to Garwin Corbin, Apr. 20, 1708, T 70/58, 331–332, VCRP; *A True State of the Present Difference between the Royal African Company and the Separate Traders* (London, 1710).

46. *True State of the Present Difference,* 35; Wood, "The Changing Population of the Colonial South," in Wood, Waselkov, and Hatley, eds., *Powhatan's Mantle,* 38.

CHAPTER 3

Cyclical Crises, 1680–1723

Although the great planters had secured property in people by importing blacks from the Caribbean and Africa and by fastening legal shackles on them, slavery was not a panacea for the instability of the tobacco economy. Rather, it proved the rub causing friction between the great planters and English merchants, whose interests diverged as the new century proceeded and the slave trade expanded. Its economic significance grew after 1680, becoming the determinant in the tobacco industry's cyclical pattern of boom and bust.

The periodic crises in the tobacco economy and the growing slave population spelled a credit problem in the colony. Although boom-and-bust cycles had been common since the beginning of the tobacco economy, the expanded slave trade after 1680 added a new dimension, rising to a fever pitch after 1698, when planters indulged in a craze for purchasing blacks that exceeded their ability to recover their investment. These fluctuations worsened in the early eighteenth century and reached a crisis during the 1720s, shaping the structure of the slave society. In this cyclical pattern, increases in European demand stimulated recurring booms in the Chesapeake economy, leading to increased productivity — and chronic overproduction in peacetime. A plant-cutting action in 1682 was the first time that violence was used against the crown's position on the regulation of the tobacco market. Continental wars closed the European market, with depression following. The economic impact changed the configuration of the tobacco and slave trades, organizing them along class lines. The great planters brokered this commerce for their correspondents in London, but over time new merchants cut into their market share by going directly to small and middling planters. The tension between the slave and tobacco trades thus created class conflicts both inside and outside Virginia.[1]

Tobacco Is a Drug

"This is a country well water'd and so fertile yet it does or might be made [to] yield anything that might conduce to pleasure or necessity of life," observed John Banister, the naturalist, from the Falls in 1679. "But want of peace, too much Land [under cultivation] and the great cropps of tobacco men strive to make hinder Virginia from improving." In a nutshell, Banister had analyzed the problem with the tobacco economy. The social conflicts generated during Bacon's Rebellion permeated the colony. Commercial conflicts between the English and the Dutch stifled the outflow of tobacco to the Continental markets, causing the surplus to be dumped in England. Continuing expansion into new land and concomitant overproduction of tobacco to offset its declining price put Virginia into a depression.[2]

The great planters promoted slavery as a remedy for the troubled tobacco economy. Enslaved laborers could produce the crop cheaper than servants could, but slavery carried with it a plethora of problems. The great planters had turned toward slavery at a time when they were anxious to restrict production, aggravating their economic situation. They continued to buy more enslaved workers, first from Barbados and then directly from Africa. Anxiety over a glutted tobacco market led an imperial administrator to an early prognosis of an impending problem: "Our purchase of negroes, by increasing the supply of tobacco," Governor Thomas Culpeper wrote in 1681, "has greatly contributed" to its low price.[3]

Planters were unable to control their tobacco habit. Culpeper used this metaphor of addiction for the compulsion of the planters to invest in pro-

1. Allan Kulikoff, *Tobacco and Slaves: The Development of Southern Cultures in the Chesapeake, 1680–1800* (Chapel Hill, N.C., 1986), 79–80; John M. Hemphill II, *Virginia and the English Commercial System, 1689–1733: Studies in the Development and Fluctuations of a Colonial Economy under Imperial Control* (1964; reprint, New York, 1985), chap. 1.

2. John Banister to Dr. Robert Morrison, Apr. 6, 1679, BR 256 (6), Miscellaneous File, 4, HL.

3. Thomas, Lord Culpeper to BT [instructions of Dec. 6, 1679, with marginal comments for each article], Dec. 12, 1681, in Elizabeth Donnan, ed., *Documents Illustrative of the History of the Slave Trade to America*, 4 vols. (Washington, D.C., 1930–1935), IV, 56 n. 2.

duction despite its ill effects. Tobacco prices had become so depressed by the summer of 1680 that he began seeking assistance from the crown. "All goes well but that Tobacco is a drugge, and that [weakens] this colony most dangerously." He advised the Board of Trade that the gravity of the situation required expanding the market. His report reflects deep frustration: "The thing is so fatal and desperate that there is no remedy; the market is overstocked and every crop overstocks it more. It is commonly said that there is tobacco enough in London now to last all England for five years; too much plenty would make gold itself a drug." Only through expansion into new markets could tobacco hold its value. "Free importation into Russia would revive our drooping spirits, for we want nothing but a vent."[4]

To salvage the bumper crop of 1680, the great planters requested a cessation on tobacco planting in 1681. Their commercial experience made them cognizant of the tie-in between the colonial supply and the Continental demand: they wanted to raise the price of tobacco by cutting off production. In the fall of 1681, organizers from Middlesex, Gloucester, and New Kent Counties collected a "greate many" signatures for a moratorium on tobacco production for one year. The petitions were presented to Sir Henry Chicheley, sitting in for Culpeper, who had returned to England. Chicheley called a session of the General Assembly to address the grievance, but the crown ordered him not to convene the session.[5]

If the planters had refrained from acting precipitately, change was imminent. The crown had instructed Culpeper to accept the great planters' solution to the problem and to suspend tobacco production. Lord Baltimore was to follow his lead by allowing a moratorium in Maryland. But a rebellion occurred while Culpeper was en route to Virginia. By this time, transactions in the colony had been reduced to barter and planters to desperation. Some planters, pessimistic from past dealings either that the crown would offer relief or that the other tobacco-producing colonies

4. Culpeper to William Blathwayt, July 8, 1680, William Blathwayt Papers, XVII, folder 2, reel 4, CWF; Thomas Culpeper, "Present State of Tobacco" (1681), in Donnan, ed., *History of the Slave Trade*, IV, 56 n. 2; Jacob M. Price, *The Tobacco Adventure to Russia: Enterprise, Politics, and Diplomacy in the Quest for a Northern Market for English Colonial Tobacco, 1676–1722* (American Philosophical Society, *Transactions*, N.S., LI, pt. 1 [1961]), 4–5, 17, 21; Russell R. Menard, "Farm Prices of Maryland Tobacco, 1659–1710," *Maryland Historical Magazine*, LXVIII (1973), 80–85.

5. Darrett B. Rutman and Anita H. Rutman, *A Place in Time: Middlesex County, Virginia, 1650–1750* (New York, 1984), 158–161; Edmund S. Morgan, *American Slavery, American Freedom: The Ordeal of Colonial Virginia* (New York, 1975), 284–288.

would agree to restrict production, resolved to destroy tobacco plants. Others supported crown authority, fearing anarchy more than they desired the benefits from the higher prices that the plant cutting would afford. Robert Beverley I bridged the gap between Bacon's Rebellion and the plant-cutting rebellion. Beverley was typical of the emerging gentry who were gathering together offices of profit and great estates in the late seventeenth century. He immigrated to Virginia in 1663 from Yorkshire, England, settling near the Piankatank River in what would later become Middlesex County. By the year of his death in 1687, he had accumulated fifty thousand acres of land and forty-two enslaved workers. Obtaining the rank of major as a staunch supporter of Governor William Berkeley during Bacon's Rebellion, Beverley endeared himself to the populists in 1677 when, as the clerk of the House of Burgesses, he refused to turn over its journals to the Royal Commissioners investigating the rebellion. The crown removed him from his post, but the burgesses reelected him in 1680.[6]

If Beverley's role as instigator in the cessation petition is unclear in the documentary record, his actions afterward place him in a leadership role. As a justice of the peace in Middlesex County, Beverley, along with justices Robert Smith, Matthew Kemp, and Ralph Wormeley, all great planters, received the cessation petition and presented it to the people for their approval in December 1681. If the other justices hesitated, remaining loyal as the crisis thickened, Beverley manipulated authority to his own advantage. Acting on a proviso of a law establishing towns, which provided that tobacco collected outside official sites would be seized after January 1682, Beverley confiscated tobacco that winter and shipped it to London. He was motivated more by the windfall profits on his large consignment of contraband than by populist pleas for fair prices. When Henry Chicheley, acting on the crown's instructions, canceled the April session, thwarting the burgesses' action on the cessation petitions, Beverley led the planters in rebellion.[7]

6. Robert Beverley, *The History and Present State of Virginia* (1705, 1722), ed. Louis B. Wright (Chapel Hill, N.C., 1947), 92; T. H. Breen, "A Changing Labor Force and Race Relations in Virginia, 1660–1710," *Journal of Social History*, VII (1973–1974), 12–13; Rutman and Rutman, *A Place in Time*, 161; Morgan, *American Slavery, American Freedom*, 274, 286; James Hagemann, *The Heritage of Virginia: The Story of Place Names in the Old Dominion*, 2d ed. (Chester, Pa., 1988), 11.

7. Rutman and Rutman, *A Place in Time*, 156–161, 210–211; Morgan, *American Slavery, American Freedom*, 284–286.

The rebels were poorer planters, former servants who had earlier supported Bacon. Now, following Beverley, they acted when the plants were still in their beds but when it would be too late for resowing, targeting the sweet-scented plants exclusively grown in Virginia. Nicholas Spencer, secretary of the colony, reported: "On May Day, a Rabble made a May sport, to dance from plantation to plantation to cut up Tobacco Plants." By the month's end, he wrote: "The present state of our affaires [is still] unsettled and unquiet, from a sick brain'd people uneasy, under the low and mean price of Tobacco."[8]

It took some time for the militia, raised by Chicheley from distant, unaffected counties, to overtake the rebels. Spencer wrote in August that there is "fresh fooleing in Gloucester County with open boldness of shewing themselves in the day time." Not until February 1683 could he report that it was "all entirely quiet," as "some of the principal Actors in the late disorders are now in prison." After one year of defiance and two executions, Spencer issued in May a "general pardon for the late disorder," exempting Beverley, "who was the principal mover of the plant cutting."[9]

The plant cutting of 1682 was a rebellion against crown commercial policy. The poor planters following Beverley acted from a populist sense of a just price, even though the great planters would benefit more because they produced a greater amount of tobacco. Destroying their own crop was a rational reaction of planters small and large to the cause of their grievance, a glut of tobacco plants, but it also bellowed their frustration at royal regulation. They were incensed that imperial administrators, so far away, determined their livelihood. Thus, the rebellion vented the planters' frustration and expressed their political outrage; in doing so, they directly challenged royal mercantile policy.[10]

By the spring of 1683, it was clear that another bumper crop was in the making. Culpeper, who had returned from England the previous November, now discouraged cessation as detrimental to the crown's revenues and

8. Beverley, *History and Present State of Virginia,* ed. Wright, 92; Spencer to Blathwayt, May 29, 1682, Blathwayt Papers, XVI, folder 1, reel 4; Breen, "A Changing Labor Force," *Jour. Soc. Hist.,* VII (1973–1974), 3–25; Rutman and Rutman, *A Place in Time,* 161; Morgan, *American Slavery, American Freedom,* 286.

9. Spencer to Blathwayt, Aug. 12, 1682, Feb. 15, May 9, 1683, Blathwayt Papers, XVI, folders 1, 2, reel 4.

10. Beverley, *History and Present State of Virginia,* ed. Wright, 92; E. P. Thompson, "The Moral Economy of the English Crowd in the Eighteenth Century," *Past and Present,* no. 50 (February 1971), 76–136.

beneficial only to the great planters, the "Engrossers" of tobacco, whom he blamed for the turbulence. Reports of the planters' distress had encouraged the Board of Trade to break into the Dutch-controlled European market and to develop new markets in France, northern Europe, and Russia. This expansion, combined with a hurricane in the summer of 1683, which blew down tobacco houses and destroyed half of the crop, caused a rise in prices.[11]

The anxiety generated by the populism of the plant-cutting rebellion, coming on the heels of Bacon's Rebellion, made the great planters eschew violence as a tool in changing economic policy. They reconciled themselves to the crown's position on cessation. Although they had empathy for the rebels and benefited from the Board of Trade's response to the rebellion, they feared the dangerous consequences of class unrest. They suppressed the uprising and pledged their allegiance to the crown. The council found evidence of "high misdemeanors" in Beverley's conduct. He had fabricated and tampered with official letters and writs intended for the burgesses and sheriffs, usurping the will and authority of the secretary, and had refused delivery of the journals of the House of Burgesses to the governor and council. The General Court found Beverley guilty but promptly issued a reprieve after he begged pardon "on bended knee, in a most submissive manner." His pardon was owing to his class ties, for two others from the small-planter class had been hanged. The great planters moved against future plant-cutting rebellions by labeling such action as treasonous. The General Assembly passed a statute in 1684 that "deemed . . . traytors" parties of eight or more that destroyed tobacco plants.[12]

Despite the relationship between tobacco prices and the number of hands employed in its production, planters continued to invest in enslaved blacks. Given the examples of other slave societies, where mortality rates required large annual slave imports to maintain even a static slave population, Virginia's policymakers assumed the slave trade was necessary to ensure a steady supply of labor. During the 1680s, growers purchased an increasing supply of blacks, especially during the boom year of 1683. But the boom was short-lived, with the expanded production playing no small part in its demise. By 1687, Nicholas Spencer could write: "Our now

11. Spencer to Blathwayt, Aug. 14, 1683, Blathwayt Papers, XVI, folder 2, reel 4; Morgan, *American Slavery, American Freedom,* 287; Price, *The Tobacco Adventure to Russia* (APS, *Trans.,* N.S., LI [1961]), 4–5.

12. *SAL,* III, 11–12; *EJCCV,* I, 36, 55 (quotation), 489–492, 498–499.

feared enimi is our poverty falling violently on us by the small or rather no value of our only commodity tobacco."[13]

The Slave Trade Has Ruined the Credit of the Country

From the great planters' perspective, the slave trade and slavery emerged as a way to maintain their hegemony in land and labor. But the slave trade only aggravated the economic crisis inherent in tobacco production. Before 1689, both white indentured servants from England and enslaved blacks from the British West Indies were purchased on contract. After 1689, when the number of servants declined rapidly, blacks were increasingly brought directly from Africa on consignment. Servants had been sold for tobacco, but the greater capital investment in enslaved labor required a monetary transaction, most often realized in bills of exchange. Not only did blacks produce more tobacco for a glutted market, but they also involved a higher initial capital outlay, compared to servants, increasing the planters' indebtedness to English merchants. Slave purchases would add a heavy coil of debt to the economic cycle, one that would become determinant in the new century.[14]

Indeed, the turn of the century saw a mania for purchasing blacks. Governor Francis Nicholson wrote to the Board of Trade in 1700 that there were as many buyers as there were blacks: even if 2,000 Africans were imported, they would find buyers. Francis Louis Michel of Berne, Switzerland, gave the reason for this enthusiasm: "Most of the wealth consists in slaves or negroes, for if one has many workmen, much food-stuff and tobacco can be produced." The opening of the slave trade after 1698 made this frenzy possible. The success of the independent slave traders greatly increased the number of blacks in Virginia. They sent 6,835 of the 7,514 (91 percent) new imports during the first decade, despite the "oppressions

13. Nicholas Spencer to Henry [Robert Spencer], earl of Sunderland, secretary of state, May 13, 1687, Blathwayt Papers, XVI, folder 4, reel 4.

14. Jacob M. Price, *Perry of London: A Family and a Firm on the Seaborne Frontier, 1615–1753* (Cambridge, 1992), 31; Susan Alice Westbury, "Colonial Virginia and the Atlantic Slave Trade" (Ph.D. diss., University of Illinois at Urbana-Champaign, 1981), 21–22; Rutman and Rutman, *A Place in Time*, 75; Morgan, *American Slavery, American Freedom*, 3–70, 108–130; Edmund S. Morgan, "Headrights and Headcounts," review of *White, Red, and Black: The Seventeenth-Century Virginian*, by Wesley Frank Craven, *VMHB*, LXXX (1972), 369.

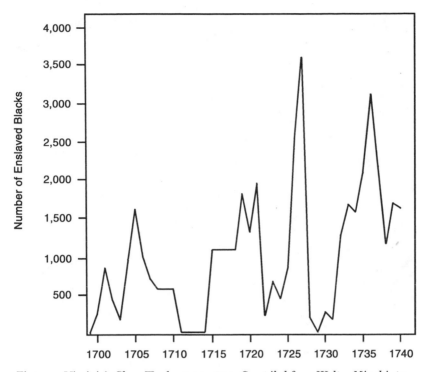

Figure 4. Virginia's Slave Trade, 1700–1740. *Compiled from Walter Minchinton, Celia King, and Peter Waite, eds.,* Virginia Slave-Trade Statistics, 1698–1775 *(Richmond, Va., 1984), xii–xv. Drawn by Peter Schweighofer*

of the [Royal African] Company on one hand and the Calamitys of the War on the other Hand."[15]

The authorities immediately saw in the slave trade a means of raising revenue by imposing a duty on imported blacks. Such a tax would provide for buildings, salaries, and defense. When the General Assembly put a twenty-shilling duty on enslaved blacks in 1699, and again in 1701, 1704, 1705, and 1706, there is no indication that it intended to restrict the slave trade. The principal motive in these acts was to raise money for building

15. Lt. Gov. Francis Nicholson to BT, Aug. 1, 1700, CO 5/1360, 31, VCRP; Wm. J. Hinke, ed., "Report of the Journey of Francis Louis Michel from Berne, Switzerland, to Virginia, October 2, (1), 1701–December 1, 1702," *VMHB,* XXIV (1916), 116; An Answer of the Separate Traders to Several Queries, Dec. 31, 1708, CO 390/12, 263–273 (quotation on 265), VCRP; Walter Minchinton, Celia King, and Peter Waite, eds., *Virginia Slave-Trade Statistics, 1698–1775* (Richmond, Va., 1984), 3–20.

LONDON'S VIRGINIA.

Plate 10. London's Virginia. English woodcut tobacco label. Ca. 1700.
Courtesy, The Granger Collection, New York

the new Capitol at Williamsburg and to defray the cost of building the governor's mansion. The importance of the slave trade as a source of revenue can be gleaned from the penalty enacted for concealing the entry of blacks: a fine of one hundred pounds sterling. The duty proved so "useful and advantageous" in raising revenue that the General Assembly asserted in 1705 that "no better expedient" could be found.[16]

After 1705, the War of the Spanish Succession choked the European market, depressing the tobacco trade and severely affecting Virginia's economy. White servants were not to be had at any price, despite a decision by policymakers to waive the duty on them. High slave prices, reflecting the ability of African merchants, especially on the Gold Coast, to take advantage of the demand, increased the indebtedness of planters. The competitive trade on the coast had led African merchants to raise prices on captives, prompting an increase from ten pounds to twenty pounds during the monopoly period and twenty pounds to forty pounds afterward. The influx of blacks and the expansion into fresh lands resulted in lower prices for the crop. The poor returns on tobacco and the defaults on slave purchases, in turn, led to a crisis in colonial credit in 1706.[17]

In that year, the Royal African Company ceased operating in Virginia, when planters' defaults on slave purchases had become manifest. The company believed that it could better invest its venture capital elsewhere, competing with the French for the Spanish *Asiento* (the contract to deliver enslaved Africans to the Spanish colonies). Feeling the pinch of depression in Virginia, it canceled supplies shipped on credit and demanded payment on debts. Many blacks had been purchased with bills of exchange, but, increasingly, these bills, more than one-quarter during the decade, were returned protested. Yet the planters were slow to react to the declining market and continued to purchase enslaved blacks and to increase production. Indignant about their difficulty in securing labor because of the cessation by the Royal African Company and the inconsequential English immigration, the planters demanded in 1708 a sufficient

16. *SAL*, III, 229.

17. Thomas Pindar, Royal African Company, to Garwin Corbin, Apr. 20, 1708, T 70/58, 331–333, VCRP; Robert Vaughan and Thomas Carney et al., "The Humble Petition of Several Planters, Barbados, 1 August 1710, Barbados," in John Roberts, *Considerations on the Present Peace as Far as It Is Relative to the Colonies and the African Trade* (London, 1763), 67–68, HL; Elizabeth Louise Suttell, "The British Slave Trade to Virginia, 1698–1728" (master's thesis, College of William and Mary, 1965), 22–24; *JHB, 1702/3–1705, 1705–1706, 1710–1712*, 180, 183, 201, 203.

supply of Africans at moderate prices. The separate traders continued to pour Africans into Virginia, another 1,902 from 1707 to 1710. Oblivious to the changing economy, these merchants pointed to the numbers with relish while agitating for an open slave market.[18]

Virginia authorities, struggling to comprehend their economic world, fingered the slave trade as the culprit. The Council of State in October 1708 attributed the crisis in tobacco to the "very plain" reason that "the great number" of blacks had increased the hands employed in tobacco, resulting in overproduction and lower prices. Edmund Jenings, president of the council, responding to a circular from the Board of Trade, complained in November about Virginia's dependence on merchants and the rising prices of enslaved blacks. "The prevailing humour of our Inhabitants," he wrote, to buy blacks "even beyond their ability [to recoup their cost] . . . has ruined the Credit of the Country." Governor Alexander Spotswood agreed. The "great number" of blacks imported had not only consumed the credit of the country but also contributed to the depression. They had been solely employed in cultivating tobacco, producing a supply disproportional to the vent that "the War had left open, and by a Natural Consequence lower'd the Price to a great Degree."[19]

The assembly in 1710 put a five-pound duty on the head of each imported enslaved black, trying to rescue tobacco from its depressed state. The assembly's action signaled the first time policymakers recognized that a tax could be used to limit importation of the enslaved. Economic realities had tempered their enthusiasm for unlimited importation, but the duty had implications for the nature of the colonial system. Spotswood discerned that the tax was an infringement on Parliament's right to control trade and lobbied the burgesses to moderate the duty. He suggested

18. Thomas Pindar, Royal African Company, to Garwin Corbin, Apr. 20, 1708, T 70/58, 331–332, VCRP; Royal African Company to Richard Corbin, Feb. 20, 1705/6, T 70/58, 217, VCRP; *A True State of the Present Difference between the Royal African Company and the Separate Traders* (London, 1710); "Copies of Instructions from the Royal African Company . . . to the Captains of Ships in Their Service," 1705–1709, T 70/63, [1v–4v], VCRP; Minchinton, King, and Waite, eds., *Virginia Slave-Trade Statistics,* xii–xiii, 14n, 15, 16n, 25; Colin Palmer, *Human Cargoes: The British Slave Trade to Spanish America, 1700–1739* (Urbana, Ill., 1981), 9.

19. *EJCCV,* III, 194; Edmund Jenings to BT, Nov. 27, 1708, CO 5/1316, 49–50, transcript, LC; Colonel Alexander Spotswood to BT, Mar. 20, 1710/1, CO 5/1363, 317–324 (quotation on 318), VCRP; John Mickle Hemphill II, "Virginia and the English Commercial System, 1689–1733" (Ph.D. diss., Princeton University, 1964), 34–35; Suttell, "The British Slave Trade to Virginia," 30.

Plate 11. Slaves Stringing and Rolling Tobacco. *From Pierre Pomet,* Compleat History of Drugs *(London, 1738). Collection of the Richmond Academy of Medicine, on deposit, Virginia Historical Society, Richmond*

amendments, concerned that the high duty might be "Interpreted as a prohibition" on trade, for the colony must show "Just Deference" to the crown. He reminded them that, since British mercantile policy did not allow for a discriminatory tax on owners of British vessels higher than that imposed on Virginia owners, it could not "be Justifyed by any Parallel Instance in *Great Brittain.*" The burgesses insisted that they had passed the duty act because of the relationship between the debt and the slave trade, arguing that the recent importation of blacks had ruined the country. It would be impossible to satisfy the debt incurred on these "if Fresh supplies be still pour'd in upon them while their Tobacco continues so little Valuable."[20]

Spotswood, ultimately persuaded by their argument and assured that the duty would not discourage the slave trade once "tobacco becomes valuable," supported the duty. He emphasized the economic motive behind the fivefold increase on imported blacks in his correspondence to

20. *JHB, 1702/3–1705, 1705–1706, 1710–1712,* 281; Spotswood to BT, Mar. 6, 1710/1, CO 5/1363, 284–301 (quotation on 290), VCRP; Hemphill, "Virginia and the English Commercial System," 34–35.

the crown. He ventured that the duty, if maintained for only three years, would allow the country to satisfy earlier debts. The alternative was a permanent increase in Virginia's self-sufficiency, a concern of the mercantile empire. Enslaved blacks and white servants could be put to work planting cotton, making clothing, and manufacturing petty goods, a system that would be "introduced by their owners [from] necessity rather than inclination." This intimation of increased manufacturing was enough for the Board of Trade to allow the duty. The ability of the assembly to put a high import duty on enslaved Africans with the crown's tacit approval represented the relative weakness of the separate traders in crown politics and the Royal African Company's lack of interest in Virginia.[21]

The five-pound duty, reaffirmed in 1712 and again in 1714, had an immediate effect on the slave trade. For the past two years, Spotswood reported in 1712, except for "a few from Barbados," there had not been any enslaved persons imported into Virginia, nor was there "likely to be while the price of tobacco is so low, and the country so much in debt." Fewer than three hundred blacks were imported into Virginia from 1710 to 1713. Indians were just as likely as Africans to be brought into the colony during these years, such as the fifty-nine Tuscaroras for "the usual price of slaves" after the Tuscarora War in North Carolina (1711–1713). Virginia authorities had successfully restricted the slave trade. Spotswood reiterated his position to the Board of Trade: "There's no reason to expect many more while the price of tobacco continues so low, and the country by that means so poor."[22]

Planters expanded production with the rise in tobacco prices after 1713, owing in part to a drought that limited the supply and to the opening of the French market. This revival aroused the interest of slave traders, especially in London and Bristol. The Royal African Company had in 1713 commissioned Robert Richardson as chief merchant of its African operations because of, among other qualifications, his "understanding Negroes proper for Virginia and Mary Land." Now, with a viable market, merchants increased the supply of enslaved Africans to Virginia. The planters continued to buy Indians, but a limited number; only ten were brought from

21. Spotswood to BT, Mar. 6, 1710/1, CO 5/1363, 284–301 (quotation on 290), VCRP; Hemphill, "Virginia and the English Commercial System," 35.

22. Spotswood to BT, July 26, 1712, CO 5/1316, 363–368, VCRP; James H. Merrell, "Some Thoughts on Colonial Historians and American Indians," *WMQ*, 3d Ser., XLVI (1989), 103; Minchinton, King, and Waite, eds., *Virginia Slave-Trade Statistics*, xiii–xiv, 20–21, 35–45; Suttell, "The British Slave Trade to Virginia," 38.

South Carolina, captives of the Yamasee War (1715–1718). More important, the merchants had renewed the direct trade from Africa: about four thousand arrived between 1715 and 1718. The sudden increase in slave trading during these years highlights the different effects duties had in times of depression and times of expansion.[23]

The planters were once again buying all the blacks they could put their hands on in spite of the duty, which was scheduled in any case to expire in 1718. Garwin Corbin, resident agent for the company, reported Virginia's economic prospects to his employers in June of that year. The duty is "near Expiring; and it is well assured [that it] will not be revived and that Negroes will sell very Well, and the bills will be good, Tobacco yielding a Good price both there [Virginia] and in England." By September, the planters were realizing the highest prices in recent memory. To capitalize on the boom in prices, they cultivated more land and declined to renew the duty.[24]

The new prosperity in the tobacco trade was built upon a foundation of sand. Increased production soon created a surplus, leading to a decade-long depression beginning in 1720. After the five-pound duty expired in 1718, 5,170 Africans arrived on thirty-five ships from 1719 to 1721. This flash of enslaved laborers rekindled the bonfire of economic problems that the duty act of 1710 was supposed to have smothered. African slave dealers demanded higher prices from English traders as the "liberty" of the open trade increased competition; these, in turn, were passed on to the planters, increasing their indebtedness. The great planters' economic house was in shambles. Purchases of blacks from 1719 to 1721 had yet to be paid for. Recruitment of enslaved workers, wrote Robert "King" Carter in 1721, "swallows a great deal of money."[25]

The great planters faced a crisis in credit similar to the one in 1706. Reacting to the crisis, they purchased only 329 enslaved blacks on two ships

23. Minchinton, King, and Waite, eds., *Virginia Slave-Trade Statistics*, xiii–xiv n. 28, 20–21, 35–45, 48n.

24. Garwin Corbin to the Royal African Company, June 4, 1718, T 70/8, 221, VCRP; Richard L. Morton, *Colonial Virginia*, 2 vols. (Chapel Hill, N.C., 1960), II, 456.

25. William Yary, "Regulation, for the Better Carrying on of the African Trade . . . Proposals for the Service of the Royal African Company," Dec. 19, 1722, 92–93, in James Brydges, "A Collection of Remarkable Papers" (ca. 1735), Stowe Collection, ST 29, HL; Louis B. Wright, ed., *Letters of Robert Carter, 1720–1727: The Commercial Interests of a Virginia Gentleman* (San Marino, Calif., 1940), 13; Minchinton, King, and Waite, eds., *Virginia Slave-Trade Statistics*, 47–51; Hemphill, "Virginia and the English Commercial System," 65–66.

in 1722. Merchants had no desire to supply the great planters, once tobacco became underpriced and bills would likely be returned protested to
the planters. The failure of the great planters to prevent the credit crisis
weakened their position as brokers in Virginia, for they could not procure
supplies easily on credit and had difficulty collecting outstanding debts
from small and middling planters.[26]

The assembly passed a new duty act on enslaved blacks in 1723 to slow
the traffic and to raise revenue. The forty-shilling duty, paired with the
tobacco act limiting production to six thousand tobacco plants per taxable field hand, was tailored to limit production by reducing black immigration. The General Assembly hoped, by lessening the number of the
enslaved, to reduce the output of tobacco, the indebtedness on slave purchases, and the outflow of capital to Great Britain. It also earmarked the
duty for salaries and for defense against black insurrection, providing a
source of revenue other than the poll tax at a time when planters' tobacco
was of "little value." An unidentified Virginian wrote to Richard Harris,
a London slave-trade merchant, that the money from the duty could increase revenue as much as four thousand pounds. The burgesses would
use this money to pay themselves, since, for the last three sessions of the
assembly, they "think Money better pay than Tobacco."[27]

The great planters, anticipating a negative response from the slave-trade
merchants, defended the duty as a tried-and-true method of raising revenue in Virginia while limiting tobacco production by constraining the influx of new field hands. They contended that planters would absorb the
cost of the duty in higher slave prices, and the price of tobacco would
rise accordingly. Robert "King" Carter made plain the great planters' position on the act in a letter to William Byrd II, Virginia's representative
in London. The measure was their "constant Law" for raising revenue
when needed. His rumination—that the tax would be absorbed by the
country rather than the importer and that the price of tobacco would rise
even higher than its proportion to the duty—was, he wrote, the planters'
"Constant Experience." Carter attacked the merchants for their opposi-

26. Hemphill, "Virginia and the English Commercial System," 65–66; Minchinton,
King, and Waite, eds., *Virginia Slave-Trade Statistics*, 51.

27. Waverly K. Winfree, comp., *The Laws of Virginia: Being a Supplement to Hening's
The Statutes at Large, 1700–1750* (Richmond, Va., 1971), 237–253; Lt. Gov. Hugh Drysdale
to BT, June 29, 1723, CO 5/1319, 111–117, transcript, LC; Extract of letters to Richard Harris, June 25, 1723, CO 5/1319, 133, transcript, LC; Darold D. Wax, "Negro Import Duties
in Colonial Virginia . . . ," *VMHB*, LXXIX (1971), 35.

tion, for "there's no doubt but the African Company will break the neck of this Law."[28]

The debt crisis and the efforts of great planters to rescue their economy were confined neither to Virginia nor to tobacco but were systemic to British mercantilism, slavery, and the slave trade. At the same time in Barbados, great planters attempted to deal with their debt crisis by legislating for paper money to inflate their currency and thereby ease the planters' debt burden. Their debt was at twenty-four thousand pounds, with some planters owing interest at 10 percent. They also proposed a five-pound-per-head duty upon all enslaved laborers imported and an excise tax on Madeira to pay the salaries of the great planters who controlled the government. A factor employed by the Royal African Company in Barbados saw this paper-currency law as detrimental to the company's "African Stocks" and a greater "Infringement upon the Liberty of the Subject as the Parliament of England ever attempted."[29]

Thus, the great planters in both Virginia and Barbados tried to tilt the balance of trade back to their favor by taxing slave imports, increasing the price of tobacco and sugar, and reducing their indebtedness as a result. Although such strategies had worked during the 1710s, the great planters now encountered resistance. Indeed, subsequent battles over the regulation of the tobacco and slave trades would reveal class conflict both among planters and between planters and merchants within and outside Virginia.

The Madness of the People

The tobacco trade that evolved in Virginia over the seventeenth century can be categorized basically by two marketing modes: direct trade (bartering tobacco for goods) or consignment (selling tobacco on commission). The great planters, because of their role as merchant-planters, corresponded directly with specific British merchant houses. Typically, the middling planters bought merchandise from and shipped tobacco to British merchants on consignment. Small planters sold their tobacco to the great or middling planters or directly to factors involved in the carrying trade or agents stationed in Virginia. These marketing modes were not mutually exclusive. Planters ventured across lines when necessary or con-

28. Robert Carter to [William Byrd II], July 2, 1723, Carter to Micajah Perry, July 3, 1723, Robert Carter's Letter Book, 1723–1724, 8–9, 10–11, CWF.

29. "A Short View of the Present State of Barbados" (1723), Barbados Factor to BT, Jan. 9, 1723, 1–2, both in Brydges, "Collection of Remarkable Papers," ST 28, HL.

venient. The great planters had the most flexibility. They could sell their tobacco on their own account to a British firm or sell their tobacco "in the country" to an agent. Some became agents for British merchants. They could even sell their tobacco to a factor or freighter. Without access to the correspondence trade, except through a merchant-planter, middling planters could consign their tobacco or sell it only to factors or agents. Smaller planters, with the least flexibility, might, after satisfying rents and local debts, sell their surplus to the vendor offering the best price in the neighborhood.[30]

The great planters and their correspondents in England, beginning in the 1630s, served each other in their mutual business interests. These planters were also the largest merchants in Virginia. Many of them began as tobacco merchants or factors, especially before 1660, brokering their accounts into considerable estates. They shouldered Virginia's economy by organizing commerce, by marketing tobacco, and by selling goods and blacks. They bought merchandise wholesale and sold it to smaller planters and tenants. They produced tobacco with slave labor, collected it as rent from tenants, or purchased it from small planters. They found merchants to handle their business in London and, in the eighteenth century, in Bristol and Liverpool. The great planters, as correspondents, helped plan inventories, placing orders for goods, servants, and enslaved persons, and shipped their tobacco to the merchants. In return, they could count on the firms to vouch for their enterprise as guarantor. No fewer than 125 men could be counted great planters. Contemporary historian John M. Old-mixon wrote: "On every River of this Province there are Men in Number from ten to thirty, who by Trade and Industry have got very compleat Estates."[31]

30. Jacob M. Price, "A Revolution of Scale in Overseas Trade: British Firms in the Chesapeake Trade, 1675-1775," *Journal of Economic History*, XLVII (1987), 4-8; Price, *Perry of London*, 32-40 (quotation on 32); Walter E. Minchinton, ed., "The Virginia Letters of Isaac Hobhouse, Merchant of Bristol," *VMHB*, LXVI (1958), 278-301.

31. John M. Oldmixon, *The British Empire in America* . . . , 2 vols. (London, 1708), I, x, 322-323; Col. Robert Quary to BT, 1704, CO 5/1314, 63, transcript, LC; William Byrd [II], "On Suspending the Laws for Paying Debts in Country Commodities of Virginia . . ." (ca. 1700-1705), Miscellaneous Papers, in T. H. Wynne, ed., *History of the Dividing Line, and Other Tracts; from the Papers of William Byrd, of Westover, in Virginia, Esquire*, II, *Journey to the Land of Eden and Other Tracts*, Historical Documents from the Old Dominion, no. III (Richmond, Va., 1866), II, 163; Beverley, *History and Present State of Virginia*, ed. Wright, xvii-xix; Price, *Perry of London*, 31-32. See also Rutman and Rutman, *A Place in Time*, 143-144, 206; Thomas J. Wertenbaker, *The Planters of Colonial Virginia* (1922),

The great planters dominated the countryside by their position on the major rivers and by their control of the trade to smaller planters. The depth of the James, York, Rappahannock, and Potomac Rivers, enhancing the planters' commercial advantage, allowed oceangoing vessels to dock at their wharves, reducing the need for towns. River frontage helped secure the great planters' economic hold on the hinterland, where most small and middling planters lived. They built wharves to serve as central storehouses, where imported merchandise, servants, and enslaved blacks could be exchanged. The great planters handled about half of the tobacco crop, at least until the 1720s. William Byrd II understood the commercial advantage of his water frontage and his stores. In 1718, he wrote: "In a few years the value of it [my estate] will grow to be double what it is at this time, by the increase of the inhabitants of the country, and by the great distance from water carriage, all the land lys that remains now to be taken up."[32]

With the advent of the triangular trade, the traffic in Virginia came under the control of the great planters. In the triangular trade, which connected the colonies to the British and African markets, factors did not accompany ships as they did in the two-way trade between Virginia wharves and British ports. Merchant houses sent ships laden with British goods to the African coast to purchase blacks. Once in Virginia, these ships relied on the great planters for direction to the best markets. The planters had in advance stocked tobacco in their waterfront warehouses. Adding enslaved blacks to the mix of merchandise and tobacco contrived a good commission. The high capital cost of blacks required greater familiarity with the buyer than the two-way factor trade. The great planters issued credit in the company's name, enhancing their local power and prestige, and looked after their correspondents' interests, acquiring tobacco and fitting out ships for their return voyages.[33]

The middling planters trafficked in the consignment or freight trade.

in Wertenbaker, *The Shaping of Colonial Virginia* (Princeton, N.J., 1958), 157; Jackson T. Main, "The One Hundred," *WMQ*, 3d Ser., XI (1954), 354–384.

32. Henry Hartwell, James Blair, and Edward Chilton, *The Present State of Virginia, and the College* (1697; orig. pub. 1727), ed. Hunter Dickinson Farish (Williamsburg, Va., 1940), 12–13; William Byrd II to Vigilante [John Smith], Feb. 18, 1718, to Lord Tipparari, [Michael Bourke, Baron Dunkellin], Feb. 18, 1718, in Marion Tinling, ed., *The Correspondence of the Three William Byrds of Westover, Virginia, 1684–1776*, 2 vols. (Charlottesville, Va., 1977), I, 312, 313–314.

33. Minchinton, ed., "The Virginia Letters of Isaac Hobhouse," *VMHB*, LXVI (1958), 282–284.

If the great planters were business associates of the merchants, the consignee planters were their clientele. The middling and great planters were distinguished by their ability to secure credit from the English merchant houses. The middling planters could reckon on goods with collateral on hand; the great planters, with their equity in land and enslaved labor and their capacity to produce tobacco, had better access to surety. The middling planters purchased goods at retail prices from the freighters and maintained stores of goods that they sold to small planters, tenants, and former servants. Trucking with kin and neighbors, less anonymous than the trade of the great planters, reinforced community ties. William Byrd II wrote around 1704 "that there is at least 400 or 500 of the Inhabitants that trade [on consignment] to England, and have Goods and Merchandizes hence."[34]

The consignment trade over time cut into the correspondence trade of the great planters. Spurred on first by the inflated prices of merchandise during the war years of the 1690s, the consignment trade hit its stride after 1713, producing high profits on goods and tobacco until about 1725. As a result, merchants increased their trade on consignment, bypassing the large tobacco ships commissioned by the great planters. By 1721, Robert "King" Carter reported to Micajah Perry III the effect of the consignment practice on the great planters. He referred to this increased practice of bypassing the great planters as the "madness of the people, that they will be freighters and not freighters as the price [of tobacco] rises and falls here."[35]

Although by the mid-seventeenth century the great planters controlled a substantial part of what the small planters produced, the majority of small planters were able to sell a portion of their tobacco directly to factors. The small planters were often former servants who had become petty proprietors. Some had been tenants who had paid rent in tobacco, escaping tenancy by selling the surplus. The direct trade emerged in the mid-seventeenth century and continued throughout the period because of the dispersed population. Factors, sent by a syndicate or firm, accompanied their goods from England and obtained lodging and storage on a river,

34. Byrd, "On Suspending the Laws," in Wynne, ed., *History of the Dividing Line*, II, 163; Rutman and Rutman, *A Place in Time*, 206; Price, *Perry of London*, 29, 31–33.

35. Carter to Perry, Feb. 13, 1720/1, to William Dawkins, Feb. 13, 1720/1, both in Wright, ed., *Letters of Robert Carter*, 74–75; Jacob M. Price, *France and the Chesapeake: A History of the French Tobacco Monopoly, 1674–1791, and Its Relationship to the British and American Tobacco Trades*, 2 vols. (Ann Arbor, Mich., 1973), I, 662–774.

where they traded merchandise for tobacco. They were sojourners who stayed only long enough—usually several months—to make their transactions and then return to England, carrying tobacco and paper on next year's crop. The factors had a decided advantage in these transactions. As early as 1696, William Byrd II applied a metaphor that highlighted the small planters' plight as well as evoked the oppression of blacks, observing: "Some of the poor Planters are already So in debt for necessarys for their familys that the Slavery of their whole life will never pay for it." The factor trade was the most common method of doing business among ordinary planters in the Chesapeake, as Byrd and Perry explained in 1717. "The trade to Virginia is usually carryed on by sending Factors with their goods from Brittain, who had been brought up [in the trade] and understood the different nature of Tobacco: by which means they made return in Exchange for their goods in such sort of Tobacco, as was proper for that Market, for which it was designed."[36]

Even as the great planters attained leadership through the correspondence system, the small planters who produced most of the tobacco still had other options for shipping their product. Seventeenth-century surveying rules allowed smaller planters river frontage and therefore access to trade ships, circumventing complete great-planter control. Before 1650, few plots were patented without shoreline. By the 1690s, tidewater lands without water access were still unclaimed. As much as one-half of the tobacco crop bypassed the great planters, partly because the survey system had allowed smaller planters river frontage and partly because the smaller planters "had always" traded directly with peddlers, factors, and "transient" ships. The great planters' half-share of the tobacco market was jeopardized in the late 1720s, when tobacco merchants aggressively wooed smaller planters and the planter consignment system broke down. During this period of expansion, as planters moved into the upper reaches of the Rappahannock and York Rivers and westward along the James and Potomac Rivers, tobacco factors were becoming more prominent on Virginia's waterways, increasing merchant access to small producers.[37]

36. William Byrd II, Notebook, 1696–1702, BR 744, 2–4, HL; Price, *Perry of London*, 31.

37. Jacob M. Price, "Merchants and Planters: The Market Structure of the Colonial Chesapeake Reconsidered," in Price, *Tobacco in Atlantic Trade: The Chesapeake, London, and Glasgow, 1675–1775* (Aldershot, Eng., 1995), chap. 4: 10–14, 29–31; Price, "The Last Phase of the Virginia-London Consignment Trade: James Buchanan and Co., 1758–1768," *WMQ*, 3d Ser., XLIII (1986), 64–65; Rutman and Rutman, *A Place in Time*, chap. 7;

New merchants in Virginia gained a foothold through the positioning of agents. Although London remained the leading tobacco and slave-trading port, Glasgow and Bristol cut into its business during the 1720s by posting agents on the waterways. The two ports were alike in that representatives operated from permanent facilities and received a commission. But they differed in the focus of their trade: Bristol specialized in enslaved laborers, and Glasgow, in tobacco. Moreover, with regard to the selection of agents, Bristol chose members of the great-planter class, but without giving them the independence of correspondents; Glasgow sent its own countrymen to establish stores on Virginia's rivers.[38]

When the slave-trade merchants started once again to invest their capital in Virginia in the 1720s, they began exercising greater control in the Atlantic economy. Bristol had become the most important slave-trading port after London during the early years of the eighteenth century. After the opening of the slave trade in 1698, Bristol steadily increased its market share from about 12 percent in its first decade to 35 percent from 1708 to 1717. After 1718, Bristol made 70 percent of the slave voyages to Virginia. Firms such as Isaac Hobhouse and Company were syndicates or limited partnerships engaged in the slave and tobacco trades. These firms supplied its agents, usually great planters with stores or other commercial interests, who received a commission of 8 to 10 percent for handling blacks and tobacco. Hobhouse's agents included John Tayloe of Mount Airy on the Rappahannock River and Augustine Moore in New Kent County. Not only had the merchants successfully shaved the market share of the great-planter correspondents but, in doing so, had splintered the power of the great planters, for some of their class had become agents for the merchants.[39]

When tobacco prices improved after 1713, Scottish firms began investing in agents and developing permanent stores. The 1707 Act of Union

---

Sarah S. Hughes, *Surveyors and Statesmen: Land Measuring in Colonial Virginia* (Richmond, Va., 1979), 43–44.

38. Price, *France and the Chesapeake,* I, 662–663.

39. Suttell, "The British Slave Trade to Virginia," 45–46; Elizabeth Donnan, "Eighteenth-Century English Merchants: Micajah Perry," *Journal of Economic and Business History,* IV (1931–1932), 70; Wright, ed., *Letters of Robert Carter,* ix; Minchinton, ed., "The Virginia Letters of Isaac Hobhouse," *VMHB,* LXVI (1958), 281; C. M. MacInnes, *Bristol and the Slave Trade* (Bristol, 1963); Herbert S. Klein, "Slaves and Shipping in Eighteenth-Century Virginia," *Journal of Interdisciplinary History,* V (1974–1975), 406–410; Minchinton, King, and Waite, eds., *Virginia Slave-Trade Statistics,* 48n.

had given Glasgow the opening needed to compete with English ports. Scottish merchants supplied their agents with goods, authorizing them to determine pricing on the spot. In taking this step, they were able to deal directly with small planters, cutting into the profit of the great planters and English merchants. With permanent facilities from which to operate, the Scottish merchants supplied a more sophisticated method of credit sales, using tobacco and sometimes wheat from next year's crop as collateral. Small planters preferred this system of using agents to the earlier one resembling barter, where they had simply traded merchandise for tobacco. These stores replaced the previous consignment trade that had supplied the great planters, siphoning off a considerable portion of the correspondence trade. Because of their focus on tobacco, the Glasgow firms were outpacing the Bristol firms in the triangular trade, making Glasgow the most important new port in the tobacco trade by the 1720s.[40]

*   *   *

THE NEW MERCHANTS over time loosened the great planters' grasp on Virginia's tobacco economy. As a result, Micajah Perry III testified before a House of Commons committee that in 1723 all five vessels sent to Virginia returned to England half-empty, despite the relative largeness of that year's tobacco crop. The great planters were in chronic debt owing to the crisis in credit induced by the slave trade and the persistently low price of tobacco. The merchants' interests were beginning to diverge from those of their partners in the correspondence trade.[41]

40. Price, *Perry of London,* 31; Price, *France and the Chesapeake,* I, 662, 663–774; Rutman and Rutman, *A Place in Time,* 206–207, 209; *Oxford English Dictionary,* s.v. "Scot peddler"; Michael Garibaldi Hall, *Edward Randolph and the American Colonies, 1676–1703* (Chapel Hill, N.C., 1960), 140–141.

41. Price, *Perry of London,* 64–65.

II

Conflicts

Race and Class

CHAPTER 4

The Laws of Slavery

Robert Beverley II described Virginia in 1705 as a pastoral community recently wrested from the wilderness. Certainly he remembered the "confu-
sions" and "Calamities" that had led to Bacon's Rebellion in 1676 and the
plant-cutting "Accident" of 1682–1683, but Beverley now proclaimed Virginia resolved of its land and labor problems. "Tenure of their Land there,
is free and common Soccage," he wrote. "The work of their Servants, and
Slaves, is no other than what every common Freeman do's." These pre-
sentments belie historical reality. Indeed, land had become unfettered and
free in the marketplace, but great planters had engrossed and entailed it
by 1705, much to the detriment of smaller planters and to the chagrin of
colonial authorities. At the same time, the distinction between servants
and the enslaved and the labor each performed had become pronounced
in 1705 with the passage of a comprehensive slave code.[1]

Although unfree labor had a long history in England, there were no legal
precedents for enslaving a class of people for life and making that status
inevitable. The great planters' turn to racial slavery was thus accompanied
by their willingness to create institutions compatible with the subjection
of an alien and rebellious laboring class. Their decision to enslave blacks
involved a choice to establish a coercive state. In doing so, colonists departed from a trend in English law toward greater freedom, their need
to secure economic dominion prompting them to initiate discriminatory
innovations in the legal code.

From ambivalent views about dark-skinned people, the great planters'
racism developed rapidly into a buttress of the Virginia superstructure.

1. Robert Beverley, *The History and Present State of Virginia* (1705, 1722), ed. Louis B.
Wright (Chapel Hill, N.C., 1947), 92, 239–240, 272–274, 277.

The English had a cultural predisposition to view blackness as symbolic of things dirty and evil. Carrying this inherited prejudice into the wilderness, anxious settlers found the Africans' animism, blackness, and customs threatening. Searching for a salve for their solicitude, they began associating light-skinned people with civilization and dark-skinned people with savageness. This racism figured significantly in their decision to enslave Africans and to eschew the possibility of enslaving Europeans or native Americans, even though Ireland and the Powhatan Confederacy, for example, provided alternatives for forced labor. Both the Irish (1641) and the Powhatans (1622 and 1644) waged war with the English, giving the English just cause to enslave them. (Indeed, the Puritans in Massachusetts had used the rationale of just war to enslave the Pequots after the Pequot War of 1637.) Although a few Indians were enslaved in Virginia after the 1644 war, the colonists would not systematically move to enslave Indians until Bacon's Rebellion in 1676. The English attributed to the Irish and the Powhatans the same traits of laziness, savagery, and flawed ancestry that they applied to Africans; yet, adhering to their notions of a hierarchy of color, they chose to make them subjects rather than enslaved laborers.[2]

Such racial attitudes weighed more heavily as the colony developed, braced by the evolving slave statutes. These laws denied blacks the traditional English rights of association, assembly, bearing arms, expression, and mobility and the rights against unreasonable search and seizure. They

2. Alan Watson, *Slave Law in the Americas* (Athens, Ga., 1989), 63–64; Robin Blackburn, "The Old World Background to European Colonial Slavery," and Alden T. Vaughan and Virginia Mason Vaughan, "Before Othello: Elizabethan Representations of Sub-Saharan Africans," *WMQ*, 3d Ser., LIV (1997), 29, 84–90, 92, 96; Winthrop D. Jordan, *White over Black: American Attitudes toward the Negro, 1550–1812* (Chapel Hill, N.C., 1968), 47–89; Robert Olwell, *Masters, Slaves, and Subjects: The Culture of Power in the South Carolina Low Country, 1740–1790* (Ithaca, N.Y., 1998), 57–102; Thomas D. Morris, *Southern Slavery and the Law, 1619–1860* (Chapel Hill, N.C., 1996), 38–46; David Barry Gaspar, "'Rigid and Inclement': Origins of the Jamaica Slave Laws of the Seventeenth Century," in Christopher L. Tomlins and Bruce H. Mann, eds., *The Many Legalities of Early America* (Chapel Hill, N.C., 2001), 78–96; Nicholas P. Canny, *The Elizabethan Conquest of Ireland: A Pattern Established, 1565–76* (New York, 1976), 160–162; Canny, *Kingdom and Colony: Ireland in the Atlantic World, 1560–1800* (Baltimore, 1988), 106; Canny, *Making Ireland British, 1580–1650* (Oxford, 2001), 205, 436–437; Ronald Takaki, "*The Tempest* in the Wilderness: The Racialization of Savagery," *Journal of American History*, LXXIX (1992–1993), 893–895; Ronald Dale Karr, "'Why Should You Be So Furious?' The Violence of the Pequot War," *JAH*, LXXXV (1998–1999), 907–908; Alden T. Vaughan, *Roots of American Racism: Essays on the Colonial Experience* (New York, 1995), 105–127, 177–199.

attempted to squeeze out class similarities between blacks and whites by bringing racial distinctions to bear against the former. In guaranteeing the expansion of the enslaved labor force, the great planters had to drive a wedge between laboring whites and blacks. The consolidation of the slave codes reinforced a developing racial system of justice in Virginia.

A Sufficient Distinction

The status of blacks was ambiguous in Virginia before 1640. Census takers distinguished blacks by identifying them as "Negroes," but they were not legally defined as enslaved. Such an appellation did not necessarily lead to slavery. Neither statutory nor judicial law consigned the charter generation of blacks in Virginia to enslavement. Without a law, civil act, or court precedent marking them as enslaved, blacks could have the same expectations as other immigrants to Virginia. In the first legal case in which the term "Negro" is used as a distinction, for example, the court in 1624 allowed John Phillip, a "Negro," to testify against Symon Tuchinge, a white man accused of illegally seizing a Spanish ship. The court determined that, because Phillip had twelve years earlier been "Christened in England," his Christian status allowed him the right to testify, a right that non-Christian Africans were presumably denied. Some Africans came as indentured servants and others as involuntary servants, not unlike "spirited" Englishmen, their transportation paid in exchange for a customary term of service. Serving out their terms proved their indentured status. Some of these, such as "Antonio a Negro," later known as Anthony Johnson, even became freeholders and slaveholders. The majority of Africans, however, were non-Christians and were enslaved without statutory basis. Planters relied instead on the precedent of enslaving non-Christian captives of war.[3]

3. *MCGC*, 33; John Thornton, *Africa and Africans in the Making of the Atlantic World, 1400–1680* (Cambridge, 1992), 147; Ira Berlin, *Many Thousands Gone: The First Two Centuries of Slavery in North America* (Cambridge, Mass., 1998), 32; Kathleen M. Brown, *Good Wives, Nasty Wenches, and Anxious Patriarchs: Gender, Race, and Power in Colonial Virginia* (Chapel Hill, N.C., 1996), 107–108, 112–114; Joseph Douglas Deal III, "Race and Class in Colonial Virginia: Indians, Englishmen, and Africans on the Eastern Shore during the Seventeenth Century" (Ph.D. diss., University of Rochester, 1981), 198–201; T. H. Breen and Stephen Innes, *"Myne Owne Ground": Race and Freedom on Virginia's Eastern Shore, 1640–1676* (New York, 1980), 7–18; A. Leon Higginbotham, Jr., *Shades of Freedom: Racial Politics and Presumptions of the American Legal Process* (New York, 1996), 19–20;

If before 1640 slavery was not encoded in law, in at least one instance the General Court, made up of great planters, began to differentiate "negroes" as a group. As early as 1630, the court sentenced Hugh Davis, a white man, to be "soundly whipt before an assembly of negroes and others" for "abusing himself" and "defiling" his body by copulating with a Negro. The record is unclear whether this punishment was for fornication or for buggery, but its focus on blacks is suggestive. Davis had soiled himself by lying with a black. His action might have been an affront to English morality, but the court wanted his transgression, whether done by force or by consent, to be punished in front of blacks. The court targeted "negroes" as witnesses to Davis's humiliation and to the exercise of their authority.[4]

The General Assembly watched with intense interest Barbados, where slavery was quickly changing the fortunes of the nabobs, but Virginians had little to draw on from the island's legislation. Barbados had incorporated all provisions dealing with the status and behavior of blacks from English laws concerning indentured servants. Although blacks had arrived as early as 1627, their status remained vague for almost a decade. They were treated as enslaved but were not legally defined as such until 1636, when the governor and council acting jointly issued a resolution that blacks and Indians would serve for life unless they had contracted for time before entering Barbados. This resolution and the earliest known statute, "An Act concerning Negroes" (August 1644), are no longer extant. A 1652 act levied a heavier fine for anyone who knowingly harbored an enslaved laborer for more than one night: it cost an offender five hundred pounds, as opposed to one hundred pounds of sugar for a servant. By making it more costly to harbor a fugitive black or Indian, the legislators tried to impress on whites that interference with enslaved property was not to be tolerated. The articulation of a slave code in 1656 drove this distinction home.[5]

In the first instance of race as a delimiter in Virginia law, the General

---

George M. Fredrickson, *White Supremacy: A Comparative Study in American and South African History* (New York, 1981), 76–77; Vaughan, *Roots of American Racism*, 128–174.

4. *MCGC*, 479; Richard Godbeer, "'The Cry of Sodom': Discourse, Intercourse, and Desire in Colonial New England," *WMQ*, 3d Ser., LII (1995), 259–286. Sodomy in seventeenth-century New England was a "filthiness committed by parties of the same sex" (Godbeer, 263). See also Jordan, *White over Black*, 78–79; cf. Brown, *Good Wives, Nasty Wenches*, 195.

5. Jerome S. Handler, *The Unappropriated People: Freedmen in the Slave Society of Barbados* (Baltimore, 1974), 12–13.

Assembly in 1640 prohibited blacks, except for freeholders, from bearing arms, a basic common-law right. The legislators, acting in their class interest, required masters to furnish guns and ammunition to able-bodied members of their households, "excepting negros." Although, technically, black landholders had the same privileges as their white counterparts, lawmakers were beginning to see blacks as a people apart. As a harbinger of changing attitudes, the statute may indicate that the great planters were trying to degrade blacks' status or were beginning to fear them, although their numbers were still negligible, only about three hundred by 1649. Clearly, however, the law made it more difficult for blacks to defend themselves, and thereby easier to enslave.[6]

Great planters also began fashioning racial slavery in the courts in 1640. They began to assume lifelong servitude for blacks and, at the same time, devised more debasing punishments for them than the customary extension of service meted out to transgressing white servants. For example, affairs between bound laborers inevitably crossed racial lines. Bastardy was not uncommon in early Virginia because of the disproportionate ratio of men to women and laws disallowing bound laborers to marry. In these cases, the courts were concerned with assigning the costs of maternity and child support. The parents were responsible to the master and the parish for these charges; they would be bound to serve extra time. Both also could anticipate public penance according to English law. Shrouded in white sheets of shame, they would be expected to acknowledge their sin in front of the parish congregation. The jurists in 1640, however, ordered that Robert Sweat, a white man, perform penance wearing white sheets at James City Parish Church for impregnating a woman belonging to Lieutenant Robert Sheppard. The absence of any discussion of compensation to Sheppard or to the parish suggests that the mother was an enslaved woman and that her child would be Sheppard's property at birth. Presumably a non-Christian, she was not allowed the ritual sheets of shame in church; rather, the jurists sentenced that she "be whipt at the whipping post."[7]

Discriminatory treatment can also be seen in jurists' dealing with inter-

---

6. *SAL,* I, 226; "Acts of General Assembly, Jan. 6, 1639–40 (Concluded)," *WMQ,* 2d Ser., IV (1924), 147. Cf. Breen and Innes, *"Myne Owne Ground,"* 24–27.

7. *SAL,* I, 552; *MCGC,* 477, 483. Brown notes that in at least one instance in 1649 an African woman convicted of fornication was sentenced to the penance "normally" assigned to whites (*Good Wives, Nasty Wenches,* 130–131; see also Higginbotham, *Shades of Freedom,* 22).

racial escapes. Black and white laborers had much in common in seven-teenth-century Virginia, and they sometimes formed alliances to escape bondage. Authorities found such collaboration intolerable. John Punch and Emanuel, both blacks, each conspired in separate incidents with white servants to run away. The court sentenced Punch's white accomplices to three additional years of labor but condemned Punch to lifelong servi-tude. The court ordered a whipping for Emanuel and the six whites in-volved in a plot to escape to New Amsterdam and extended the whites' terms for an additional year. Emanuel, who already served for life, was to be "burnt in the cheek with the letter R. and to work in shackle for one year or more as his master shall see cause."[8]

Nonwhites recognized their precarious position in a society where courts were instituting lifelong servitude based on racial characteristics. In response, blacks sought means to preserve their freedom. Conversion to Christianity was one important way they could contest slavery for them-selves and their children. Since the English used non-Christian affiliation as justification for enslavement and associated Protestant Christianity with liberation, blacks and Indians seeking redress from slavery by pleading their Christianity provided whites with a dilemma in creating a closed racial society. John Graweere, a black servant to William Evans, tried to secure the freedom of his child, born of a black woman belonging to Lieutenant Robert Sheppard, through Christianity. After purchasing his child's freedom with the savings he accumulated from the selling of hogs, he petitioned the county court in 1641 for his child to be baptized and raised in the Christian faith. The court, in turn, stipulated that he or the godfather had custodial responsibility. Emmanuel Driggus, an enslaved man who did not become free until 1661, apprenticed his two adopted chil-dren, eight-year-old Elizabeth (for thirteen years) and one-year-old Jane (for thirty years), to Francis Potts; Potts was to furnish meat, drink, cloth-ing, lodging, and Christian instruction. Driggus purchased Jane's contract in 1652 through the sale of his cattle. He was unable to protect his two natural children, nine-year-old Ann and three-year-old Edward, whom Potts sold as enslaved laborers in 1657. In yet another instance, William, born and baptized in 1655, was set free with his father Mihill Gowen in 1658 because they were Christians. That blacks used Christianity to es-

<hr />

8. Warren M. Billings, ed., *The Old Dominion in the Seventeenth Century: A Documen-tary History of Virginia, 1606–1689* (Chapel Hill, N.C., 1975), 172; *MCGC*, 466–467.

cape slavery made slaveowners, always ill at ease, even more anxious about their peculiar property.[9]

At the same time, the General Assembly, promoting peaceful relations between the colony and the tributary tribes, protected Indian children as indentured servants and promoted their proselytism. The English had not moved to enslave the Powhatans after the war of 1644, continuing to treat them as tributary subjects, although they had the precedent of the Massachusetts Bay Colony, which enslaved Indians after the Pequot War of 1637. The Puritans, coveting the Indians' farms in land-scarce New England, racially demonized the Pequots and exchanged them in Providence and Tortugas for blacks. Three years later, the act "Liberties of Forreiners and Strangers" spelled out the justification for selling Pequots as enslaved laborers and buying enslaved blacks. The legislature in 1641, bowing to English law, prohibited "bond-slavery, villenage or captivitie" but acknowledged as justifiable the enslavement of "lawful captives taken in just warrs, and such strangers as willingly sell themselves, or are solde to us." Such enslavement as part of international law stood above state prohibitions. The legislators thus declared that those justly enslaved could not seek freedom even though they "shall have the libertyes and Christian usages which the law of God established in Israell concerning such persons doth morally require."[10]

Cognizant of the Massachusetts policy, the great planters were yet unwilling to enslave the tributary Indians. Rather, they tolerated the Indians, who, living on reserved land, were considered culturally deprived, and tried through Christianity to assimilate them. To this end, in the 1655 act "for better securing the peace," the assembly allowed Indian children, serving for a term of years agreed upon with their parents, to be educated

9. Brown, *Good Wives, Nasty Wenches,* 131–132, 135; Blackburn, "Old World Background," *WMQ,* 3d Ser., LIV (1997), 67–72; Jerome W. Jones, "The Established Virginia Church and the Conversion of Negroes and Indians, 1620–1720," *Journal of Negro History,* XLVI (1961), 20; Joseph B. Earnest, Jr., *The Religious Development of the Negro in Virginia* (Charlottesville, Va., 1914), 17–18; Billings, ed., *Old Dominion,* 164; Deal, "Race and Class in Colonial Virginia," 327–331.

10. Jordan, *White over Black,* 67–71; Max Savelle, *The Origins of American Diplomacy: The International History of Angloamerica, 1492–1763* (New York, 1967), 203; Lorenzo Johnston Greene, *The Negro in Colonial New England* (New York, 1942), 15–20; Karen Ordahl Kupperman, "Errand to the Indies: Puritan Colonization from Providence Island through the Western Design," *WMQ,* 3d Ser., XLV (1988), 75; Takaki, "Tempest in the Wilderness," *JAH,* LXXIX (1992–1993), 901–912.

and reared as Christians. The assembly legislated in 1658 that "Indians
not be assigned over" to others. Employers of indentured children were
not only unable to transfer them, but the children were limited to a term
of service until their twenty-fifth birthday, when they were to be set free
and put at their "owne disposall." The assembly additionally found testimony in 1658 that unscrupulous Englishmen have "violently and fraudulently" kidnapped Indian children, pretending to have purchased them
from their parents or tribal officials, "rendering religion contemptible, and
the name of Englishmen odious." To eliminate this scandal of "Stealing
Indian Children," the assembly outlawed the purchase of an Indian from
another Englishman. In at least one case, an Indian sued for emancipation because an Indian king wrongly sold him to an Englishwoman. This
suit, argued before the House of Burgesses in 1661, further demonstrates
the perceived relationship between acculturation, Christianity, and freedom. Weetoppen, an Indian boy, petitioned that the king of the Weyanokes
had unfairly sold him to Elizabeth Short, who registered the deed in the
Surry County court in 1659. Weetopen's argument was that he was Powhatan, not Weyanoke. The king had "no power to sell him being of another
nation," wrote the burgesses; just as important, "he speak[s] the English
tongue perfectly and desir[es] baptism."[11]

The cases of Manuel and Fernando demonstrate how the enslaved used
in court the strategy of previous Christian status to seek freedom. Manuel
and Fernando were typical of many Atlantic Creoles who accepted Christianity and sued their owners in court. Their Latin names suggest that they
had previously lived in a Hispanic society where they converted to Christianity. Manuel, as a Christian, petitioned the General Assembly for emancipation because William Whittacre had wrongfully enslaved him in 1644.
Whittacre claimed that he had purchased Manuel, a mixed-race man, from
Thomas Bushrod, who had bought him from William Smith, believing
him assigned "as a Slave for Ever." The assembly adjudged that Manuel
was "to serve as other Christian servants do" and fined Whittacre twenty-
five pounds sterling. Whittacre unsuccessfully petitioned the governor and
the council for relief; Manuel was freed in 1665. Two years later, Fernando
sued his master, John Warner, in Lower Norfolk Court for his freedom
not only because he was Christian but also because he had resided free in
several Latin American countries before his enslavement in Virginia. He

11. "The Northern Neck of Virginia," *WMQ*, 1st Ser., VI (1897–1898), 214–215; *SAL*, I,
410, 455–456, 481–482, II, 155.

presented documents in Portuguese, or "some other language which the Court could not understand," allegedly in the hand of the respective governors of the colonies where he had lived as a free man. He also claimed that he had spent several years in England and should serve no longer than other English servants. After the Lower Norfolk Court "Judge[d] him a slave for his life," he appealed to the General Court, but that ruling is not extant.[12]

In the same year Fernando instituted his suit and two years after Manuel won his freedom, the General Assembly sought to dispel the notion that Christianity implied freedom. Because of the uncertainty cast on the status of christened children enslaved "by birth," Virginia's legislators passed a statute in 1667 stipulating that the sacrament of baptism "doth not alter the condition of the person as to his bondage or freedome." With one stroke, this act allowed conscientious masters, "freed from this doubt," to christen enslaved laborers. The law protected slaveholders' property rights while they endeavored to inculcate blacks with Christian precepts.[13]

The English custom of not enslaving coreligious, adopted from the Muslims during the Crusades, became problematic in Virginia during the 1660s. Alert to the contradiction implicit in Christianity of not enslaving Christians while retaining that condition for those Christians already enslaved, colonial authorities began after 1667 to correlate religious designations of pagan, heathen, and infidel with the geographic origins of the enslaved. Subsequent acts hammered out the rationale behind the enslavement of blacks, associating enslavement with non-Christian origins. The General Assembly in 1670 classified non-Christians carried in by sea as enslaved and those carried over land as servants. This act did not account for Christians coming from Africa, including the Kingdom of the Congo; rather, it was meant to distinguish between Africans and Indians, for Africans arrived in Virginia by sea and Indians by land. This distinction, which affirmed the 1655 and 1658 statutes classifying indigenous Indians as indentured, had more to do with the recognition that a native

12. Thornton, *Africa and Africans*, 269–270; Berlin, *Many Thousands Gone*, 27–46; Brown, *Good Wives, Nasty Wenches*, 114–115; "The Randolph Manuscript: Virginia Seventeenth-Century Records: To the Honourable Sir Wm. Berkeley Knight Governor, etc., and the Honourable Council of Virginia; the Humble Petition of Wm. Whittacre Sheweth," *VMHB*, XVII (1909), 232; Billings, ed., *Old Dominion*, 169.

13. *SAL*, II, 260; Brown, *Good Wives, Nasty Wenches*, 135–136; Warren M. Billings, "The Law of Servants and Slaves in Seventeenth-Century Virginia," *VMHB*, XCIX (1991), 58.

people, familiar with the terrain near their homeland, could more effectively disrupt the plantation system than with any benevolence toward Indians. Nevertheless, the distinction further alienated blacks racially.[14]

The great planters in 1682 repealed the 1670 act that made "Indians and others free." Still suspicious about the status of enslaved Indians following Bacon's Rebellion (1676) and cognizant of enslaved Christians' suits for freedom, the legislators refined the religious and geographic rationale of the 1670 act. During Bacon's Rebellion, the assembly had allowed soldiers to enslave Indian captives as spoils of war, coining this practice in 1679 as the right of "free purchase." According to the 1682 statute, non-Christian origins were a predicate of enslavement. Any captives "whose parentage and native country are not christian at the time of their first purchase" were enslaved for life, as were Africans and Indians "taken in warre." The status of Muslims was qualified. Turks and Moors were exempted from slavery "whilest in amity with his majesty," but Muslims from African nations not recognized by the crown could be enslaved. The act was principally aimed at black converts, however. The new law was clear: conversion to Christianity alone did not warrant freedom for the enslaved. The new stipulations would prevent both "great losse and damage" to owners and "great discouragement" to merchants "bringing in such slaves for the future."[15]

Later, with the slave code of 1705, the General Assembly sought to remove any lingering equivocation that Christianity could in any way lead to freedom. In doing so, it reopened a controversy a generation of legislation had tried to resolve. The General Assembly legislated that blacks coming to Virginia from the West Indies could sue for freedom only if they had embraced Christianity in England or some other European country before their arrival. This exception troubled the great planters, for, after forty years of legal maneuvering, the basis for Fernando's suit, free Christian status before arrival in Virginia, was still recognized in law. The only way to deal with the problem was to exclude these people from the colony.

14. *SAL,* II, 283; John K. Thornton, "African Dimensions of the Stono Rebellion," *American Historical Review,* XCVI (1991), 1105–1106; Thornton, *Africa and Africans,* 254; Wesley Frank Craven, *White, Red, and Black: The Seventeenth-Century Virginian* (Charlottesville, Va., 1971), 74–75; Morris, *Southern Slavery and the Law,* 19; Edmund S. Morgan, *American Slavery, American Freedom: The Ordeal of Colonial Virginia* (New York, 1975), 329; Brown, *Good Wives, Nasty Wenches,* 136.

15. *SAL,* II, 283, 490–491; Morris, *Southern Slavery and the Law,* 19; Morgan, *American Slavery, American Freedom,* 328–329.

Thus, the Council of State in 1706 prohibited the sale in Virginia of blacks and people of mixed ancestry who were free in other Christian countries.[16]

If there was to be clarity in marking the enslaved in Virginia, sexual relations further muddled the distinction between black and white. Some blacks had resisted slavery by claiming free white paternity. Elizabeth Key, for example, using as evidence an expired contract made with her late owner, successfully sued for her freedom in 1655, partly because of her white paternity. Thus, to erase "doubts" that free white paternity might introduce, the burgesses in 1662 for the first time stipulated that children were "bond or free only according to the condition of the mother."[17]

This matrilineal law, at first glance, seems an interesting departure, given the patriarchal basis of society, but, on closer inspection, it is the great planters' first move in the direction of asserting their authority over the progeny of enslaved women. The assembly tried to tie up the loose ends concerning bound-labor maternity in 1662. Punishment for impregnating a servant not only carried additional service or compensation for lost labor but also security for the maintenance of the child. The father was liable for the child's support and any expenses that might be incurred by the master, mistress, or parish. Earlier, in 1658, the assembly had legislated that the answerable father, whether indentured or free, was to serve the mother's employer for one year or to pay him fifteen hundred pounds of tobacco and an indemnity to "defray all charge about keeping the child." With this paternal responsibility in effect the authorities now specified that two years be added to the mother's term if she was unable to pay two thousand pounds of tobacco to her master so that he might recoup the "losse and trouble" sustained because of maternity. The assembly also enacted legislation removing servants impregnated by "dissolute masters" and selling them for two-year terms with the proceeds paid to the parish. Their sale was to discourage "loose" women from laying "all their bastards on their masters." On the other hand, since paternity of a child born to an enslaved woman was mooted, she could not name the responsible father and became more vulnerable to sexual exploitation by her master. Since she could not make up additional time because she already served for life, enslaving her child not only compensated the owner but also natu-

16. *SAL*, III, 447–448; *EJCCV*, I, 110; Earnest, *Religious Development of the Negro*, 31–32.

17. *SAL*, II, 170; Billings, "The Law of Servants and Slaves," *VMHB*, XCIX (1991), 57; Warren M. Billings, "The Cases of Fernando and Elizabeth Key: A Note on the Status of Blacks in Seventeenth-Century Virginia," *WMQ*, 3d Ser., XXX (1973), 467–474.

ralized slavery as a condition of birth. Exceptions did exist, of course, as illustrated in the 1672 legacy of Colonel Thomas Gerrad to his namesake: "I leave and give unto my negro boy baptized and named Tho: One thousand pounds of Tobc to be bestowed uppon [him] for his learning and Education." But, unless a master intervened, the status of a child of mixed race was determined by the mother.[18]

Stipulating that a child follow the condition of the mother blurred the racial distinction between enslaved and free. As a result, the 1662 statute also threatened "any Christian" (white) with a heavy fine for interracial fornication, double the amount customarily assessed for this behavior. This penalty and those in subsequent acts were primarily directed against white women engaged in interracial affairs whose progeny would increase the free population. (Targeting whites also presumed that nonwhites were likely enslaved and unable to pay fines or to serve additional time.) The responsibility for a mixed-race child of an enslaved man was clearly problematic, particularly when the woman was an indentured servant. Since enslaved men were incapable of compensating the woman's master, authorities thus felt compelled to curtail the sexual activity of white women. The great planters who dominated the assembly thought that any sexual connection between a black male and a white female was "implicitly most dangerous to the social order . . . [and] threatening to patriarchal authority, property, and the security of labor." Indeed, legislators had been alarmed by several instances in Norfolk and on the Eastern Shore in which black men had successfully courted white women. Free black men might have been choosing white women strategically because a 1643 act taxing black and mixed-ancestry women burdened the family. One-half of the ten black householders on the Eastern Shore married white women, including Richard Johnson, Emmanuel Driggus, Philip Mongan, and Anthony Longo. Since any child born of such a union would, following the law, be either free or indentured according to the mother's status, the prohibition against fornication was meant to preserve the racial character of the free population. The 1662 act sought to control sexual access and guarantee the expansion of the labor force.[19]

18. *SAL*, I, 438–439, II, 114–115, 167–168, 170; Brown, *Good Wives, Nasty Wenches*, 132–135, 195–196; "Washington and His Neighbors . . . : Will of Col. Thomas Gerrard," *WMQ*, 1st Ser., IV (1895–1896), 82.

19. Morgan, *American Slavery, American Freedom*, 336; Douglas Deal, "A Constricted World: Free Blacks on Virginia's Eastern Shore, 1680–1750," in Lois Green Carr, Philip D. Morgan, and Jean B. Russo, eds., *Colonial Chesapeake Society* (Chapel Hill, N.C., 1988), 277; Brown, *Good Wives, Nasty Wenches*, 126–127, 187, 195, 196, 432 n. 19.

To further discourage miscegenation, the General Assembly in 1691 legislated that white women be punished for having a biracial child. A free white woman that had a mixed-race bastard was fined fifteen pounds sterling, due within a month of the birth. Failure to pay this fine could result in bondage for five years. If she was a servant, the churchwardens sold her for five years' additional service after her contracted time had expired, and her child was bound to the churchwardens until the age of thirty. To clear up any confusion that might be caused by the language of the act, the assembly repeated the dictum of the 1662 statute: children follow the condition of their mothers. Furthermore, the 1691 law also prohibited interracial marriage to prevent "abominable mixture and spurious issue." Any white marrying a nonwhite was within three months to be banished from Virginia "forever."[20]

Confusion reigned as Virginians contested the miscegenation statute, but authorities remained steadfast in their resolve to prohibit interracial sexual relations. George Ivie, a white man from a distinguished family, and several others from Norfolk (where the great planters prosecuted four white indentured women for bearing mixed-race bastards from 1681 to 1691) unsuccessfully petitioned in 1699 that the council rescind the 1691 act without result. John Bunch, of mixed ancestry, and Sarah Slayden, a white woman, challenged the statute by petitioning the council in 1705 to order the minister at Blissland Parish to publish their marriage banns. After evaluating their petition, Attorney General Stevens Thomson gave his opinion that Bunch was not a true mulatto but a "Mustee" (that is, the offspring of a mulatto and a white), and therefore the marriage was not restricted by the 1691 act, although it might have been "within the intent." When the General Assembly met in October 1705, it had not yet clarified the status of mustees, but it remained adamantly against interracial marriage and passed a new act that instead of deportation threatened free whites that married nonwhites with six months in prison without bail and a fine of ten pounds Virginia currency. Moreover, an Anglican minister who blessed an interracial marriage could be fined ten thousand pounds of tobacco.[21]

Although lawmakers tried, they could not reconcile slavery consistently with the condition of religious conversion or of mixed-race ancestry. As they grappled with Christianity and interracial sexual relations, they began making distinctions between whites and nonwhites with dogged determi-

20. *SAL,* III, 86–88 (also 453–454).
21. *LJCCV,* I, 262; *EJCCV,* III, 28, 31; *SAL,* III, 453–454.

nation. Indeed, in promoting a society based on race, the great planters had recognized the need to diminish distinctions made between Europeans, English-born or not. This need was compounded by the concomitant one to people the colony. As early as 1660, the House of Burgesses, while encouraging the Dutch and other foreign traders to bring Africans to Virginia, repealed an act (first passed in 1655 and renewed in 1658) that required Irish servants without indentures to serve terms of six or seven years. (The legislators had found that the regulation discouraged immigration and "retarded" the population.) Hoping to attract Europeans even if they were not English or Protestant, the assembly legislated that in 1660 servants from a Christian nation should serve no longer than English servants did. Those who arrived before the passage of the act were to work no more time than stipulated in the act and were to be paid "competent wages" for having "overserved" their masters.[22]

The authorities, attempting to create solidarity among poor whites and the great planters through racial consciousness, prohibited blacks from owning or supervising whites regardless of their status, driving deeper the wedge between the races. In a 1669 case indicative of the emerging racial climate, Hannah Warrick, a white servant runaway, escaped punishment because her overseer was black. One year later, the General Assembly ordered that nonwhites could not buy whites but are "not debarred from buying any of their owne nation." On this point, the authorities were clear: blacks were not to be masters of whites.[23]

Virginia's tax laws further divided the races. Along with all men sixteen years or older, the legislature in 1643 taxed "all negro women" in the first law discriminating by race. English women were exempt, because, according to English custom, they were considered household dependents. Implicit in the tax was the belief that owners of enslaved women, who typically worked in the tobacco fields, could contribute to the colony's welfare. Some masters put white women servants in the field, benefiting doubly from their productive but tax-free labor. The scarcity of white women in the colony, however, encouraged authorities to accord them special treatment by inhibiting their use in the fields. To this end, the assembly in 1662 imposed a tithe on female servants "working in the crop." James Revel, a transported convict serving in Virginia from about 1666 to 1680, lam-

22. *SAL*, I, 411, 471, 538–540; Alden T. Vaughan, "The Origins Debate: Slavery and Racism in Seventeenth-Century Virginia," *VMHB*, XCVII (1989), 340n.

23. *MCGC*, 513; *SAL*, II, 280–281; Beverley, *History and Present State of Virginia*, ed. Wright, 271–274, 281–284; Jordan, *White over Black*, 86–88.

pooned the excess of women servants working in the house while male servants and blacks worked in the fields by highlighting the disparity in numbers: "Besides four transport women in the house, / To wait upon his daughter and his Spouse." The law elevated the status of white servant women by providing a "Sufficient Distinction" between them and black and Indian women, who were now expected to work "out of Doors."[24]

In 1668, the assembly reinforced the 1662 act's racial impact when it affirmed the 1643 statute that free black women, unlike free white women, were to be tithed as laborers, for they "ought not in all respects to be admitted to a full fruition of the exemptions and impunities of the English." Indeed, free black women were accorded the same tithable status as enslaved women, leading to the deterioration of the free black class. Wives of small planters, black and white, often worked in tobacco fields with their husbands, thereby contributing to their families' survival. The law, by penalizing black families, discouraged them from accumulating property and eventually contributed to their economic devastation.[25] Insensitive to the hardship that this tax imposed on free blacks, county authorities demanded payment. In one instance, Francis Stipes received an order from the Lower Norfolk court demanding payment for his wife, "shee being a negro." In another case, Susannah, a free black, petitioned the Charles City County court for an exemption from the levy in 1677 because of her lack of "strength and ability" and was denied. The world of the free blacks, a highly conspicuous and acculturated class, became increasingly constricted and desperate by the 1680s. The tithing of free black women remained a problem until 1705, when the assembly, finding free blacks a demoralized group, lifted the imposition for the moment. In 1723, the tax was revived, specifying the wives of nonwhite householders.[26]

24. *SAL*, II, 170; Beverley, *History and Present State of Virginia*, ed. Wright, 271–272; James Revel, "The Poor Unhappy Transported Felon's Sorrowful Account of His Fourteen Years Transportation at Virginia in America," in Billings, ed., *Old Dominion*, 139; Brown, *Good Wives, Nasty Wenches*, 86–88.

25. *SAL*, II, 267; Lois Green Carr and Lorena S. Walsh, "The Planter's Wife: The Experience of White Women in Seventeenth-Century Maryland," *WMQ*, 3d Ser., XXXIV (1977), 542–571; Brown, *Good Wives, Nasty Wenches*, 125–128.

26. *SAL*, III, 258; Billings, ed., *Old Dominion*, 157–158. The assembly once again tithed free women of color in 1723 after receiving complaints from Northampton County of "the great Numbers of free Negros of which the women pay no Taxes" (*JHB, 1712–1714, 1715, 1718, 1720–1722, 1723–1726*, 369). See also Philip J. Schwarz, "Emancipators, Protectors, and Anomalies: Free Black Slaveowners in Virginia," *VMHB*, XCV (1987), 321; Brown, *Good Wives, Nasty Wenches*, 123. Several free blacks, members of the charter generation,

Regulating manumission was another way authorities were able to undermine free black society. In 1691, the assembly acted to end the mean-spirited and cruel practice of manumitting the enslaved that, "being grown old," were put off plantations to fend for themselves. This decision was not a humanitarian gesture, however, but an effort to halt superannuated blacks from becoming wards of the parish. Limiting the local burden was only part of the government's larger project to restrict the manumission of the enslaved and thus impede the accretion of free blacks. The General Assembly also ruled in 1691 that a manumitted black must be transported out of the colony within six months or the emancipator would be fined ten pounds sterling, which was to be paid to the churchwardens, who could then use the money for the transportation. Thereafter, only a special bill would allow manumission without transportation from the colony, such as the one in 1710 for the enslaved Will, who betrayed an incipient insurrection of that year. A loophole in the 1691 act on manumission existed in the preamble, however, which stated that the emancipated should not become either a charge or a nuisance to the community. In 1713, the Council of State, responding to a directive from the governor, reviewed a report from the justices of Norfolk County in which it was related that the late John Fulcher, a planter in Norfolk, had used this qualification to free, through his will, sixteen blacks and had given them a "considerable Tract of Land in fee simple." The council asked the assembly to pass a law against such manumissions, fearing the potential danger over time of the freed slaves' "increase and correspondence with other Slaves." Codifying the principle set forth in the precedent of manumitting Will, the great planters in 1723 disallowed manumission of the enslaved "under any pretense whatsoever, except for some meritorious services, to be adjudged and allowed by the governor and council."[27]

The slave code of 1705 consolidated Virginia's racial system by denying blacks the civil rights accorded to whites. Free blacks, for example, were

---

demonstrated their uneasiness by fleeing from Northampton County to Somerset County, Maryland, in 1683. See Deal, "A Constricted World," in Carr, Morgan, and Russo, eds., *Colonial Chesapeake Society,* 275; Michael L. Nicholls, "Passing through This Troublesome World: Free Blacks in the Early Southside," *VMHB,* XCII (1984), 51–53; James H. Brewer, "Negro Property Owners in Seventeeth-Century Virginia," *WMQ,* 3d Ser., XII (1955), 575–580; Breen and Innes, *"Myne Owne Gound,"* 107–109.

27. *SAL,* III, 87–88, 537–538, IV, 132; *EJCCV,* III, 332; *JHB, 1702/3–1705, 1705–1706, 1710–1712,* 270; Adele Hast, "The Legal Status of the Negro in Virginia, 1705–1765," *Jour. Negro Hist.,* LIV (1969), 221.

denied due process; those accused of felonies continued to be tried and punished in the county along with the enslaved, unlike white felons, who were sent to the capital, Williamsburg. At the same time, the 1705 slave code forbade nonwhite people from holding any ecclesiastical, civil, or military office, regardless of their status, thus denying them any substantial role in running the colony. The statute implied that they were incapable of authority and needed the direction of whites.[28]

Although poor whites were often denied access to these same positions of authority for reasons of class, the prohibition for them was not permanent, not tied to race. Indeed, to make Virginia more attractive to European immigrants, legislation enhanced the status of white servants at this time. Continuing the effort to create a common identity among European immigrants, the General Assembly in 1705 further defined the rights of "christian white servants"; they were to receive from their masters "competent" provisions and lodging, and, more important, they were not to receive "immoderate" corporeal punishment. Whipping a "naked" white servant could be punishable by a fine of forty shillings sterling paid by the master to the abused servant. Moreover, to "further christian care and usage of all christian servants," the assembly repeated the 1670 stipulation that nonwhites, "although christians," could not purchase anyone "except of their own complexion."[29]

To be sure, according to authorities, non-Christian, non-English-speaking, non-European enslaved workers in large numbers required regulation, supervision, and even repression by white workers, who were becoming even scarcer. Consequently, the assembly dropped the fifteen-shilling impost on servants "not born in England or Wales" while retaining one on enslaved workers. By exempting white servants from import duties, the act was an affirmative attempt to attract them to the colony to counterbalance the large number of imported blacks. Because their enhanced status had everything to do with their policing power, freed white male servants, by order of the Council of State in 1706, were issued a gun at the end of their indenture.[30]

The 1705 code tied up loose ends concerning property rights in en-

---

28. *SAL,* III, 447–462. White convicted felons had the same exclusionary status as blacks; see Morgan, *American Slavery, American Freedom,* 328.

29. *SAL,* III, 448–450.

30. Ibid., 193, 233, 235, 346, IV, 126; Waverly K. Winfree, comp., *The Laws of Virginia: Being a Supplement to Hening's The Statutes at Large, 1700–1750* (Richmond, Va., 1971), 22–23, 257–259; Schwarz, *Twice Condemned,* 85–88.

slaved laborers. Although the dictum that a child follow the condition of the mother had appeared in the statute books in 1662, 1691, and 1696, the code of 1705 affirmed it. The effect of the law was to maintain the integrity of the great planters' estates. The assembly declared the enslaved were property, with the line of descent to heirs and widows "according to the manner and custom of land inheritance, held in fee simple." Moreover, wrote William Gooch, reflecting upon this act twenty-two years later, "inasmuch as Lands without Slaves are of little value," the assembly bound the enslaved adscript to their owners' land (that is, the enslaved's service was transferable with the land from one owner to another). If a slaveowner died intestate, the enslaved were to be divided equally among his children after their inventory and appraisal, excepting the widow's dower, which was taken first. Such a stipulation was necessary to preserve intestate properties intact, curbing the "ill practices" of executors who kept the enslaved and gave to the heirs their appraised value. This "former practice of Executors and administrators appraising and selling the slaves of Testators," the council opined, had been "fatal to severall familys."[31]

The great planters, using laws of entail and personalty, defined the in-

31. *SAL*, II, 288, III, 333–335; William Gooch to BT, June 8, 1728, CO 5/1321, 44–45, VCRP; *JHB, 1702/3–1705, 1705–1706, 1710–1712*, 201, 206, 208, 210, 212, 213, *1712–1726*, 15–16, *1727–1740*, 28, 36, 39, 40, 45, 130; *LJCCV*, I, 464, 465, 541–543; *EJCCV*, III, 111. A widow risked forfeiture of her dower of enslaved blacks if she sent them from Virginia. If she remarried and she or her husband were to send them from Virginia, they would both forfeit rights to them. Several exemptions maintained blacks as chattel. Because enslaved laborers belonging to merchants or factors could not be bound to land, they remained personal property. To prevent ship captains from carrying an enslaved black from the state, authorities assessed a forfeiture penalty of fifty pounds for every servant, one hundred pounds for every enslaved worker, and liability for every debtor. Sales of the enslaved were not recorded as land transactions but continued as personal property. The same was true of enslaved blacks sold to satisfy debts. Enslaved blacks were not to be considered as escheat property, nor given in apportioning franchise, nor recovered in suits as with real estate; in each of these instances, they were regarded as chattel (*SAL*, IV, 222; see also "An Act Declaring Slaves to Be Personal Estate and for Other Purposes Therein Mentioned," CO 5/1330, 177, typescript, CWF).

Burgesses from York and Warwick Counties believed in 1711 that treating enslaved laborers as real estate was "very prejuditiall" (*JHB, 1702/3–1705, 1705–1706, 1710–1712*, 331). Their attempt to repeal the act dealt with issues of ownership in the delivery of the enslaved as freight-on-board, intestate death, and the transfer of property to widows. The council vetoed their bill. The burgesses unsuccessfully tried to repeal the act again in 1720 and 1727 but ultimately acquiesced in 1732, when they passed a resolution against the repeal of the enslaved as real estate (*JHB, 1727–1734, 1736–1740*, 28, 36, 39, 40, 45, 130; *LJCCV*, I, 541–543).

tegral unit of their estates to be lands with enslaved laborers. The great planters passed the 1705 act because they could envision the productivity of their land—and thus ensure the survival of their estates—only in relation to an enslaved laboring class. They invented this community of enslaved laborers whose condition could be reproduced in perpetuity, regardless of free paternity or religious affiliation. The resistance of African-descended and mixed-race people to enslavement and discrimination, however, would continue. If the great planters were to maintain their slave society, they would have to construct a racial system of justice and enforce sanctions against transgressors.

Dangerous Consequences

Servants and the enslaved suffered similar material conditions and, as mentioned earlier, often acted in concert to escape. To discourage this continuing practice and to further the campaign to make distinctions between blacks and whites, protect enslaved property, and conscript whites into policing blacks, the great planters once again turned to the courts and the legislature. In 1660, the General Assembly moved against interracial alliances to escape bondage by targeting white servants. To compensate owners for lost time, white servants who ran away with blacks were required to serve not only for their time absent but also for the time of their black accomplices. The runaway problem became so pervasive that the General Assembly amended the legislation in 1661. Servants who ran away with blacks "incapable of makeing satisfaction by the addition of time" must serve for the enslaved's time in proportion to the number of fugitives and pay for those who escaped or died with four years' service or five hundred pounds of tobacco.[32]

The apprehension and correction of runaway indentured and enslaved laborers prompted state intervention and discriminatory public punishment. As "the diverse good lawes . . . made to prevent runaway servants" have "hitherto in greate parte proved ineffectuall," legislators in 1669 offered a reward of one thousand pounds of tobacco to anyone who apprehended a fugitive servant. Once captured, the fugitives would be conveyed from county constable to county constable until reaching their home county. They were required to serve their masters for the time absent and were then sold in order to reimburse the counties for the cost of re-

32. *SAL,* II, 26.

turning them to their masters. The persistence of the problem caused authorities one year later to deal more harshly with servants "that hath runaway twice." Using English vagrancy laws as precedents, punishments became more severe for recidivists. Replacing the 1642 punishment of branding second-time offenders on "the cheek with the letter R," the assembly ordered masters to crop the hair of the runaways so that they "may be the more easily detected." If a servant was caught escaping again, each constable en route toward his master's home was enjoined to "whip [him] severely" and then convey him to the next constable, "who is to give him the like correction." Because the enslaved could not be saddled with additional time and their flight threatened insurrection, the great planters considered enslaved runaways more dangerous and dealt with them more severely. Unlike the servant, the enslaved fugitive was punished with specified whippings on the first offense. As a way of "preventing . . . Insurrections," the assembly in 1680 charged the constable in the county where an enslaved person was apprehended without a pass from his owner to apply "twenty lashes on his bare back well layd on" before sending him to the next county for like treatment, continuing until he reached his master's plantation. Outraged by the havoc caused by "negroes, mulattoes, or other slaves" who "lie hid and lurk in obscure places," the assembly in 1691 empowered "lawfull authority" to kill any who resisted recapture. In a draconian measure, the assembly legislated in 1705 that an owner could apply to the county court to have a habitual fugitive dismembered. Court-ordered dismemberment, which often meant cutting off a foot but could even result in castration, was the most heinous practice for disciplining runaways, but the General Assembly reasoned in 1705 that it would not only reclaim the fugitive but also would have the effect of "terrifying others from the like practices."[33]

33. *SAL*, I, 254–255, II, 273, 278, 481, III, 86, 461; Sally E. Hadden, *Slave Patrols: Law and Violence in Virginia and the Carolinas* (Cambridge, Mass., 2001), 26–29; Philip J. Schwarz, *Slave Laws in Virginia* (Athens, Ga., 1996), 22. In rescinding this punishment (dismemberment) in 1769, even the assembly called it "disproportioned to the offence, and contrary to the principles of humanity" (*SAL*, VIII, 358). See Billings, "The Law of Servants and Slaves," *VMHB*, XCIX (1991), 51; Allan Kulikoff, "The Origins of Afro-American Society in Tidewater Maryland and Virginia, 1700 to 1790," *WMQ*, 3d Ser., XXXV (1978), 238; Schwarz, *Twice Condemned*, 22, 80–81; Darrett B. Rutman and Anita H. Rutman, *A Place in Time: Middlesex County, Virginia, 1650–1750* (New York, 1984), 176–177. Cf. J. H. Plumb, "How Freedom Took Root in Slavery," review of *American Slavery, American Freedom*, by Edmund S. Morgan, *New York Review of Books*, Nov. 27,

Such terror did not always have its intended effect. Robert "King" Carter habitually butchered recidivists. He boasted: "I have cured many a negro of running away by this means," including Bambara Harry and Dinah, whom he mutilated in 1710. Carter obtained an order in 1725 to dismember outliers Will and Bailey, "hid and Lurking in Swamps and Woods and other obscure places killing hogs and committing other injuries to his Matys subjects." And, in 1727, he wrote: "Ballazore is an incorrigeable rogue nothing less than dismembring will reclaim him." Nevertheless, Carter, in the same year, refused to have Madagascar Jack, who had suffered dismemberment at his order, at a new slave quarter. Jack was still a problem and would cause trouble, even though he had lost his toes five years before.[34]

Poor blacks and whites, suffering from chronic hunger, often stole meat, but their punishments and their owners' liability differed. As with the fugitive issue, the legislators divvied up punishment and liability along racial lines. The penalties for hog stealing reveal the calculus of the 1705 racial code. The authorities held owners culpable for their bound laborers' theft, charging a fine of 400 pounds of tobacco for a transgressing servant. The servant had to reimburse the master with an additional month's service in which he would produce 150 pounds of tobacco. The owner of an enslaved black caught stealing a hog paid half, 200 pounds of tobacco. Whites caught stealing a hog, shoat, or pig — a misdemeanor — for the first offense had the option of receiving twenty-five lashes or paying a fine of ten pounds current Virginia money. Nonwhites did not have the choice of paying a fine and received thirty-nine lashes "well laid on, at the common whipping-post of the county." Repeat offenders, black or white, suffered the same fate: they were to stand for two hours with their ears nailed to the pillory and then have their ears cut loose from the nails. The third offense was a felony, and the penalty was death. Christopher Robinson's enslaved man Charles served as an example of the law's practice. The jurists in Middlesex County had him whipped in 1711 for hog stealing. A year later,

1975, 3–4; Willie Lee Rose, ed., *A Documentary History of Slavery in North America* (New York, 1976), 4; Billings, ed., *Old Dominion*, 161–163.

34. Robert Carter to Robert Jones, Oct. 10, 1727, M-113, CWF; "Order to Cut Off Toes of Madagascar Jack," Sept. 12, 1722, "Order to Dismember Negroes," July 4, 1725, Lancaster County Order Book, 1721–1729, 59–60, 83, 183, VSL; Schwarz, *Twice Condemned*, 80–81. See Rutman and Rutman, *A Place in Time*, 176–177, for dismemberments and castrations in Middlesex County, Virginia.

as a repeat offender, he was pilloried and had his ears cut off; five years later, he was hanged as a habitual felon.[35]

The authorities made no distinction when punishing free whites trading with servants and the enslaved in the black market. William Byrd II believed that these whites were chiefly exiled convicts from Old and New England. "Some of these Banditti Anchor Near my estate," he wrote, "for the advantage of trafficking with my slaves, from whom they are sure to have a good Penny-worths." Governor Francis Nicholson threatened to punish severely those indulging in the "disolute Practices" to "harbour[,] Entertaine[,] truck[,] trade[,] or deale" with servants and the enslaved. The assembly made good this threat with the 1705 statute. They ordered anyone engaged in the trade of "coin or commodity" with a servant or an enslaved black to be jailed until able to post a bond of ten pounds for the first offense or, for the second, to pay a penalty of four times the value of the contraband.[36]

The legislature also tightened the laws concerning assemblies of blacks and developed new ones to deal with insurrectionists, outlying enslaved blacks, and other criminals. With the influx of Africans during the 1680s, authorities became apprehensive of black rebels. Gatherings of blacks for cultural rituals terrified them. Indeed, outliers or maroons preying on plantations and insurrectionists organizing to seize control of the colony were their worst nightmare. When blacks rebelled, their punishment assumed dramatic exposure with branding, hanging, and dismembering. Public trial and punishment were designed to cow the most recalcitrant enslaved black. The "majesty" of the law and its instruments of control— the court, the whipping post, and the gallows—combined to prop up the authority of the slaveowners.[37]

After discovering an intended insurrection in the Northern Neck in

35. *SAL,* III, 276–277; Rutman and Rutman, *A Place in Time,* 177; Paul C. Palmer, "Servant into Slave: The Evolution of the Legal Status of the Negro Laborer in Colonial Virginia," *South Atlantic Quarterly,* LXV (1966), 355–370; Hast, "The Legal Status of the Negro in Virginia," *Jour. Negro Hist.,* LIV (1969), 225–227. The General Assemby had also attempted to stem the "unseasonable" killing of deer (Feb. 1 to July 31) in 1699 by fining the offender five hundred pounds of tobacco for each deer killed. Servants and enslaved laborers incapable of paying such a sum received the same penalty: thirty lashes by order of the justice of the peace. Their masters were responsible for fines (*SAL,* III, 180).

36. *EJCCV,* I, 148, 149, II, 182; William Byrd II to [Benjamin] Lynde, Feb. 20, 1735/6, William Byrd II Letter Book, VHS; *SAL,* III, 451; Schwarz, *Twice Condemned,* 75.

37. Schwarz, *Twice Condemned,* 53; Gwenda Morgan, *The Hegemony of the Law: Richmond County, Virginia, 1692–1776* (New York, 1989), 111–112.

1680 designed to spread throughout the colony, the assembly passed "An Act for Preventing Negroes Insurrections." It focused on the congregation of blacks for feasts and burials, which could be used as a cover for insurrection. Blacks were forbidden to arm themselves "with any club, staffe, [or] gunn" or leave the plantation without a pass from their masters or overseers. Blacks raising their hand in opposition to any white could receive thirty lashes, inflicted by a court-appointed person, and whites could lawfully kill blacks "lying out and resisting."[38]

Outlying enslaved laborers were a particular problem for magistrates. Many killed hogs and robbed houses beyond the ability of their individual owners to control. Governor Nicholson authorized that, in the event of marauding blacks, sheriffs in several counties be given notice at once, and he empowered them without further warrant to deputize others as they saw fit to deal with the offenders. He also gave the sheriffs authority to hold transgressors in irons until they were charged and to whip them before turning them over to their owners or to the secretary of state. The assembly then passed an act in 1691 for "suppressing outlying Slaves" who "lie hid and lurk in obscure places killing hoggs and committing other injuries to the inhabitants of this dominion." This act, like Nicholson's executive order, empowered the sheriff to issue warrants for the apprehension of these fugitives and to raise a posse to pursue them.[39]

To ensure slaveholders against the loss of their investments, the General Assembly stipulated that, if a posse killed outlying enslaved blacks, their owners would be compensated four thousand pounds of tobacco for each by the government. The outlawing of Billy offers a case in point. Billy had terrorized whites for several years in James City, New Kent, and York Counties. In 1701, the assembly issued a bill of attainder, offering a reward of one thousand pounds of tobacco for either his capture or his death; if Billy died at the hands of the bounty hunter, his owner would be compensated four thousand pounds.[40]

Distinctions between nonwhites and whites were most pronounced in

38. *SAL,* II, 481, 482.

39. *EJCCV,* I, 317, 525; *SAL,* III, 86.

40. *SAL,* III, 210–211; see also *EJCCV,* I, 459. Cf. Marvin L. Michael Kay and Lorin Lee Cary, "'The Planters Suffer Little or Nothing': North Carolina Compensations for Executed Slaves, 1748–1772," *Science and Society,* XL (1976), 288–306; Kay and Cary, *Slavery in North Carolina, 1748–1775* (Chapel Hill, N.C., 1995), 77–90. On the other hand, Robert Shields sought a pardon for his enslaved black Samson, convicted of stealing fifty shillings; see "Court of Oyer and Terminer at York County," Aug. 9, 1744, Williamsburg, BR 256, Miscellaneous File, HL.

the execution of the criminal code. To deter blacks from committing capital crimes, the assembly passed an act in 1692 for the "speedy prosecution of negroes and other slaves." Inspired by the General Assembly's convening of a special court to prosecute offenders after the insurrectionary activity of 1687, the county courts picked a commission to try blacks in the county of offense, a precursor to the oyer and terminer courts. White felons accused of the same crimes, on the other hand, went to the capital, James City, and, later, Williamsburg, for trial. The significance of trying blacks and punishing them at the scene of the crime is readily apparent; the gallows served as symbolic reminders of white power and of the penalty for those who challenged it. The authorities reasoned in April 1692 that the speedy prosecution and punishment of black felons were "absolutely necessarie." Not only did this deter others from like crimes, but it was an incentive for them to "vigorously proceed in their labours."[41]

In 1705, the authorities closed the loopholes in the law regarding the disposition of felonious enslaved blacks. Slaveholders were reluctant to uncover the crimes of their laborers, for the 1662 law did not allow compensation to the owner of a condemned black. The assembly rectified this omission in the 1705 law; after the execution, a valuation was made, and the owner was compensated accordingly. After reviewing this statute, Governor William Gooch wrote that it served as an "encouragement to People to discover the Villainies of their slaves." The assembly affirmed the necessity of trying blacks accused of capital crimes in county courts because it afforded quick justice and avoided the "extraordinary charge" of taking them to the General Court. Moreover, the assembly allowed two "credible" white witnesses or one white with "pregnant circumstances" as sufficient to convict a nonwhite. Masters were now allowed to defend their enslaved before the commission but were restricted "only . . . to matters of fact" and could not challenge judicial procedure. This stipulation was qualified, however, shortly afterward in November 1705. Philip Lightfoot of James City County petitioned for a writ of supersedeas to stop the order to give his enslaved James thirty-one lashes, which was granted. He referred to the 1680 "Act for Preventing Negroes Insurrections," most likely the clause that required the testimony by the aggrieved "christian" before a magistrate when an enslaved person was accused of injuring him. For the most part, commissioners still exercised discretion and made fine distinc-

41. *SAL,* III, 102–103; Schwarz, *Twice Condemned,* 15, 81–82; Olwell, *Masters, Slaves, and Subjects,* 73–74.

tions between enslaved individuals, as the Westmoreland County court of oyer and terminer shows. Three enslaved blacks appearing "not . . . so notoriously Criminal" were pardoned, whereas two principals were sentenced to death, for they did not appear as "fitt objects of mercy."[42]

With public punishment sheltered behind compensation, officials visited upon enslaved blacks brutal treatment rarely if ever experienced by whites. Commissioners tortured blacks to extract confessions and whipped, exiled, dismembered, and hanged them. It was not uncommon for an enslaved black convicted of theft to be paraded through the county to the gallows and there hanged. Indeed, four of five blacks convicted of "major" theft by a commission of oyer and terminer between 1706 and 1739 were hanged. If a black assaulted a white, the black's body might be exposed on a common pathway after hanging. In extreme cases, officials beheaded, quartered, or burned them, punishments not bestowed on whites in the eighteenth century. Black women suffered public burning. One woman was burned in 1737 for the "petit treason" of murdering her mistress; the same fate befell another in 1746 for poisoning her master. Authorities punished black men with quartering. Salvadore and Scipio were hanged and quartered for "treason" in 1710. James, who inexplicably died in prison, was posthumously ordered quartered in 1730, allegedly for murdering his owner's daughter. Each quarter and his head were displayed in different sections of Richmond County.[43]

Armed with a formidable array of laws and punishments, white society in 1705 was prepared to preserve racial slavery to the death. Restricted in their movement and assembly and excluded from the possession of arms, enslaved blacks were legally confined to their quarters and fields of labor. Transgressors were viciously dealt with at the local level to serve as a warning to others. Whites, on the other hand, were fully empowered to patrol slave quarters and to break up assemblies. If a white killed a black in the course of a reprimand, the white was protected; authorities could not risk blacks' seeing whites divided on the issue of the death of an enslaved person.[44]

42. *SAL,* II, 481, III, 269–270; Gooch to BT, July 23, 1730, CO 5/1322, 53–67, VCRP; *EJCCV,* III, 58, 128; Schwarz, *Twice Condemned,* 20.

43. Winthrop D. Jordan, review of *A Rumor of Revolt: The "Great Negro Plot" in Colonial New York,* by Thomas J. Davis, *WMQ,* 3d Ser., XLIII (1986), 315–316; Schwarz, *Twice Condemned,* 17–18, 53–54, 70–71, 74–75, 81, 316; Morgan, *Hegemony of the Law,* 111–113; Rutman and Rutman, *A Place in Time,* 176–177.

44. Schwarz has likened group escape plots to "forcible breakouts from prisoner-of-

Indeed, the threat of murder lies at the base of the relationship between master and enslaved. The 1669 act concerning the "casuall killing of slaves" best illustrates this truth. Since the punishment for a "refractory" servant included extended terms of service not applicable to the enslaved, suppression of blacks' "obstinacy" required "violent meanes." The 1669 law gave the owner or overseer the power to kill an incorrigible enslaved black with impunity. To free the master or his hired ruffian from legal prosecution, the assembly ordered that this type of homicide should not be considered murder, "since it cannot be presumed that prepensed malice (which alone makes murther felony) should induce any man to destroy his owne estate."[45]

The unequivocal determination of slaveholders to fix their brand of slavery in place—a system based on brute force—was vividly demonstrated by the flogging death of Rose and her mistress's eventual trial. On January 13, 1714, Andrew Woodley, justice of the peace and coroner of Isle of Wight County, told John Clayton, a lawyer, that Frances Wilson "was suspected to be Guilty of whipping one of her Husbands Slaves to death." Woodley the previous fall had convened a coroner's jury to consider the evidence and returned the findings to the secretary's office. The coroner's jury exhumed Rose's body, which had been "suddenly and secretly Buried," and questioned how a "hail Negro gave up the Ghost" under a "very Moderate Correction." The inquest of November 26, 1713, concluded that "by hard usage she is come to her death, we finding no mortall wounds but only stripes," and the jury returned a verdict of murder. Half of the fourteen jurors could give only their mark to the judgment, indicating a substantial presence of small farmers. They perhaps sympathized with a laborer subjected to the power of a wealthy slaveowner. Despite the verdict, both the county and secretary's office failed to issue a warrant for Wilson's arrest. Given the divisions manifested among the county's white inhabitants, Governor Alexander Spotswood saw an opening to corral the great planters as he did following the 1711 proposed legislation allowing slaveholders to hunt on their neighbors' land. Spotswood asserted that

---

war camps or large prisons"; see *Twice Condemned*, 85. Cf. Peter H. Wood, "Slave Labor Camps in Early America: Overcoming Denial and Discovering the Gulag," in Carla Gardina Pestana and Sharon V. Salinger, eds., *Inequality in Early America* (Hanover, N.H., 1999), 230–234.

45. *SAL*, II, 270.

the great planters should not be above the law, using as his foundation the crown's instruction to him that he get an act passed that the "willful Killing of Indians and Negroes may be punish'd with Death." Spotswood appointed Clayton attorney general, who, recalling Woodley's conversation, obtained a copy of the inquest. He found it defective, for it not only failed to spell out the details of the case but also did not follow the legal procedure for a felony case. Clayton sought and got Spotswood's assent to prosecute after giving his opinion "that no Subject has power over the Life of his Slave."[46]

When the grand jury was called into session in March 1714, Mary Lupo, a white neighbor, gave evidence that Frances Wilson gave Rose "40 mortal strokes on the back part of her body"; Lupo "plainly accused" Wilson of murder. The grand jurors differed sharply over their disposition. John Custis IV and some others had opposed the charge to the grand jury, which stated "that in this Dominion no Master has such a Sovereign Power over his Slaves as not to be liable to be called to an Account whenever he kills him that at the same time, the Slave is the Master's property, he is likewise the King's Subject, and that the King may lawfully bring to Tryal all Persons here, without exception, who shall be suspected to have destroyed the Life of his Subject." It was not worth pressing. They urged on behalf of Wilson that she should not be "molested" for killing her enslaved black, for the law of Virginia precluded a charge of murder. The master's self-interest in the preservation of his property (1669) or an enslaved black's resistance during correction (1705) removed premeditation—that is, the charge of felony murder—and they moved that her counsel speak to that point. But Spotswood's supporters drew up a "very fine" petition to the General Court, for which he "treated and caressed" his backers. At the same time, he labeled Custis and the other jurors malcontents and marked them for their opposition.[47]

46. Gov. Alexander Spotswood to BT, Feb. 7, 1716, in R. A. Brock, ed., *The Official Letters of Alexander Spotswood, Lieutenant-Governor of the Colony of Virginia, 1710–1722*, 2 vols. (Richmond, Va., 1882–1885), II, 202–203; John Clayton to BT, Dec. 20, 1716, CO 5/1318, 95–96, VCRP.

47. Clayton to BT, Dec. 20, 1716, CO 5/1318, 95–96, VCRP; John Custis to Byrd, Mar. 30, 1717, in Marion Tinling, ed., *The Correspondence of the Three William Byrds of Westover, Virginia, 1684–1776*, 2 vols. (Charlottesville, Va., 1977), I, 297; Brock, ed., *Official Letters of Spotswood*, II, 203; Gwenda Morgan, "Law and Social Change in Colonial Virginia: The Role of the Grand Jury in Richmond County, 1692–1776," *VMHB*, XCV (1987), 453–480.

The majority of the grand jurors having judged that Wilson ought to be tried on the indictment, the colonial office succeeded in bringing her in. Although the General Court "gave judgement that she ought not be tried," the trial proceeded. Clayton finally got Wilson into General Court in October 1714, where she pleaded not guilty. William Byrd II presided over the case and from the bench opposed the indictment. In the end, the jury ruled that Frances Wilson was not guilty, and the court discharged her. That no other white person had been "prosecuted for the death of a Slave by Correction" since Spotswood's arrival in 1710, Clayton wrote, "is the plain and whole truth of that matter."[48]

The outcome of the trial for Rose's murder demonstrates that she was totally subject to her owner's wrath, despite the crown's opposition to the exemption of slaveowners from responsibility for deaths of the enslaved. Even though the governing class was divided, in part because of co-optation by the governor's office, they ultimately supported the policing of the enslaved to the point of murder. The racial solidarity that was integral to the maintenance of the slave society was beginning to show fault lines, however. In 1723, the great planters, responding to an attempted insurrection, revisited the issue with "An Act Directing the Trial of Slaves, Committing Capital Crimes." In instances "touching the death of slaves under correction, or lawful punishment," the owner shall be blameless, unless one credible witness under oath in county court gives evidence that the enslaved was "killed wilfully, maliciously, or designedly." Although this act now specified the terms by which a master could be charged with the murder of an enslaved black, if the trial resulted in the lesser conviction of manslaughter the defendant got off with no punishment. The new act also departed from previous legislation by no longer exempting from liability agents of the slaveholders, such as patrollers who manhandled fugitives, overseers who whipped recalcitrant laborers, and surgeons who amputated recidivists. These killers were now liable both for civil damages to the slaveholders and for criminal charges of murder.[49]

The death sentence of Andrew Bourne (Bryn), an overseer, for the murder of an enslaved black suggests the dangerous fissures within Virginia's white society. The case of Frances Wilson juxtaposed to this case shows

48. Great Britain, PRO, *Calendar of State Papers,* Colonial Series, *America and West Indies,* ed. W. Noel Sainsbury et al. (London, 1860-), XXIX, 248–249; Clayton to BT, Dec. 20, 1716, CO 5/1318, 95–98, VCRP.

49. *SAL,* IV, 132–133.

that the law would grant a mistress, but not an overseer, the right to kill a recalcitrant enslaved laborer. The great planters feared that Bourne's execution would alienate lower-class whites, who were essential in policing the enslaved and ensuring the great planters' security. As a result, after Bourne was convicted of murder by a commission of oyer and terminer, the judge who presided over the case and then the Council of State appealed the conviction. Both argued that the judgment had been more in response to the property rights of the owner than the death of the enslaved, implicitly denying any recognition of the black man's humanity. The overseer, it was claimed, had corrected him for running away and had not intended to kill him. Moreover, if overseers did not have the shield of the law to protect them, they would be demoralized, and blacks would be encouraged to challenge their overseers' punishments. "The taking away the life of this man will, in all probability stir up the Negro's to a contempt of their Masters and Overseers," wrote the council, "which may be attended with dangerous consequences to this Colony, where the Negroes are so numerous." Such class divisions within white society would open the way to rebellion and, worst of all, might inspire dangerous alliances of the enslaved and lower-class whites.[50]

* * *

GREAT PLANTERS had sought to secure their property in enslaved blacks by impressing a racial system of justice into the statute books. The evolution of the slave code reveals the planters' endeavors to consolidate lower-class white interests with theirs, to subjugate all blacks, to separate blacks and whites, and to parry royal governors' control over them. Yet, the case

50. *EJCCV*, IV, 206; "Virginia Council Journals," *VMHB*, XXXIV (1926), 209; Gooch to the secretary of state, June 29, 1729, CO 5/1337, 132–133, VCRP. Only two years before, Gooch had received instructions from the Board of Trade that anyone who murdered an enslaved laborer might be put to death. Nevertheless, in requesting a pardon from the Colonial Office, Gooch echoed the sentiments of the councillors: "The executing of [Bourne] for this offense may make the slaves very insolent and give them an occasion to condemn their Masters and Overseers; which may be of dangerous Consequence in a Country where the Negroes are so numerous and make the most valuable part of People's Estates" ("Commission to Orkney," 1727, CO 5/1365, VCRP). Nevertheless, the General Court did not hesitate in 1739 to sentence another overseer and his accomplice to death for the murder of an enslaved man of Charles Braxton's in Essex County. Charles Quin and David White were hanged in Williamsburg for "Whipping him to Death, in a most cruel and Barbarous Manner" (*Virginia Gazette*, Nov. 16–23, 1739).

of Rose in 1714 and of Bourne in 1729 demonstrate that the great planters' authority was vulnerable to challenge from above and below. They based the laws of Virginia on white racial supremacy, but to uphold them, as the ever more stringent terms of those laws indicate, they created a system of violence, resistance, and oppression.

CHAPTER 5

Revolt and Response, 1676–1740

A history of early Virginia must give slave rebellion a central place for illuminating both the black struggle for freedom and white determination to maintain slavery despite its costs. Indeed, events from 1676 to 1740 are a tapestry of black resistance and white response. Slave traders and planters knew insurrection was endemic to the system and vigilantly guarded against it.

Yet, more often than not, historians of Virginia have regarded black insurgency during the colonial period as inconsequential. When they note rebellious events at all, they describe them as episodic, unworthy of serious response from contemporary and later authorities. A reexamination of the behavior of both blacks and whites during the late seventeenth and early eighteenth century offers persuasive evidence that blacks were not only conscious of their racial and class degradation but collectively attempted to change their condition.[1]

1. David Geggus, "The Enigma of Jamaica in the 1790s: New Light on the Causes of Slave Rebellions," *WMQ*, 3d Ser., XLIV (1987), 292; Gerald W. Mullin, *Flight and Rebellion: Slave Resistance in Eighteenth-Century Virginia* (New York, 1972), 59; Edmund S. Morgan, *American Slavery, American Freedom: The Ordeal of Colonial Virginia* (New York, 1975), 309; Rhys Isaac, *The Transformation of Virginia, 1740–1790* (Chapel Hill, N.C., 1982), 109–110; Darrett B. Rutman and Anita H. Rutman, *A Place in Time: Middlesex County, Virginia, 1650–1750* (New York, 1984), 174–177; Philip D. Morgan, *Slave Counterpoint: Black Culture in the Eighteenth-Century Chesapeake and Lowcountry* (Chapel Hill, N.C., 1998), xxii; Alan Kulikoff, *Tobacco and Slaves: The Development of Southern Cultures in the Chesapeake, 1680–1800* (Chapel Hill, N.C., 1986), 329; Kathleen M. Brown, *Good Wives, Nasty Wenches, and Anxious Patriarchs: Gender, Race, and Power in Colonial Virginia* (Chapel Hill, N.C., 1996), 216–218. Philip J. Schwarz, on the other hand, does give collective rebellion greater weight in *Twice Condemned: Slaves and the Criminal Laws of Virginia, 1705–1865* (Baton Rouge, La., 1988), 84–89.

Resolved to Regain Their Liberty

Although we can never completely document the extent of black resistance on the outward voyage, the testimonials of slave traders Thomas Phillips, Willem Bosman, Jean Barbot, and William Snelgrave give witness that Africans habitually conspired and rebelled aboard slave ships. These men were merchants, veterans of the slave trade, who memorialized the trials and tribulations of that traffic. Phillips wrote specifically in response to an inquiry from the Board of Trade. Barbot, Bosman, and Snelgrave wrote for other merchants and the European public. With an eye on mercantile policy, their purpose was to promote the access of independent merchants. None of the four had any reason to exaggerate shipboard insurrection. Rather, it was more likely, given their interest in encouraging the slave trade, that they would underestimate the dangers involved.

Slave traders had to guard against insurrection diligently, often through force of arms and terror, lest their captives overrun them, seize the ship, and save themselves. "When our slaves are aboard we shackle the men two and two, while we lie in port, and in sight of their own country," wrote Thomas Phillips, master of the *Hannibal* in 1693-1694, "for 'tis then they attempt to make their escape, and mutiny." Slave traders considered mealtime, when the ship was still in sight of land, most dangerous. They had the sailors "stand to their arms; and some with lighted matches at the great guns," which were trained upon the captives until they were once again forced below deck. Phillips believed that such vigilance was the key: "I never heard that they mutiny'd in any ships of consequence, that had a good number of men, and the least care." "But in small tools where they had but few men, and those negligent or drunk, then they surpriz'd and butcher'd them, cut the cables, and let the vessel drive ashore, and every one shift for himself."[2]

Jean Barbot, who traded from Gorée Island to the Congo to America from 1678 to 1712, observed that Africans from the inland countries, especially the Pawpaws (Fons) of Dahomey (Benin) who were brought down to Ouidah between the Gold Coast (Ghana) and the Slave Coast (Nigeria), conspired among themselves and were the most likely to revolt aboard ship. The weapons were stored in the captain's cabin under armed guard to discourage them. The captives watched for an opening and, given the

2. Thomas Phillips, "Voyage of the *Hannibal*, 1693-1694," in Elizabeth Donnan, ed., *Documents Illustrative of the History of the Slave Trade to America*, 4 vols. (Washington, D.C., 1930-1935), I, 406-407.

opportunity, would kill the ship's entire crew to secure liberty. "We have almost every year some instances [of rebellion], in one *European* ship or other, that is filled with slaves."[3]

Willem Bosman, a Dutchman who traded on the Gold, Slave, and Ivory Coasts, also believed that shipboard insurrection was imminent near the African shore. All nations were at risk, but the Portuguese were the most unfortunate, having lost four ships in as many years. He agreed with Barbot's depiction of the belligerence of war captives from an "inland country" brought down to Ouidah. He wrote that these captives, in a panic about cannibalism, "resolve and agree together (and bring over the rest of their party) to run away from the ship, kill the Europeans, and set the vessel ashore; by which means they design to free themselves from being our food." Bosman witnessed two insurrections. He and the ship's captain quelled the first by shooting its leader in the head. The Africans in the second uprising were more successful. They were able to act because of the "carelessness" of the captain who had stored a salvaged anchor in the hold where the men were locked down. Making an anvil of the anchor and using a pilfered hammer, they "in short time broke all their fetters into pieces." Then they ascended from the hold to the deck, attacked the crew, "greviously" wounding several, and would have taken the ship if crews of French and English ships anchored nearby, alarmed by the distress of gunfire, had not intervened. The international counteroffensive quashed the uprising, killing twenty insurgents and driving the rest back into the hold.[4]

William Snelgrave, who from 1704 to 1734 trafficked in the enslaved from Sherbro Island in Sierra Leone to Cape Lopez in Angola, concurred that Africans were apt to rebel and would kill the crew, unless prevented by proper diligence and violent repression. "I knew several Voyages [that] had proved unsuccessful by Mutinies; as they occasioned either the total loss of the Ship and the white Mens Lives; or at least," he wrote, rendered it "absolutely necessary to kill or wound a great number of the Slaves, in order to prevent a total Destruction."[5]

3. [Jean] Barbot, *A Description of the Coasts of North and South-Guinea* . . . (1688), in [Awnsham Churchill, ed.], *A Collection of Voyages and Travels* . . . , V (London, 1732), 339.

4. Willem Bosman, *A New and Accurate Description of the Coast of Guinea, Divided into the Gold, the Slave, and the Ivory Coasts* . . . , 2d ed. (London, 1721), 339–345.

5. William Snelgrave, *A New Account of Some Parts of Guinea, and the Slave-Trade* . . . (London, 1734), 4, 173; Walter Minchinton, Celia King, and Peter Waite, eds., *Virginia Slave-Trade Statistics, 1698–1775* (Richmond, Va., 1984), 14n, 15, 17, 19; Donnan, ed., *History of the Slave Trade*, IV, 121n, 174n.

The slavers used the terror of grotesque punishment to intimidate rebellious captives. They flogged the enslaved to within an inch of their lives or dismembered them. Phillips advocated dismemberment because Africans believed that they could not return to their ancestral home unless whole. "The form of punishment that scares Africans most," Barbot recalled, "is by chopping parts off a living man *(couper un homme vif)* with blows from an axe and presenting the separated parts to the others." The whites sacrificed the lives of the "most mutinous" to "terrify" the others. The condemned were dismembered, Snelgrave wrote, "for many of the Blacks believe, that if they are put to death and not dismembered, they shall return again to their own Country, after they are thrown overboard."[6]

Snelgrave's observations have greater relevance than Barbot's, Bosman's, or Phillips's for a discussion of Virginia because he regularly traded to the colony. He commanded the *Eagle Galley* for at least three voyages to Virginia from 1704 to 1708 and was commissioned in 1713 by Messieurs Bradley, merchants of Virginia, to carry enslaved Africans from Accra to Virginia on the *Anne*. He observed four attempted rebellions, one aboard the *Eagle Galley* in the Bight of Biafra in 1704 and three on the *Henry* off the Gold Coast in 1721–1722. All four attempts took place in the port. He found that the Africans acted when the whites had let down their guard, when they were in a weakened state, or when they were divided against themselves. He noted the difficulties that the rebels encountered—not only from their captors but also from other captives—and recorded what the rebels thought of their enslavement, allowing a rare glimpse into their mental state. He was sensitive to the ethnic differences among his captives and the effect those differences had on rebellion. He also described his reasons and choices for punishing the rebels. The stories of the *Eagle Galley* and the *Henry* show that blacks' struggle against enslavement by whites began in Africa.

The rebels aboard the *Eagle Galley* began their uprising during mealtime while still in port in the Bight of Biafra. The 400 Africans on board (likely Igbos) had been bought on the Cross River in Old Calabar and were destined for Virginia. The 10 white men on the ship had survived a sickness that had emaciated the crew. Recognizing their numerical advantage, 20 chained captives struck for freedom as they went to supper by

6. P. E. H. Hair, Adam Jones, and Robin Law, eds., *Barbot on Guinea: The Writings of Jean Barbot on West Africa, 1678–1712*, 2 vols., Hakluyt Society, 2d Ser., nos. 175, 176 (London, 1992), II, 775; Royal African Company to Mr. Paul Sorel, Dec. 16, 1701, T 70/62, 106–109, VCRP; Snelgrave, *New Account of Guinea*, 180–184 (quotation on 184).

surprising the 3 guards armed with cutlasses. The rebels seized the chief mate and tried to throw him overboard, when one of the guards, a heavyset man on the forecastle, beat them "heartily" with the flat side of his cutlass until they released the chief mate, allowing him to run to the quarterdeck for arms. A seventeen-year-old African, while receiving a blow on his arm, interfered with a rebel who was attacking the captain with a billet; a sailor then shot the rebel, ending the uprising. Two of the leaders disappeared, apparently having "jumped overboard," the only "Loss[es] we suffered." The *Eagle Galley* landed in Virginia with only 229 captives. For his part, the seventeen-year-old man, who appears to have acted on impulse, was freed when he reached Virginia, and Colonel Robert Carter took him into his service until he became acquainted with the country and capable of providing for himself.[7]

At Mumfort on the Gold Coast in 1721–1722, Snelgrave had taken on board the *Henry* Koromanti captives, a group whom he described as not easily enslaved. This time fifty white men stood guard over five hundred captives, "all in health." Four of the Koromantis struck for freedom at midnight under a bright moon after being given permission to go to the privy. Four others, "who had got their irons off," followed them but jumped overboard when the guards arrived and were found clinging to the cables of the ship. The Koromantis, like the rebels on the *Eagle Galley*, failed in part because they were unable to strip the cutlasses from the guards, in this case because the yard-length cords that bound the handles were fastened to the guards' wrists.[8]

The Koromantis, undaunted, tried again. A few days after the first uprising, they proposed to a free African, who was hired because of his ability to speak English, that he procure an ax for them so that they could cut the cables that anchored the ship at night and run it aground. In return, they proposed he return to their country as their servant. Offering him freedom would have made no sense to the Koromantis; instead, they offered him what in their minds was more valuable, a place in society. They could not conceive of freedom as a personal liberation, of neither belonging nor having a connection to a lineage. For them the autonomy

7. Snelgrave, *New Account of Guinea*, 164–171 (quotations on 165, 167); Minchinton, King, and Waite, eds., *Virginia Slave-Trade Statistics*, 14–15; Daniel C. Littlefield, *Rice and Slaves: Ethnicity and the Slave Trade in Colonial South Carolina* (Baton Rouge, La., 1981), 9; Mechal Sobel, *The World They Made Together: Black and White Values in Eighteenth-Century Virginia* (Princeton, N.J., 1987), 245n.

8. Snelgrave, *New Account of Guinea*, 169.

of personal freedom was social suicide. Slavery's opposite was corporate membership with lineage rights, including inheritance, protection, and participation. The translator's alien origins precluded his participation in the society's productive and reproductive cycles with an age-group cohort. What they offered him was the position of "not-slave" servant, who would pay them homage, honor, and deference. They did not comprehend that he was free, or that becoming their servant was not incentive enough, and he betrayed them. Snelgrave should not have been surprised by the second rebellion, for, after the first attempt when he asked the rebels through the translator "what had induced them to mutiny," they answered that he "was a great Rogue to buy them, in order to carry them away from their own Country; and that they were resolved to regain their Liberty if possible."[9]

Snelgrave witnessed a mutiny and a third rebellion under a full moon a month later when he attempted to procure 120 captives from Captain Thomas at Anomabu, the principal English outlet on the Gold Coast, a few miles east of Cape Coast Castle. The crew had befriended the 100 or so Africans from the Windward Coast during their long sojourn in port and, led by the cooper, refused to deliver them to the captain. Other captives, perhaps intending either to pirate the vessel or simply to rescue their friends, sensed dissension and seized the opportunity to strike. A few Koromantis, who had been purchased but two or three days before and who were divided from the Windward Coast Africans by language, killed the cooper, who was acting as a sentry, with a cook's hatchet during an escape attempt. The death of the leader ended the mutiny, and Captain Thomas took back the ship. Four of the Koromantis jumped overboard and tried to swim ashore. The sharks ate two of them, and the two survivors were sentenced to death. When told by the translator that they would be executed in an hour, one of them spoke up to Snelgrave: "He must confess it was a rash Action in him to kill him [the cooper]; but he desired me to consider, that if I put him to death, I should lose all the Money I had paid for him." He was roped under his arms and led to the foreyard arm, where, showing no concern for his imminent death, he was

9. Ibid., 170–171; Orlando Patterson, *Freedom*, I, *Freedom in the Making of Western Culture* (New York, 1991), 23–28; Suzanne Miers and Igor Kopytoff, eds., *Slavery in Africa: Historical and Anthropological Perspectives* (Madison, Wis., 1977), 17; Claude Meillassoux, *The Anthropology of Slavery: The Womb of Iron and Gold,* trans. Alide Dasnois (1986; reprint, Chicago, 1991), 23–26.

shot to death. His head was cut off and his body thrown overboard "to let our Negroes see, that all who offended thus, should be served in the same manner."[10]

Shipboard rebellion indicated a predilection among captives to regain their freedom. That Snelgrave published his observations in England meant that literate Englishmen, including the Virginia planters, were cognizant that Africans were not only willing to use violence to save themselves on the outer voyage but would have carried this proclivity to Virginia. That Robert "King" Carter harbored the seventeen-year-old man who had thwarted the *Eagle Galley* revolt in 1704 proves the planters had firsthand knowledge of Africans' resistance. The struggle continued in Virginia, but blacks had to surmount not only the ethnic divide that had made resistance difficult aboard ship but also a widening racial rift. Throughout the tidewater, blacks traveled two roads of insurrection. The first road, well trod in Virginia, had its source in interracial efforts to escape servitude and its heyday during Bacon's Rebellion in 1676, when racial boundaries had yet to become fixed between black and white tobacco workers. The second, newer road of black resistance began with the increased concentration of Africans owing to the rising slave trade in the 1680s. Masses of Africans gathered in the countryside, celebrating feasts, burials, and African traditions—and plotting insurrection.

Freedom Wears a Cap

The specter of class war with blacks and whites fighting side by side against the great planters was a real threat, and colonial authorities did all in their power to prevent such an alliance. The early 1660s were rife with lower-class unrest. The great planters had begun breaking up interracial alliances in 1661, when the General Assembly doubled the time for servants who escaped with enslaved workers. A year later, the assembly consigned the children of enslaved mothers to lifelong slavery, regardless of the race or status of their fathers. To deal with the rising labor and religious discontent, the assembly also legislated in 1662 that each county erect a whipping post, a pillory, and a pair of stocks near the courthouse and a ducking stool where convenient. That year, the colony arrested a former New Model Army soldier, George Wilson, for preaching the Quakers' New Light gospel to the poor and confined him in a "dirty . . . nasty stink-

10. Snelgrave, *New Account of Guinea,* 180–184 (quotations on 182, 183–184).

ing" close and breathless "dungeon" where he died. Other exiled soldiers and sailors carried the leveling doctrine of the Commonwealth era into the colony.[11]

The great planters had their first taste of organized resistance in 1663 when nine laborers in Gloucester, including Cromwellian Roundheads recently exiled owing to the Restoration policies of Charles II, plotted an uprising of the tobacco workers. Their recruits included indentured laborers and transported felons, and possibly some of the enslaved. "Several mutinous and rebellious *Oliverian* Soldiers" riled up the workers, who were "very uneasie" from their unrequited labor, poor diet of corn-meal and water, religious persecution, and draconian punishments. The plot's martial structure betrayed its New Model Army provenance: companies were formed, captains elected, drummers recruited, marching orders given, and arms and ammunition strategically collected. John Gunter and William Bell, either of whom the company was willing to accept as captain, put into motion a plan at least a month old that would terrify the great planters. The insurrectionists intended to strike on September 6, resolving to depose Governor William Berkeley if he should oppose their demand for freedom. The nine leaders, taking a death oath of secrecy, met at Peter Knight's little house in the woods near Cook's Quarter on September 1 to plot "a designe for their freedom." That plan called for them to rendezvous at Poplar Spring on the next Sunday at midnight, bringing "what Company, armes, ammunicon wee could gett." From there they were to go to the houses of Lieutenant Colonel Francis Willis, a member of the Council of State, Katherine Cooke, a widow, and Colonel John Walker to seize "all the Gunns, Weapons, and other armes and amunicons of Warr," enough for a company of thirty men. They also planned to take a drum from Willis's house, having already recruited Major John Smith's drummer, and then march from house to house, killing anyone who opposed them. They would then proceed to Governor Berkeley's house in

11. Warren M. Billings, "A Quaker in Seventeenth-Century Virginia: Four Remonstrances by George Wilson," *WMQ*, 3d Ser., XXXIII (1976), 127–130; *SAL*, II, 75; Robert Beverley, *The History and Present State of Virginia* (1705, 1722), ed. Louis B. Wright (Chapel Hill, N.C., 1947), 69; Peter Linebaugh and Marcus Rediker, *The Many-Headed Hydra: Sailors, Slaves, Commoners, and the Hidden History of the Revolutionary Atlantic* (Boston, 2000), 135–136; Herbert Aptheker, *American Negro Slave Revolts*, rev. ed. (New York, 1974), 164–165; Morgan, *American Slavery, American Freedom*, 246; T. H. Breen, "A Changing Labor Force and Race Relations in Virginia, 1660–1710," *Journal of Social History*, VII (1973–1974), 8–9.

Green Spring to "demand our freedome." If Berkeley refused their demand, they would overthrow him, raise up the bound laborers to their
cause, and "make and wholy submit and distroy the State of this Country
of Vir'g."[12]

Before they could act, a servant, Thomas Birkenhead, betrayed them.
Notified of the intended insurrection, Berkeley secretly issued orders to
set up an ambush to capture the insurgents as they "singly" approached
the spring. Only a few were taken, because "several" others escaped and
warned accomplices en route. The General Court tried the plotters for
treason, hanged four, and exiled five. The General Assembly passed legislation requiring passes for servants abroad, especially on Sunday. They
memorialized the day that the conspirators were arrested, September 14—
inscribed in their minutes as Dies Lunae, the day of the moon—as an annual Thanksgiving Day and rewarded Birkenhead with his freedom and
five thousand pounds of tobacco. Charles II, alarmed by the event, commanded the building of a fort at Jamestown, but the great planters, believing that they had dealt with the threat, erected only a battery of a few
cannons about the town. Their sense of relief was short-lived, for by 1670
the Council of State received several petitions concerning the rowdiness
of transported felons from York, Gloucester, and Middlesex Counties.
The councillors recalled the Gloucester plot and banned the importation
of any "jaile bird" from England because of the "horror yet remaining
amongst us."[13]

Sir Henry Chicheley, who learned the importance of military might
fighting Roundheads in the English Civil War, wrote in 1673 to his brother
Sir Thomas Chicheley that Virginia should raise a militia of freeholders,
using perhaps a few English servants but no enslaved blacks. His fear of
the "multitude" was prescient: "a Rebellious Party" of blacks and white
servants soon materialized in 1676. Though Bacon's Rebellion is often
portrayed as a struggle between competing planters, it had crucial importance for workers. Had their integrated ranks gained the upper hand, it
might well have been necessary for Stuart officers to offer freedom to loyal
servants and enslaved blacks. Instead, crown officials quashed the rebel-

12. "Virginia Colonial Records: The Servants' Plot of 1663," *VMHB*, XV (1907-1908),
38-43; *MCGC*, 511; Beverley, *History and Present State of Virginia*, ed. Wright, 69.

13. *MCGC*, 209-210, 511; *SAL*, II, 204, 509-511; Thomas Ludwell to [Lord Arlington?], Apr. 29, 1670, *VMHB*, XIX (1911), 353-356; Beverley, *History and Present State of
Virginia*, ed. Wright, 69-70.

lion without having to play this last card, and the Stuart regime instituted further legal distinctions between whites and blacks in Virginia.[14]

Bacon's Rebellion began in April 1676 as a result of the white planters' hunger for Indian land, which conflicted with the ruling elite's Indian policy, but by the fall it had become a war waged by Virginia's "multitude" for freedom. Andrew Marvell, relying on the testimony of a ship captain who left "without knowing further of the event," reported that Nathaniel Bacon, in a "heady attempt" to seize the colony, "proclaimed liberty to all Servants and Negroes" two days before his attack on Jamestown. Motivated by the promise of freedom and an opportunity for landownership, about 250 blacks, or 10 percent of the enslaved, joined the rebellion. These enslaved laborers as well as servants and men recently "out of their time" composed the rebel army that captured Jamestown in September and sent Governor Berkeley into exile across the Chesapeake Bay. The inclusion of enslaved and indentured laborers in the rebellion transformed the conflict into one of class struggle, uniting the planters in opposition.[15]

The crown understood that the enslaved desired emancipation and was willing to use the cause to divide the rebel army. Charles II had issued a proclamation in October, giving Governor Berkeley discretion in offering freedom to servants and the enslaved who fought for loyalists in the conflict. Berkeley refused to issue the proclamation, for he knew its implications were far greater than the rebellion at hand. But Thomas Grantham, captain of an armed English merchantman employed for the suppression of the uprising, did not hesitate to mention emancipation strategically to deceive diehard groups of black and white rebels into surrender. Grantham's behavior and the rebels' outraged response open a window

14. Sir Henry Chicheley to Sir Thomas Chicheley, July 16, 1673, CO 1/30, 113, transcript, LC; Commissioners Report, Dec. 11, 1677, BR 766, 142, 143, HL; Proclamation of King Charles II, Oct. 27, 1676, CO 5/1355, 129–132, transcript, LC; "Note: Sir Henry Chicheley," *VMHB*, XVII (1909), 144–146; Brown, *Good Wives, Nasty Wenches*, 180–181. See also Theodore W. Allen, *Class Struggle and the Origin of Racial Slavery: The Invention of the White Race* (Hoboken, N.J., 1975), 3–4; Breen, "A Changing Labor Force," *Jour. Soc. Hist.*, VII (1973–1974), 22; Aptheker, *American Negro Slave Revolts*, 164–165; Schwarz, *Twice Condemned*, 69.

15. Commissioners Report, July 11, Dec. 11, 1677, BR 766, 57–58, 142, 144, HL; Andrew Marvell to Sir Henry Thompson, Nov. 14, 1676, HM 21813, HL; *JHB, 1659/1660–1693*, 86; Philip D. Morgan, "British Encounters with Africans and African-Americans, circa 1600–1780," in Bernard Bailyn and Morgan, eds., *Strangers within the Realm: Cultural Margins of the First British Empire* (Chapel Hill, N.C., 1991), 195; Breen, "A Changing Labor Force," *Jour. Soc. Hist.*, VII (1973–1974), 3–25. Cf. Morgan, *American Slavery, American Freedom*, 250–270.

into the final phase of the rebellion, giving voice to the rebels' desire for liberty.[16]

First, by deceitfully promising them freedom, Grantham secured the surrender of three hundred rebels at West Point. He then took on the rebels' stronghold a few miles away, where four hundred black and white rebels in arms accused him of treachery at West Point and threatened either to shoot him or to cut him into pieces. He disarmed them by giving them notes promising freedom, rundlets of brandy, and himself as hostage until they had received satisfaction from His Majesty. He thus persuaded all of them to return to their homes, except for eighty blacks and twenty whites who refused to lay down their arms. Grantham tricked these remaining one hundred to board a sloop with the promise of carrying them to a rebel fort a few miles down the York River. In perfidy, he pulled them behind his sloop, not to the refuge of their own fort, but to a loyalist ship lying in wait, compelled their surrender by force of arms, and delivered them to their owners. He later recalled that "they yielded with a great deal of discontent, saying had they known my resolution, they would have destroyed me."[17]

With the memory of Bacon's Rebellion still fresh, the crown recognized the need to secure stability in Virginia. Ironically, crown policy had contributed to the shortage of whites needed for defense by discouraging immigration to the colony. The principal merchants in transporting servants and the enslaved touted the security risks of a restricted servant trade. Unless the crown acted "speedily," Virginia would not have enough whites to oversee the blacks and to serve in the militia and thus could not guard against the combined threat of invasion and black insurrection. Such a situation would soon replicate the deplorable social circumstances prevailing in Jamaica, where blacks outnumbered whites twenty to one.[18]

Thus, the crown, recognizing the political importance of a racial sys-

16. Proclamation of King Charles II, Oct. 27, 1676, CO 5/1355, 129–132, transcript, LC; Proclamation of Sir William Berkeley, Feb. 10, 1676/7, CO 1/39, 39, transcript, LC; Petition of Richard Clark to King's Commission, ca. 1677, CO 1/40, 5–6, transcript, LC.

17. See "£200 Reward to Capt Thomas Grantham, for Services during the Rebellion," Privy Council Register, June 11, 1679, PC 2/68, VCRP; Allen, *Class Struggle and the Origin of Racial Slavery*, 3–4; Breen, "Changing Labor Force," *Jour. Soc. Hist.*, VII (1973–1974), 15–18.

18. "Observations on Two Petitions of the Principal English Merchants Trading to the Plantations Who Are Liable to Prosecution for Landing Servants to Those Plantations" (ca. 1681), Owen Wynne Collection, 211, 75r–76r, Codrington Library, All Souls College, Oxford University, VCRP.

tem for the production of staples in the colonies, began encouraging two legal categories of labor: servant and enslaved. Servants were to be treated humanely as crown subjects and included in the civic tasks of the militia. The Board of Trade in 1676, ruminating on the plight of Jamaica's servants, expressed its displeasure with the "word servitude, being a mark of bondage and slavery, and think fit rather to use the word service, since those servants are only apprentices for years." To discourage emigration from Virginia, the Privy Council instructed Thomas Culpeper in 1679 to get a bill enacted restraining "inhuman severity" on white servants and stipulating that "all Planters and Christian [white] servants . . . bee listed under Officers; and as often as you shall think fit, Mustered and Trained." At the same time, the great planters redoubled their efforts to divide workers by race by encouraging and employing whites to restrict further the activities of blacks. They recognized that coercive regulations lay at the heart of the plantation system and used their powers of state to keep blacks enslaved.[19]

The crown's distinction between servants and the enslaved had little effect on the immediate material conditions of servants, for they were used brutishly, bought and sold as chattel. Indeed, the law of servitude was a model for the emerging slave statutes. However, reaction to rebellious black behavior in 1672, the first instance of blacks massing together, demonstrates how the great planters moved away from the servant law and began distinguishing between indentured and enslaved laborers. Although the enslaved had not organized any insurrections, the great planters were fearful of their concourse in various parts of the colony. Since no satisfactory means had been found to prevent their assembling, the General Assembly passed "An Act for the Apprehension and Suppression of Runawayes, Negroes, and Slaves." Servants were excluded from the act, although the danger of their joining the enslaved was noted in the act's preamble. The assembly offered to indemnify owners of any enslaved wounded or killed resisting: forty-five hundred pounds of casked tobacco for a black and three thousand pounds for an Indian. They also offered the tributary tribes a bounty of twenty yards of roanoke (*rawranoke,* beaded white shells) or its value in goods for each fugitive they apprehended and returned. Moreover, as a preventive measure, the Surry Court tried to hold

19. Instructions of the Privy Council to Thomas, Lord Culpeper, Dec. 6, 1679, CO 5/1355, 326-356 (quotations on 336-337, 348), transcript, LC; "Historical Notes and Queries," *WMQ*, 1st Ser., VIII (1899-1900), 273; Winthrop D. Jordan, *White over Black: American Attitudes toward the Negro, 1550-1812* (Chapel Hill, N.C., 1968), 80-81.

the owners of enslaved runaways accountable and applied to the enslaved the 1663 act, a consequence of the Gloucester Rebellion, which required servants to carry passes when away from their plantations. The court fined Mathias Marriott, a prominent planter, two hundred pounds of casked tobacco for giving his enslaved man "a Note to goe abroad and having noe business." According to the court, Marriott's action was symptomatic of the "too Careless and inconsiderate Liberty given to Negroes" that allowed them to assemble on Saturday and Sunday and that had brought several other planters to court. The jurists believed that the enslaved used these assemblies to consult about projects and alliances to the "danger and damage of the neighbors" as well as their masters. Attempts to restrict the enslaved went beyond their freedom of movement to their choice of apparel. The court found that the enslaved commonly favored fine linen and accessories, which not only heightened their "foolish pride" but also encouraged them to steal. The enslaved were thus ordered to wear blue shirts, shifts, caps, and scarves or, if that color was unavailable, clothes made of lockram, a coarse woven linen, or canvas.[20]

Although whites and blacks toiled in the same tobacco fields, such legal distinctions as the color or texture of slave clothing and the indemnity or bounty for the suppression of the enslaved at once degraded blacks and began to raise the status of whites. Moreover, through these distinctions class tensions between great planters and their indigent fellow Englishmen were muted, or at least contained. By employing poor whites as overseers and patrollers, the authorities divided the class of exploited, making them enemies rather than allies.[21]

Although the racial rift was widening between blacks and whites, their paths would intersect one more time on Ralph Wormeley II's Middlesex County plantation in 1687. In perhaps the last vestige of interracial co-operation, John Nickson, a white servant on the plantation, and "diverse other ill disposed Servants and others," including the enslaved, planned to secure guns, powder, shot, and other arms and to escape by force of arms. Before they could act, county authorities discovered the plot, confined Nickson to the common jail, held him over until the next court

20. *SAL,* II, 299–300; "Management of Slaves, 1672," *VMHB,* VII (1899–1900), 314.

21. Rutman and Rutman, *A Place in Time,* 130, 153, 264 n. 7; "Historical Notes and Queries," *WMQ,* 1st Ser., VIII (1899–1900), 273; "Observations on Two Petitions," Wynne Collection, 211, 75–76; Warren M. Billings, "The Law of Servants and Slaves in Seventeenth-Century Virginia," *VMHB,* XCIX (1991), 46–53; Morgan, *American Slavery, American Freedom,* 21–82, 126–129, 346.

date (his fate is unknown), and pursued the other conspirators. Possibly among them were Mingoe, Lawrence, and an unnamed servant, who escaped from the Wormeley plantation two years later, gathered followers, and raided plantations in Rappahannock County for cattle and hogs. They became notorious in November 1691 when they stole, among other things, two guns and a carbine. The theft of the weapons caused the authorities to intensify their search and to capture the three outlaws. The three were tried in the Middlesex County court. The jurists sentenced Mingoe to receive thirty-nine lashes and the servant to an additional term of five years and twelve days. Lawrence, who was found in possession of a stolen gun, was confined as a felon to the county jail until he could be sent to the General Court for sentencing. Although his fate is unknown, Lawrence was probably hanged.[22]

By the 1680s, the road to interracial resistance was beginning to give way to the road of African mass resistance. The increased activity of the slave trade brought more blacks into Virginia, first from Barbados and then from Africa, carrying with them the customs of their homelands. As the proportion of the enslaved that came directly from Africa increased, blacks began organizing to celebrate traditional African rituals such as feasts and burials, opportunities to recall their lost African world and to rekindle ties with friends and relatives. It was not long before they used these gatherings to plot strategies for escaping to freedom. The apprehension among whites that these assemblies engendered, first perceived in 1672, persisted throughout the late seventeenth and early eighteenth century.[23]

The ever-present threat of slave insurrection can be deduced by the consistent efforts of whites to thwart it, particularly measures aimed at preventing the enslaved from assembling. Governors spoke of the threat of black assemblies in proclamations to their subjects and in reports to the crown. Complaints and petitions made mention of it from counties

22. Warren M. Billings, ed., *The Old Dominion in the Seventeenth Century: A Documentary History of Virginia, 1606–1689* (Chapel Hill, N.C., 1975), 147; Aptheker, *American Negro Slave Revolts,* 167; Schwarz, *Twice Condemned,* 70; Rutman and Rutman, *A Place in Time,* 171. Wormeley was the earliest plantation to invest fully in slavery. Its history of resistance began with the "rioutous and rebellious conduct" of the enslaved during the Indian wars of 1644–1646 (*MCGC,* 502).

23. Sidney W. Mintz and Richard Price, *An Anthropological Approach to the Afro-American Past: A Caribbean Perspective,* Institute for the Study of Human Issues Occasional Papers in Social Change, no. 2 (Philadelphia, 1976), 1–21; Allan Kulikoff, "The Origins of Afro-American Society in Tidewater Maryland and Virginia, 1700 to 1790," *WMQ,* 3d Ser., XXXV (1978), 239.

throughout Virginia. The Council of State and the House of Burgesses debated the best way to keep blacks from meeting together, the length of time blacks could be away from their plantations without a pass, and the frequency of patrols and militia musters. Indeed, the variety of evidence from governors' reports and proclamations, legislative debates, statutes, petitions, and court testimonies points to a real, not imagined, threat.

In 1680, the council issued a proclamation disallowing the enslaved "to hold or make any Solemnity or Funeralls for any [deceased] Negroes." The threat of insurrection had reached a crisis by 1686, when the burgesses debated the expediency of blacks "going armed." A year later, when the Nickson plot was discovered in Middlesex, Nicholas Spencer presented "Intelligence" to the council of a conspiracy of blacks in the Northern Neck intent on "Distroying and killing his [Majesties] Subjects . . . [and] Carrying it through the whole Collony of [Virginia]." The councillors believed that such activity was prompted by the "great freedome and Liberty" of the enslaved to "Consult and advise" one another on Saturday and Sunday and "under [the] pretention" of funerals. They urged Governor Howard Effingham to issue a proclamation enforcing the laws against black assembly, which he did in November 1687.[24]

During the 1687 insurrection scare, the enslaved were rounded up, interrogated, and punished. Frank, an enslaved black belonging to Henry Gibbs, was imprisoned and questioned in Warwick County concerning his role in organizing the enslaved in Charles City and New Kent Counties, but the council declined to issue warrants for him or his cohort of Cussan, Robin, and Tom. The council did find Sam, a black belonging to Richard Metcalfe in Westmoreland County, guilty in 1688 because he "several times endeavored to promote a Negro insurrection in this Colony."[25]

Sam's case proves instructive in how great planters dealt with insurrectionists. He had been found guilty of insurrection, yet they spared his life. The councillors, representing the interests of the slaveholders, sentenced him to be severely whipped and taken to the gallows in James City, not to be hanged, but to be displayed. From there, Sam was to return to prison to recover until he could be severely whipped again at the next court session. After this whipping, it was ordered "that hee have a strong Iron collar

24. *EJCCV*, I, 87; *JHB, 1659/60–1693,* 266, 268, 269, 271; *EJCCV*, I, 86–87, 511.

25. Schwarz, *Twice Condemned,* 70; "Punishment for a Negro Rebel," *WMQ,* 1st Ser., X (1901–1902), 177–178.

affixed about his neck with four spriggs." He was neither to take off the collar nor leave his owner's plantation for the rest of his life, under the threat of hanging. The clerk for the General Court informed the council that Sam had received "twenty-nine lashes on the bare back well laid on [which] was performed accordingly with a halter about his neck, and the collar put on." The colonial authorities had made him into a permanent example of an incorrigible black.[26]

The noncompliance of poorer whites and laxity among slaveholders undermined the authorities' campaign to stop blacks from gathering together. Poorer planters had no stake in policing blacks, and slaveholders did not have the wherewithal to control the movements of the enslaved during the weekend. Two generations of custom had allowed laborers Saturday evenings and Sunday as holidays; to force both nonslaveholders and slaveholders to comply thus required state sanction. The burgesses and the councillors differed on the method for doing so. The elected burgesses, hard-pressed by their constituencies' concern about Africans massing in the countryside, introduced in 1688 and 1693 more "severe" laws to restrict blacks from gathering in "Considerable Numbers." They laid the responsibility on the great planters, who owned the majority of enslaved laborers, by calling for a poll tax on each of the enslaved to pay for defense. The council, without the worry of an electorate, represented its class interest by opposing the poll tax and insisting that the current laws be obeyed, for the 1680 act had "sufficiently" dealt with the issue.[27]

Governor Edmund Andros agreed with his predecessor Effingham's assessment on the need to enforce the current laws. In 1694, he chided the slaveholders' "remissnessnes and Licenciousness" in allowing black assemblies throughout the colony. What concerned him most was the owners' laxity in policing the enslaved who were visiting another plantation for more than four hours. Blacks should be allowed to leave the plantation for a specific purpose, and only then with passes detailing time and place. Failure to enforce the laws, especially the acts of 1680 and 1682 for preventing insurrections, he believed, would result in "dangerous consequences."[28]

Amid such warnings, the black struggle for freedom culminated in an-

26. "Punishment for a Negro Rebel," *WMQ*, 1st Ser., X (1901–1902), 177–178.

27. *JHB, 1659/60–1693*, 299, 305, 405; *LJCCV*, I, 127.

28. "Affidavit of Dudley Digges Submitted to Sir Edmund Andros, Governor of Virginia," Mar. 22, 1694, VHS; *JHB, 1659/60–1693*, 299, 305; *LJCCV*, I, 127; *EJCCV*, I, 317.

other insurrection plot in 1710 on the lower James River, the region that had imported the largest number of Africans in the previous decade. The rebels in James City, Isle of Wight, and Surry Counties, who included Africans, African-Americans, Indians, and at least one free black, conspired to escape by force of arms and settle in the North Carolina frontier area of the Great Dismal Swamp.

Like most other insurrection plots in colonial Virginia, however, the enslaved were betrayed and discovered before they could act. With trepidation, an enslaved black, Will, approached his master, Robert Ruffin, with information certain to strike terror into the heart of a Virginia planter: an insurrection was afoot. With Will's help, the planters rounded up suspects from several counties and put them under armed guard. Despite efforts to hide Will's identity, his betrayal was soon known to the other blacks. Ruffin had to secrete him in the Northern Neck for "More Safety" because "in a short Time [he was] so much Suspected That Several Negro's Laid Wait for his Life."[29]

Edmund Jenings, president of the council, launched a full investigation to determine the breadth of the conspiracy and to isolate the leaders. Leading a commission of oyer and terminer with three other planters from James City County, Phillip Ludwell examined the enslaved belonging to Dr. James Blair and Mr. Jacqueline along with three of his own and three others whom he had learned about from his enslaved blacks. The commissioners, satisfied with their testimony and confident that they would not run away, believed that they should be discharged. Two of Ludwell's blacks, afraid that they would not be released, confessed to what they knew, implicating John Brodnax's enslaved black Jamy and Edward Ross's Essex. Ludwell released the confessors, promising Jenings that they would be punished, partly because he believed that they would not "stir" and because, being confined during the sickly season, they were in danger of falling ill. But, most important, Ludwell, following Jenings's expressed intention, wanted to minimize the plot's significance by carrying on business as usual. The commissioners pumped and browbeat Jamy, Essex, and Jacqueline's enslaved black Will, piecing together their case. Although no one confessed, the white men concluded that Jamy and Essex were "very instrumental in the designe and are doubtless great Rogues." Jenings issued an order for the arrest of suspected blacks in Bruton Parish, some

29. *JHB, 1702/3–1705, 1705–1706, 1710–1712,* 270.

of the names of whom—Angola Peter, Pamla, his wife, Bumbara, and Mingo—suggest an influential African-born constituency in the plot.[30]

The investigation spread to Surry and Isle of Wight Counties, where commissions met on March 24. After examining enslaved blacks and Indians at the Surry courthouse, the commission determined that the planned breakout was designed by "great numbers" of them, who were going to kill any white attempting to stop them. The commissioners discharged all the blacks and Indians examined except Scipio, Jackman, Salvadore (an Indian), and Tom Shawn, whom they believed were the principal leaders, and they outlawed Samuel Thompson's enslaved black Angola Peter of Surry County, who had run away. They believed Angola Peter and Scipio to be the leaders because of their rude and insolent behavior; Salvadore, on the other hand, was less conspicuous, encouraging and promoting the design without drawing attention to himself. Significantly, the other person convicted in Surry was Booth, a free black. The court found that Booth knew of the planned breakout and entertained several conspirators at his home. For his complicity, Booth was sentenced to receive twenty-nine lashes. On the same day, the commissioners examined and tried blacks at the Isle of Wight courthouse. Again, they released all but the principals. They found Manuell, an enslaved black belonging to John Googo, guilty of "knowing" about the planned escape, based on Scipio's confession and his own self-incriminating statements, for which he received forty lashes.[31]

To prevent further seditious activities, Jenings issued colonywide directives for the more effectual policing of the enslaved. In his first order of business, he issued a proclamation on March 21 that restricted slave assembly. He had acted upon "Intelligence" gathered of "Severall Illegall, Unusuall and Unwarrantable" slave meetings where whites were not present, thus giving the blacks the opportunity to plan insurrection. The proclamation was directed at owners and overseers who had been lax in policing their enslaved, threatening those who "knowingly" allowed their

30. "Proceedings in an Investigation of an Insurrection of Negroes and Indians, Slaves, in Surrey and Isle of Wight," Mar. 19, 1709, Colonial Papers, folder 20, no. 11, VSL; *EJCCV*, III, 234–235; "Order Signed by E. Jenings for the Arrest of Certain Negroes in Bruton Parish," Mar. 20, 1709 [1710], Colonial Papers, folder 20, no. 12, VSL; Schwarz, *Twice Condemned*, 53–54.

31. "Examination of Slaves concerning the Conspiracy of the Surrey County Persuant to an Order of the Hon. in Councill," Mar. 24, 1709, Colonial Papers, folder 20, nos. 13–14, VSL; "Return from Isle of Wight County Court concerning the Conspiracy of Negroes, and the Orders of the Court," Mar. 24, 1709, Colonial Papers, folder 20, no. 13, VSL.

enslaved off the plantation for more than four hours with a fine of 150 pounds of tobacco paid to the informer. The enslaved were not to go armed away from the plantation, nor to leave their quarters without a signed certificate, nor to stay on someone else's grounds without proper permission. The investigations of the commissions of oyer and terminer confirmed Jenings's fear that the blacks had planned their insurrection when they were absent from their plantations longer than the law allowed.[32]

The Council of State issued an order superseding the county jurisdiction on April 18. It directed the suspected leaders to be arraigned in General Court for high treason, both because the conspiracy crossed county lines and because of the enormity of the threat. High treason, the most egregious crime, was a curious charge for an enslaved laborer who owed no allegiance to the state. Three days later, after acquitting three of the accused, the General Court found Salvadore and Scipio guilty and sentenced them to be hanged and then drawn and quartered, the penalty for high treason. The General Court ordered that Salvadore's sentence be carried out in Surry. His rent body was to be sent to the sheriffs and displayed: his head in the capital, Williamsburg, one quarter next to the great guns in James City, another in "the most publick place" in New Kent County, and the remainder in Surry where the justices "think fitt." Scipio was to be executed in Gloucester, where his head would be displayed. His shattered corpse was to be exhibited in Middlesex, Lancaster, and King and Queen Counties in "the most publick" places.[33]

Colonel Jenings placed a reward on Angola Peter's head for his role in "Stirring up and abetting" the blacks in James City County "to levy warr" against Her Majesty's government. The council offered to pay ten pounds to the bounty hunter that brought in Angola Peter alive and less, five pounds, if dead. The councillors preferred that Angola Peter be captured alive so that he would suffer the same gruesome punishment as Salvadore and Scipio. They set free Will, the betrayer of the plot, to encourage "like Fidelity."[34]

Salvadore's and Scipio's fate served as the decisive end to the intended uprising. The president of the council intended their example to stifle the

32. "Proclamation [against the] Illegal, Unusual and Unwarrantable Concourses, Meetings and Assembling Together of Negro, Mulatto, and Indian Slaves . . . ," Mar. 29, 1709 [1710], CO 5/1316, 166–169, transcript, LC; *EJCCV*, III, 573–574.

33. *EJCCV*, III, 242–243.

34. *JHB, 1702/3–1705, 1705–1706, 1710–1712,* 270; *SAL,* III, 537–538; *EJCCV,* III, 575.

longing for liberty in other enslaved blacks. Jenings wrote to the Board of Trade: "I hope their fate will strike such a terror in the other Negroes, as will keep them from forming such designs for the future, without being obliged to make examples of any more of them." The Board of Trade, echoing Jenings, expressed to the newly installed governor, Alexander Spotswood, its happiness that the insurrection was suppressed and prayed that the two chief conspirators would serve as "an Example to the rest, and deter them from attempting anything of the like nature for the future."[35]

The atmosphere of fear and guilt after Salvadore's and Scipio's execution caused many to shiver for their society. William Byrd II's June nightmare exposes the anxiety felt by slaveholders at the time. He feared the divine punishment of the apocalypse, but its prospect was too frightening for conscious reflection. "I dreamed I saw a flaming star in the air at which I was much frightened and called some others to see it but when they came it disappeared." The flaming star figures as a sign of judgment that threatened Virginia, but he was unable effectively to warn his fellow planters. His consciously recording the dream in his diary indicates that, even as the portent of disaster burned bright over Virginia's slave society, his inability to alert his class haunted him. His impotence was just as unnerving as the catastrophe on the horizon. Five days after his nightmare, he had yet to come to terms with its horror. Struggling to make sense of his vision, he confessed, "I fear this portends some judgement to this country or at least to myself."[36]

Governor Spotswood also sensed the danger. The 1710 conspiracy demonstrated the ability of the enslaved to organize across ethnic lines—and at a time when their numbers were rapidly increasing—making them a "Most Dangerous" enemy. He chided slaveholders for their lax vigilance

35. Colonel Edmund Jenings to BT, Apr. 24, June 10, 1710, CO 5/1316, 141–142, 144–145, transcript, LC; BT to Colonel Alexander Spotswood, Aug. 28, 1710, CO 5/1363, 198–203, VCRP.

36. Louis B. Wright and Marion Tinling, eds., *The Secret Diary of William Byrd of Westover, 1709–1712* (Richmond, Va., 1941), 194. Byrd was not the only one with an apocalyptic vision in 1710, observed Dr. Francis Le Jau, SPG missionary of St. James Parish in Goose Creek, South Carolina. "The best scholar of all the Negroes in my Parish and a very sober and honest Liver . . . told his master abruptly there wou'd be a dismal time and the moon wou'd be turned into Blood, and there wou'd be dearth of darkness and went away." A black that witnessed the encounter gave out the story "publicly blazed abroad that an Angel came and spake to the Man, he had seen a hand that gave him a Book, and he had heard Voices, seen fires, etc." (Frank J. Klingberg, ed., *The Carolina Chronicle of Dr. Francis Le Jau, 1706–1717* [Berkeley, Calif., 1956], 70).

in restricting slave assemblies, just as Jenings had done earlier that year. Even the "Babel of Languages" among them, he warned the burgesses, should not lull whites into a false sense of security. Their desire for liberty or power might spur them "to any Attempts." The burgesses must prevent assemblies of the enslaved, for "freedom Wears a Cap which Can Without a Tongue, Call togather all Those who Long to Shake of[f] The fetters of Slavery."[37]

Enslaved Virginians continued to collaborate, determined to shake off the fetters of slavery. Led by Robin and Mingo, six blacks belonging to John Smith and Christopher Robinson, both of Middlesex County, made good their escape in April 1713. They broke into the merchant storehouse of Arthur Bickerdike and stole thirty pounds sterling. They resisted capture with guns, assaulting the undersheriff of Gloucester County and his posse. They were believed headed for Totusky or the Dragon Swamp, a dragon-shaped tributary of the Piankatank River. The Council of State issued an order that the sheriffs from Middlesex, Gloucester, King and Queen, and Essex Counties raise a "sufficient" militia to search the Dragon Swamp. The sheriffs of Richmond and Lancaster were ordered to do likewise in Totusky. If the fugitives resisted, the sheriffs had permission "to kill and destroy" them. The council put five pounds current money on the heads of Robin and Mingo and five shillings on each of the others as a bounty; information leading to the capture of the fugitives was worth one-fifth the reward. The fate of the runaways is unknown, but it is likely that they escaped.[38]

A conspiracy involving enslaved blacks in Middlesex and Gloucester Counties was uncovered in the fall of 1722. "Great numbers" of the enslaved had held "frequent" secret meetings to plot their freedom. Governor Hugh Drysdale reported to the Board of Trade on October 16 that the enslaved intended to "rise and cutt off the English in Virginia," but the suspects were now in jail. On December 20, he repeated this information. The problem for the authorities was one of evidence, which was obtained from "only Negros, and those not Christians." After 1705, the law forbade non-Christian enslaved blacks to serve as witnesses (although Christian blacks could still testify). Since the evidence was thus inadmissible, the

---

37. *JHB, 1702/3–1705, 1705–1706, 1710–1712,* 240–241.

38. *EJCCV,* III, 336–337; Rutman and Rutman, *A Place in Time,* 175; Schwarz, *Twice Condemned,* 75. Perhaps the blacks' escape route is the provenance of "the negro road" that runs between the main road and the Dragon Swamp referred to in a land transaction in 1716 (Rutman and Rutman, *A Place in Time,* 164).

transgressors could not be convicted of high treason, and Drysdale sought the Council of State's advice on how to proceed.[39]

The Council of State ordered the attorney general to get an indictment for misdemeanors and procure all evidence that could be found against the suspects. Although they were charged only with misdemeanors, the application for bail was denied "upon Consideration . . . and the Circumstances of their Case." Three blacks, two Sams and Will, were found guilty of "Congregating . . . Communicating contriving and Conspiring among themselves and with the said other Slaves to kill murder and destroy very many" Englishmen. The two Sams were both transported to the West Indies, and Will's fate is unknown.[40]

Hoping for more information, the authorities held over other blacks until the next General Court in April 1723. Dick and five other "principall ringleaders," Robin, Tom (alias Jack and Bambara Tom), Isaac, Jeffrey, and Sancho, were acquitted, since "the Evidence against them being only of their own Condition and Complexion" combined with their secrecy and their "Threatening" witnesses from prison was insufficient for conviction. Yet, the "pregnant Circumstances of their Designs," to wage war against whites, made it imprudent to discharge them despite the lack of legal evidence. The General Assembly thus found a way not only "to free the Country of such dangerous Rogues, but [also] to prevent and to punish the like secret Conspiracys for the future." The assembly, acting upon the presumption "That if these escape with Impunity not only they but others by their perswasion and Example will be encouraged to more daring Attempts," exiled them to the West Indies under penalty of death if they returned. At the same time, the assembly compensated their owners. This punishment of the blacks not only prevented them from entering into new plots, but it would also "discourage others by this example," wrote Drysdale, "for an exile from their wifes and Children, is almost as terrible to them as death itself."[41]

The want of legal evidence in 1723 does not rule out a conspiracy. The

39. Waverly K. Winfree, comp., *The Laws of Virginia: Being a Supplement to Hening's The Statutes at Large, 1700–1750* (Richmond, Va., 1971), 257; "Abstract of Letter from Mr. Drisdale, Williamsburg, Dec. 20, 1722," CO 5/1370, 77–78, VCRP; *EJCCV*, IV, 20.

40. *EJCCV*, IV, 29; Aptheker, *American Negro Slave Revolts*, 176.

41. *EJCCV*, IV, 31; *JHB, 1712–1714, 1715, 1718, 1720–1722, 1723–1726*, 367–368; Drysdale to BT, June 29, 1723, CO 5/1319, 111–117 (quotation on 115), VCRP; Winfree, comp., *Laws of Virginia*, 257–259; Schwarz, *Twice Condemned*, 86–87; Aptheker, *American Negro Slave Revolts*, 176.

commissions were hindered in the prosecution by their own legal trappings. If the evidence is ambiguous whether the two groups of men tried in 1722 and 1723 were connected, between them their actions were sufficient to lead Governor Drysdale to push for a more stringent law and for the burgesses to enact one. At the same time, the great planters were using the danger of insurrection to consolidate their power, strengthening regulations and disabilities against blacks, free and enslaved, and dragooning lower-class whites into supporting a racially ordered society. The fear of rebellion was not merely paranoia; whites were apprehensive with good reason. The nature of conspiracy demands clandestine and secret activity. Authorities and slaveowners in the 1723 case left enough evidence in their reports and the court records to indicate what the enslaved were doing and thinking. Enslaved blacks met in secret, planning to seize the country and cut off the English. Once caught, they remained mum and threatened witnesses from prison. The reaction of the lawmakers after the event suggests that slaveholders took the threat seriously.[42]

Indeed, the conspiracy to seize the country alarmed whites throughout Virginia. In at least two counties straddling the fall line, they began agitating through their representatives for stricter enforcement of the slave code. The landowners of Hanover and Prince George Counties, concerned that blacks were "going abroad Carrying Arms and Convening in great Numbers," sent to the House of Burgesses in 1723 "several propositions" for suppressing outliers and compensating owners if their enslaved were killed.[43]

In response to the propositions from those two counties and Governor Drysdale's insistence that the laws be tightened, the General Assembly in 1723 reexamined the slave code. In the 1710 insurrection case, to convict Salvadore and Scipio of a capital crime authorities had to charge them with high treason. Recognizing the difficulty of doing so, the burgesses had in the November 1710 session debated and amended a bill that would have made insurrection a felony punishable by death, but, in the end, the bill was rejected. In 1723, for the first time, perhaps recognizing the absurdity of indicting a slave insurrectionist for high treason, the General Assembly made conspiracy by six or more of the enslaved a capital crime. More likely, however, it was provoked into enacting the statute because convictions might have been more easily obtained in the April trials

---

42. *SAL*, IV, 129–131.
43. *JHB, 1712–1714, 1715, 1718, 1720–1722, 1723–1726*, 369.

of the six blacks. Indeed, the bar of evidence was lowered, requiring now the oath of only one witness and admitting the non-Christian testimony of blacks and Indians.[44]

Also in 1723, the legislators further restricted the mobility, assembly, and manumission of blacks, withdrawing the few rights they retained after 1705. The enslaved could be castrated or killed for consulting, plotting, and conspiring in a group of six or more. The same punishment could be meted out to "incorrigible runaways." All meetings of blacks were made illegal unless specifically licensed by a master on his own quarters, and even then not at night. The assembly also revoked the franchise of free blacks, reinstated the tax on free black women, and restricted manumissions to grants by the governor and Council of State for "meritorious service." The assembly, suspicious of free blacks' empathy for the insurrectionists, restricted gun ownership and forbade all nonhouseholders from serving in the militia, although this law was later amended so that they could be drafted as laborers in time of invasion. Governor William Gooch, reflecting upon the deprivation of rights, thought it was necessary for the assembly "to fix a perpetual Brand" upon free blacks, partly because of their mixed racial origin and partly because they "adhere to and favour the slaves."[45]

At the same time, the assembly also passed "An Act for Laying Duty on Liquors and Slaves," which imposed a new duty of forty shillings or two pounds on each imported black to raise funds for the defense of the colony, especially against slave insurgency. With the revenue collected from the duty, arms and ammunition would be provided to the poorer whites to guard against the threat of blacks and Indians. Drysdale wrote that the "chiefe [view] of this bill" was to provide the needed funds to arm "the Militia for the guard of the Country as well against forreign invasions of Indians and others, as [against the] intestine commotions of slaves."[46]

44. *JHB, 1702/3–1705, 1705–1706, 1710–1712,* 264, 266, 268, 272, 275, 278, 280, 281; *SAL,* IV, 126, 127; Winfree, comp., *Laws of Virginia,* 257–259; Schwarz, *Twice Condemned,* 85–88.

45. William Gooch to Allured Popple, May 18, 1736, CO 5/1324, 19–22, VCRP; Adele Hast, "The Legal Status of the Negro in Virginia, 1705–1765," *Journal of Negro History,* LIV (1969), 261; *JHB, 1712–1714, 1715, 1718, 1720–1722, 1723–1726,* 367; *SAL,* III, 258, IV, 126–134; Billings, ed., *Old Dominion,* 158; Schwarz, *Twice Condemned,* 88–89. See also Philip J. Schwarz, "Emancipators, Protectors, and Anomalies: Free Black Slaveowners in Virginia," *VMHB,* XCV (1987), 321; Brown, *Good Wives, Nasty Wenches,* 123.

46. Drysdale to BT, June 29, 1723, CO 5/1319, 111–117 (quotation on 112), transcript,

Relations between blacks and whites remained tense during the late 1720s. The persistent problem of slave assembly caused the General Assembly to improve the flawed militia acts in 1727. Before then, white men were required to furnish their own arms in drills and musters. Now, arms and ammunition would be provided for all white men from age twenty-one to fifty-one, and they were liable with little exception for muster once a year and for drills four times a year. White men were required to restrict the activities of blacks during the Christmas, Easter, and Whitsuntide holidays. At other times, they were "to patrole in such places as commanding officer shall think fit to direct" and disperse "all unusual concourse" of the enslaved. Company commanders were given discretion to patrol when they believed it necessary to prevent "any dangerous combinations which may be made amongst them at such meetings."[47]

One such meeting occurred during the winter of 1729 in Prince George County. William Harrison, sheriff and justice of the peace, disrupted an assembly of blacks, seizing some and dispersing the rest. In retaliation, the blacks burned Harrison's tobacco house on the following night. By doing so, the arsonists not only demonstrated their indignation but also indicated that they conceded no legitimacy to white rule. Like other cases involving acts of violence by blacks against the state, there was an informant; Peter, an enslaved black belonging to Nicholas Hatch, gave information leading to the discovery and punishment of the arsonists. This was the first instance of arson by a group, an act of resistance that would become more pronounced after 1740. Of this event, Gooch wrote: "We are in no small danger from our Slaves."[48]

The blacks' struggle for freedom reached a climax with the Chesapeake rebellion of 1730, the largest slave uprising during the colonial period. Blacks began massing throughout Virginia in September. During what John Brickell, the naturalist, characterized as "the most agreeable and pleasant Summer that has been known for many Years," whites, wrote Gooch to the Board of Trade, "discovered many meetings and Consulta-

LC; Darold D. Wax, "Negro Import Duties in Colonial Virginia . . . ," *VMHB*, LXXIV (1971), 35.

47. *SAL*, IV, 118–126, 197, 202 (quotations).

48. *JHB, 1727–1734, 1736–1740*, 63; Gooch to BT, Mar. 26, 1729, CO 5/1321, 110, VCRP; E. P. Thompson, "The Moral Economy of the English Crowd in the Eighteenth Century," *Past and Present*, no. 50 (February 1971), 76–136; Schwarz, *Twice Condemned*, 115–118.

tions of the Negros in several Parts of the Country in order to obtain their Freedom." The meetings had been spurred by a rumor that the king had sent by former governor Alexander Spotswood an edict emancipating the enslaved as soon as they became Christians, but the edict had been suppressed. The authorities were unable to determine the "first Author" of the rumor. The timing of the political activity suggests that it possessed the rudiments of a work slowdown, for the "alarm" occurred during the harvest. This "occasioned a good deal of Fatigue to the Militia and some loss in their Crops," wrote Gooch, "as happening at a time when their Labour and Industry were much wanted in their Grounds."[49]

That blacks assigned to Spotswood the role of emancipator is not surprising. The enslaved were likely aware of his part in prosecuting Frances Wilson for the murder of her enslaved woman Rose and his attempts to curb whites' unrestrained violence against blacks. But rumors often distort reality; by 1730, Spotswood had become a great landholder and slaveowner and had negotiated with the Indians to return fugitive blacks to Virginia. Also predictable was the belief among the enslaved, inspired by the increasing proselytism of the late 1720s and the example of earlier generations, that their conversion to Christianity should guarantee their freedom.[50]

Indeed, recently enslaved Christians from the Congo would have been quick to rally under the banner of liberty for Christians. The Kingdom of the Congo had sustained a Christian state from the era of King Nzinga a Kuwu and his son Nzinga Mbemba in the early sixteenth century. Owing in part to civil wars, both the kingdom and Christianity collapsed during the 1710s, when English merchants representing the South Sea Company earnestly began trafficking in "black Christians of the Congo." Congolese made up the majority of Africans enslaved by the English from 1710 to 1740, and it is likely that many found their identity in Christianity. Without doubt, a sizable number of Christians were sold in Virginia, for nearly half of the enslaved imported into the colony from 1727 to 1740 came from Congo. Many of these captives took pride in their Christian heritage and comprehended the rumored emancipation in 1730 in religious terms.[51]

49. John Brickell, *The Natural History of North-Carolina; with an Account of the Trade, Manners, and Customs of the Christian and Indian Inhabitants* . . . (1737) (New York, 1969), 25; Gooch to BT, Sept. 14, 1730, CO 5/1322, 156, VCRP.

50. James Blair to the bishop of London, June 28, 1729, FPP/15, 109, Gooch to the bishop of London, July 20, 1730, FPP/13, 131, VCRP; Schwarz, *Twice Condemned,* 79.

51. John K. Thornton, "'I Am the Subject of the King of Congo': African Political Ide-

The insurrection threatened in early September came to fruition six weeks later. For blacks, ill disposed and uneasy in their condition, the possibility of freedom was "sufficient to Incite them to Rebellion." Two hundred assembled in Norfolk and Princess Anne Counties, where they chose "Officers to Command them" in their "intended Insurrection." This strategy could have reflected the Congolese martial pattern in waging war, which not only included elections but also the practice of dividing participants into units under officers. They planned their breakout on a Sunday while the whites were unarmed at church and thus most vulnerable.[52]

More than three hundred of the rebels escaped en masse into the Dismal Swamp, John Brickell wrote, "where they commit[ted] many outrages against the [white] *Christians*" and "did a great deal of Mischief in that Province [of Virginia] before they were suppressed." The authorities, with the aid of Indians, put down the rebellion quickly and violently and recruited Indians to hunt down the fugitives. The Pasquotanks, in particular, were noted to be "very expeditious" in finding the rebels. The pursuers meted out vigilante justice. "I saw four and twenty of these *Negroes* hanged in Virginia for conspiring against their Masters," Brickell wrote. They "had taken Sanctuary in the Woods for some time before they were discovered, or hunted out by the *Indians.*" Governor Gooch reported the aftermath of the insurrection to the crown. In addition to the twenty-four that Brickell saw summarily hanged in the woods, the five leaders were captured, tried, and hanged. The rounding up of the "most Suspected" in other counties where they were less well organized had brought the blacks into "desperate Combinations," leading to the capture of the principal conspirators.[53]

Gooch reasoned that the "greater boldness" shown by the enslaved in meeting together was the result of a security breakdown: the failure of overseers and patrols to enforce the statutes concerning slave mobility and

ology and Haitian Revolution," *Journal of World History,* IV (1993), 188–189; Thornton, "African Dimensions of the Stono Rebellion," *American Historical Review,* XCVI (1991), 1104–1106; Kulikoff, *Tobacco and Slaves,* 321–322.

52. Gooch to the bishop of London, May 28, 1731, FPP/15, 111, VCRP; Gooch to BT, Feb. 12, 1731, CO 5/1322, 161, VCRP; John K. Thornton, "The Art of War in Angola, 1575–1680," *Comparative Studies in Society and History,* XXX (1988), 366; Thornton, "'I Am the Subject of the King of Congo,'" *Jour. World Hist.,* IV (1993), 200.

53. Brickell, *Natural History of North-Carolina,* 357; Gooch to BT, Feb. 12, 1731, CO 5/1322, 161, VCRP (Gooch's earlier dispatches on the insurrection were lost at sea).

the failure of county authorities to publish militia responsibilities as the law required. Once again Gooch called out the militia to patrol two to three times a week to prevent night meetings. With the advice of the Council of State, he ordered all overseers and militiamen "repairing to their respective Churches or Chappels on Sundays or Holy Days to carry with them their Arms to prevent any Surprise thereof in their absence when slaves are most at Liberty and have greatest opportunity for that purpose." He berated the slaveholders for their negligence in policing the enslaved and threatened that the grand jury would prosecute owners "who either by Connivance encourage or by Negligence Suffer any unlawful assembly of Slaves at their plantations or who knowing of such unlawful meeting neglect to suppress [it]." With the attempted insurrection fresh in his mind, Gooch sought to safeguard the mouth of the James River with a fort or a "substantial Battery . . . [with] some Cannon and other Stores" to guard against piracy during times of peace and, especially, to "secure us against the Insurrection of our slaves, the Enemy I do assure your Lordships we have great reason to be apprehensive of."[54]

The mass breakout in the Chesapeake rebellion of 1730 ended a decade of rebellion in which whites combined tactics of preemption and repression in suppressing blacks. But they could not deal with the threat of insurrection alone; they also recruited Indians to catch fugitive blacks and to prevent the establishment of maroon societies in the woods, swamps, and mountains.

We Have Mountains in Virginia Too

The forests in the border region between Virginia and North Carolina served as hiding places for black fugitives for months at a time—at the planters' expense. Moreover, many white Virginians feared that these outlaws would establish permanent maroon settlements in the area. The counties most exposed to danger were those in the frontier region, Spotsylvania, Brunswick, and Prince William Counties, shadowed by the Blue Ridge Mountains. This was also the area most vulnerable to Indian attack. The English, increasingly anxious about Indian invasion and black

54. Gooch to BT, July 10, 1731, CO 5/1322, 202, VCRP; Gooch, "A Proclamation for Preventing the Unlawful Meetings and Combinations of Negroes and Other Slaves," Oct. 28, 1730, CO 5/1322, 405, transcript, LC. See also Peter H. Wood, *Black Majority: Negroes in Colonial South Carolina from 1670 through the Stono Rebellion* (New York, 1974), 301–303.

insurrection, thus over time developed a strategy to deal with these two threats. They increased military preparedness in this most vulnerable region, enlisted Indians in hunting maroons in the woods and mountains, and promoted settlement in the areas between the mountains and tobacco settlements. The manipulation of the Indians was the key to this strategy, first in opening up plantation settlement and protecting the land from attack and then in capturing and securing the enslaved.[55]

As early as 1712, during the Tuscarora War in North Carolina (1711–1713), Governor Spotswood "dreaded" the combined threat of black insurrection and Indian invasion. Yet he found the General Assembly "stupidly adverse" to raising the funds necessary to guard "against either of these two events." He took the children of the tributary Indians as hostages and, exercising "great Prudence," brought them to the College of William and Mary, where they were educated in Christianity. Their lives depended on their nations' pledge not to engage in war. After the war, Spotswood relocated the tributary Indians near Fort Christiana on the Meherrin River to intimidate both the blacks escaping to the mountains and "the skulking parties" of the Five Nations of the Iroquois Confederacy (which included the Senecas, Cayugas, Onondagas, Oneidas, and Mohawks) who were using the eastern side of the Blue Ridge Mountains as a road for their fur-hunting expeditions. Also, to guard against escaping blacks, the commissioners of the Indian trade "seated" the Winyaws on the Santee River for the express purpose of "keeping the Negroes there in Awe."[56]

To serve as a buffer between the blacks and the mountains and to block the southern migration of the Iroquois in search of furs and captives, the first white settlement in the piedmont, Germanna, was established in 1714

---

55. Eugene D. Genovese, *From Rebellion to Revolution: Afro-American Slave Revolts in the Making of the Modern World* (Baton Rouge, La., 1979), 101; Wood, *Black Majority*, 301–303; Herbert Aptheker, "Maroons within the Present Limits of the United States," *Jour. Negro Hist.*, XXIV (1939), 168; Mullin, *Flight and Rebellion*, 41–46.

56. Spotswood to BT, Oct. 15, 1712, in William L. Saunders, ed., *The Colonial Records of North Carolina*, 10 vols. (Raleigh, N.C., 1886–1890), I, 886; William Byrd, *Histories of the Dividing Line betwixt Virginia and North Carolina* (ca. 1728–1736), ed. William K. Boyd (1929; reprint, New York, 1967), 116, 118; W. L. McDowell, ed., *Journals of the Commissioners of the Indian Trade: September 20, 1710–August 29, 1718*, Colonial Records of South Carolina, 2d Ser., *The Indian Books* (Columbia, S.C., 1955), 80. The commissioners also proposed building a "small Factory" for trading purposes. See Daniel K. Richter, "War and Culture: The Iroquois Experience," *WMQ*, 3d Ser., XL (1983), 557–558; Richter, *The Ordeal of the Longhouse: The Peoples of the Iroquois League in the Era of European Colonization* (Chapel Hill, N.C., 1992), 238–240; James Axtell, *The Invasion Within: The Contest of Cultures in Colonial North America* (Oxford, 1985), 191, 262.

with forty Germans on the Rapidan River, twenty miles above the falls of the Rappahannock. In 1721, Spotswood reported that blacks from this town, including some of "his own" employed as furnace workers at a mining and smelting concern, had run away to the Blue Ridge Mountains, where they were hard to apprehend. Their increase there would have ill consequences for Virginia, he wrote, and, especially, would be a "detriment to Frontier Inhabitants." As a result, he requested that the governors of Maryland, Pennsylvania, and New York enlist their Indian allies to hunt for the fugitives and reward them whether the blacks were brought back dead or alive—an offer likewise extended to the deputies on patrol.[57]

In an attempt to bring under control runaways, to separate warring Indians, and to protect white settlement, in 1721 New York governor William Burnet struck an agreement in Spotswood's name with the sachems of the Five Nations. They agreed that the Indians under their dominion would stay on the western side of the "high Mountains" (the Appalachians, also known as the "Great Mountains" and, previously, the Cherokee Mountains) and the northern side of the Potomac River, unless the governor granted them permission to enter eastern Virginia. The Indians also promised to assist the colonists in hunting for fugitive blacks in the "Great Mountains" and to deliver them to the whites at Germanna. Notice would be sent to the deputies on patrol to notify the Indian hunting parties that they should capture fugitives on their return home. As a token of their consent, the Indians were given a belt of wampum. The English promised that the Indians would be "well rewarded." But the sachems of the Five Nations did not capture the black outlaws, reporting in September 1722 that they were unable to do so "because they lye very much out of our way."[58]

In response, Governor Spotswood traveled six hundred miles to Albany, New York, reminding the sachems of their agreement not to enter Virginia without a passport from the governor and to find the maroons who had escaped from Germanna. As an incentive, he proposed that fugitives be returned to George Mason's house on the Potomac River, where the Iroquois would receive a bounty for each runaway of "one good Gun and two Blankets, or the value thereof." Spotswood laid on the table five guns and five hundred flints to sweeten the deal, but not before he ac-

57. *EJCCV*, III, 549–550.

58. Ibid.; John Romeyn Brodhead, ed., *Documents Relative to the Colonial History of the State of New-York*, 15 vols. (Albany, N.Y., 1853–1887), V, 635, 637–639, 676; Richter, "War and Culture," *WMQ*, 3d Ser., XL (1983), 552–556.

cused the Iroquois of "hostilities, Robberies, and Repeated Breeches" of the treaty agreed upon the year before. He singled out the depredations against Colonel Robert Hicks of Virginia, in which the Indians murdered his enslaved black, killed seventy of his horses, and stole a "considerable cargoe of Goods." Spotswood, in the interest of a renewed relationship, offered to bury these "past misdeeds."[59]

The Five Nations agreed to the renewal of the treaty. They owned up to their theft of Colonel Hicks's property but said that they lost it through negligence in setting fire to dry woods. They offered to make reparations to Hicks when they could afford it, but they made no mention of his murdered black. They again accepted the boundaries north of the Potomac and west of the "great Ridge," understanding that trespassing could result in death or deportation as enslaved laborers. They agreed to return runaways to Mason's house but averred once again that the Germanna fugitives were not within their jurisdiction: the outlaws "may be had more easily by other Indians."[60]

The "other Indians" referred to by the sachems included the Cherokees. In September 1730, the seven chiefs of the Cherokee Nation, traditional enemies of the Iroquois, in negotiating a treaty with the English resigned themselves to the English presence on both sides of the "Great Mountains." The treaty included a fugitive slave clause: "If any Negro

59. George Mason had led a fifty-horse exploratory expedition across the Blue Ridge Mountains for which he was made a Knight of the Golden Horseshoe by Alexander Spotswood in 1716. To commemorate the event, Spotswood gave him a brooch inscribed "Sic Juvat Transcendere Montes" ("For your service in crossing the mountains"). At the treaty meeting in 1722, Spotswood gave to the Indian spokesman a golden horseshoe, which symbolized the key to Virginia (Helen Hill, *George Mason, Constitutionalist* [Cambridge, 1938], 10-11). Spotswood was relieved as governor while in New York in 1722 to negotiate a treaty with the Five Nations; see Brodhead, *Colonial History of New-York,* V, 674-676; Sarah S. Hughes, *Surveyors and Statesmen: Land Measuring in Colonial Virginia* (Richmond, Va., 1979), 74.

60. These efforts could not have been very successful. New York governors William Burnet in 1723 and William Cosby in 1733 requested that the Five Nations return the fugitive blacks that they had heard were among them, without result. "To the best of our knowledge," the sachems replied in 1733, "we know not that there is one among any of the Six Nations" (Kenneth W. Porter, "Relations between Negroes and Indians within the Present Limits of the United States," *Jour. Negro Hist.,* XVII [1932], 308). See Porter, "Notes Supplementary to 'Relations between Negroes and Indians,'" ibid., XVIII (1933), 290; Brodhead, *Colonial History of New-York,* V, 675-676, VII, 964-965, 968; William Renwick Riddell, "The Slave in Early New York," *Jour. Negro Hist.,* XIII (1928), 82. The Five Nations became the Six Nations after the Tuscaroras, trekking north from North Carolina after 1715, joined the confederacy.

slaves shall run away into the woods from their English masters the Cherokee Indians shall endeavour to apprehend them and either bring them
back to the Plantation from whence they run away or to the Governor." For
the privilege of capturing and returning fugitive blacks, the English gave
to the Cherokees "a box of vermillion ten thousand of gun flints and six
dozen hatchets," and, as the bounty for each black returned, the Cherokees asked for a gun and a matchcoat (from the Powhatan *matshcore*), a
loose-fitting mantle made of furs and feathers.[61]

During the negotiations, the Cherokees contrasted images of the chain
and the rope to distinguish themselves from the English. After hearing the
English present a series of linking metaphors—a chain without "rust or
foulness" fastened to the breast of the king, his nation, his council, his provincial authorities, and his people and a "chain of friend ship" fastened
to the king and the Cherokee Nation—the Cherokees produced a "small
rope." They said that the Cherokees had no need for chains; Colonel
Robert Johnson, governor of South Carolina, could attest that this was
all that they used to bind their enslaved, and they reminded the English:
"You have iron chains for yours." The Cherokees manipulated the metaphor of a chain to denote the bind that the English authorities were in
because of their dependence on the Cherokees to capture enslaved blacks
that English masters themselves could not control. In the end, they capitulated tongue in cheek: "However if we catch your slaves we shall bind
them as well as we can and deliver them to our friends again and have no
pay for it."[62]

After these treaties, Indians routinely searched for fugitive blacks, but
only after the search was deemed futile by white bounty hunters. John
Brickell explained how invaluable the Indians were in finding blacks who
"frequently run away from their Masters into the Woods, . . . as it happened in *Virginia* not long since [in 1730]." The Indians, who knew the
headwaters of rivers six or seven hundred miles away from their homes,
could find a fugitive in one-tenth the time that it took white men. Moreover, they were relentless in their pursuit, continuing to search for the
runaways until "they destroy[ed] or hunt[ed] them out of the Woods."[63]

61. The Seven Indian Chiefs of the Cherokee Nation, Sept. 7, 9, 1730, in Saunders, ed.,
Colonial Records of North Carolina, III, 129–133 (quotations on 130, 131).

62. Ibid., 130, 132–133. The Five Nations referred to their alliance with the English as
the "Covenant Chain." See Brodhead, *Colonial History of New-York*, V, 638.

63. Herbert Aptheker, "Maroons within the Present Limits of the United States," *Jour.
Negro Hist.*, XXIV (1939), 168; Brickell, *Natural History of North-Carolina*, 356–357.

The Indians shoot blacks on sight in the woods or "take Pleasure in putting them to the most exquisite Torments," claimed Brickell. He represented this cruelty as the Indians' "natural aversion" to blacks. Possibly, the Pasquotanks, who were the most likely bounty hunters in the Dismal Swamp, acted out of frustration and displaced aggression. They had once raised milk cows and churned butter until they were dispossessed of their land. Suffering at the hands of whites who "not only beat and abuse them, but commonly rob them of their *Furs, Deer Skins,* and other commodities," they could have reacted violently by hunting down runaway blacks. If the tone of the Five Nations was cautious and the Cherokees ironic, the Pasquotanks, according to Brickell, were exuberant: they reveled in the chase.[64]

The use of Indian slave catchers in the Dismal Swamp and the woods dividing North Carolina and Virginia terrified blacks. When they learned that Indians were on their trail, the runaways often surrendered to the "injured" whites rather than risk capture by the Indians. Brickell thought that this terror was decisive in maintaining security in Virginia, discouraging "great Numbers" from becoming outliers. Without the Indians to "suppress them when they Rebel against their Masters, which they frequently do in Virginia," Brickell believed, the blacks "wou'd destroy" the planters.[65]

Despite the militia and the fear of Indian bounty hunters, fugitives still attempted to establish settlements in the Blue Ridge Mountains. In one instance, about fifteen blacks belonging to a new plantation at the head of the James River escaped to the mountains, carrying with them provisions, clothing, bedding, and tools as well as arms and ammunition. They built shelters and had just begun to clear the ground when their owner, with a search party, having made "such a diligent Pursuit," found them in a "very Obscure place." The posse forced the surrender of the blacks after an exchange of shots, during which one of the maroons was wounded. The fugitives' efforts were in the tradition of the aborted escape plots of 1687, 1710, 1713, and 1722 in which the goal was to break out of slavery, using guns if necessary, and escaping to a region far from the authorities.

William Byrd concurred with Brickel's assessment: "It is certain many Slaves Shelter themselves in this Obscure Part of the World" (Byrd, *Histories of the Dividing Line,* ed. Boyd, 56).

64. Brickell, *Natural History of North-Carolina,* 314–315.

65. Ibid., 263, 315, 356–357; William S. Willis, "Divide and Rule: Red, White, and Black in the Southeast," *Jour. Negro Hist.,* XLVIII (1963), 162–171.

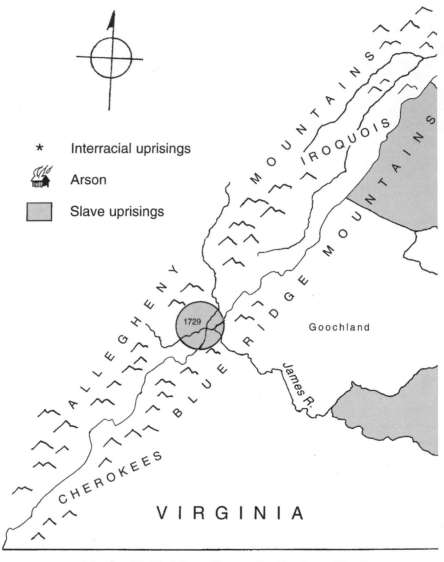

Map 2. Rebellion and Containment, 1663–1730. *Drawn by Richard Stinely*

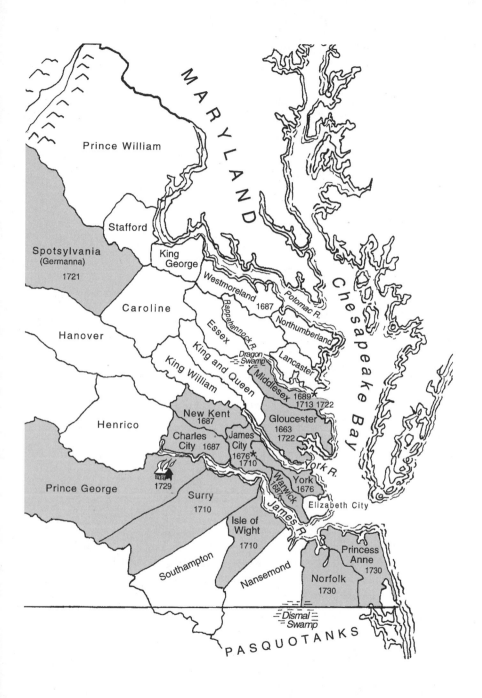

Prince William

Stafford

Spotsylvania
(Germanna)
1721

Caroline

Hanover

Henrico

Prince George

MARYLAND

Chesapeake Bay

King
George

Westmoreland
1687

Potomac R.

Rappahannock R.

Essex

King and Queen

King William

Northumberland

Lancaster

*Dragon
Swamp*

Middlesex
1689
1713 1722

New Kent
1687

Gloucester
1663
1722

Charles
City   1687

James
City
1676
1710

1729

Surry
1710

York R.

Warwick
1681

York
1676

Elizabeth City

Isle of
Wight
1710

James R.

Southampton

Nansemond

Norfolk
1730

Princess
Anne
1730

*Dismal
Swamp*

PASQUOTANKS

The whites, recognizing the danger that the fledgling settlement posed to the slave system, quickly destroyed it and returned the runaways to slavery.[66]

With the recently routed settlement in mind, Gooch wrote in 1729 that the Blue Ridge Mountains could prove as dangerous as the Blue Mountains in Jamaica, where maroons engaged the British in a protracted war; it was "certain that a very small number of Negroes once settled in those Parts, would very soon be encreas'd by the Accession of other Runaways and prove dangerous Neighbours to our frontier Inhabitants." He employed an adjutant at a salary of £150 per year to teach "the Officers in those Counties most expos'd to danger" to counter slave insurgency and reported: "I am training and exercising the Militia in the several Counties as the best means to deter our Slaves from endeavouring to make their Escape, and to suppress them if they should."[67]

William Byrd II, in letters to the earl of Egmont and Johan Rudolph in July 1736, gives evidence of the great planters' anxiety about the mountains as a base of rebellion for the enslaved and their desire to secure it with Europeans. Byrd reported: "We have mountains in Virginia too, to which they may retire as safely, and do as much mischief as they do in Jamaica." The English should encourage the settlement of foreign Protestants in the valleys as a buffer between the blacks and the mountains, he wrote, an opinion that he had developed as a young man. Settling the valley lands with Europeans, bearing capital to purchase land or working off an indenture, served both security and speculative purposes. Forts should be built to command passes through the mountains as a precaution against the loss of lives and money. This strategy would enable the planters to "engross" the western Indian trade, secure the silver mines, guard against invasion by the French, and "prevent the Negroes taking Refuge there, as they do in the Mountains of Jamaica." "These [maroons] will be more dangerous, because the French will be always ready to supply them with arms, and to make use of them against us upon all occasions."[68]

The General Assembly attempted to restrict further the movements of the enslaved with a new militia act in 1736. The existing law was not being

---

66. Gooch to BT, June 29, 1729, CO 5/1321, 9–12, VCRP; *EJCCV*, III, 553.

67. Gooch to BT, Mar. 26, June 29, 1729, CO 5/1321, 10, 110, VCRP.

68. William Byrd II to John Perceval, earl of Egmont, July 12, 1736, William Byrd II Letter Book, 1735–1736, VHS; Byrd to Johann Rudolph Ochs, July 15, 1736, in Marion Tinling, ed., *The Correspondence of the Three William Byrds of Westover, Virginia, 1684–1776*, 2 vols. (Charlottesville, Va., 1977), II, 490–492.

enforced, for attendance at muster "in great measure [had] ceased for near Fifteen Years past." The burgesses, sensitive to the needs of the small planters, explained that they had not enforced the law out of "Compassion," for it had been a burden on the poor, who had to attend muster both "armed and accoutred," leaving their crops when their labor was essential. For this reason, as over the last thirty years, the militia remained in the "same defenseless State."[69]

The burgesses thus wanted to pass the cost of security on to the great planters in the form of a poll tax on the enslaved while providing relief to the small and middling planters who participated in slave patrols. The burgesses did not include in the new bill—believing it "unequal"—the high fines on planters who were absent from the muster. Rather, they recommended a poll tax of six pence upon blacks for two years to buy arms for poorer whites. They also proposed that patrollers visit the slave quarters and that whites arm themselves when going to church "at certain Seasons; the want of which, has been long complained of." A militia act was also drawn up, establishing a formal patrol system for the first time and exempting patrollers from public levies. But the Council of State would not agree to the tax on the enslaved, which would fall heaviest on the great planters, nor to the patrollers' exemption from taxes, which would have lifted the tax burden from the small and middling planters, and the measures failed.[70]

In the same year, because the burgesses and the councillors were unable to come to terms, Gooch issued a proclamation restating what he had already said in 1730. With the Council of State's advice, his executive order of October 29, 1736, ordered the counties to strengthen the militia against the two primary threats: slave insurrection and Indian invasion. Musters were to be called when and where the county militia commanders thought necessary. The people were to be supplied with arms and ammunition, as the law prescribed, and were obligated to attend muster. County courts-martial were to enforce discipline by fines. Because the repression of slave insurrection was the central concern of the proclamation, Gooch ordered that the county commanders break up any "unusual Concourse" of blacks, "preventing any dangerous Combinations amongst them, especially during the Holy-Days, wherein they are exempted from Labour." Gooch recalled his earlier 1730 proclamation and ordered that all militia-

69. *JHB, 1727–1734, 1736–1740*, xxviii, 301–303 (quotations on 302, 303).
70. Ibid., 302.

men and officers carry "Arms, Ammunition, and Accoutrements" to their parish churches or chapels during holy days.[71]

By 1738, the General Assembly once again felt the need to revise the code for policing the enslaved. Burgesses from Spotsylvania County had proposed that a "white Overseer, or other white Person, be constantly kept at every Negro Quarter." The final bill required the militia, including free white males over twenty-one years old, to select a system of four-man teams "to patrol, and visit all negro quarters, and other places suspected of entertaining unlawful assemblies of slaves, servants, or other disorderly persons." The Council of State in 1739 was still adamantly against enlisting white servants in the militia "upon any pretence whatsoever" because the great planters remained suspicious of the alliance that might be forged between enslaved blacks and servants in Virginia.[72]

* * *

BLACKS WERE ever ready to resist and rebel to attain their freedom. The great planters were thus obliged to take preventive measures to repress the enslaved's resolve. County commissions sentenced rebels to gruesome, torturous deaths; the General Assembly ordered batteries built at the heads of the rivers; governors enlisted Indian nations to hunt out runaways in the woods, swamps, and mountains. This last development extended beyond Virginia, for the crown made treaties with Indian nations along the frontier from New York to the Carolinas for the return of fugitives to their respective jurisdictions.

The enslaved had thus threatened the order of Virginia society, touching the most sensitive source of the great planters' anxieties, their fear of a servile insurrection. This pressure continually threatened the elite class, who turned this threat of insurrection to their advantage by using it to divide, control, and set against each other blacks, Indians, and lower-class whites.

71. *EJCCV*, IV, 470–471.
72. *JHB, 1727–1734, 1736–1740,* 331; *SAL,* V, 19; *EJCCV,* V, 6.

CHAPTER 6

Class Conflicts,
1724-1740

He [George III] has waged cruel war against human nature itself,
violating it's most sacred rights of life and liberty in persons of a
distant people who never offended him, captivating and carrying
them into slavery in another hemisphere, or to incur miserable
death in their transportation thither.... Determined to keep open
a market where MEN should be bought and sold, he has prostituted his negative for suppressing every legislative attempt to prohibit or to restrain this execrable commerce.

—Thomas Jefferson, 1776

The dependence of Virginia's planters on enslaved blacks would lead to
an important question, one that would be a perennial source of contention
for the colonists and the crown, climaxing in Thomas Jefferson's deleted
clause in the Declaration of Independence cited above, which damns
George III for fastening the slave trade on the colonies. Were mercantile
interests or planter interests to blame for the upsurge in racial slavery?
Since no cargo of healthy enslaved laborers ever lacked buyers, not all
planters wanted to restrict importation. At first, the great planters alone
bought enslaved blacks, but by the 1720s small and middling planters,
especially those in the inferior tobacco-growing regions like the piedmont, began purchasing human labor. These newcomers, along with slave
traders, would oppose the great planters by agitating for a duty-free slave
trade, and the crown would support them to further mercantilist interests
in Great Britain.[1]

1. Merrill D. Peterson, ed., *Thomas Jefferson: Writings* (New York, 1984), 22; Thad W.
Tate, *The Negro in Eighteenth-Century Williamsburg* (Charlottesville, Va., 1965), 30;
Darold D. Wax, "Negro Import Duties in Colonial Virginia . . . ," *VMHB,* LXXIV (1971),
43; James Curtis Ballagh, *A History of Slavery in Virginia* (1902; reprint, New York, 1968),
11, 15n, 16–21.

Moreover, the ability of the British slave-trade merchants to maintain a duty-free slave trade would deprive the great planters of an essential device for controlling tobacco prices. Fewer imported enslaved Africans would have meant fewer hands to work in tobacco fields, decreasing production and thereby increasing the value of the crop. But merchants began to challenge the great planters' control of the hinterland by buying tobacco and trading enslaved blacks directly to smaller and parvenu planters, lowering the price of their chief commodity, tobacco.

Direct confrontation between the great planters and merchants over the regulation of the slave and tobacco trades would thus expose increasing class tensions within Virginia society. The new administration of Robert Walpole (1722–1740) would use these divisions to weaken the elite's provincial foundation, subordinating them to a colonial position. To curb the power of the great planters, policymakers began to promote a mercantile policy that placed the economic burden on the planters rather than the merchants: the advantage would go to the seller and creditor rather than to the buyer and debtor. At the same time, the great planters, consolidating their gains, planned policies that excluded lower-class whites from the benefits of slavery, even as they tried to instill in these lesser planters the discipline and deference necessary for repressing blacks.

So Sweet to Those Concerned

As noted previously, in 1723 the General Assembly, with the support of the great planters, passed "An Act for Laying Duty on Liquors and Slaves," which imposed a forty-shilling duty on imported enslaved laborers to restrict the trade in Virginia as well as to finance the colony's defense. The great planters, with their gangs of enslaved blacks, had a vested interest in restricting importation. Not only did they have adequate hands employed in tobacco production, but their enslaved were beginning to reproduce, increasing the workforce naturally. At the same time, as the most prominent participants in the slave trade, they had greater access to credit—given by the British merchants "according to the number of slaves . . . possessed"—and could replenish their supply of laborers as needed. London slave-trade merchant Richard Harris wrote that the "overgrown" planters had ample reserves of the enslaved to produce tobacco for their estates. "Divers merchants, Trading to Africa and Virginia" believe this act is in the "Interest of the great Planters who have passed this Law, so as thereby the Less Tobacco being made by . . . [the great planters] who are so well furnished with Hands would sell so much the Dearer at Markett."[2]

To be sure, slave traders protested vehemently against the 1723 duty. Basing their argument on their experience with the duty act of 1710, traders warned that the new tax would discourage the slave trade, hurting both the merchants and the colony, which required a rapid augmentation of labor. Tobacco production would decrease, as would customs, and prices would increase, all helping rivals in the tobacco market. Applying mercantilist principles, they argued that Virginia's problems should be considered within the context of the empire. The duty was in direct conflict with the Order in Council of 1717 forbidding American assemblies from passing laws that adversely affected the trade of Great Britain. They warned that a colonial duty, which even a friendly nation should not place on trade, was a dangerous precedent. They also noted that it was the policy of the mother country to collect revenue from duties placed on exports, but not on imports. The duty would discourage the importing and exporting of hemp and other naval stores by making labor expensive. Harris proffered that a duty of forty shillings made the slave trade to Virginia prohibitive when added to the inherent risks involved with "Infinite Casualtys and dangers which other Trades are not." Moreover, restricted access to new enslaved labor would discourage small and middling planters from planting tobacco. Robert Cary, a leading London merchant with ties to Virginia, argued that the duty could result in the "Ruin of the poorer planters" because they would not be able to buy a "sufficient Number" of blacks to cultivate their plantations, especially in the newer counties of Spotsylvania and Brunswick.[3]

2. Richard Harris to Allured Popple, Sept. 23, 1723, CO 5/1319, 128, transcript, LC; "A Memorial of Divers Merchants, Trading to Africa and Virginia," with "A Computation under Different Distinctions in What Manner and Proportion the Duty of Forty Shillings Head on Negroes to Be Imported into Virginia after March Next Will Affect the Negroe Trade in That Colony, Presented to the Commissioners of Trade and Plantations," Dec. 5, 1723, CO 5/1319, 130–132, transcript, LC; Minutes of BT, Jan. 17, 1723/4, CO 391/33, 11–19, transcript, LC; William Gooch to BT, June 8, 1728, CO 5/1321, 44–45, VCRP.

3. EJCCV, IV, 40. The following are transcripts at the LC: Mr. Lynn, secretary to the Royal African Company, to Mr. William Popple, secretary to BT, Aug. 29, 1723, CO 5/1319, 126–127; Harris to Allured Popple, Sept. 23, 1723, CO 5/1319, 128–129; "A Memorial of Divers Merchants," Dec. 5, 1723, CO 5/1319, 130–132; Petition of the Merchants of the City of Bristol, Presented to BT, Dec. 18, 1723, CO 5/1319, 140–141; Minutes of BT, Jan. 10, 17, 1723/4, CO 391/33, 10–19; "Petition of the Mayor, Alderman, and Merchants of the

Merchant interests drove the criticism of the great planters as a class, but the critique could just as readily have come from ambitious small and middling planters and those in newly settled regions. Although these planters wanted a good price for their tobacco, they had no interest in a duty that would raise prices on the enslaved. This predicament set up the elite's desire for a duty to control expansion because part of the problem had to do with the internal web of debt, with smaller planters depending on and owing money to the great planters. John Custis IV tried to explain the predilection to debt to Micajah Perry III, waxing wroth in 1721 that his financial situation would greatly improve if he could just get people to pay him his "just debts." "But," he added, "at this time it is the most difficult thing in notary to get one's debts in; people will buy Nigros at the same time they owes the money to other people." The great planters in the older regions were not buying blacks in 1723, observed Robert Carter; the "small folks and middling people have been the only buyers." But their influence did not extend to the chamber of the Board of Trade, as did that of the great planters, represented by colonial agents Peter Leheup and William Byrd II and their associates in the tobacco trade. On the other hand, their influence could be felt in Virginia. The assembly had passed the duty act of 1723 by a slim majority of two or three. Although the record does not indicate whether the vote was divided along regional lines, the nays probably came from the piedmont counties, where the small and middling planters had their strength and were purchasing the bulk of the enslaved.[4]

Not all merchants opposed the duty act of 1723. The London tobacco merchants, such as Micajah Perry III, who were associated with some of Virginia's most powerful families, favored the duty. Because they handled tobacco shipments, these merchants sought a higher price for their staple

Antient and Loyall Corporation and Port of Liverpool in the County of Lancaster, Traders to Guinea, Virginia and Other [of] His Majesties Forreign Plantations," Jan. 22, 1723/4, CO 5/1319, 158.

4. John Custis to Micajah Perry, John Custis Letter Book, 1717-1742, LC; Robert Carter to Perry, July 13, 1723, Robert Carter Letter Book, 1723-1724, typescript, CWF (see also *Southern Planter: A Monthly Periodical Devoted to Agriculture, Horticulture, and the Household Arts* [Richmond, Va.], II [February 1842], 41-42); Philip D. Morgan and Michael L. Nicholls, "Slaves in Piedmont Virginia, 1720-1790," *WMQ*, 3d Ser., XLVI (1989), 238-239. Carter was not thinking of Alexander Spotswood, who had contracted for four hundred slaves to be delivered from the Gambia on the *Dove* in 1723; see Walter Minchinton, Celia King, and Peter Waite, eds., *Virginia Slave-Trade Statistics, 1698-1775* (Richmond, Va., 1984), 48.

—a potential benefit of the duty act. In alliance with the great planters, they sought to maintain their role as guarantors in the Virginia trade. Harris wrote that as correspondents of the great planters their purpose was to "prevent and discourage the great" importation of the enslaved so that money usually drawn for bills by slave-trade merchants would remain in the hands of the tobacco merchants.[5]

They gave a number of reasons for supporting the duty. They recalled that the crown objected to neither the 1710 nor 1714 duty acts. A duty was simply a tried-and-true method to raise funds. In this case, the funds collected from the duty were necessary for settling the new piedmont counties and supporting the militia. They contended that the duty would not adversely affect British commerce, citing Maryland as an example of a tobacco colony where a comparable duty had not hurt the slave trade. If the duty was rejected, the need for revenue would result in a property tax placed directly on tobacco or enslaved laborers, and the tobacco market, already heavily taxed, would not bear the burden. The duty was not prohibitive, given its proportion to the price of blacks; on the contrary, the improved price of tobacco would most likely help the trade, for "the Virginians [were] always ready to buy Slaves when they have money."[6]

The key question for the crown to consider was whether the forty-shilling duty created a burden on trade that diminished royal revenues. Richard West, the royal attorney, reported to the Board of Trade that he found no other objection to the duty set in Virginia than its mercantile effect. After considering the petitions and counterarguments of the merchants, the Virginia planters, and the crown's attorney, the Board of Trade recommended a repeal of the Virginia duty, listing three chief objections: its "great Hindrance" to the slave trade, its burden on the "poorer Planters," and its discouragement to the development of naval stores, especially in Brunswick and Spotsylvania Counties, "where great Numbers of Negroes will be wanting." The board had accepted in toto the slave-trade merchants' argument. The Privy Council, in turn, recommended and ap-

5. "Memorial of Several Merchants of London Trading to Virginia and Others," Jan. 9, 1723/4, CO 5/1319, 142, transcript, LC; "Meeting of the Lords Commissioners of Trade and Plantations to Discuss the Duty," Nov. 19, 1723, CO 391/32, 212–217, transcript, LC; Minutes of BT, Jan. 10, 17, 1723/4, CO 391/33, 10–19, transcript, LC; Harris to Allured Popple, Sept. 23, 1723, CO 5/1319, 128, transcript, LC.

6. "Memorial of Several Merchants," Jan. 9, 1723/4, CO 5/1319, 142, transcript, LC.

proved the repeal of the duty in 1724. The stiff opposition of the slave-trade merchants had defeated the great planters' attempt to raise revenue and control production by limiting slave importation.[7]

The crown's revocation of the duty coincided with the broader strategy of Prime Minister Walpole to assert fiscal control over colonial assemblies. His ministry had not been able to end the practice of assemblies' nominating revenue officers, for example, but could use the factionalism introduced by the interest of the slave-trade merchants and lesser planters to rein in the great planters' power. Earlier efforts by Governor Alexander Spotswood to control the elite on the council had failed. The great planters had vigorously defended their turf against Spotswood, who raised their ire with his prosecution of Frances Wilson for the murder of her enslaved woman Rose, his opposition to councillors' serving as jurists in oyer and terminer cases, and his dismissal of William Byrd II from the Council of State. They succeeded in having Wilson acquitted of the murder charge and preserving their tenure as jurists in the oyer and terminer courts. Byrd and Commissary James Blair lobbied the crown for Byrd's reinstatement. As a result of their agitation, the crown recalled Spotswood, just as he moved from contentious governor to fellow great planter. Walpole chose subsequent governors Hugh Drysdale (1723–1726) and William Gooch (1727–1749), who were careful not to offend local interests but who used political suasion to negotiate consensus and conformity to the crown's position.[8]

Meanwhile, Virginia's economic problems intensified in 1724, the only year in which tobacco fetched high prices in this decade. Governor Drysdale wrote to the Board of Trade that a violent storm in August had almost destroyed the tobacco crop. The limited supply of tobacco would cause a rise in prices, which would lead to expansion into "new ground," where planters could expect a better return on their investment than in the "old

7. Richard West to BT, Dec. 10, 1723, CO 5/1319, 143–144, transcript, LC; Order in Council, Court of Saint James's, Apr. 30, 1724, PC 2/88, 506–507, transcript, LC; Minchinton, King, and Waite, eds., *Virginia Slave-Trade Statistics*, xiv; John Mickle Hemphill II, "Virginia and the English Commercial System, 1689–1733" (Ph.D. diss., Princeton University, 1964), 71; Representation of BT to the king, Jan. 29, 1723/4, CO 5/1365, 269–271, transcript, LC.

8. James A. Henretta, *"Salutary Neglect": Colonial Administration under the Duke of Newcastle* (Princeton, N.J., 1972), 17, 27; Jeremy Black, *British Foreign Policy in the Age of Walpole* (Edinburgh, 1985), 99–100; Michael Jubb, "Economic Policy and Economic Development," in Black, ed., *Britain in the Age of Walpole* (London, 1984), 123–124.

impoverished settlements." During the year, the colony invested in only 464 newly enslaved Africans, but, owing to the expected price increase, importation almost doubled in 1725 to 856 shackled recruits.[9]

The assembly, discouraged by the low price of tobacco after 1724 and hoping to raise revenue, once again imposed a forty-shilling duty on the enslaved in March 1728 with "An Act for Laying a Duty on Slaves Imported." The importation of 6,614 blacks during the preceding season, 1726–1727, was also a contributing factor in precipitating the duty. The responses in the two legislative branches to the bill manifested divergent class interests in Virginia. The Council of State, representing the great planters, was especially interested in the duty's passage because it would enhance the vested value of slave property. The burgesses, cognizant of this consequence and backed by the interest of small and middling planters in maintaining duty-free trade, used the issue as a lever to obtain a pay hike for themselves. They refused to pass the bill until an agreement was struck at the next session to pay them in money rather than tobacco.[10]

The battle in London in 1728 over the duty was not as intense as it had been in 1724. Although the issues were just as important, the great planters halfheartedly defended their position and were unable to muster new evidence for the necessity of the tax. The leadership of the great planters had dissipated. By 1728, Edmund Jenings's senility forced his removal as council president, James Blair was seventy-six years old, and Philip Ludwell and Nathaniel Harrison had died. Sensing this decline, the burgesses moved to assert greater authority in the General Assembly. The Council of State, demonstrating the resignation of the great planters, did not even provide instructions to its agent, John Randolph, who pleaded no contest before the Board of Trade. With precedent on their side, the slave-trade merchants were determined to deter the great planters' efforts to employ the duty. They protested the duty as contrary to the crown's instructions to the governor and asked the crown to enjoin Governor Gooch from allowing this or any other act "prejudicial" to the slave trade and the trade of Great Britain and "highly Injurious to the true Interest of the Plantations."[11]

9. Governor Hugh Drysdale to BT, Jan. 29, 1724, CO 5/1319, 425, transcript, LC; Minchinton, King, and Waite, eds., *Virginia Slave-Trade Statistics,* xiv.

10. *JHB, 1727–1734, 1736–1740,* xvii, xviii, 131–133, 139, 145, 165, 188, 219, 221–222, 225, 233.

11. Warren Billings, John E. Selby, and Thad W. Tate, *Colonial Virginia: A History* (New York, 1986), 234–236; "Meeting of the Lords Commissioners of Trade and Planta-

The crown's attorney, Francis Fane, submitted a legal opinion that embodied the slave-trade merchants' arguments. Fane recalled that the importation of the enslaved to Virginia from 1710 to 1718 was "inconsistent" and reminded the crown of Virginia's position in the British colonial system. The duty should not be allowed, he argued, because it would "discourage" merchants from sending a "sufficient number" of blacks to Virginia. "This Colony cannot Subsist or be improved" unless the "planters are furnished with large and constant supplies of Negroes and at the Easiest Rates."[12]

After review, the Board of Trade sent its objections to the Privy Council. The commissioners, recalling the issues raised in the 1723 act, determined that the duty would discourage settlement in the two new counties of Spotsylvania and Brunswick, "as the Poorer People will not be able to buy Sufficient Stocks of Negroes, should they be charged with this Duty." The Privy Council, in turn, repealed the act because it restrained trade. That the matter might not surface again, the Board of Trade sent an order to the colonies stating mercantile policy. They advised the assemblies not to pass import duties on the enslaved that "do in some Measure enhance the Price of Labour and consequently the Price of Sev[era]l Commodities produc'd in the Plantations, Wherein Our Neighbours rival Us in Foreign Markets."[13]

The crown's rejection of the 1723 and 1728 slave-duty acts dealt a blow to the great-planter class, severely weakening its control of the Atlantic economy. The dovetailing of the interests of the slave-trade merchants and the crown hindered the planters' attempt to deal with the tobacco economy by restricting the slave trade. The great planters could, at first, rest assured that the market would curtail the slave trade: only 691 blacks were purchased between 1728 and 1731. But, with the expansion of the trade

---

tions to Discuss the Slave Duty Act of 1728," May 21, 1729, CO 391/38, 128–129, transcript, LC; "Petition of the Severall Merchants of London Trading to the Coast of Africa and Your Majestys Plantations," "Petition of the Incorporated Society of Merchants in the City of Bristol," "Petition of the Severall Merchants of Liverpool Trading to the Coast of Africa and Your Majesty's Plantations," "Order in Privy Council to the Lords Commissioners of Trade and Plantations" [enclosures], Sept. 26, 1728, CO 5/1321, 62–73 (quotations on 71), transcript, LC.

12. Francis Fane to BT, Dec. 10, 1728, CO 5/1321, 108–109, 217, transcript, LC.

13. BT to the queen, May 23, 1729, CO 5/1366, 28–29, transcript, LC; Order in Council, July 31, 1729, PC 2/91, 37, transcript, LC; Order in Council, Oct. 14, 1729, CO 391/38, 261–263, transcript, LC.

to smaller planters, by 1732 the total number of imported blacks almost doubled to 1,287.[14]

Gooch, responding to the revitalized slave trade, devised a new strategy for raising revenue and restricting importation. He advised the assembly that, although the crown had been explicit in its instructions prohibiting a duty on the enslaved paid by the importer, it had not proscribed a tax on the buyer. The great planters thus regained control of slave importation to Virginia in 1732 by passing the tax burden on to local buyers as an ad valorem assessment of 5 percent, which increased to 10 percent in 1740.[15]

The planters' appetite for enslaved laborers prompted them to avoid regulations and default on debts. Robert Carter reported in 1736 that "diverse fraudulent Concealments" of enslaved blacks shipped into Virginia from the British West Indies and continental colonies evaded entry into the records. Also, the Naval Office collected no duty for captives shipped in "for their own Use," which was clearly a loophole for great planters who could order enslaved blacks from their correspondents on their own account. Another accounting by Carter from 1736 to 1738 compiled a four-page list of persons in arrears, for a total debt of £1,399. Despite the ad valorem tax, the number of enslaved blacks imported into Virginia from 1733 to 1740 was the highest to date: 16,522 captives. Small and middling planters invested every penny of their spare capital in them.[16]

Because the great planters were often the source of credit for the smaller planters, the indebtedness of these lesser planters undermined the great planters' credit. The merchants, in turn, had increasing difficulty collecting debts from their Virginia correspondents. This difficulty was rooted in the law of entail. Since both land and the enslaved were entailed, merchants were unable to seize them if a decedent correspondent defaulted on a loan, making the bulk of a great planter's estate off-limits.

John Baylor, for example, correspondent of Isaac Hobhouse and Company and eulogized as the "great negro seller, and in all respects the greatest merchant we had among us," left an estate of entailed land and enslaved laborers valued at £6,500 to his nephew, the son of his brother Robert. At

14. Minchinton, King, and Waite, eds., *Virginia Slave-Trade Statistics*, xv.

15. *EJCCV*, IV, 265; *JHB*, *1727–1734*, *1736–1740*, xxiii, 116, 188, 219, 225, 233, 333, 407; *SAL*, IV, 310–322; Wax, "Negro Import Duties in Colonial Virginia," *VMHB*, LXXIV (1971), 31–37.

16. *JHB*, *1727–1734*, *1736–1740*, 259, 384; Minchinton, King, and Waite, eds., *Virginia Slave-Trade Statistics*, xv; Allan Kulikoff, *Tobacco and Slaves: The Development of Southern Cultures in the Chesapeake, 1680–1800* (Chapel Hill, N.C., 1986), 82–85.

the time of his death in 1723, Baylor was heavily indebted to Isaac Hobhouse and Company for the enslaved Africans and goods extended to him for sale to great planters (which were then resold to lesser planters). Baylor had employed at least thirteen ships in his business and supplied his stores in Gloucester, King and Queen, and New Kent Counties from his principal warehouse, "Baylors" on the Mattapony River. The Bristol ships that he used — *Twerton, Prince Eugene, Anne and Sarah, Little John, Hunter, Greyhound, Berkley,* and *Calabar* — delivered 2,163 Africans, principally from the Bight of Biafra, from 1718 to 1721. This supply was almost one-half of the 5,170 Africans that arrived on thirty-five ships during the period of expansion following the expiration of the £5 duty in 1718. The guardians of the estate, Robert Baylor and Augustine Moore, a great planter from New Kent County, had difficulty collecting from their clients in order to satisfy the balance owed to Hobhouse. Moore wrote to Hobhouse on May 3, 1723, that their efforts to rein in the delinquents had led to "Nothing but disappointments here [in Virginia] and that Chiefly from Some of our Great Men." But the executors had little incentive to pay Baylor's debts. Without the force of law, they refused to sell new tobacco or land. The estate did manage to pay John Dixon, an agent of Hobhouse, £300 in 1723 but failed to collect another £150 due that year. After three years of legal haggling, Dixon believed the company would not receive half of what it was owed unless the land was sold, which, given the law, was highly unlikely. Although the Baylors had a vested interest in maintaining the estate intact, Robert, hoping to secure his brother's lucrative commercial correspondence, offered to pay off "as fast as the debts are rec[eive]d." He assured the company that "if at any time here after y[ou] should think me worthy of Serveing you in any Commission business . . . none should be more faithfull and Just."[17]

The Baylor matter ended favorably for the merchants, yet it did not solve their debt-collection problems associated with entail. The merchants thus began to look for a legal remedy. They usually granted credit based on the number of enslaved laborers a planter owned, yet they had no way of knowing whether the enslaved were entailed. William Gooch observed in

17. Louis B. Wright, ed., *Letters of Robert Carter, 1720–1727: The Commercial Interests of a Virginia Gentleman* (San Marino, Calif., 1940), 54; Walter E. Minchinton, ed., "The Virginia Letters of Isaac Hobhouse, Merchant of Bristol," *VMHB,* LXVI (1958), 291, 292, 299; Minchinton, King, and Waite, eds., *Virginia Slave-Trade Statistics,* 43, 45, 47, 49, 51; W. G. Stanard, ed., "Abstracts of Virginia Land Patents," *VMHB,* VI (1898–1899), 297–299.

1728 that "many Creditors would be defrauded and especially the British merchants, who can't be informed or always made acquainted with such Settlements." Consequently, the merchants, acting less like commercial partners than colonial rivals, were able to persuade Parliament to pass the Colonial Debts Act of 1732, despite the great planters' overwhelming opposition. Debtors' property, including land and enslaved laborers, now could be seized. The great planters found the act "threatening," especially because a creditor could simply present an oath before a British magistrate to prove his claim in court.[18]

The merchants' debt-collection strategies, culminating in the Colonial Debts Act, made the great planters feel like quarry and contributed to their declining status in the 1730s, when merchants forced them to sell off land and enslaved blacks formerly protected by entail. The effect of the act was evident in the deteriorating relationship between business associates Micajah Perry, author of the Colonial Debts Act, and William Byrd II. The history of the Parke estate, which Byrd inherited from the family of his wife, Lucy Parke, explains Byrd's financial woes. He got more than he bargained for by assuming both the debt of his father-in-law, Daniel Parke, and the responsibility of "Nigros all dead and past their Labor." In 1736, Byrd expressed biting criticism of Perry when Byrd was forced to sell land and blacks to satisfy a debt to "that hungry magistrate." As of 1740, Byrd had reduced the debt to one thousand pounds, but Perry, impatient for the balance, continued to press him. Byrd wrote that he might yet again have to sell blacks to satisfy Perry's importunity.[19]

During this period of expansion, the great planters believed that the slave trade was destabilizing Virginia. At least two of them, anticipating Jefferson, wished in 1736, when 3,125 blacks entered Virginia, that Parliament would step in and end the trade. Indeed, hoping to stem Virginia's economic decline and the possibility of black insurrection, William Byrd II wrote that Parliament must "put an end to this unchristian Traffick of making Merchandize of Our Fellow Creatures." John Custis IV also

18. William Gooch to BT, June 8, 1728, CO 5/1321, 44–45, VCRP; Jacob M. Price, *Perry of London: A Family and a Firm on the Seaborne Frontier, 1615–1753* (Cambridge, 1992), 82–89. Alderman Micajah Perry III gave up his assets to his creditors in 1744 because of his inability to collect debts from the planters and because of his losses in the consignment trade.

19. Custis to Hon[ore]d Madame, ca. 1730, Custis Letter Book, 1717–1742, LC; William Byrd II to [Sir Charles Wager?], July 2, 1736, May 26, 1740, in Marion Tinling, ed., *The Correspondence of the Three William Byrds of Westover, Virginia, 1684–1776*, 2 vols. (Charlottesville, Va., 1977), II, 485, 547–548 (hereafter cited as *Byrd Correspondence*).

Plate 12. William Byrd II. By Hans Hysing, circa 1724.
Courtesy, Virginia Historical Society, Richmond

Plate 13. Lucy Parke Byrd (with unidentified woman).
By the Studio of Godfrey Kneller, circa 1716. *A. C. Stewart Estate,
on deposit, Virginia Historical Society, Richmond*

lamented his class's position. The small and middling planters will buy all the blacks that are sent over, which, he observed, will lead to "our ruin." Like Byrd, he wished that the slave trade could be stopped; "but it is so sweet to those concerned; and so much concerns the trade and Navigation of Great Brittain; that it will bee next to impossible to break the neck of it."[20]

A Dead Commodity

As with the duty acts on the enslaved, the interests of merchants and planters diverged on the regulation of tobacco. The planters proposed measures to restrict production, hoping to raise the price of tobacco. The tobacco merchants opposed the limitation because they had a vested interest in maintaining production at current levels and keeping prices low. With the reduction of the quantity of tobacco, they had much more to lose than the differential in the price. Their profits from freight, handling charges, and commissions on tobacco would be shaved, and they would lose some bargaining power over the planters, for the colonials could effectively limit production to available shipping, thereby reducing the premiums merchants could charge. The merchants also sold the inferior leaf and stalk, pressed and shredded, to the English poor, reserving the premium leaf for the well-to-do and the foreign markets. During the 1720s, the English annually smoked about two pounds of tobacco per capita. Tobacco might have been "the first [of] new mass consumed groceries"; smoking, thought Governor William Gooch, was as "necessary as food to the laborer and mechanick." Encouraged by the merchants, especially the Scots, Parliament in 1723 prohibited the importation of tobacco stripped from the stalk, thus preserving high carrying charges on the bulky plants and allowing cheap trash to be passed off on laboring men. The planters protested this statute and by 1729 had an ally in Gooch.[21]

The tobacco stinting act of 1723, "An Act for the Better and More Effec-

20. Byrd to John Perceval, earl of Egmont, July 12, 1736, William Byrd II Letter Book, 1734–1736, VHS; Custis to Thomas L[l]oyd, 1736, Custis Letter Book, 1717–1742, LC; Minchinton, King, and Waite, eds., *Virginia Slave-Trade Statistics,* 85–91.

21. Gooch to the secretary of state, Feb. 28, 1728/9, CO 5/1337, 130–131, VCRP; Richard L. Morton, *Colonial Virginia,* 2 vols. (Chapel Hill, N.C., 1960), II, 510–513; Hemphill, "Virginia and the English Commericial System," 94–95, 161; Price, *Perry of London,* 80; Carole Shammas, "Changes in English and Anglo-American Consumption from 1550 to 1800," in John Brewer and Roy Porter, eds., *Consumption and the World of Goods* (New York, 1993), 180–181.

tual Improving the Staple of Tobacco," further divided the English and Virginia correspondents. It was designed to enhance the value of tobacco by stinting, or limiting, the number of plants each year to six thousand per taxable hand, three thousand per male child from ten to fifteen years old, and ten thousand to "all single Housekeepers having no Servants or Slaves," not unlike modern tobacco allotments. The tobacco act favored the great planters' economies of scale because there was no limitation to the number of hands or plants per estate. In order to protect their advantage in the labor force, the great planters sought to undercut the stint act's incentive to buy more blacks by enacting the forty-shilling duty on imported blacks. Although many planters supported the limitations on tobacco production in principle—provided the proprietary colonies of North Carolina and Maryland followed suit—few felt they could afford to reduce tobacco production in practice. The intention of the planters who supported the stint act was to produce a better-quality and more valuable plant. Certainly this had been the anticipation of Robert "King" Carter: "We shall then plant the best of all our Lands, tend it with All Imaginable nicety and probably make more and to be sure much better, than now We do off of ten or twelve thousand plants, besides there will be abundance more [laborers] put in for the Makeing of Tob[acc]o than now are Employed that way in hopes of that becoming a good commodity."[22]

Carter attacked the merchants for their opposition to the stint. He complained to Micajah Perry that the "Extraordinary nature of the act" had been necessitated by "Calamitious circumstances." Carter made plain the planters' position on the stint. Writing from his Rappahannock plantation to a London correspondent, most likely William Byrd II, he asked him to lobby the crown's ministers on behalf of the stint act, for tobacco was now a "dead commodity." Carter expressed his concern about Glasgow's edge in the Chesapeake market. The Scottish agents' ability to offer on-the-spot pricing and terms, whether bills or goods, made them more competitive than the great-planter correspondents, such as Carter, who were often unable to satisfy their consignments. They believed that the Scots were able to offer the higher prices only because they were evading customs in Great Britain. He mused that, even if there were "some diminution" of revenues collected, would not a wise crown weigh that against the perils of the

22. *EJCCV*, IV, 47; Waverly K. Winfree, comp., *The Laws of Virginia: Being a Supplement to Hening's The Statutes at Large, 1700–1750* (Richmond, Va., 1971), 247–253; Carter to [Byrd], July 2, 1723, in Carter Letter Book, 1723–1724, 8–9; Hemphill, "Virginia and the English Commercial System," 93–94.

great planters' predicament in light of the Scottish agency? "What must we come to? Must we starve? Must we not be Allowed to live upon our Labours? Must all the Gent[le]m[en] of the Country be swallowed up by the North Brittains frauds?"[23]

The crown allowed the 1723 stint act to stand, yet low tobacco prices continued to plague the planters. Thwarted in the attempt to limit production by inhibiting the slave trade, the General Assembly passed another stint act in 1728. To allay the concern of the Board of Trade that the act was simply a "great hardship" imposed by the great planters on the smaller ones, Gooch argued that small planters too would benefit from the stint. The act exempted single housekeepers, or "People having no Slaves" or other taxable laborers, from the six-thousand-plant limit, allowing them to cultivate as many as ten thousand plants. Because of the limitations of their land and labor, they could not "afford" in any case to cultivate much more than the six thousand plants allowed in the act. Otherwise, they would risk "destroying that they have" through soil exhaustion. Indeed, Gooch explained, the great planters, with their larger tracts and "good" land, were "more cramp'd" by the stint than smaller planters were. Only by their wherewithal to make "prompt Payment" at the customhouse, which would earn them an additional discount of 7 percent from the crown, would they be compensated for abiding by their quota and thus profit more than the "industrious" smaller planters. The only planters "aggrieved" by this act were the parvenu planters in the piedmont that had "great Tracts of Fresh Land and many Slaves." Without the restriction of the stint act, "they would have indeed the advantage of planting more Tobacco on such fresh Grounds and tending it more easily than others can on Lands that have been cultivated before; and having abundance of Hands to employ on their new Lands, whenever the Price of Tobacco gives encouragement they can make greater Crops than now they are allow'd to do." To the merchants' chagrin, the crown once again allowed the act to stand.[24]

But the stint acts proved no antidote to the poison of oversupply and debt ailing the economy. Supply continued to exceed demand. The inability to regulate the slave trade only increased labor, nullifying the tobacco limitation. "The daily encrease of the number of People Employed

23. Carter to Perry, June 19, 1723, Carter to [Byrd], July 2, 1723, in Carter Letter Book, 1723-1724, 8-9, 10-11; Price, *Perry of London,* 64-65.

24. Winfree, comp., *Laws of Virginia,* 295-305; Gooch to BT, Aug. 9, 1728, CO 5/1321, 149, VCRP.

in making of Tobacco by the importation of Negros, as well as the encrease of the Inhab[i]t[ant]s who being chiefly employed in the making
of Tobacco," opined the Council of State in 1723, "will always supply the
European Market with as much as can be vended." Possibly, Virginia authorities did not recognize how rapidly the population was increasing.
Gooch, for example, relying upon local sources, severely underestimated
the population in 1730, positing a total of 114,000 persons. The best modern estimate for that year is 153,000 inhabitants. The increased number of
planters, more than anyone realized, made the stint act ineffective. In the
end, the total amount of tobacco planted exceeded the reduction intended
by the act's stipulations.[25]

A look at William Byrd's market analyses in 1728 and 1729 reveals the
difficulties involved for great planters trying to control their economic des-
tiny and their ambivalence about attempting to impose rational planning
upon an agrarian, colonial world. Inspired by their commercial interests,
the great planters were developing proto-free-market notions. With the
passage of the tobacco act of 1728, for example, John Custis wrote in favor
of a natural market. "I think wee have no need of a Law. God Almighty
Seems not to." Byrd chimed in that the market was a better mechanism for
regulating tobacco, for the crop would be stronger in the long run, disre-
garding his remonstrations against a duty-free slave trade. Not only would
tobacco improve in an open market, but the navigation and trade of Great
Britain would benefit as well. Byrd pointed to the need to cut costs by
shifting labor from the production of an unprofitable commodity to a re-
munerative one. Perhaps the planters would flood the tobacco market if
they were left to their own devices. But, eventually, they would shift labor
and resources "to make hemp and other naval stores so necessary for our
mother country, which now pays for those commoditys for the most part
in mony."[26]

By 1729, Byrd had qualified his enthusiasm for the market. "Out of
humour with tobacco," he had employed a "great part" of his enslaved

25. *EJCCV*, IV, 49; Gooch to BT, July 23, 1730, CO 5/1322, 53–67, Aug. 22, 1743, CO
5/1326, 12–19, VCRP; Hemphill, "Virginia and the English Commercial System," 71, 72;
Price, *Perry of London*, 80; Peter H. Wood, "The Changing Population of the Colonial
South: An Overview by Race and Region, 1685–1790," in Wood, Gregory A. Waselkov, and
Thomas M. Hatley, eds., *Powhatan's Mantle: Indians in the Colonial Southeast* (Lincoln,
Nebr., 1989), 38.

26. John Custis to Mr. L[l]oyd, [1728], Custis Letter Book, 1717–1742, LC; Byrd to
[Capt. James Bradley], July 3, 1728, in *Byrd Correspondence*, I, 377; Michael Greenberg,
"William Byrd II and the World of the Market," *Southern Studies*, XVI (1977), 429–456.

laborers in making hemp, yet he was unsure whether he could profit. He believed that producing hemp was more costly in Virginia—even with slave labor—than in Russia, where wages were exceedingly "cheap." He could counter this disadvantage only by building a mill and investing in an engine from Holland, "where the art of easing of labor is so much improved."[27]

Since most planters were not in a position to diversify by investing in capital equipment, any economic upturn would have a direct relation to tobacco output. By limiting the quantity of tobacco plants in the 1728 stint act and in the following year successfully petitioning for the repeal of the parliamentary statute against stemmed tobacco, the great planters aimed at improving quality. Governor Gooch wrote that the 1728 act had intended to curb the "very mean stuff" dumped on the market and boost quality tobacco, but it had failed. "Bad as it is, [the trash tobacco] brings them Money or Goods and helps to maintain their Families," though, when used at home, it "produces very small returns, [and] frequently brings them in Debt." Besides, even if the planters held back the bad tobacco, Gooch surmised that it would end up on the black market. "The purpose would be defeated by their Slaves, who in spite of the Vigilance of their Overseers, would be the Vendors of it." As a result, under his prodding, the General Assembly repealed the 1728 stint act and passed the Virginia Inspection Act of 1730. The purpose of the new act was to prevent the exportation of "bad and trash tobacco" by inspecting tobacco at public warehouses before it could be exported or used as currency. Gooch wanted to impose a premium on tobacco from within Virginia.[28]

The difficulty that the great planters had with the Inspection Act of 1730 reveals their ambivalence about how to deal with the economy. Splits within their class were becoming increasingly evident. Great planters with wharves and warehouses opposed inspection because of the cost of transporting their tobacco to inspection stations. On the other hand, those who produced fine, high-quality tobacco wanted to eliminate trash tobacco to enhance the value of their product. Moreover, planters who had the capital to diversify their production into hemp and flax wanted the urban devel-

27. Byrd to [Jacob] Senerff, [ca. June 25, 1729], *Byrd Correspondence*, I, 410.

28. Gooch to BT, Aug. 9, 1728, CO 5/1321, 74–75, to the secretary of state, Feb. 28, 1728/9, CO 5/1337, 130–131, VCRP; *SAL*, IV, 247; Philip J. Schwarz, *Twice Condemned: Slaves and the Criminal Laws of Virginia, 1705–1865* (Baton Rouge, La., 1988), 76; Richard L. Morton, *Colonial Virginia*, 2 vols. (Chapel Hill, N.C., 1960), II, 511; Kulikoff, *Tobacco and Slaves*, 108–109.

opment that tobacco inspection might generate to exploit the hinterland. Some great planters, such as Byrd, who would found the towns of Richmond, Petersburg, and Manchester, were hopeful that tobacco inspection would encourage market diversity and generate an entrepôt on their land. Both flax and hemp called for processing. Not only did pressed flaxseed yield linseed oil, but also the fibers of its stalk could be spun into linen thread. Hemp fiber could be made into rope and sailcloth.[29]

As they grappled with the 1730 Inspection Act, the great planters believed they were becoming less effective in provincial politics. Small and middling planters had become more powerful in the burgesses with westward expansion, and Gooch at the helm exercised greater mastery in negotiating with the General Assembly than previous governors. The great planters' language betrayed their feelings of impotence. Robert "King" Carter and John Custis both implored their English correspondents to help overturn the passage of the Inspection Act, for they now believed that they were powerless to stop it themselves. Carter, arrogant in his support of the 1723 tobacco act, lamented the passage of the 1730 law. He wrote to Edward Tucker that his peers had no control over the disposition of the act that was before the crown. If he was uncertain of the act's standing from his informants in England, he was sure that, unless the merchants persuaded the crown to rescind the law, "it will create such abundance of trouble for us Planters and heave the Country into such great Charges." The great planters would have to "submit to the directions of our Legislators." Custis also expressed anxiety that the great planters were losing their mastery over the governor and burgesses in a letter to Richard Fitzwilliams. Gooch had massaged the General Assembly for four years until it passed the Inspection Act, wrote Custis, even though it should never have left committee. Despite the assembly's aversion to it, he mused, the "perplexing" tobacco law had been passed and "with Submission" sent to England. The law was no more like the 1723 tobacco act "than an apple is like an oyster." "May it travell to England and like the air so well it may never return to Virginia."[30]

Gooch reached out to the dissident great planters by offering the Coun-

29. Hermann Wellenreuther, with a letter from Fred Siegel and a reply from Joseph A. Ernst and H. Roy Merrens, "Urbanization in the Colonial South: A Critique," WMQ, 3d Ser., XXXI (1974), 653–668.

30. Carter to Edward Tucker, Aug. 16, 1731, Carter Letter Book, 1731–1733; Custis to [Richard Fitzwilliams], 1730, Custis Letter Book, 1717–1742; Hemphill, "Virginia and the English Commercial System," 160–161.

cil of State the power to appoint inspectors. He thus gave them the ability
to protect their interests and a reason to support the 1730 act. But dissension among planters over the law remained. Planters in the tidewater with
older tracts of land competed with parvenu planters in the piedmont with
fresh tracts, and small planters and those in inferior-growing regions remained outside the power circle. The act garnered little popular support,
and, eventually, it elicited violent protest.[31]

In March 1732, planters in the Northern Neck rose in rebellion. Sensitive to the discriminatory impact of the Inspection Act, they feared a disproportionate destruction of their tobacco, owing to its inferior quality.
The ringleaders were small planters without enslaved blacks, and the majority of their followers were most likely tenants, also without enslaved
laborers, who produced no more than two hogsheads of tobacco. The
rebels burned warehouses in Lancaster, Northumberland, Prince William,
and King George Counties. In one instance, the burning of the Burr public tobacco warehouse at Deep Creek, Lancaster County, the Council of
State offered one hundred pounds for the capture of the arsonists, indicating the seriousness of the crime. As a result of the rebellion, the General
Assembly made burning tobacco warehouses a capital crime punishable
by death. The governor called out the militia. This show of force, together
with the threat of hanging the arsonists, was enough to end the rebellion.
Frightened by the social unrest, the great planters became conciliatory
toward inspection and began to consolidate as a class.[32]

Despite the social unrest, in 1734 the General Assembly renewed the
Inspection Act for four more years. The House of Burgesses received petitions for repeal from all the counties in the Northern Neck and Eastern
Shore as well as Hanover County. Five counties asked for a new stint act.
In the 1735 election, small planters throughout the colony replaced numerous pro-regulation assemblymen; these new burgesses, joined by those
from regions that produced inferior tobacco, voted to repeal the Inspection Act. Of the election Governor Gooch wrote that people were not de-
ferring to the great planters but were reacting to the tobacco law, as "the

31. Kathleen M. Brown, *Good Wives, Nasty Wenches, and Anxious Patriarchs: Gender,
Race, and Power in Colonial Virginia* (Chapel Hill, N.C., 1996), 253; Kulikoff, *Tobacco and
Slaves,* 109–110; Morton, *Colonial Virginia,* II, 511–512; Billings, Selby, and Tate, *Colonial
Virginia,* 236–240.

32. *EJCCV,* IV, 259; Brown, *Good Wives, Nasty Wenches,* 253; Kulikoff, *Tobacco and
Slaves,* 108–112; Morton, *Colonial Virginia,* II, 512–513; Rhys Isaac, *The Transformation
of Virginia, 1740–1790* (Chapel Hill, N.C., 1982), 18n.

gentlemen here having no influence over the meaner people [who were] vastly the majority of electors." The Council of State, unaccountable to any constituency, rejected the repeal bill.[33]

To avoid this kind of reaction among burgesses in the future, the General Assembly in 1736 changed the election code. In a 1736 electoral law with ramifications for class power ("An Act to Declare Who Shall Have a Right to Vote in the Election of Burgesses to Serve in the General Assembly . . ."), the great planters restricted the vote to those white men that owned fifty acres of land, or twenty-five acres and a house. Half of the electorate was thus effectively disenfranchised. At the same time, the assembly eliminated the residency qualification—a boon to the great planters who owned land in more than one county. The law also allowed plural voting. A single planter could vote in every county where he met the property qualification. It even allowed fractional voting if property was jointly held and the owners could come to agreement. Since suffrage was now determined by propertyownership rather than residency, the great planters had increased their power in the assembly. The great planters had taken the offensive and seemingly regained control of politics in Virginia. Challenged by the smaller planters who had pressed their own interests, the great planters had coalesced along class lines to maintain their influence.[34]

Yet the agitation against the Inspection Act persisted through 1738, when it was up for renewal in the General Assembly. With the flame of struggle extinguished and the voice of the ballot hushed, the inspection opponents turned to lambasting the regulations. Edwin Conway, a burgess from Lancaster County in the Northern Neck, with "express Instructions" from his constituents to repeal the Inspection Act, contributed to the debate by writing an article in the *Virginia Gazette*. He argued that the inspection offered no advantage for the planter, causing him "great Trouble and Risque" in carrying his tobacco from his plantation to a warehouse for inspection. Moreover, his tobacco had to be inspected again in Britain. Conway contended that prices were not uniform even for tobacco of the same weight and questioned whether the laws for safe packing and tarring were sufficient to detect "Roguish Planters." "If, by Misfortune, I can't

33. Kulikoff, *Tobacco and Slaves*, 112–113; Brown, *Good Wives, Nasty Wenches*, 253; Morton, *Colonial Virginia*, II, 514.

34. *SAL*, IV, 475–482; J. R. Pole, *Political Representation in England and the Origins of the American Republic,* rev. ed. (Berkeley, Calif., 1971), 141–142; Douglas R. Egerton, *Gabriel's Rebellion: The Virginia Slave Conspiracies of 1800 and 1802* (Chapel Hill, N.C., 1993), 4.

make my Tobacco as good as my Neighbour's Tobacco," he queried, "is it reasonable and just to burn it, and I go Naked, when a Merchant would willingly give me Goods for it?" "There is no Standard for Tobacco; it depends altogether upon Humour and Fancy."[35]

An anonymous planter, also writing in the *Virginia Gazette,* asked, since the Germans and French had challenged the British in the marketplace, shouldn't they improve the quality of their cloth, for example, by limiting the number of sheep kept by the shepherd, or by limiting to six the number of hours in a day that a manufacturer could work? Yet, if anyone were to propose such a scheme, "would they not send the Wronghead back to his Borough of Guzzle down, and bid him meddle only with Matters within his own Comprehension?" The legislators sponsoring the act were promoting the business of their rival Maryland and of the poorer tobacco producers such as Pennsylvania and North Carolina, he argued, for these colonies would "fill up the Gap" left by the stint. Despite the spirited criticism, the assembly renewed the inspection act.[36]

Such critical commentary indicated that the great planters had not done enough to quell the resistance to their tobacco policy. They had tried to regulate the tobacco and slave trades only to find splits within their class and opposition from merchants, small planters, and those from inferior tobacco-growing regions. Losing a good share of the profits and increasingly subjected by the crown to the role of colonial, the great planters thus began to develop a provincial ideology, one that would at once articulate their dominant status in society and justify the subjection of an enslaved laboring class that was increasing in both size and influence.

35. *Virginia Gazette,* Nov. 17–24, 1738.
36. Ibid., Oct. 27–Nov. 3, 1738.

III

Reactions

Ideology and Religion

CHAPTER 7

The Emergence of Patriarchism, 1700–1740

The expansion of the tobacco economy, the growth of slavery, the return of prosperity, and the rapid increase of native-born populations, enslaved and free, triggered social changes in Virginia in the 1720s. As the great planters grappled with these changes, they tried to maintain their dominance in a society where their authority was under contest.[1]

A century before, the Puritans saw America as a refuge from England, a chance for redemption that would carry them on an errand into the wilderness. Unlike the Puritans, the English that came to Virginia did not do so to create a City on a Hill. Their plans were mundane and materialistic. They were after the main chance and felt no need to differentiate themselves from their English counterparts.[2]

The great planters thus did not at first feel the need to justify their dominant place in society. The raw power of husbands, fathers, speculators, and enslavers, expressed in land titles and slave statutes, ensured control over wives and children, the poor, and enslaved blacks. Through their assertion of male prerogative, these wealthy planters assumed their dominance in the plantation household. Their authority as officials, conveyed in royal appointments and electoral seats, secured their control over small

1. Allan Kulikoff, *Tobacco and Slaves: The Development of Southern Cultures in the Chesapeake, 1680–1800* (Chapel Hill, N.C., 1986), 78–85, 167–183; Holly Brewer, "Entailing Aristocracy in Colonial Virginia: 'Ancient Feudal Restraints' and Revolutionary Reform," *WMQ*, 3d Ser., LIV (1997), 297–298, 301–303, 317, 325.

2. Mary Beth Norton, *Founding Mothers and Fathers: Gendered Power and the Forming of American Society* (New York, 1996), 4–14; Perry Miller, *Errand into the Wilderness* (1956; reprint, Cambridge, Mass., 1975), 4–6; Martin H. Quitt, "Immigrant Origins of the Virginia Gentry: A Study of Cultural Transmission and Innovation," *WMQ*, 3d Ser., XLV (1988), 638–639; Lewis P. Simpson, *The Dispossessed Garden: Pastoral and History in Southern Literature* (Athens, Ga., 1975), 3–13.

and middling planters, who perceived their own interests in tobacco production were best served by allying with those in power. The threat of violence kept the enslaved in check.

With the 1720s, however, the maturation of the colonial system shifted the equation of power that supported the great planters in their slave society. Following a dramatic increase in their numbers, the enslaved began pushing for their freedom, organizing insurrections in 1722 and 1730. The crown's unwillingness to allow the duty acts of 1723 and 1728 to regulate the slave trade, proven measures to deal with both potential slave uprisings and declining tobacco prices, aggravated the great planters' social and economic concerns. The tobacco regulation acts of 1723, 1728, and 1730, poor substitutes for raising prices, increased divisiveness, as planters in inferior-growing regions pressed for their repeal. Factors, or agents, including maverick great planters representing merchant interests, increased their presence on Virginia's great rivers by selling provisions and enslaved blacks to small and middling planters and buying tobacco directly from them. These middlemen siphoned off trade previously dominated by the great planters and loosened the elite's economic foundation. Moreover, by the 1720s, in an effort to create ancestral estates, Virginia's elite had instituted entail in both land and enslaved laborers, inadvertently making their family members less dependent upon them because inheritance was assured.

The great planters thus began looking for something distinctive in their culture as they became weaker in their dealings with the crown, more dependent on English merchants, more anxious about their women and children, less masterful over small and middling planters, and more threatened by blacks. They found it in an ideology, one that would at once distinguish them from English merchants and secure their power in Virginia society. That ideology was patriarchism.[3]

3. The emergence of patriarchism should also be distinguished from the later development of paternalism. Philip D. Morgan argues that patriarchism is the key to understanding eighteenth-century master-slave relationships in Virginia. He describes patriarchism as more authoritarian, more distant, and more realistic in understanding the slave demeanor than paternalism, which was more intimate, more engaging, and dissimulate. These distinctions, however, are "complex and confused." Accepting that paternalism might have emerged after 1750, Morgan believes that it does not become pronounced until the nineteenth century (Morgan, "Three Planters and Their Slaves: Perspectives on Slavery in Virginia, South Carolina, and Jamaica, 1750–1790," in Winthrop D. Jordan and Sheila L. Skemp, eds., *Race and Family in the Colonial South* [Jackson, Miss., 1987], 39–40 [quotation on 40]; Morgan, *Slave Counterpoint: Black Culture in the Eighteenth-*

Like One of the Patriarchs

Patriarchism, a term that first appeared in print in 1666, can be defined as an organizational belief system in which society is structured around the supremacy of the patriarch, or father. Its emphasis on organization more aptly describes the formative nature of this type of society in early-eighteenth-century Virginia than the more commonly used *patriarchalism,* a word dating from as late as 1847 and suggesting an established patriarchal social hierarchy and government. The root of both words, *patriarchal,* is derived from *patriarchical,* a term in use by 1606, on the eve of Virginia's founding. *Patriarchal,* meaning of or belonging to the patriarch or characteristic of the patriarchs and their times, appeared in print fifty years later, after the English Civil War, suggesting its ideological construction was related to Sir Robert Filmer's political treatise *Patriarcha,* written during the 1630s but published posthumously in 1680. As Filmer developed it, patriarchism was a compendium of English political thought promoting the idea of natural inequality embedded in a hierarchical, organic social order and structuring both state and familial relationships. When Filmer was composing *Patriarcha,* the old order was under attack; he was reacting to rapid changes in English life. The shift from patronage in feudal society to commercial market relations, together with the changing class structure, eventually eroded the political power of aristocratic kinship and clientage and increased the power of middle-class merchants. To counteract this shift, a flood of pamphlet literature inspired by Filmer emphasized obedience to the king in the realm and to the father in the nuclear family. *Patriarchal* and *patriarchism,* then, would have been current terms in the eighteenth-century world inhabited by Anglo-Virginians.[4]

Century Chesapeake and Lowcountry [Chapel Hill, N.C., 1998], 273–296 [esp. 284]). On the other hand, Kathleen M. Brown concludes: "An examination of the full complement of planters' social relations reveals paternalism—in the guise of the ideals of domestic tranquillity—to be one face of patriarchy, not a softer replacement of it" (Brown, *Good Wives, Nasty Wenches, and Anxious Patriarchs: Gender, Race, and Power in Colonial Virginia* [Chapel Hill, N.C., 1996], 322–323, 366 [quotation]).

4. *Oxford English Dictionary,* compact ed., *Oxford Universal Dictionary on Historical Principles,* 3d ed., s.v. "patriarchal," "patriarchalism," "patriarchical," and "patriarchism." Daniel Defoe used *patriarchal* in 1727: "Some are of the opinion, by the sons of God, there is meant the patriarchal heads of families" (*The History and Reality of Apparitions* [Oxford, 1840], quoted in *OED,* compact ed., s.v., "patriarchal"). See also Michael McKeon, "Historicizing Patriarchy: The Emergence of Gender Difference in England, 1660–1760,"

Indeed, in the 1720s and 1730s, the great planters, attempting to hold on to the reins of power, invoked the notion of patriarchism and adapted it to their own society. Contained in this emerging Virginia patriarchism were ideals of patriarchy and good nature, or virtue. The great planters likened themselves to the biblical patriarchs; they were the heads of their families and the governors of society. They governed through mutual responsibilities and obligations, charging themselves with supplying for the needs of society and regulating the lives of its members and expecting deference and obedience in return. To be the leaders of their society, the planters had to possess good nature, which, in a meaning obsolete today, had its equivalent in virtue, denoting the quality of persons whose lives conformed with the principles of morality.[5]

Other aspects of the great planters' patriarchism were order, the pastoral, provincialism, and providence. The planters' emphasis on order carried a double meaning: they were not only an order or class of persons distinguished from others by nature or character; they were first in order or rank in their relationship with other classes. Provincialism emphasized their separateness from Britain, which they turned into attachment to their own province of Virginia, its institutions and interests. They celebrated

Eighteenth-Century Studies, XXVIII (1995), 295–298; Peter Laslett, ed., *Patriarcha and Other Political Works of Sir Robert Filmer* (London, 1949); Laslett, "Sir Robert Filmer: The Man versus the Whig Myth," *WMQ,* 3d Ser., V (1948), 523–546; Laslett, "The Gentry of Kent in 1640," *Cambridge Historical Journal,* IX (1947–1949), 148–164; Gordon J. Schochet, *Patriarchalism in Political Thought: The Authoritarian Family and Political Speculation and Attitudes, Especially in Seventeenth-Century England* (New York, 1975), 10–16; Peter Walne, ed., "'Henry Filmer of Mulberry Island, Gentleman': A Collection of Letters from Virginia, 1653–1671," *VMHB,* LXVIII (1960), 408–428; Lawrence Stone, *The Crisis of the Aristocracy, 1558–1641* (Oxford, 1965); Stone, *The Family, Sex, and Marriage in England, 1500–1800* (New York, 1977); Bernard Bailyn, "Politics and Social Structure in Virginia," in James Morton Smith, ed., *Seventeenth-Century America: Essays in Colonial History* (Chapel Hill, N.C., 1959), 90–115; Rowland Berthoff and John M. Murrin, "Feudalism, Communalism, and the Yeoman Freeholder: The American Revolution Considered as a Social Accident," in Stephen G. Kurtz and James H. Hutson, eds., *Essays on the American Revolution* (Chapel Hill, N.C., 1973), 256–288; Michael Walzer, *The Revolution of the Saints: A Study in the Origins of Radical Politics* (New York, 1973), 148–195; Arthur O. Lovejoy, *The Great Chain of Being: A Study of the History of an Idea* (Cambridge, Mass., 1936), chap. 4.

5. Most historical discussions on virtue focus on early-eighteenth-century Britain or late-eighteenth-century America; almost none focus on British America from the 1720s to the mid-1760s. See Jack P. Greene, "The Concept of Virtue in Late Colonial British America," in Richard K. Matthews, ed., *Virtue, Corruption, and Self-Interest: Political Values in the Eighteenth Century* (Bethlehem, Pa., 1994), 27–54.

this distinctiveness in the pastoral, a romance of rural life. Paul Fussell posits that the retreat to the pastoral is the English way of dealing with unthinkable cataclysms by imagining a prosaic alternative: "Pastoral reference . . . is a way of invoking a code to hint by antithesis at the indescribable; at the same time, it is a comfort in itself." The great planters repressed the thought of servile insurrection by imagining Virginia as a pastoral garden dutifully tended by faithful servants. Divine providence ordained this structure, which served as a justification of the great planters' rule and as a model: as God directed, controlled, and guided, so did the elite execute their function in society.[6]

William Byrd II, whose mother happened to be the widow of Filmer's son Samuel, captured the essence of Virginia's patriarchism in a 1726 letter to Charles Boyle, the earl of Orrey. Byrd's writings were prototypical of the retreat from history, when the great planters were investing in the myth of the plantation slave society rather than dealing with its reality. For Byrd, the English errand into paradise could be realized exclusively in terms of Virginia's slave society. Independent of all but God, the great planter assumed the mantle of patriarch, shepherding his herds and directing his people. He referred to the biblical patriarch in a pastoral setting. He mixed metaphors of Scriptures-old patriarchs with proto-industrial timekeepers. He had withdrawn from a debased, self-indulgent England and advanced to a superior, self-sufficient Virginia.

> Like one of the patriarchs, I have my flocks and my herds, my bond-men and bond-women, and every soart of trade amongst my own servants, so that I live in a kind of independance on every one, but Providence. However tho' this soart of life is without expence yet it is attended with a great deal of trouble. I must take care to keep all my people to their duty, to set all the springs in motion, and to make every one draw his equal share to carry the machine forward. But then tis an amusement in this silent country, and a continual exercise of our patience and oeconomy.[7]

6. Paul Fussell, *The Great War and Modern Memory* (New York, 1975), 235; Simpson, *The Dispossessed Garden*, 15–25.

7. William Byrd II to Charles Boyle, earl of Orrery, July 5, 1726, in Marion Tinling, ed., *The Correspondence of the Three William Byrds of Westover, Virginia, 1684–1776*, 2 vols. (Charlottesville, Va., 1977), I, 354–355 (hereafter cited as *Byrd Correspondence*); Simpson, *The Dispossessed Garden*, 20–23; Mechal Sobel, *The World They Made Together: Black and White Values in Eighteenth-Century Virginia* (Princeton, N.J., 1987), 25–26, 84–85; Gerald W. Mullin, *Flight and Rebellion: Slave Resistance in Eighteenth-Century Virginia*

Byrd used biblical and pastoral imagery to distinguish Virginia from London, Paris, and the sugar islands, which he believed were uninhabitable dens of vice. His letters should be considered in light of their times, when the great planters suffered in their dealings with merchants, manufacturers, and even sugar planters who used their vast fortunes to make a home in London and buy seats in Parliament. Too often scholars have missed the negative part of Byrd's allusion, his contrasting referents, choosing to concentrate on his Virginia ideal.

In the aftermath of his final return from London in 1726, his letters should also be read as a justification of his circumscribed ambitions. After Lucy Parke Byrd died of smallpox in 1716 in London, Byrd sought a second wife with the intention of bettering his material situation and settling permanently in England. Spurned twice in his courtship of well-born, wealthy Englishwomen, in 1724 he married Maria Taylor, who was from a solid English family but without a fortune, and returned two years later to Virginia. Byrd's sense of personal defeat at the hands of English society, along with lifelong debt to English creditors inherited through his first marriage to Daniel Parke's daughter, sharpened his animosity toward the English gentry. In the same period, Byrd not only failed in his political aspiration to become Virginia's governor but also found himself under attack by Governor Alexander Spotswood, who had removed him from the Council of State. He operated from a position of weakness as the colony's agent, failing to prevail in the oyer and terminer and slave-duty disputes. Only later did the crown reverse itself by advising Spotswood to continue the practice of allowing councillors to serve as oyer and terminer justices and to return Byrd to his council seat.[8]

(New York, 1972), 3–33; Jan Lewis, *The Pursuit of Happiness: Family and Values in Jefferson's Virginia* (Cambridge, 1983), 11–15, 23; Kenneth A. Lockridge, *On the Sources of Patriarchal Rage: The Commonplace Books of William Byrd and Thomas Jefferson and the Gendering of Power in the Eighteenth Century* (New York, 1992), 21.

8. Byrd to "Vigilante" [John Smith], Feb. 18, 1718, John Custis to Byrd, Mar. 30, 1717, Byrd to BT, Feb. 24, 1718, all in *Byrd Correspondence,* I, 95–98, 312, 314; Byrd to Sabina Smith, July 2, 1717, Smith to Byrd, July 4, 1717, in Maude H. Woodfin, ed., *Another Secret Diary of William Byrd of Westover, 1739–1741, with Letters and Literary Exercises, 1696–1726,* trans. Marion Tinling (Richmond, Va., 1942), 302–304; Richard R. Beeman and Rhys Isaac, "Cultural Conflict and Social Change in the Revolutionary South: Lunenburg County, Virginia," *Journal of Southern History,* XLVI (1980), 525–550; Lockridge, *On the Sources of Patriarchal Rage,* 23; Brown, *Good Wives, Nasty Wenches,* 248; Kevin Berland, Jan Kirsten Gilliam, and Kenneth A. Lockridge, *The Commonplace Book of William Byrd of Westover* (Chapel Hill, N.C., 2001), 10–12.

After ten years of political and personal frustration, he reconciled himself to a life of moderation in the provinces. Rejecting the extremes of wealth and corruption in the Indies, he wrote to the earl of Egmont, "We have . . . nothing like this Inhumanity here, that is practiced in the Islands, and God forbid we ever should." He urged his friend Peter Beckford of Jamaica to consider Virginia for his progeny. If, for sentimental reasons, Beckford wanted to end his days in his birthplace in the "Torrid Zone," then at least he should send one of his sons to Virginia. Here "you may make him a Prince for less money than you can make him a Private Gentleman in England."[9]

Byrd contrasted images of an idyllic Virginia invigorated by patriarchs, bondmen, and tradesmen with images of a depraved England vitiated by beggars, housebreakers, and highwaymen, unredeemed by Daniel Defoe's escape valve to a virtuous life in the Chesapeake. He wrote to Boyle in July 1726: "We can rest securely in our beds with all our doors and windows open, and yet find every thing exactly in place the next morning. We can travel all over the country, by night and by the day, unguarded and unarmed, and never meet with any person so rude as to bid us stand. We have no vagrant mendicants to seize and deaften[?] us wherever we go, as in your island of beggars."[10] With allusions to the Exodus and his personal weakness, Byrd described England as the Egypt of the Pharaohs, replete with the tempting sensations from which the chosen people had fled to their Promised Land of Virginia. Byrd continued to Boyle: "We are very happy in our Canaan, if we could but forget the onions, and the flesh-pots of Egypt. There are so many temptations in England to inflame the appetite, and charm the senses, that we are constant to run all risques to enjoy them. They always had I must own too strong an influence upon me, as your Lordship will belive when they could keep me so long from the more solid pleasures of innocence, and retirement." Nearly ten years later, he explained to Beckford the difference between metropolitan and provincial society by the absence of cities, those Enlightenment sites of both civili-

9. William Byrd II to Peter Beckford, Dec. 6, 1735, Byrd to John Perceval, earl of Egmont, July 12, 1736, William Byrd II Letter Book, 1735–1736, VHS.

10. Byrd to Boyle, July 5, 1726, *Byrd Correspondence*, I, 355, 356–359. Daniel Defoe (1660–1731) published two novels in 1722 in which the protagonists, a servant girl and a street urchin, grow into master thieves who are convicted and transported to the Chesapeake, where, repentant, they become plantation owners (*The Fortunes and Misfortunes of the Famous Moll Flanders* [London]; *The History and Remarkable Life of the Truly Honourable Colonel Jacque, Commonly Call'd Col. Jack* [London]).

zation and corruption: "We live here in health and in Plenty, in Innocence and security, fearing no Enemy from abroad or Robbers at home. . . . We all lye securely with our Doors unbarred, and can travel the whole country over without either Arms or Guard, And all this not for want of Mony, or Rogues, but because we have no great Citys to shelter the Thief, or Pawn-Brokers to receive what he steals."[11]

Byrd took umbrage at the merchant class, or the "men [that stand] behind counters." He criticized merchant capital, more angered with Virginia's weakness under British mercantilism than displeased with nascent capitalism. Byrd himself had dabbled as a land speculator and merchant. He was surely aware of the contemporary view in which merchant wealth was celebrated for supporting liberty and promoting arts and sciences. Nonetheless, Byrd described merchants as cheats, pickpockets, and pirates, which was consistent with his theme of Britain as a harbor of thieves. Once, in a fit of pique about a shipment of tobacco and an order of goods for his plantation, Byrd urged that merchants be prevented from sending their "refuse" to Virginia. He reiterated that England had sent Virginia its convicts and reprobates and had let moral and economic restraints give way to lavishness there, all at a cost to honest Virginia labor: "'Tis hard we must take [all] the worst of their people, and the worst of their goods too. But now shopkeepers have left off their bands, their frugality, and their spouses must be maintaind in splendour, 'tis very fit the sweat of our brows shoud help to support them in it." Reacting to the great planters' inability to limit the trade, Byrd was most critical of the slave-trade merchants. He likened the slave traders to African dealers whom he condemned for allegedly selling their own relatives. Even the merchants' spouses were figuratively at risk. These men were so avaricious that they "would sell their Fathers, their Elder Brothers, and even the Wives of their bosoms, if they could black their faces and get anything by them."[12]

In constructing their provincial identity, the great planters attempted to reconcile themselves to their growing impotence in the mercantile system. They did not, however, consider independence from the crown. On the contrary, the king was the epitome of a good-natured man, and the great

11. Byrd to Boyle, July 5, 1726, *Byrd Correspondence,* I, 355–356; Byrd to Beckford, Dec. 6, 1735, Byrd Letter Book, 1735–1736.

12. Byrd to ———, Sept. 3, 1729, *Byrd Correspondence,* I, 417–418; Byrd to Egmont, July 12, 1736, Byrd Letter Book, 1735–1736; Lockridge, *On the Sources of Patriarchal Rage,* 23–45; David Dabydeen, *Hogarth's Blacks: Images of Blacks in Eighteenth Century English Art* (Athens, Ga., 1987), 100.

planters sought to fashion their communities from the cloth of the mother country—even though their cut was that of a slave society. In comparison with the Caribbean slave societies, the more favorable racial demographics for white-settled Virginia encouraged the planters to think of themselves as autonomous provincials rather than dependent colonials. Their province would be at once self-sufficient but also part of the British community.[13]

Increasingly concerned, though, with royal control over local administration, the great planters had to reconcile patriarchism with their opposition to the crown's appointed rulers of the province, especially the governor. Where in the natural order of things do these royal appointees fit? As the king's representatives, should they not be superior in the scheme of patriarchal organization? The answer was not to be found in Filmer; the earlier ideology of patriarchism did not figure on colonialism. Even if the great planters recognized the power of the king to make these appointments, they could challenge whether the recipients were worthy surrogates of the king. The great planters viewed these rulers as illegitimate if they strayed from the path of the provincial interest. Antagonism between Virginia's elite and royal governors dated back to John Harvey's administration in the 1630s, but, with the growing alienation of the great planters from the English mercantile system, criticism of imperial authority became part of the planters' ideology. They argued that royal appointees interrupted the ordained flow of authority. The provinicals' claims of the inversion of the natural hierarchy more often than not resulted from their perceptions of a corrupt or ineffective governor. The author of "Virginia's Complaint against the Plaintiffs" (1705), for example, disgusted with Governor Francis Nicholson's land policies, accused him of intervening in the natural order from king to subjects, not only preempting local authority but also corrupting racial order. (Note the contradistinction of ill nature to good nature.)

> You quite invert the highest Ends of State
> Subjecting Judges to the Subjects Heat
> Ill Natur'd Haughty men
> Transfus'd this Evil blood in many a vein

13. *Virginia Gazette,* Nov. 19, 1736; Benedict Anderson, *Imagined Communities: Reflections on the Origin and Spread of Nationalism,* rev. ed. (New York, 1991), 52–53, 55; C. Duncan Rice, review of *American Negro Slavery: A Documentary History,* ed. Michael Mullin, *WMQ,* 3d Ser., XXXV (1978), 402.

Let us amend or Law will Stop and drain
Bad juice flowes up apace
And runs in Poisoned Groves from Race to Race
Bark the Trees Or'e they their Saplings raise
Thus Guards must Guards ensure
Each lower Orb Supports the High Power
He Shakes the Throne that rudely treads the floor.[14]

William Byrd was also highly critical of the crown's appointed governors. His assessment, no doubt, was tainted with unrequited ambition, for
he desperately wanted the appointment for himself and used much of his
political influence attempting to secure it. In petitioning for the council's
control over appointments to the courts of oyer and terminer in 1718, Byrd
wished that "the good inhabitants of that colony [Virginia] may not have
their lives their libertys and fortunes so intirely in the hands of their governour." Although many of the great planters, including Byrd, respected
Governor William Gooch, Byrd wrote to one correspondent in 1736: "I
am sorry to say it, but most of the worthy gentlemen sent to govern in this
part of the world, are more inclind to represent the kings authority than
they are his vertues. They are generally so intent upon makeing their fortunes, that they have no leizure to study the good of the people, and how
to make them useful to their mother country."[15]

Viewed from the overall scheme of patriarchism, the royal appointees
had failed Virginia. As he had done with the merchants, Byrd saw the governors' characteristic venality as the legacy of English culture and society.
To drive the point home, Byrd lumped the governors in the same category as transported convicts, spared from English gallows and prisons.
Through them the English had imported criminality into Virginia. The
provincials suffered solely from the vices put on them by England, for
only virtue sprang from the soil of Virginia. Virginia had "neither publick robbers nor private," he wrote in 1726, only the "pilfering convicts"
and "needy governours" sent from England to live among them. "It is sus-

14. "Virginia's Complaint against the Plaintiffs," 1705, Frank J. Klingberg Collection,
Charles E. Young Research Library, UCLA; Wesley Frank Craven, *White, Red, and
Black: The Seventeenth-Century Virginian* (Charlottesville, Va., 1971), 1–2. See also Clif-
ford Lewis III, "Some Recently Discovered Extracts from the Lost Minutes of the Virginia
Council and General Court, 1642–1645," *WMQ*, 2d Ser., XX (1940), 69.

15. Byrd to BT, Feb. 24, 1717/8, Byrd to [Sir Charles Wager?], July 2, 1736, *Byrd Correspondence*, I, 314–315, II, 485; Lockridge, *On the Sources of Patriarchal Rage*, 23.

pected [that these governors] have some-times an inclination to plunder, but want the power," claimed Byrd, "tho' they may be tyrants in their nature, yet they are tyrants without guards, which makes them as harmless as a scold would be without a tongue." By implication, he suggested Virginians were too virtuous to ally with royal appointees in their pursuit of illicit power. "Our Government Too is so happily constituted," Byrd wrote to Beckford in 1735, "that a governor must first outwit us, before he can oppress us. . . . And if ever he squeeze money out of us he must first take care to deserve it."[16]

William Parks, publisher of the newly established *Virginia Gazette* (1736), also professed the ideology of patriarchism. Printer-journalists were significant to the development of prenationalist identity in Creole societies, especially in North America, where presses took on a crucial function in forging communications and a sense of shared concerns among colonials.[17] Parks articulated for his readers, chief among them the great planters, the tenets of the elite's provincial ideology. He wrote that human existence is ordered by "divine, and human, moral, and political" ties of obligation. For this reason, a socially responsible gentleman must at once reconcile the well-being of the "whole Community" generally and at the same time its "constituent Parts . . . separately." A good-natured or virtuous man avoided "Savageness of Temper, . . . Pride, Envy, or Jealousy, or any other baser Passion, or Motive" that might "obstruct or defeat the Happiness of his Fellow Creatures" and be a "Subverter of Society." Moreover, in Virginia a patriarch, or "a man . . . born to an Estate," presided over land and laborers under the guidance of providence. This self-conscious plantation pastoralism was a cultural innovation of the great planters, not a mimicking of the English aristocracy. Within this idealized setting, agriculture was in part responsible for the beneficent state of society, for "it conducts to Morality and every social Vertue, and inforces a due Regard to and Dependance on the supreme Being, in which consists the Essence of Religion." Indeed, providence and revealed religion served as the model and wellspring for the patriarchal myth. God as Father and

16. Byrd to Boyle, July 5, 1726, *Byrd Correspondence,* I, 354–359; Byrd to Beckford, Dec. 6, 1735, Byrd Letter Book, 1735–1736.

17. Newspaper traits included provinciality, plurality, or a "full awareness of provincials in worlds parallel to [a reader's] own," and, eventually, political awareness. They "created an imagined community among a specific assemblage of fellow-readers." See Anderson, *Imagined Communities,* 61, 62.

Judge embodied the characteristics of a good-natured man who directed society.[18]

Parks encouraged the great planters to embrace virtue. In a series of essays beginning in 1736, he promoted the concept of "Good Nature," which he defined as a "Complication of Virtues." These virtues included disinterestedness, benevolence, patience, forbearance, humility, and moderation. Parks, chiding the great planters for lacking a "proper Education," pointed to the want of gentility in Virginia society. He cautioned them that, just because a man is born into an estate, it does not follow that all things are "subservient" to him. To be the patriarchs of their society, they needed both a thorough reexamination of mind and soul and a thorough reformation of behavior and expression.[19]

With this reformation in mind, Parks published a poem by David Mossom, minister of St. Peter's Parish in New Kent County. Mossom had honored Governor Gooch with a poem alluding to Horace. In it he expressed what was lacking in Virginia society, despite the bountiful returns of the pastoral. He denied the threat of invasion or insurrection by referring to the peace Virginia enjoyed. The Indians were vanquished and the blacks were contained, and both contributed to the crown through their tribute and their labor respectively. Yet, he minimized them. The labor of blacks was less important than nature's bounty. Mossom, parroting Horace's reference to India's Indians, remarked that Virginia's Indians had capitulated to their moral superiors. All acquiesced in the natural order embedded in rank and power. Law and force of arms curbed moral turpitude and vice within society. Perhaps now gentility, through virtue, might flower in its place.

> Blest by thy Government, our Soil
> With Plenty crowns the Lab'rers Toil,
> The Savage Indians too adore
> Thy Virtues, and confess thy Pow'r:
> Return Obedience to the King,
> And ev'ry Year their Tribute bring.
> Now Wars and Tumults wholly cease,
> And all the Land enjoys sweet Peace.
> Just Order holds its curbing Reins,

18. *Va. Gaz.*, Nov. 19, 1736, "On Good Nature," Jan. 28, 1737, "Praise of Agriculture," Mar. 23, 30, 1739.

19. *Va. Gaz.*, Nov. 19, 1736, "On Good Nature," Jan. 28, 1737.

And wild Licentiousness restrains.
Vice out of Countenance is fled,
And Virtue rises in its Stead.[20]

By recalling an anachronistic model of biblical-era patriarchal estates, the great planters of Virginia found an ideological justification for asserting their place as the rightful leaders of a province in social crisis during the 1720s and 1730s. In projecting a virtuous society, they sought to distinguish their class from money-grubbing merchants in Great Britain, cruel slaveholders of the West Indies, and venal royal appointees to the province. To minimize, even deny, internal conflict, as Mossom did in his poem, the great planters had to assure their dominance in the ascending order of the body politic within Virginia. They therefore would seek to further control small and parvenu planters and contain women within the domestic sphere. In doing so, they would have to reconcile patriarchism with the competing ideology of republicanism and changing conceptions of affection.

The Difference between Gentle and Simple

Republican ideals, including autonomy, honor, and disinterestedness, or a selfless passion for the commonweal, were well known to English colonial leaders before 1740. This notion of public virtue was grounded in an ideal of landed independence as developed by James Harrington in *Oceana* (1656) and as elaborated by other English republicans of the seventeenth century. Their ideas were not inconsistent with classical, organic notions of political authority. Republicanism presumed that the propertied virtuous few should have power over the many, who would naturally defer to them.[21]

20. David Mossom, "This Imitation of the 15th Ode of the 4th Book of Horace Is Humbly Addressed to the Honourable William Gooch, Esq.; Governor of This Colony . . . ," *Va. Gaz.*, Nov. 26, 1736; David S. Shields, *Oracles of Empire: Poetry, Politics, and Commerce in British America, 1690–1750* (Chicago, 1990), 272. James Kennelly has brought to my attention that Mossom also alluded to Horace's *Carmen Saeculare*, esp. ll. 50–60.

21. J. G. A. Pocock, "The Classical Theory of Deference," *American Historical Review*, LXXXI (1976), 516; Pocock, *The Machiavellian Moment: Florentine Political Thought and the Atlantic Republican Tradition* (Princeton, N.J., 1975), 515; James Harrington, *The Commonwealth of Oceana; and, A System of Politics*, ed. Pocock (New York, 1992); Joyce Appleby, *Liberalism and Republicanism in the Historical Imagination* (Cambridge, Mass., 1992), 22, 124–139; Daniel Walker Howe, "European Sources of Political Ideas in

But republicanism did not countenance a preordained gentry. On this point, the contradiction in patriarchism is clear, for, in the great planters' emerging ideology, the patriarchs were the men *born* to estates. Although the great planters seemed to agree with the republican premise that the ownership of an estate was a natural selector for leadership, they in fact favored a landed aristocracy. The self-described patriarchs frowned on men who amassed estates but were not from the great families, even though they themselves were but nouveaux riches. In the great planters' idealization of the hierarchic polity in Virginia, they perceived themselves as "the self-evident leaders" of "respectful but . . . [not] uncritical" middling and small planters. Yet, in reality, elections, supposed to endorse the standing order, proved to be "insufficient" evidence of deference. Conflicts such as slave uprisings and agitation over tobacco legislation underscored the fragility of the great planters' dominance in society.[22]

Perhaps recognizing the contradiction between patriarchism's claims and Virginia's social conditions, William Parks, in a 1739 issue of the *Virginia Gazette,* referred to an anonymous verse usually attributed to John Ball in the Wat Tyler Rebellion of 1381: "When *Adam* dug and *Eve* span / Who was then the Gentleman?" At the beginning of human history, he implied, class distinctions did not exist. Glossing over the class origins of the gentry, their ruthless engrossment of Virginia's land, and their enslavement of blacks, Parks instead suggested that their virtue had its origins in honest labor. The great-planter class derived its leadership from divine natural order. Parks, distinguishing the great planters from poorer whites, wrote: "True Virtue can have no mercenary Considerations. . . . But some look, with an envious Eye, upon their prosperous Neighbours; others, upon Offices of Profit and Honour, etc. These are the most miserable of Men being."[23]

For the great planters to successfully impose their hierarchic scheme on lesser planters, they had to distinguish themselves by outward symbols and appearances. People increasingly gauged the great planters' status by visible signs and marks of respect: salutations, dress, and manner of play. The first generation of great planters engrossed English appellations of

---

Jeffersonian America," *Reviews in American History,* X, no. 4 (December 1982), 33–34; Richard R. Beeman, "Deference, Republicanism, and the Emergence of Popular Politics in Eighteenth-Century America," *WMQ,* 3d Ser., XLIX (1992), 405.

22. Beeman, "Deference," *WMQ,* 3d Ser., XLIX (1992), 408.

23. *Va. Gaz.,* Sept. 24, 1736, "Praise of Agriculture," Mar. 23, 30, 1739.

gentility just as they engrossed the land. The men pretentiously affixed "gentleman" after their names, although they could hardly claim such rank through the College of Heralds. The women, as their wives, widows, or daughters, became "ladies," the title of English nobility. Councillors signed "Esquire" after their names, an English honorific indicating the chief landowner in the district, and the chief militia officer in the county appropriated the title of colonel. They passed these marks onto their children as they passed on the titles to land and offices of profit and power. In public, the gentry could expect the etiquette of deference at every turn. The gentlemen saluted their social inferiors with a cultivated condescension that the classes returned with the proper obeisance: the substantial planter with an admiring gaze, the common planters with doffed hat, and the enslaved with averted eyes. The ladies did not greet those of lesser status directly but from behind the protective facade of an escort. Clothing and personal effects, such as wigs, also marked a person's rank and commanded deference. The gentry wore laces, linens, silks, ruffled cuffs, and wigs that marked them as free from manual labor. The common planters wore cottons, woolens, and yarns suitable to working in the fields. The enslaved wore the coarse canvas German-imported Oznabrigs that marked their degradation. Reverend Devereux Jarratt, a longtime minister of Bath Parish, Dinwiddie County, recalled the awe-inspiring effect of such elite symbols as a child growing up in New Kent County.

> We were accustomed to look upon, what were called gentle folks, as beings of a superior order. . . . A *periwig,* in those days, was a distinguishing badge of *gentle folk*—and when I saw a man riding the road, near our house, with a wig on, it would so alarm my fears, and give me such a disagreeable feeling, that, I dare say, I would run off, as for my life. Such ideas of the difference between *gentle* and *simple* were, I believe, universal among all of my rank and age.[24]

24. C. G. Chamberlayne, ed., *The Vestry Book and Register of St. Peter's Parish, New Kent, and James City Counties, Virginia, 1684-1786* (Richmond, Va., 1937), 659-660 (emphasis in original); T. H. Breen, "Horses and Gentlemen: The Cultural Significance of Gambling among the Gentry of Virginia," *WMQ,* 3d Ser., XXXIV (1977), 239-257; Beeman, "Deference," ibid., XLIX (1992), 410-411; Rhys Isaac, "Evangelical Revolt: The Nature of the Baptists' Challenge to the Traditional Order in Virginia, 1765 to 1775," ibid., XXXI (1974), 345-368; Isaac, *The Transformation of Virginia, 1740-1790* (Chapel Hill, N.C., 1982), 43-138; Beeman and Isaac, "Cultural Conflict and Social Change," *Jour. So. Hist.,* XLVI (1980), 526-530; A. G. Roeber, "Authority, Law, and Custom: The Rituals of Court Day in Tidewater Virginia, 1720 to 1750," *WMQ,* 3d Ser., XXXVII (1980), 29-52.

The great planters participated in rituals of play unique to their rank, such as horse racing. Only wealthy planters could afford to breed horses or host races. Sporting events such as horse races might be seen by all but were the separate purview of the gentry, who staged them. An earlier generation of great planters during the era of the landgrab had cultivated the traits of their class in this sport: competitiveness, individuality, and acquisitiveness. Off-the-cuff competitors covering wagers raced shaggy sprinters on straight quarter-mile makeshift pathways. By the 1720s, the great planters had raised the level of competition to ritual, evoking their new patriarchal traits: order, moderation, and productivity. The impromptu challenge had given way to the scheduled event, the pathway to the track, and the shaggy horse to the larger galloping breed, improved with the introduction in 1730 of Bulle Rock, an Arabian. Horse racing allowed the great planters to elevate physical prowess as a natural symbol, with women and smaller planters as unequal participants. By including women and lesser planters as witnesses to their prowess, performance, and patronage, the great planters reinforced deferential decorum. The *Virginia Gazette,* for example, giving insight into the sport's societal function, publicized horse races in 1736 and 1737. "Some merry-dispos'd gentlemen" in Hanover prompted an annual festival on November 30, St. Andrew's Day, which included a quarter-mile race, activities of "Exercise and Agility," and "several other Diversions, for the Entertainment of the Gentlemen and Ladies." The public could attend but would be expected to comport themselves with proper decorum, for this was a celebration of class cohesion. "All persons resorting there are desir'd to behave themselves with Decency and Sobriety; the Subscribers being resolv'd to discountenance all Immorality with the utmost Rigour." The reason for the festivities was given: "Hanover County is large, well-seated, and inhabited by a considerable Number of Gentlemen, Merchants, and credible Planters who being desirous of cultivating Friendship; and innocent Mirth, propos'd annual meeting of the best Sort, of both Sexes."[25]

25. *Va. Gaz.,* Nov. 19–26, 1736, Sept. 30–Oct. 7, 1737; Breen, "Horses and Gentlemen," *WMQ,* 3d Ser., XXXIV (1977), 243, 250–251; Jane Carson, *Colonial Virginians at Play* (Charlottesville, Va., 1965), 103–119; Isaac, *Transformation of Virginia,* 43–46, 52–57, 98–101; Louis B. Wright, *The First Gentlemen of Virginia: Intellectual Qualities of the Early Colonial Ruling Class* (San Marino, Calif., 1940), 41–66. Elite women were, however, able to compete with gentlemen by betting on races, which exposed tension within the plantation household, covert female aspiration, and a challenge to male dominance; see Linda L. Sturtz, "The Ladies and the Lottery: Elite Women's Gambling in Eighteenth-Century Virginia," *VMHB,* CIV (1996), 165–184.

The amplification of architecture during the 1720s and 1730s ramified the values of patriarchism in the landscape. The great planters built about a dozen great mansions, including Mann Page's Rosewell, Gloucester County, Thomas Lee's Stratford, Westmoreland County, William Byrd's Westover, Charles City County, and Robert "King" Carter's Corotoman, Lancaster County. Hugh Jones wrote in 1724 that "the gentlemen's seats are of late built for the most part of good brick," perhaps indicating that the elite needed the stability of brick to shore up their shaky social foundations. Their architects began to employ a design of arcaded piazzas, which connected the main house with the dependent working buildings, further affirming the authority of the great-planter family and the dependence of the enslaved. This arched design also could be found in the newly built courthouses of the 1720s. Wooden courthouses were giving way to formal brick ones modeled after the Williamsburg public buildings. Churches formerly plain and made of wood were now refined and bricked. For the first time, the parish vestries began to plan their foundations with bricks rather than posts. Fifteen churches were built in the 1730s—more than any other decade—and were designed according to Anglican custom and tradition, from the tall elegant windows to the hierarchical seating structure and raised pulpit, but also according to a new Virginia vernacular style, with cruciform shapes and vaulted doorways of molded brick or wood. Christ Church (built ca. 1732–1735), Lancaster County, served as the prototype of this new provincial architecture. Although the cruciform structure, or T plan, symbolizes the cross, the architects' main concern was to build a structure that allowed most of the congregants a clear view of the pulpit and of the gentry in the front pews. This building efflorescence was thus not just an expression of increased wealth; the elite used the new architecture of the 1720s and 1730s to elevate their status and to distinguish themselves from others while proclaiming the value of stability, order, rank, and power.[26]

26. Fraser D. Neiman, "Domestic Architecture at the Clifts Plantation: The Social Context of Early Virginia Building," in Dell Upton and John Michael Vlach, eds., *Common Places: Readings in American Vernacular Architecture* (Athens, Ga., 1986), 292–314; Upton, *Holy Things and Profane: Anglican Parish Churches in Colonial Virginia* (New York, 1986), 13, 31–34, 70–73, 79–98; Vlach, *Back of the Big House: The Architecture of Plantation Slavery* (Chapel Hill, N.C., 1993), 3–5; Beeman and Isaac, "Cultural Conflict and Social Change," *Jour. So. Hist.,* XLVI (1980), 529; Roeber, "Authority, Law, and Custom," *WMQ,* 3d Ser., XXXVII (1980), 36–37; Isaac, *The Transformation of Virginia,* 16 (quotation), 58–65, 73–74, 323–357; Sobel, *The World They Made Together,* 127; Richard L. Bushman, "American High-Style and Vernacular Cultures," in Jack P. Greene and J. R.

A hierarchical class structure was only one aspect of patriarchism. The role of women within the gentry was also delineated. Parks's use of John Ball's verse again is illustrative: "When *Adam* dug and *Eve* span / Who was then the Gentleman?" Eve, of course, could not be the gentleman, so, in the natural order, patriarchy existed from the beginning. By refining patriarchism, the great planters hoped to subordinate women's role to hearth and home.

Several demographic changes in Virginia had significance for the development of patriarchism. The gender imbalance of the early seventeenth century had social consequences, for women generally exerted a stabilizing influence on community life. Fewer women in a society often meant an increase in general restlessness and mobility, weak authority, and frequent acts of violence. When women were proportionately represented, their presence tended to emphasize the virtues of home and settled life. Seventeenth-century commentators regarded the domesticating influence of good wives as the key to restoring the social order. With the increase of blacks working on plantations, white women were, for the most part, removed from the fields and relegated to the domestic sphere. As their role as guardians of culture became more pronounced with settled life, they undoubtedly influenced the emerging patriarchism.[27]

During the early seventeenth century, the scarcity of white women and the high mortality rate among white men had enabled a few women to accumulate huge estates by arranging profitable marriages. With the increasing life expectancies of white men after 1700, there was, in essence, a transition from "widowarchy" to patriarchy. Women's influence in familial and economic life diminished, as the number who outlived their husbands, held families together singlehandedly, or amassed wealth decreased.[28]

Pole, eds., *Colonial British America: Essays in the New History of the Early Modern Era* (Baltimore, 1984), 360–365, 370–373; Edmund S. Morgan, *American Slavery, American Freedom: The Ordeal of Colonial Virginia* (New York, 1975), 368.

27. Mary Beth Norton, *Liberty's Daughters: The Revolutionary Experience of American Women, 1750–1800* (Ithaca, N.Y., 1980), 3, 5–7, 38, 110, 112, 126–127; Morgan, *American Slavery, American Freedom,* 166; Herbert Moller, "Sex Composition and Correlated Culture Patterns of Colonial America," *WMQ,* 3d Ser., II (1945), 137–138, 153; Brown, *Good Wives, Nasty Wenches,* 31, 80–82, 128; Kulikoff, *Tobacco and Slaves,* 161–174.

28. Daniel Blake Smith, *Inside the Great House: Planter Family Life in Eighteenth-Century Chesapeake Society* (Ithaca, N.Y., 1980), 79–81; Kulikoff, *Tobacco and Slaves,* 161–174; Morgan, *American Slavery, American Freedom,* 162–168; Brown, *Good Wives, Nasty*

Nevertheless, women in the gentry retained a great deal of power. Men protected the continuity of their estates by naming their wives as executors and, often, their daughters as beneficiaries. Perhaps as many as 16–20 percent of the entailed bequests named heiresses. The widow, at least during her lifetime, had control of the estate. The decedent, by assuring his inheritance and shielding the estate from a second husband, had unwittingly empowered his widow.[29]

The property rights of widows put the great planters in a quandary with regard to the patriarchal claims of new husbands. In a 1727 debate over a widow's rights to an intestate husband's enslaved laborers, the General Assembly gave priority to a man's right to an estate over the needs of a woman. A widow had been able to retain her intestate husband's enslaved blacks as real property since 1705. The new act rendered the enslaved as "absolute property" to her new husband, unless they were adscripted to entailed lands. (Yet, even here, these enslaved blacks were still liable for the debts incurred by the estate, ostensibly to protect British merchants who had given credit based on the number of enslaved laborers the planter owned). Opponents of the act had argued unsuccessfully that the new husband could "squander" his wife's estate and "leave her a Beggar." Proponents had countered that her inconvenience was no greater if her estate consisted only in money; the "greater" "hardship" belongs to a husband who marries a woman whose estate "portion is only in Slaves." The husband had to be protected, for "after maintaining [a wife] many Years suitable to her Rank and Degree and then she dying without Issue, her whole Estate shall be taken away from the Husband." Lawmakers thus tried to circumscribe female propertyholding, though the law of entail still had precedence. Despite the 1727 act, many women retained control of their deceased husband's estate, and some men continued to leave their estates

Wenches, 31, 80–82, 128; Linda L. Sturtz, *Within Her Power: Propertied Women in Colonial Virginia* (New York, 2002), 29–30.

29. Brewer, "Entailing Aristocracy," *WMQ*, 3d Ser., LIV (1997), 322–323. Brewer's findings suggest that elite women might have had greater property rights under patriarchism than they would have later under republicanism. See also Joan R. Gundersen and Gwen Victor Gampel, "Married Women's Legal Status in Eighteenth-Century New York and Virginia," *WMQ*, 3d Ser., XXXIX (1982), 116–127; Linda L. Sturtz, "'As Though I My Self Was Pr[e]sent': Virginia Women with Power of Attorney," in Christopher L. Tomlins and Bruce H. Mann, eds., *The Many Legalities of Early America* (Chapel Hill, N.C., 2001), 250–271; Marylynn Salmon, *Women and the Law of Property in Early America* (Chapel Hill, N.C., 1986), 151–154.

in the care of their wives on behalf of their children, crimping the authority of new husbands.[30]

To deal with increasing anxiety over the real and imagined power of women, the great planters used patriarchism to demonstrate their authority. They did so by promoting women as guardians of virtue, confining them to housewifery and child rearing, and castigating their carnal disposition. Parks, for example, giving voice to the patriarchal values promoted by the great planters, published a verse in the *Virginia Gazette* by an unnamed Irish bard that emphasized both the civilizing effects of women on society and their need for male authority. The feminine role of domesticating men had its roots in essential male vulgarity, which resulted from men's competition in public affairs. The poem also stresses male responsibility for female viciousness. Although by nature women are virtuous, they could be corrupted through sexual provocation, thus bringing the female carnal instinct to the surface. Only through male self-control and vigilance could women become champions of virtue and return society to the Edenic ideal.

> The Woman promise, but the Men obey.
> By them the World has ever since been led,
> And cully'd Men content with the name of Head.
> Our wits by our Employments may appear,
> Our Days of Labour, and our Nights of care,
> Fatigues of War, and Drudgeries of State,
> Wifely endured to make our Women Great:
> All that is Good in Life, for Life they chuse;
> We Glean up all the Bad which they refuse;
> Suppose them in their Taste not over nice,
> Say, Is not want of Taste our common Vice?
> Suppose in Women you no Faith can find;
> Say, are not Men less faithful than the Wind?
> No Wonder that their Frailties go astray,
> On our own Conduct chiefly hangs our Fate;
> Neglect them, and our Title's in debate:
> Not Heat, but Provocation fires their Blood;
> Good were all Men, all women would be good.

30. *SAL,* III, 333–335, IV, 222–225 (quotation on 223); William Gooch to BT, June 8, 1728, CO 5/1321, 44–45, VCRP; Brown, *Good Wives, Nasty Wenches,* 287–289; Kulikoff, *Tobacco and Slaves,* 188–189.

By Nature, virtuous, virtuous as they're fair;
We make them vicious, vicious when they are,
Cou'd Man but once resolve to sin no more,
Woman wou'd soon lost Innocence restore.[31]

Within the great-planter class, expressions of political anxieties and inadequacies found formulation in sexual terms. They attributed women's reproductive capacity and projected sexual prowess as sources of their own impotence, describing women as sphinxlike monsters capable of annihilating them. They brooded over the prospect of being cuckolded and the resulting bastards corrupting their line of inheritance to estate and rank. The writings of William Byrd II, particularly in his Commonplace Book and his essay titled "The Female Creed," gave vent to the frustrations underlying the emerging patriarchal ideology in eighteenth-century Virginia. Unlike the nineteenth century, when women would be regarded as the weaker sex, Byrd defined women as sexually powerful, lustful, and lascivious. Black women, especially, he described using sensual and erotic images. Men, on the other hand, were easily tempted and could be overcome by sexual impulse. Female lasciviousness meant anarchy and chaos. Unnatural, lustful women, he believed, were not fecund. If order and authority were to prevail, men of the great-planter class had to avoid promiscuous white women; if they were to preserve the white race and society, women had to be forced to submit to strict patriarchal control.[32]

Since building estates was a central goal in which marriage and inheritance played crucial roles, fathers also exerted control over their children.[33] Ideally, sons were to be assertive and self-reliant; in turn, they inherited property and became patriarchs of estates. Daughters were counseled to

31. "On Woman," *Va. Gaz.*, Feb. 16, 1739, "Praise of Agriculture," Mar. 23, 1739.

32. Byrd even recommended that men take women from behind sexually, for this not only rendered them submissive but made reproduction more likely. Lockridge, *On the Sources of Patriarchal Rage*, 1–45; William Byrd, "The Female Creed," in Woodfin, ed., *Another Secret Diary*, trans. Tinling, 445–475; Sobel, *The World They Made Together*, 147. See also Kenneth A. Lockridge, "Colonial Self-Fashioning: Paradoxes and Pathologies in the Construction of Genteel Identity in Eighteenth-Century America," in Ronald Hoffman, Mechal Sobel, and Fredrika J. Teute, eds., *Through a Glass Darkly: Reflections on Personal Identity in Early America* (Chapel Hill, N.C., 1997), 288–301; Brown, *Good Wives, Nasty Wenches*, 328–334.

33. Byrd, anxious about their marriage settlements, dominated his children, daughters included. He even discouraged Daniel Custis's courtship with his daughter Anne in 1741 because he believed that his personal difficulties with John Custis would diminish her settlement. See Brown, *Good Wives, Nasty Wenches*, 258.

Plate 14. John Custis, IV, "Tulip" Custis, at Age Forty-eight. Portrait by an
unknown American artist. Ca. 1725. *Courtesy, Washington-Custis-Lee Collection,
Washington and Lee University, Lexington, Va.*

marry well and assist their husbands in the management of the estate.
The different expectations of the Custis children illustrate the range of
patriarchical identity invested in emerging gender and racial roles. Al-
though John Custis IV offered little affection to his daughter Frances Parke
(Custis) Winch Danise, he focused on seeing her satisfactorily married.
On the other hand, he sent his son Daniel Parke Custis to the College of

William and Mary rather than abroad to keep him close at hand. He left him 275 acres of land in St. Peter's Parish, New Kent County (worth about two thousand pounds), "for the naturall love and affection" that he bore for him. Underscoring the line of descent between father and son, this land was a supplement to Daniel's expected inheritance and more than a sentimental gesture in the older region of Virginia, where few fathers gave bequests to their sons because most of the land was already entailed.[34]

Fewer fathers still recognized their children born of enslaved women. Such offspring most certainly were not expected to become or marry patriarchs. More often than not, they continued in their enslaved status. Custis, however, petitioned the governor and the Council of State to manumit his son John, "born of the body of my slave Alice." Custis provided that John be "handsomely maintained out of the profits of my estate given him." This estate included building "a handsome strong convenient dwelling house," designed by Custis, on a plantation that he purchased on Queens Creek in York County. He bequeathed that it be furnished with a dozen high-backed and a dozen low-backed Russian leather chairs, a "good and strong" Russian leather couch, "three good feather bedsteads and furniture," and "two good black walnut tables." He also provided that fences and "other appurtenanes" on the plantation be kept in "good repair." As further evidence of his attention, he commissioned a miniature portrait of John. In his bequest to John, whom he affectionately called his "dear black boy Jack," he clearly signaled his paternity, if not patriarchism. Jack died in 1751 before he received his inheritance. By these arrangements for his progeny's future, Custis exerted his power over the next generation for his daughters through marriages, for his white son through property and supervised education, and for his black son through freedom and a maintenance.[35]

With the emergence of patriarchism, great planters viewed providing for their white children's education as a parental duty necessary to realize the divinely designed order that would enable their children to distinguish themselves in both "Class and Rank" from their underlings. Although

34. Jo Zuppan, ed., "Father to Son: Letters from John Custis IV to Daniel Parke Custis," *VMHB*, XCVIII (1990), 81, 83.

35. Ibid., 83–90 (quotations on 87–88), 97–100; Deed of trust for Jack Freedman, Custis Family Papers, 1663–1858, section 6, MSS C96898a, 38–40, VHS; Smith, *Inside the Great House*, 292; Smith, "In Search of Family," in Jordan and Skemp, eds., *Race and Family*, 30–31; Brown, *Good Wives, Nasty Wenches*, 346, 348, 359, 370; Kulikoff, *Tobacco and Slaves*, 272.

some great planters continued to send children off to England, many believed metropolitan values engendered independence from parental authority and provincial ways and thus tried to promote instead natural affection and proper breeding at home. Such education fostered parental control of children and prepared them to run the peculiar households and plantations that made up their estates. Untoward children tried their fathers' hand, eliciting from them threats of disinheritance (pronouncements limited by the rules of entail and primogeniture). Graduation speeches exemplify these patriarchal characteristics. Not only were they notorious for idealistic rhetoric; they were designed to strike a familiar chord with their audience. In an oration delivered upon graduation from the College of William and Mary in 1722, the speaker cautioned his fellows of the consequences of sending sons abroad to England for education. Not only will the returning son not "know how to manage a Virginia estate, trained in English ways," but he will not "Submit himselfe to the Paternall or Maternall Yoke." What is worse, not only will the child feel abandoned by his parents; he will "truly forget" them and act "as if he were under no filial tye or Relation." From this insensibility "there grows a Strangeness and a want of Natural affection."[36]

The contradictions inherent in patriarchism were everywhere in Virginia society in the 1720s and 1730s. Inherited privilege flew in the face of republicanism; the calculated interests of patriarchism put a damper on emerging notions of affection. The property rights of widows to the estates of their deceased husbands had to be reconciled with the patriarchal claims of new husbands; women were at once considered guardians of virtue and receptacles of vice. The tensions between control and self-assertion would be even more acute when applied to blacks.

Either a Fool or a Fury

Printed accounts of repression, rebellion, and violence in Africa, the West Indies, and North America fueled planters' fears of slave rebellions in Virginia and its most frightening consequence, black rule over white society. Planters repressed this horror by denying its possibility through patriarchism.

36. Oration, College of William and Mary, Williamsburg, Va., 1722, BV 13, SPG, Package II, Klingberg Collection; Brown, *Good Wives, Nasty Wenches*, 342–343; Brewer, "Entailing Aristocracy," *WMQ*, 3d Ser., LIV (1997), 303–317.

The source of the great planters' anxiety was unique to its time and place. In early-eighteenth-century Virginia, the enslaved were defined as real estate and no longer personal property. As such, they were legally alienated from their owners and attached to the land only, lacking the bonds of mutual obligation that existed in traditional hierarchies. Deference, which required at least a conditioned freedom, was absent from the master-slave relationship. The enslaved had to be forced into submission. Rebellious enslaved blacks do not fit the mold for which patriarchism was shaped; yet it was shaped precisely to suppress the reality of the rebellious enslaved. The great planters thus feared the combined danger of racially alienated and enslaved people, who threatened not only society but also the ideological foundation of that society. Both masters and enslaved recognized the unstable grounds of power. As Lewis P. Simpson has concluded: "Thus arose a fear compounded by the racial dimension of slavery but not produced by it: the fear of slavery as being not simply a threat to the social order but of its being a subversion of the very source of order— that is, the mind and imagination."[37]

To deal directly with the alienation of a labor force from the society they were meant to support, the great planters developed in particular one aspect of patriarchism, the responsibility of the paterfamilias, or head of household. Planters aimed at co-opting the enslaved by making them fictitious members of their families. As fictive fathers, planters were responsible for the naming, care, and supervision of the enslaved, including an invasive concern with their health and reproduction. A familial model of authority helped to satisfy the great planters' need to justify themselves and their society by invoking the concept of black dependence. As blacks' cultural distinctiveness from whites became less pronounced with the creolization of the slave population, the great planters resorted to claims of inferiority as a defense of slavery. They legitimized the enslavement of blacks by portraying themselves as patrons of a benighted people. The enslaved needed and benefited from their master's protection.[38]

37. *SAL,* III, 333–335, IV, 222–228; Simpson, *The Dispossessed Garden,* 20–23; Anderson, *Imagined Communities,* 12, 48–51.

38. William McKee Evans, "From the Land of Canaan to the Land of Guinea: The Strange Odyssey of the 'Sons of Ham,'" *AHR,* LXXXV (1980), 19–21; John W. Bennett, "Paternalism," *International Encyclopedia of the Social Sciences,* XI (1968), 472–477; David Brion Davis, "Slavery," in C. Vann Woodward, ed., *The Comparative Approach to American History* (New York, 1968), 132. Cf. Philip Morgan, "Three Planters and Their Slaves:

The great planters were especially compelled to develop this racial aspect of patriarchism because of the printed reports of black violence abroad. When William Byrd II described Virginia as New Guinea in 1736, the year that 3,125 Africans entered Virginia, he was likely aware of *A New Account of Some Parts of Guinea,* recently published in London in 1734. The author, William Snelgrave, raised the specter of black violence against slave traders. His *Account* is apologetic of the slave trade and heavy with tales of Africans' sacrificing humans, selling their children into slavery, and engaging in cannibalism. But, more important, it chronicles rebelliousness aboard slave ships and the Dahomean destruction and desolation of Ouidah, an outlet for 20,000 slaves a year, and other factories on the Slave Coast from 1727 to 1732. Snelgrave also wrote that Agada, the king of Dahomey, even executed the English governor, who had whipped a principal man of Dahomey at the flagstaff and had foolishly said he would serve the king of Dahomey likewise *"if he was in his Power."*[39]

Newspaper accounts of white slavery heightened awareness of struggles for power between blacks and whites. In the pages of the *Virginia Gazette,* discussions of Africans and Europeans in Morocco played out role reversals in racial slavery. Morocco offered the converse of Virginia: Africans enslaved Europeans, and blacks occupied positions of authority and power. The *Gazette* reported that the French and the Dutch were unable to secure "the Redemption of [white] Slaves." In February 1736, it reported that the Emperor Muley Abdallah, a white, "treated with uncommon Civility" English ships and "that the English Nation was never in higher Esteem with the Moors." In September, however, the *Gazette* reported that the "principal Officers of the Blacks" had seized power. An extract from a London letter reprinted in the October issue reported that "the black Army was well united, and firmly resolved to maintain Muli Alli on the Throne." In December, the *Gazette* juxtaposed with advertisements for runaway blacks an item about a white man who escaped slavery in Barbary and would be "presented to his Majesty at Kensington." The slavery of whites in a country where blacks held power had indeed caught the great planters' attention.[40]

Perspectives on Slavery in Virginia, South Carolina, and Jamaica, 1750–1790," in Jordan and Skemp, eds., *Race and Family,* 39–40; Brown, *Good Wives, Nasty Wenches,* 366.

39. William Snelgrave, *A New Account of Some Parts of Guinea, and the Slave-Trade . . .* (London, 1734), 130–131. See Chapter 5 for a discussion of rebellions aboard slave ships.

40. *Va. Gaz.,* Feb. 4, Sept. 10, Oct. 1, Dec. 22, 1736; John W. Blassingame, *The Slave*

The *Virginia Gazette* spelled out in vivid detail attempted insurrections even closer to home, in Antigua, Jamaica, and South Carolina. Antiguan rebels were described as grotesquely heroic; Jamaican maroons were lionized for their ability to extract a treaty from the English. The discussion of the Stono Rebellion in South Carolina in 1739 impressed upon the great planters even more the willingness of blacks to strike for freedom. When war with Spain broke out simultaneously, suspicions deepened that enemies abroad encouraged black rebels at home. Newspapers thus served to incorporate world events into readers' imaginings of their familiar world. For the great planters, these printed accounts of slave rebellions and black hegemony in other countries foreshadowed potential cataclysms in their own society.[41]

William Byrd II, for example, feared that the increasing number of blacks made them "as troublesome and dangerous" as they have "lately" been in Jamaica, where their revolt proved costly in money and lives. Particularly because blacks could take refuge in the Blue Ridge Mountains, he believed, one of them "with more advantage than Cataline, [could] kindle a Servile War . . . [and] before any opposition could be formed against him . . . tinge our rivers as wide as they are with blood." Byrd's anxious projections worked in tandem with his pastoral descriptions of Virginia society. The horror from which Byrd and his fellow great planters recoiled had its source in both realistic and moral qualms. Their ideology of patriarchism articulated their sense of danger from insurrection and their unease with making people chattel. By portraying Virginia as an idyllic society through patriarchism, the great planters could, to some extent, distance themselves from the underlying reality of having enslaved their fellow human beings and repress from their consciousness its latent explosiveness.[42] Thus, invoking scriptural images, Byrd referred to "bond-

Community: Plantation Life in the Antebellum South, 2d ed., rev. and enl. (New York, 1979), 53–55, 61–63.

41. *Va. Gaz.,* Dec. 17, 1736, Mar. 15, Apr. 8, May 27, 1737, Apr. 11, Aug. 22, Nov. 26, 1739, Aug. 22, 1745; Philip J. Schwarz, *Twice Condemned: Slaves and the Criminal Laws of Virginia, 1705–1865* (Baton Rouge, La., 1988), 61. See also David Barry Gaspar, *Bondmen and Rebels: A Study of Master-Slave Relations in Antigua, with Implications for Colonial British America* (Baltimore, 1985); Peter H. Wood, *Black Majority: Negroes in Colonial South Carolina from 1670 through the Stono Rebellion* (New York, 1974), 308–326; Thomas J. Davis, *A Rumor of Revolt: The "Great Negro Plot" in Colonial New York* (New York, 1985); Anderson, *Imagined Communities,* 63.

42. Byrd to Egmont, July 12, 1736, Byrd Letter Book, 1735–1736; Sigmund Freud, "Lec-

men" and "bondwomen" rather than "enslaved," and, as his brother-in-law Robert Beverley II and the Reverend Hugh Jones had before him, he likened the fieldwork of the enslaved to that of a gardener. In this way, he minimized their significance—even as their numbers were increasing—and, therefore, their threat. "Our Negroes are not so numerous, so enterprizing as to give us any apprehension or uneasiness," reflected Byrd. "Nor indeed is their Labour any other than Gardening, and less by far, than poor People undergo in other Countrys."[43]

But the significance of the enslaved and slavery for Virginia's emerging market economy was evident. As commodities, purchased with cash, bills of exchange, and credit, the enslaved were hired out, rented, leased, and sold to satisfy debts. Their owners expropriated their entire surplus value. Indeed, the great planters conceived of hiring slave labor in the same fashion as hiring free labor, the marked distinction being that hirers paid a wage to the owner rather than the worker. The hiring out of the enslaved allowed for the mobility of labor in Virginia, where the enslaved were bound to the estate. Skilled workers, especially carpenters and scythemen, were in great demand, and owners hired out their skills as well as their tools to other planters. Wages, contracts, profits, debits, rents, and interest all figured into the negotiations between the owner and renter of enslaved workers. The great planters would even sometimes lease out entire estates.

The anomaly of slavery in a market economy contributed to the contradictions between patriarchism and daily reality. The great planters understood that remuneration not only dignified labor but also distinguished free labor from slavery. "Honor without money is an empty thing," wrote Governor Gooch. "Every labourer is worthy of his Hire and ought to be paid in proportion to his work, without which I am no better, but in degree, than one of my slaves." Honor and power—and their antithesis, dishonor and powerlessness—are central to master-slave relationships. Not only did slavery dishonor the enslaved; it degraded labor itself. And, because slavery was the primary means by which planters made money, it

ture XXXII: Anxiety and Instinctual Life" (1932), in Peter Gay, ed., *The Freud Reader* (New York, 1989), 773–783. "The Conspiracy of Catiline [63 BCE]" appeared on a broadside in Philadelphia dated Oct. 2, 1727. It was described as "a Conspiracy that was design'd to make the *Honest Freeholders* of the Country, Slaves to those that had neither Virtue nor Common Honesty enough to be own'd by any Country." Robert Ulery brought this source to my attention.

43. Byrd to Beckford, Dec. 6, 1735, Byrd Letter Book, 1735–1736. For similar uses of pastoral imagery with reference to enslaved labor, see Chapter 2, n. 4.

was clearly associated with labor in the minds of the colonists. Indeed, Byrd once remarked that poor whites "detest work for it should make them look like Slaves."[44]

Cognizant that the cash nexus underlay the foundation of slavery in Virginia, Byrd nevertheless extolled the illusion that the system operated outside the money economy by invoking the romance of the pastoral. He exalted the cornucopia of the land and fashioned the fiction that slavery was superior to wage labor because the great planters lived off "the fruit of their labour" without the exchange of wages for work. They co-opted the enslaved by making them honorific members of their families. "Besides the advantages of a pure air," wrote Byrd, "we abound in all kinds of provisions, without expence (I mean we who have plantations)[.] I have a large family of my own, and my doors are open to every body, yet I have no bills to pay, and half-a-crown will rest undisturbed in my pocket for many moons together."[45]

Without wages, one of the main problems faced by the great planters was providing incentives for their enslaved to work. Jonathan Boucher, an Anglican minister remembered primarily for his loyalist views during the American Revolution, noted the poor economics of slavery. Without the incentive of wages, the enslaved required constant supervision. "I believe it is capable of demonstration that, except the immediate interest which every man has in the property of his slaves, it would be for every man's interest that there were no slaves," he wrote. "And for this plain reason, because the free labour of a free man, who is regularly hired and paid for the work which he does, and only for what he does is, in the end, cheaper than the extorted eye-service of a slave."[46]

Slavery was, by definition, a labor system designed to prevent the distribution of goods according to the labor that went into producing them. Robert "King" Carter instructed his overseer that the only method to make the enslaved work for their masters was "to make them stand in fear." To

44. Gooch to his brother, Jan. 9, 1738, typescript, CWF; Byrd to Egmont, July 12, 1736, Byrd Letter Book, 1735–1736; Orlando Patterson, *Slavery and Social Death: A Comparative Study* (Cambridge, Mass., 1982), 10–11; Karl Marx, *Wage-Labour and Capital and Value, Price and Profit* (1891; reprint, New York, 1976), 19–20.

45. Byrd made the connection between slavery and capital formation in Virginia in a letter to "Vigilante" John Smith, commissioner of the excise: "The usual method [of making money] . . . is to seat our own slaves upon it [the land], and send the fruit of their labour, consisting in tobacco and naval stores, to England" (Byrd to [Smith], Feb. 18, 1718, *Byrd Correspondence*, I, 312); Byrd to Boyle, July 5, 1726, ibid., 354–359 (quotation on 355).

46. R. W. Marshall, "What Jonathan Boucher Preached," *VMHB*, XLVI (1938), 8.

justify extortion of blacks' labor, the great planters used the ideology of patriarchism, pointing to blacks' indolence and dependence.[47]

John Custis IV illustrated the difficulty the great planters had in forcing enslaved blacks to work without constant supervision and violence condoned by the state. Blacks refused to work when their masters were away from the plantation, even though an overseer was present. When John Randolph was away in 1732, his enslaved black Simon asserted that he had no master, which led Custis, acting as caretaker, to reassert control and force him to work. "Your plantation business goes on tolerably well," Custis advised his fellow absentee planter Mr. Randolph in 1732. "Only some of the Nigros, and particularly Simon at Chichominy has been a little Sullen and run away, having a notion he has no master; but upon complaint of the overseer, I went immediately up and seized him to his cost." Four years later, Custis complained that absence from his plantation had ruined his tobacco crop because the blacks refused to work. "I should have gone on with the planting if I could have the liberty to make the most of my slaves' labor; but to have it destroy my bossing offers too much trouble in making it a disturbing thing." Although the great planters wanted an efficient laboring force, to keep it they sometimes had to compromise the system of absolute control in favor of preserving their hegemonic authority. The exigencies of holding a race captive encouraged them to keep the enslaved demoralized, dependent, and ignorant. In the end, the conditions in which the great planters maintained the enslaved undermined the superstructure of patriarchism, which held the master responsible for the enslaved's welfare.[48]

The attempt of the planters to assert control over slave identities also belied the probity of patriarchism. The naming and clothing of the enslaved, for example, meant first and foremost stripping them of their former identities and asserting the planters' dominion over their physical beings. These rituals were key to initiating the survivors of the Middle Passage into the ranks of the enslaved. When they arrived in Virginia, enslaved boys and girls were "all Stark naked," as were the "greatest part" of the men and women, observed William Hugh Grove. "Some had beads about their necks and arms and [Waists] and a ragg or Peice of Leather the bigness of a figg leaf." Newly purchased blacks were brought to the

47. Robert Carter to Robert Jones, Oct. 10, 1727, Robert Carter Letter Book, 1727–1728, M-113, CWF.

48. John Custis to Mr. Randolph, 1732, Custis to Micajah Perry, 1736, John Custis Letter Book, 1717–1742, LC.

plantation, where they were issued coarse cotton shirts and drawers and given names, often diminutives such as Tom, Jack, or Sue. Robert "King" Carter, writing to his overseer, insisted that blacks became familiarized with the new identities affixed to them: "I am sure we repeated them so often to them that evry one knew their names and would readyly answer to them." Masters also could mock the enslaved by naming them like pets; from classical antiquity, for example, they often assigned to blacks mythological names such as Jupiter and Pluto or historical ones such as Julius Caesar and Scipio. While demoralizing the enslaved, such practices served the planters' business interests and, at the same time, reinforced their control over the enslaved.[49]

In his autobiography, Olaudah Equiano discusses the identity conflicts he experienced because of this casual naming practice. Equiano remembered that Igbo names marked either some event or foreboding at the time of one's birth. His given name Olaudah, foreshadowing his life, suggested the following characteristics: vicissitude, fortune, favor, and loud voice. Yet, even though he had his own African names, his captors imposed other Anglicized personal names, first Jacob, then Michael, that called up a "miserable, forlorn, and much dejected state . . . which made my life a burden." After being sold by his Virginia master, Mr. Campbell, he was renamed Gustavus Vassa by Michael Henry Pascal, a lieutenant in the British navy, apparently to hide his status from the Admiralty, which frowned upon officers' having enslaved blacks at sea. Gustavus Vassa was the name of a Swedish freedom fighter (1496–1560) and thus can be seen in the same light as the degrading historical and classical names given to his contemporaries. At first, Equiano resisted his new name, which "gained me many a cuff; so at length I submitted, and by which I have been known ever

49. William Hugh Grove Diary, April 1732, microfilm, CWF; Carter to Jones, Oct. 10, 1727, Carter Letter Book, 1727–1728, M-113; Sobel, *The World They Made Together,* 157; Darrett B. Rutman and Anita H. Rutman, *A Place in Time: Middlesex County, Virginia, 1650–1750* (New York, 1984), 173; Morgan, *Slave Counterpoint,* 549–550; Ira Berlin, *Many Thousands Gone: The First Two Centuries of Slavery in North America* (Cambridge, Mass., 1998), 95–96, 112; Eugene D. Genovese, *Roll, Jordan, Roll: The World the Slaves Made* (New York, 1972), 447–450; Herbert G. Gutman, *The Black Family in Slavery and Freedom, 1750–1925* (New York, 1976), 186–191; Cheryll Ann Cody, "There Was No 'Absalom' on the Ball Plantations: Slave-Naming Practices in the South Carolina Low Country, 1720–1865," *AHR,* XCII (1987), 563–596; Carol Berkin and Leslie Horowitz, eds., *Women's Voices, Women's Lives: Documents in Early American History* (Boston, 1998), 52; Shane White, *Somewhat More Independent: The End of Slavery in New York City, 1770–1810* (Athens, Ga., 1991), 192–193.

since." Undoubtedly aware of the irony of being named after a freedom
fighter, he appropriated the name, choosing to call himself Gustavus Vassa
for the remainder of his life. With time, as Virginia's slave society matured,
many blacks did as Equiano did and appropriated naming practices for
themselves. Enslaved parents shunned classical and derisive names and
chose names of kin, especially fathers, separated from them in time and
space, for their children.[50]

Planters found other ways of extending control over the physical terms
of enslaved existence. Poor-quality clothing was a means both to saving
money and to underscoring inferior status. Planters deliberately issued inadequate clothing of the poorest quality to their enslaved: imported coarse
fabrics called Negro cottons and the plain and coarse German linens called
Oznabrigs. When searching for a suitable metaphor to allude to cloth of
the worst quality, John Custis IV used slave clothing, which he described
as "mostly cut rags." He once complained to Robert Cary that the stock-
ings he received on consignment were "the wors trash I ever saw so unfit
that they will not fit Nigros." An adamant opponent of the tobacco Inspection Act, Custis wrote in 1739 that not even Negro clothes were fit
for a tobacco inspector. When ordering blankets, William Beverley made
sure that his correspondent understood his requisition. "They are for my
negros so that I desire you will buy such as are suitable."[51]

A fine line existed between planters' patriarchical duty to supply decent
materials to cover the bodies of their enslaved and their interests to harbor
resources and degrade blacks. Overstepping too far could have negative
consequences for the master. Byrd described the "Scandal" of Colonel
Thomas Jones's blacks, who were "a kind of Adamites, very Scantily sup-

50. Olaudah Equiano, *The Interesting Narrative of the Life of Olaudah Equiano, or
Gustavus Vassa, the African; Written by Himself* (1789), ed. Paul Edwards, 2 vols. (London, 1969), I, 31, 90, 92; Olaudah Equiano, *The Interesting Narrative and Other Writings,*
ed. Vincent Carretta (New York, 1995), xx, 63, 64, 252 n. 129; Sobel, *The World They Made
Together,* 156–160; Ira Berlin, "From Creole to African: Atlantic Creoles and the Origins
of African-American Society in Mainland North America," *WMQ,* 3d Ser., LIII (1996),
251–252; Rutman and Rutman, *A Place in Time,* 173; James Walvin, *An African's Life: The
Life and Times of Olaudah Equiano, 1745–1797* (London, 1998), 31–32.

Vincent Carretta, our best authority, believes that Mr. Campbell is likely Alexander
Campbell, also owner of Quobna Ottobah Cugoano. See Quobna Ottobah Cugoano,
*Thoughts and Sentiments on the Evils and Wicked Traffic of the Slavery and Commerce of
the Human Species . . .* (1787), ed. Vincent Carretta (New York, 1999), x.

51. John Custis to ———, February 1726, Custis to Robert Cary, 1741, Custis to Gentleman, 1739, Custis Letter Book, 1717–1742; William Beverley to [Thomas] Blackhouse,
Nov. 19, 1740, William Beverley Letter Book, 1737–1744, M-1334, CWF.

Olaudah Equiano;

or

GUSTAVUS VASSA,

the African?

Published March 1 1789 by G. Vassa

Plate 15. Olaudah Equiano; or Gustavus Vassa, the African. Engraved by
Daniel Orne, after the painting by William Denton. [1789?]. *The photograph
of Olaudah Equiano is used with the permission of the Special Collections
Department, University of California, Riverside*

ply'd with cloaths and other necessaries. . . . However, they are even with their Master, and make him but indifferent Crops." Although the planters considered Jones's neglect of his enslaved reprehensible, most of them were caught in a balancing act between patriarchal ideals of responsibility and domination.[52]

As colonials, the planters were trapped in their own web of dependence within British mercantilism. They sought to shift the burden of responsibility implicit in patriarchism from themselves to the merchants and often blamed them for the poor quality of slave clothing. Indeed, because of Virginia's dependency in the mercantile system, the enslaved suffered severe deprivation, depending upon market conditions and the relative wealth of their owners. Governor Gooch emphasized the vulnerability of the enslaved when he promoted the tobacco Inspection Act in 1732. The act would improve tobacco prices and encourage planters to buy English goods, which they "have for sometime gone without, insomuch that their Negroes go naked all the Winter, have not the proper Tools to work with, and their Quarters for want of Nails are tumbling down."[53]

Food supply was another area in which the great planters asserted their dominion over the enslaved. Unlike the sugar islands, which depended upon the importation of food, Virginia produced enough grain to be an exporter of food (except in periods of crisis), but great planters provided their enslaved with only enough for subsistence. Blacks supplemented their diet by cultivating small plots near their quarters at night and on Sundays and by raising fowl. In 1701, Francis Louis Michel and George Larkin both observed that the quality of slave food was wanting in taste, nutrition, and variety. The coarse and uniform fare allowed to blacks sharply differentiated their status from those they were forced to serve. Michel reported that "many die on the journey or in the beginning of their stay here, because they receive meagre food and are kept very strictly. . . . Among such people food tastes so badly, that one can hardly stand it." Larkin reported to the Board of Trade in the same year that the enslaved's diet

52. John Spencer Bassett, ed., *The Writings of "Colonel William Byrd of Westover in Virginia Esqr."* (New York, 1901), 348.

53. Gooch to BT, May 27, 1732, CO 5/1323, 29–31, VCRP. John Custis IV once complained to Micajah Perry III that the merchants were responsible for the miserable conditions of the blacks. "We want our Cloathing easly for our slaves and other necessaries for our Plantations, [which] will force us to correspond with the other ports; or less our slaves perish; or be sick all the winter" (Custis to Micajah Perry, 1735, Custis Letter Book, 1717–1742).

consisted of hominy and water. William Hugh Grove recorded in his diary that corn was "the only support of the Negroes who Roast it in the Ear." He noted that the enslaved were "allowed a peck of Indian Corn P[er] W[eek] w[hi]ch stand the Master in 26s p[er] Ann[um]." The financial interests of the planters led them to turn over to blacks the responsibility of feeding themselves while, at the same time, doubling their workload. Grove observed: "They also allow them to plant little Plotts for potatoes or Indian pease and C[ultivate] w[hi]ch they do on Sundays or night for they work from Sun rising to setting[.] [They tend] 6000 plants of Tobacco w[hi]ch wil make 1000£ weight beside their share of Corn is a slave task. Thus, the keeping y[ou]r slaves cost Little."[54]

In the medical care of blacks, the great planters invasively extended their control over the bodies of the enslaved. For example, John Custis IV, who had "studied Phisick more than 40 years," wrote to Peter Collinson that he "had a large experience; having not less than 200 young and old in my severall familys; which I dayly assist." Nevertheless, he still concerned himself with the cost of their care. He allowed that "it is thought Ipeacuana [ipecac] is the best vomit for fluxes . . . [but] it is a dear vomit and if it were given to all our Nigros would bee very costly." Rather, "Crocus is cheap and I take it to bee the best vomit in the world." Great planters more often than not relied upon their own medical skills, which were sorely lacking, to treat the enslaved. When they did call in assistance, they might have done so as preferential treatment. William Byrd II once sent for a midwife for his enslaved black Jenny, a house servant and an apparent favorite — possibly indicative less of patriarchism than of paternity. Indeed, in what may be an admission of paternity, Byrd spoke of Jenny and his wife Lucy in the same passage as "breeding . . . likewise."[55]

Enslaved midwives and herbalists countered planters' control over black bodies — something that increasingly made slaveholders anxious. Not only did the midwife and herbalist recall the authority of the priest

54. Wm. J. Hinke, ed., "Report of the Journey of Francis Louis Michel from Berne, Switzerland, to Virginia, October 2, (1), 1701-December 1, 1702," *VMHB*, XXIV (1916), 116-117; George Larkin to BT, Dec. 22, 1701, CO 5/1360, 203-207, VCRP; Grove Diary, July 1732; Carter to Jones, Oct. 10, 1727, Carter Letter Book, 1727-1728, M-113; Robert Carter, "Corn Book, 1743," M-113, CWF.

55. Custis to Collinson, May 2, 1742, Custis Letter Book; Custis to Daniel [Parke Custis], Aug. 30, 1739, in Zuppan, ed., "Father to Son," *VMHB*, LXXXVII (1990), 92-94; Louis B. Wright and Marion Tinling, eds., *The Secret Diary of William Byrd of Westover, 1709-1712* (Richmond, Va., 1941), 549-550; Brown, *Good Wives, Nasty Wenches*, 331, 347, 353-354.

and priestess in African culture, but they also assumed the capacity to poison as well as to heal. Nevertheless, whites were quick to appropriate herbal cures from the enslaved. Papaw, an enslaved man belonging to Mrs. Frances Littlepage of New Kent County, was the most notable of the herbalists. Governor Gooch offered Papaw his freedom and an annuity for life for revealing the "several medicines he made . . . for expelling poison, and cure of other diseases." Of Papaw, Gooch observed that he has known the "Secrett . . . for many years in this country where he practiced with success."[56]

The greatest violation of black bodies lay in the great planters' control over the reproduction of the enslaved. Capital investment in the enslaved could best be realized by promoting the black population's natural increase, which the planters also sought to supervise. The pairing of male and female enslaved was less about benevolence than social control. Planters wanted to maintain a reproducing, tractable, and healthy workforce. A comment by William Byrd II in 1729 indicates that planters had an eye on profits in encouraging natural increase. In a petition concerning the Dismal Swamp, he proposed that planters buy "both sexes, that their Breed may supply the loss [because of death]." Byrd also encouraged a balanced gender ratio as a social mechanism to control slave behavior. He argued:

> Another benefit in providing wives for men [is] it will keep them at home, and prevent their rambling abroad at night from which rise many great Inconveniences. By this practice they learn to be dishonest, take cold, and loose their rest whereby they are less fit to do their work the following day. Besides when they have Wives in other Familys they are frequently poison'd by Jealousy of their Rivals, who think they have a much better right to the affections of their Fellow Servants, than any Stranger. By this many loose their lives.[57]

The great planters, assuming the roles of father and judge in their family of enslaved, promoted the concept of good nature as the proper method in dealing with enslaved blacks. As early as 1699, Daniel Parke instructed his daughter Fanny: "Behave y'rselfe soberly and like a Gentlewoman. . . .

56. Gooch to the bishop of London, June 29, 1729, FPP/13, 153, VCRP; Gooch to BT, June 29, 1729, CO 5/1322, 9–12, VCRP; "Virginia Council Journals, 1726–1753," *VMHB*, XXXII (1924), 1–64; *EJCCV*, IV, 199; Brown, *Good Wives, Nasty Wenches*, 354.

57. Byrd and others to the king, "Petition for Wastelands in Virginia and North Carolina Comprising the Dismal Swamp [1729]," BR 256 (29), HL.

Carry y'rselfe so that Everyboddy may Respect you. Be Calm and Oblige-
ing to all the servants, and when you speak doe it mildly, Even to the
poorest slave." Four years later, he reminded her: "Be kind and good-
natured to all your servants. It is better to have them love you than fear
you." Fanny's brother-in-law, William Byrd II, wrote to Peter Beckford
that blacks worked without "any cruelty exercised upon them unless by
accident they happen to fall into the hands of a Brute, who always passes
here for a Monster."[58]

Despite such pronouncements, masters often treated blacks brutishly.
Indeed, slavery could only undermine the character of the gentleman.
Black resistance was continually testing the great planters' theory of good
nature. In other words, the base of partriarchism contained its own contradiction between responsibility and domination. Masters were forced to
compromise their good conscience in correcting the enslaved, or they acquiesced to being duped by the enslaved. In a letter to the earl of Egmont
in 1736, William Byrd II expressed his anxiety over controlling recalcitrant
blacks. "These base tempers require to be rid with a Taut rein. Yet even
this is terrible to a good natured Man, who must submit to be either a Fool
or a Fury." When Byrd wrote that blacks required a taut rein, he meant it
literally. He routinely screwed a horse's bit into the mouths of captured
runaways. He confided in his diary: "My negro boy [or Betty] ran away
again but was soon caught. I was angry with John G——r——l for losing
the screw of the [bit]." This frightful routine could have its desired effect.
Olaudah Equiano, who had just arrived at the Campbell plantation, "was
very much affrighted" at seeing a woman in the "iron muzzle."[59]

The relationship between masters and the enslaved, on which Byrd reflected, existed in a state of constant tension. This tension reflected a dialectical struggle for power. Contemporaries James Blair and Jonathan Boucher, both men of the cloth, observed this struggle and lamented its moral
effects. In 1743, when Virginia's enslaved blacks numbered about eighty-
two thousand, the sagacious Commissary Blair, after fifty-eight years in
Virginia, understood too well that masters dominated the enslaved. But
he also observed the significance of enslaved labor for Virginia. He per-
ceptively commented that slavery, "from being an instrument of wealth[,]
had become a molding power, leaving it a vexed question [of] which con-

58. "Virginia Gleanings in England," *VMHB*, XX (1912), 375, 377; Byrd to Beckford,
Dec. 6, 1735, Byrd Letter Book, 1735-1736.

59. Byrd to Egmont, July 12, 1736, Byrd Letter Book, 1735-1736; Wright and Tinling,
eds., *Secret Diary*, 206; Equiano, *Interesting Narrative*, ed. Edwards, I, 91-92.

trolled society most, the African slave or his master." Blair observed both the interdependence of the enslaved and their owners in Virginia society and the struggle for power as the enslaved resisted their status. Quoting from Montesquieu, Reverend Boucher preached to his congregation that "the state of slavery is, in its own nature, bad." It undermined the character of the enslaved person, for "he can do nothing through a motive of virtue"; it undermined the character of the master, for "having unlimited authority over his slaves, he insensibly accustoms himself to the want of all moral virtues, and from thence grows fierce, hasty, severe, voluptuous, cruel." The unlimited power of masters over their enslaved servants, he wrote, guaranteed by that "great champion of liberty and advocate of humanity, Mr. Locke," had never been realized in Virginia. Boucher's disclaimer was meant, not to absolve the slaveowners for their brutality, but to acknowledge the dependence of masters and the enslaved on each other in Virginia.[60]

* * *

SLAVERY WAS above all an economic system, but it also shaped ideas about society and culture. The great planters became dependent on slavery for economic reasons and then found themselves having to justify a social system that countered their basic beliefs as Englishmen. Indeed, they developed the ideology of patriarchism to deal with the contradictions inherent in the master-slave relationship and to firmly establish the degraded status of blacks in Virginia society. Despite appearances, however, masters could never truly control their enslaved, as blacks continued to struggle for freedom and identity on their own terms.

The great planters' elaboration of patriarchism was also an attempt to come to grips with the social changes of the 1720s and 1730s, to reconcile the class conflicts of a provincial society that was increasingly treated as a dependent colony. As Kenneth Lockridge has written, the Virginia

60. Blair, quoted in Sydney E. Ahlstrom, *A Religious History of the American People,* 2 vols. (New York, 1975), I, 245; Marshall, "What Jonathan Boucher Preached," *VMHB,* XLVI (1938), 5; G. W. F. Hegel, "Independence and Dependence of Self-Consciousness: Lordship and Bondage," in Hegel, *The Phenomenology of Mind* (1807), trans. J. B. Baillie (1910; reprint, New York, 1966), 228–240; David Brion Davis, *The Problem of Slavery in the Age of Revolution, 1770–1823* (Ithaca, N.Y., 1975), 557–564; Wood, *Black Majority,* 18–19. Cf. Genovese, *From Rebellion to Revolution: Afro-American Slave Revolts in the Making of the Modern World* (Baton Rouge, La., 1979), xvi–xvii; Charles de Secondat, Baron de Montesquieu, *The Spirit of the Laws* (1748), ed. and trans. Anne M. Cohler et al. (Cambridge, 1989), 246.

elite, responding to feelings of frustration, failure, and fear, mimicked the metropolitan culture, but with an inferior's need to surpass that culture's accomplishments. Such a response is doomed to failure, for mimicry cannot lead to liberation, but only to exasperation. The provincial ideal fades in the harsh light of colonial reality, heightening the elite's feelings of inadequacy. Indeed, the great planters' attempt to compensate for this inadequacy through control of the enslaved, women, and poor whites would extend to the realm of religion.[61]

61. Lockridge, *On the Sources of Patriarchal Rage,* 96–99. See also D. A. Brading, *The First America: The Spanish Monarchy, Creole Patriots, and the Liberal State, 1492–1867* (Cambridge, 1991), 291, 297, 305; Anderson, *Imagined Communities,* 12, 48–51.

CHAPTER 8

Baptism and Bondage,

1700–1740

Early Virginia was not a secular society, for Perry Miller's dictate applies in general that Englishmen "could conceive of the society they were erecting in America only within a religious framework." The provincial ideology that the great planters were developing had to fit within the framework of Christianity, an important buttress of their class's superstructure and of their identity as English free men. "*Christianity* only," William Parks wrote, "can set us right upon this Topick" of providence, which was a significant aspect of the ideology of patriarchism.[1]

In developing their ideology, the great planters borrowed much from the Anglican Church. They found the patriarchism formulated by the English Anglicans in the seventeenth century appropriate because they had been raised in the faith and because the English gentry had called upon it when they, like the Virginia planters later, were threatened by the merchant class. The great planters also found the Anglican cosmology suitable to their developing ideology as it applied to blacks. In particular, they drew support for forming their social order from the social inequality and hierarchic character of Anglican society, where all revered and recognized authority, where all had a fixed place and personal duties.[2]

In bolstering their standing, Anglican planters constructed white patri-

1. *Virginia Gazette,* Dec. 7–14, 1739; Perry Miller, *Errand into the Wilderness* (Cambridge, Mass., 1956), 108, 138–139.
2. Jerome W. Jones, "The Established Virginia Church and the Conversion of Negroes and Indians, 1620–1720," *Journal of Negro History,* XLVI (1961), 12; Darrett B. Rutman and Anita H. Rutman, *A Place in Time: Middlesex County, Virginia, 1650–1750* (New York, 1984), 53, 122–125; Michael Walzer, *The Revolution of the Saints: A Study in the Origins of Radical Politics* (New York, 1973), 148–195; Arthur O. Lovejoy, *The Great Chain of Being: A Study of the History of an Idea* (Cambridge, Mass., 1933), esp. chap. 4; John W. Bennett, "Paternalism," *International Encyclopedia of the Social Sciences,* 472.

archism, commanding black obedience as the basis for slavery in America. Religion became an essential component in the formulation of their ideology. Englishmen at first thought of themselves in religious rather than racial terms. They were, not white, but Christian. They connected Protestant faith with Englishness and freedom and saw the papists, especially the Spaniards, as purveyors of slavery in the Americas. If the English first came to the New World with thoughts of liberating enslaved Indians and Africans, they began to follow the Iberian lead in enslavement with colonization. They acquiesced that Africans or Indians taken in war could be enslaved, for it was the right of the conqueror by "the Law of Nature and of Nations" to transfer that status by purchase. Part and parcel of the justification for enslaving Africans and Indians was that they could offer them the true faith. Yet what of those African-descended people who had prior Christian status, usually Catholic in a Hispanic colony? Could they readily be enslaved, or should they have the same standing as European Christians coming to the colony?[3]

The charter generation of blacks in Virginia was familiar with Christianity. Many who arrived in Virginia were already Christians. They believed that Christianity anchored their claim to freedom, property, and security in the colonial society. With the rise of slavery, blacks, Indians, and mixed-raced people embraced Christianity as a guard against the loss of freedom, causing authorities to fear that their enslaved property was at risk. Even the 1667 law affirming the enslavement of Christians did not ease the planters' concern. The crown had encouraged Christianity as a method of social control, but masters were still cautious, slow to baptize their enslaved. Moreover, the clergy was indifferent to the salvation of the souls of the enslaved and, with the advance of the slave trade, the African-born resisted Christianity in an effort to retain their traditional religious beliefs and cultures. But, beginning in the 1720s, with the emergence of patriarchism, the great planters' attitudes about baptizing the enslaved changed, precipitating a controversy over Christianized blacks.[4]

3. William Gooch to the secretary of state, May 26, 1735, CO 5/1334, 177–179, VCRP; Robin Blackburn, "The Old World Background to European Colonial Slavery," *WMQ*, 3d Ser., LIV (1997), 87–90; Edmund S. Morgan, *American Slavery, American Freedom: The Ordeal of Colonial Virginia* (New York, 1975), 9–24; David Brion Davis, *The Problem of Slavery in Western Culture* (Ithaca, N.Y., 1966), 100; Winthrop D. Jordan, *White over Black: American Attitudes toward the Negro, 1550–1812* (Chapel Hill, N.C., 1968), 55–63, 93–95.

4. Jon Butler, *Awash in a Sea of Faith: Christianizing the American People* (Cambridge, Mass., 1990), chap. 5; Ira Berlin, *Many Thousands Gone: The First Two Centuries of Slav-*

His Master Was Not Admitting It

From the start of the Restoration in 1660, the crown encouraged the conversion of blacks to Christianity to reduce them to greater docility. In a "Draft of an Act for the Baptizing and Better Ordering of Negroes and Infidels in the King of England's Plantations in America," the Council for Foreign Plantations in 1661 advised colonial authorities in Barbados and Virginia to bring in missionaries to convert blacks. Its reasoning was clear: the plantations are "best arrived [at] or managed by bodily labour"; blacks, increasing daily there, are "strong and able, and most fitt"; since they are "well ordered and guided" under English law and government, they should be Christianized so that "they will be reduced in short time into great civillity." Despite this deduction, the Council for Foreign Plantations knew that the great planters had to contend with local conditions and conceded that they had to run their plantations in their own way. Consequently, the council provided the disclaimer that "this Act . . . shall [not] or tend in any sort to impead, restrain, or impair the Jurisdiction, power, Authority, liberty or priviledge of a Governor, Governors, Master or Masters, planter or planters of or in those [his Majesty's] said plantations."[5]

Yet, even with the crown's encouragement and all the legal reassurances developed between 1667 and 1705 that baptism did not equal freedom, few blacks were baptized. Doubts lingered about the status of the children of the enslaved, and baptism only complicated the matter. In the seventeenth century, blacks, increasingly uneasy about the growth of racial slavery and believing Christianity served as a guarantor of freedom, baptized and raised their children in the faith. To clear up any uncertainty about the children, the General Assembly in 1667 stated plainly that baptism did not exempt blacks from bondage and encouraged owners to propagate Christianity by baptizing children and "those of greater growth if capable." Despite the law, and notwithstanding Lord Thomas Culpeper's declaration in 1681 that blacks "are daily Converted to the Christian Religion, now [that] they are to continue to be slaves forever," masters balked at bringing blacks to the baptismal font. Morgan Godwyn, author of *The Negro's and Indians Advocate* (1680), observed in a report to Governor William

ery in North America (Cambridge, Mass., 1998), 29–46; Jones, "The Established Virginia Church," *Jour. Negro Hist.,* XLVI (1961), 18–21.

5. Council for Foreign Plantations, "Draft of an Act for the Baptizing and Better Ordering of Negroes and Infidels in the King of England's Plantations in America," [ca. 1661, London], Tanner MSS 447, 53–54, Bodleian Library, Oxford University, VCRP.

Berkeley that a man who encourages the Christianizing of blacks and Indians in Virginia is considered foolhardy. The preamble to a 1682 statute "to repeale a former law making Indians and others free" pointed to the reason for slaveowners' continued reticence about conversion. The explicit link of slave status with non-Christians left owners' "just right and tytle to such slaves[s]" that were converted after purchase and brought into Virginia open to question. "Some well disposed Christian, who . . . out of a pious zeal, have wrought the conversion" beforehand, would suffer "great losse and damage" in not being able to sell his enslaved property within the colony. Encouraging baptism, wrote Godwyn, is looked "upon, by our new Race of *Christians,* as so idle and Ridiculous, so utterly needless and unnecessary, that no Man can forfeit his Judgment more, than by any proposal looking or tending that way."[6]

Slaveholders did not baptize the African-born enslaved, believing that their cultural and religious background made conversion difficult. Indeed, unlike the charter generation of blacks, pulled to the pole of Christianity for security against enslavement, the new immigrants not only resisted conversion to an alien religion but also performed their traditional religious practices. The slave trade after 1680 resulted in a critical mass of animists who expressed their religious spirit in feasts and burials. The slaveholders, fearing insurrection as a result of blacks massing together for these ceremonies, especially at night, outlawed slave assemblies in 1680. In 1699, the burgesses, responding to an official query from Governor Francis Nicholson, proffered that the cultural differences of immigrant Africans, especially in language and manners, made their conversion "impossible." In that same year, Commissary James Blair wrote that the immigrants were not converted because they were "indocile" and did not understand English.[7]

6. *SAL,* II, 260, 490–491; Thomas, Lord Culpeper to BT, Dec. 12, 1681, in Elizabeth Donnan, ed., *Documents Illustrative of the History of the Slave Trade to America,* 4 vols. (Washington, D.C., 1930–1935), IV, 56; Morgan Godwyn, *The Negro's and Indians Advocate, Suing for Their Admission into the Church* . . . (London, 1680), 172; Kathleen M. Brown, *Good Wives, Nasty Wenches, and Anxious Patriarchs: Gender, Race, and Power in Colonial Virginia* (Chapel Hill, N.C., 1996), 108; T. H. Breen and Stephen Innes, *"Myne Owne Ground": Race and Freedom on Virginia's Eastern Shore, 1640–1676* (New York, 1980), 83–88; Winthrop D. Jordan, "Modern Tensions and the Origins of American Slavery," *Journal of Southern History,* XXVIII (1962), 18–30; Jordan, *White over Black,* 48–52; James H. Brewer, "Negro Property Owners in Seventeenth-Century Virginia," *WMQ,* 3d Ser., XII (1955), 575–580.

7. *JHB, 1695–1696, 1696–1697, 1698, 1699, 1700–1702,* 174; James Blair, "A Proposi-

As late as 1724, Virginia's elites were still resistant to the proselytism of African immigrants. Virginia's custodians of language and custom, dismissing as out of the question the conversion of Africans, barred the church doors to them. In 1723, Edmund Gibson, the bishop of London, surveyed the religious condition of the Africans, Indians, and their descendants, asking each parish minster: "Are there any infidels, bond or free, within your parish; and what means are used for their conversion?" The following responses sent to him in 1724 concerning the ministry to the enslaved reflect the elites' hesitance in bringing immigrants to the baptismal font. Rev. John Bell reported that he baptized with "circumspection," for Christ Church Parish, Lancaster County, had a "great many" Africans that "understand not our language nor me theirs." Rev. William Le Neve of James City Parish, James City County, tried to explain away why he had not converted the African-born enslaved: the immigrants have so "little Doci[li]ty" and so little knowledge of God and religion that they are doubly damned.[8]

What white Virginians had described as indocile and alien were Africans' efforts to retain their religious beliefs. They were not mesmerized by their master's religion, nor were they desirous of conversion. Holding their own religious views in the face of an alien culture, they used them to comprehend their present circumstances. An all-powerful God and ancestral and other spirits including tricksters were personal deities at work in their lives. At times, they were contemptuous of the religious hypocrisy of the master class. What Rev. Francis Varnod heard and recorded about the religious views of Africans in South Carolina sheds light on their contem-

---

tion for Encouraging the Christian Education of Indian, Negro, and Mulatto Children," Sept. 6, 1699, Francis Nicholson Papers, CWF; *LJCCV*, III, 1523, 1525; Berlin, *Many Thousands Gone*, 102–105, 110, 128–129.

8. John Bell to the bishop of London, Christ Church Parish, 1724, FPP/15, 6, VCRP; William Le Neve to the bishop of London, James City Parish, 1724, FPP/15, 14, VCRP. See also to the bishop of London, all in VCRP: Zach[arias] Brooke, Saint Paul's Parish, 1724, FPP/15, 1; George Robertson, Bristol Parish, July 8, 1724, FPP/15, 11; Henry Collings, Saint Peter's Parish, June 1, 1724, FPP/15, 10; Peter Fontaine, Westover Parish, June 18, 1724, FPP/15, 18; Dan[ie]l Taylor, Blissland Parish, [1724], FPP/15, 5; Emanuel Jones, Petsworth Parish, 1724, FPP/15, 4; Alex[ande]r Forbes, Upper Parish, 1724, FPP/15, 2; Bartho[lomew] Yates, Christ Church Parish, June 15, 1724, FPP/15, 3; James Blair, Bruton Parish, July 15, 1724, FPP/14, 1; William Black, Accomack Parish, June [8?], 1724, FPP/15, 21; [Alexander Scott], Overworton Parish, Stafford County, 1724, FPP/15, 174; James Falconar, Elizabeth City Parish, May 27, 1724, FFP/15, 19; John Lang, St. Peter's Parish, Feb. 7, 1725/6, FPP/15, 68.

poraries in Virginia. One woman told Varnod her conceptions "of a Devil, and dismal apprehensions of apparitions" and "Of a God that disposes absolutely to all things." Varnod recorded the fatalism that comprehended the misfortunes of their lives: slavery, punishment, and loss. "For asking one day a negro-pagan woman how she happened to be made a slave, [she] replied that God would have it so and she could not help it. I heard another saying the same thing on the account of the death of her husband. And a Devil whereby who leads them to do mischief, and betrays them, whereby they are found out by their masters and punished." Blacks had serious reservations about Christianity, and reluctance to convert was not from ignorance. "They are also sensible that as we are Christians, we do not act accordingly," Varnod observed. He gave the example of a fourteen-year-old black boy "who has never been instructed." Unfairly chastised by his mistress as she left for church, he was heard to say, "My mistress can curse and go to church."[9]

Slaveholders also did not readily baptize Virginia-born blacks. Although they could not blame language and intractability, for the native-born spoke English and at least some desired conversion, slaveholders were suspicious of the motives of these would-be converts, believing they would press for their freedom. Although the moral dilemma posed by denying Christianity to their charges did seem to trouble some slaveholders, it was not incentive enough for them to promote conversion. Perhaps as a result, they projected the falsehood that Creoles were baptized. For example, the burgesses claimed in 1699 that the native-born were "generally" christened and brought up in the church. But the number of black Christians appears negligible. Francis Louis Michel, a Swiss visitor to Virginia, was closer to the mark when he observed in 1702: "The children like the parents must live in slavery. Even if they desire to become Christians, it is only rarely permitted."[10]

Commissary James Blair was concerned about the slaveholders' ne-

9. Francis Varnod to David Humphreys, Apr. 1, 1724, in Frank J. Klingberg, *An Appraisal of the Negro in Colonial South Carolina: A Study in Americanization* (Washington, D.C., 1941), 56; Sylvia R. Frey and Betty Wood, *Come Shouting to Zion: African American Protestantism in the American South and British Caribbean to 1830* (Chapel Hill, N.C., 1998), 10–12, 35; Olaudah Equiano, *The Interesting Narrative of the Life of Olaudah Equiano, or Gustavus Vassa, the African; Written by Himself* (1789), ed. Paul Edwards, 2 vols. (London, 1969), I, 28–29.

10. *JHB, 1695–1696, 1696–1697, 1698, 1699, 1700–1702,* 174; Wm. J. Hinke, ed., "Report of the Journey of Francis Louis Michel from Berne, Switzerland, to Virginia, October 2, (1), 1701–December 1, 1702," *VMHB,* XXIV (1916), 116.

glected duty to baptize and instruct black children in the faith. Lighting
the lamp of conversion, he encouraged the General Assembly in 1699 to
offer a financial incentive to planters who baptized slave children. He recommended that the government provide a tax exemption for each baptized enslaved child until the child's sixteenth birthday, rather than the
twelfth birthday, which was stipulated in the existing 1680 law. The baptized child would be publicly catechized by the minister and would have
to be capable by age twelve of giving a "distinct account" of the Apostle's
Creed, the Lord's Prayer, and the Ten Commandments. Blair reasoned
that, more than charity or piety, the difference of four years of tax relief
would inspire masters to perform their Christian duty, but nothing came
of his proposal.[11]

Benjamin Dennis, a missionary for the Society for the Propagation of
the Gospel in Foreign Parts (SPG) in South Carolina, found Virginia
slaveholders resistant to black baptism, even in the case of an articulate
seeker, desirous of conversion. On the way to his mission in Goose Creek,
South Carolina, after a visit to Williamsburg in 1711, Dennis crossed over
the James River, where he discussed Christianity with a "sensible fellow"
who operated the sloop.

> I ask'd him if he believed there was a God, and what his notion
> was of him,
> he answer'd he was make[r] of all things both in Heaven and
> Earth.
> I ask'd him if he believed in Christ the Son of God,
> he said yes, he did.
> I ask'd him if he profess'd my Religion
> who reply'd yes he did, and that when he had time he went to the
> Ch[urch] of Engl[an]d, but it was Seldome his Master (who was the
> Wherry man of that place) not suffering him to have any time either
> Sunday and Working days.
> I ask'd him if he was baptiz'd,
> he said not. his Master not admitting it notwithstanding his great
> desire. . . .
> I advis'd him to apply himself to the Minister of the Parish and
> that I was shure he would prevail with his Master: to admit him to
> be Baptiz'd:

11. *SAL*, II, 480; Blair, "Proposition," Nicholson Papers, CWF; *LJCCV*, III, 1523,
1525.

all which the fellow thank'd me for and assur'd me that he would [at] first opportunity and desir'd God to bless and be with me for my good advice.

After Dennis arrived in South Carolina, he was "really surprized" to find four black male communicants at his church. Not only did men and women of the great-planter class attend his church faithfully, but "the blacks were as Consistent as any."[12]

Virginia slaveholders continued to drag their heels on conversion, still believing that Christianity jeopardized their property rights in people. The English Parliament, cognizant of the planters' anxiety, drafted a bill in 1713 encouraging conversion. Parliament stated in the bill's preamble that, although all Christians had an "undoubted obligation" to propagate the gospel, on the plantations missionary efforts had been thwarted. This failure is "chiefly to be occasion'd by a mistaken opinion that the Interest of the Master in his Negro or Servant, is taken away or Lessen'd by the Negro or Servant becoming a Christian." To remove this apprehension, the bill stated that baptism should not be construed as conferring either freedom or franchise, "or in Measure or Degree be, or be construed to be any Diminution or Prejudice of . . . any just Right or Property."[13]

The notion that blacks would press for their freedom on the basis of being Christian was grounded in reality. They had already petitioned for manumission on the condition of their being free and Christian in their country of origin, prompting the General Assembly to act in 1667. But blacks continued thereafter to sue for their freedom, using Christianity to bolster their case. Well into the 1690s, the enslaved continued to claim

12. Benjamin Dennis to the secretary [SPG], July 3, 1711, SPG Letter Books, SPG Archives, London, MS A, vol. 6, VCRP. South Carolina masters rarely allowed their enslaved to be baptized despite the intense efforts of the SPG. Robert Olwell estimates that 3 percent to 5 percent of the enslaved were baptized during the colonial period (Olwell, *Masters, Slaves, and Subjects: The Culture of Power in the South Carolina Lowcountry, 1740-1790* [Ithaca, N.Y., 1998], 116-118). See Frey and Wood, *Come Shouting to Zion*, 65-68; Peter H. Wood, *Black Majority: Negroes in Colonial South Carolina from 1670 through the Stono Rebellion* (New York, 1974), 188; C. E. Pierre, "The Work of the Society for the Propagation of the Gospel among Negroes in the Colonies," *Jour. Negro Hist.*, XLVI (1961), 349-360; Faith Vilbert, "The Society for the Propagation of the Gospel in Foreign Parts: Its Work for the Negroes in North America before 1793," ibid., XLIII (1933), 171-212; Luther P. Jackson, "Religious Instruction of Negroes, 1830-1860, with Special Reference to South Carolina," ibid., XV (1930), 72-114.

13. "A Draught of a Bill For Converting the Negros in Plantations," ca. 1713, Lambeth Palace Papers 941, 72, Lambeth Palace Library, London, VCRP.

Christianity as a reason for their manumission. Some asserted their conversion in their freedom petitions and others their Christian free status in Christian countries before their arrival. William Cattilah asked the York County jurists to consider his baptism in his 1695 freedom petition. A mixed-race woman petitioned a Lancaster court for freedom in 1697, citing her child's baptism. She claimed that her white common-law husband John Beeching, the child's father, had purchased her in exchange for tanning work. As proof of her living as a free woman, the petitioner offered evidence of the christenings. The court found for the plaintiff. Governor Gooch, reflecting upon a 1719 case where planters refused to buy blacks from a Jamaican privateer because they feared that the captives, prisoners of war from a Spanish squadron, had been free people, reported, "I have known many Instances even of Negros sett at liberty by our Courts of judicature, upon Proof of their being so in the Country from whence they came."[14]

In response to the parliamentary bill, acting governor Edmund Jenings issued a proclamation in 1713 encouraging infant baptism. Jenings, emphasizing again that the baptism of the enslaved in no way jeopardized a master's property-in-people, bid owners to have the parish minister baptize babies, without fee, within three months of their birth. He exhorted owners to give their maturing American-born blacks permission to hear instruction from the minister on Sundays, to be baptized by him, and to attend the church "nearest them." If these instructions had been carried out generally, Dennis's boatman would have been allowed the instruction and baptism he desired, but slaveholders continued to oppose proselytism among blacks. Indeed, the House of Burgesses in 1715 not only rejected "at first Sight" a proposal for baptizing the enslaved but also referred to a Grand Committee a proposition for suppressing SPG activities among the Indians, as if, in Governor Alexander Spotswood's phrase, it "were a Crime which ought to be Restrain'd by Law."[15]

Early in the 1720s, however, the burgesses began hearing propositions for catechizing and baptizing blacks. The change likely had to do with the

14. Brown, *Good Wives, Nasty Wenches*, 135–136, 223, 439n; James Hugo Johnston, *Race Relations in Virginia and Miscegenation in the South, 1776–1860* (Amherst, Mass., 1970), 168; Gooch to the secretary of state, May 26, 1735, CO 5/1337, 175, VCRP. See also Chapter 4, above.

15. "Clause concerning the Negro's Delivered by Mr. Jenings," 1713, SPG Letter Books, SPG Archives, MS A, IX, 68–69, VCRP; *JHB, 1712–1714, 1715, 1718, 1720–1722, 1723–1726*, 167.

increasing number of Creoles among them. When in 1720 the Middlesex County representatives suggested that the colony provide for a catechist to instruct the enslaved, the House of Burgesses rejected it as "Impracticable." When William Todd and others in 1723 proposed that the slaveholders proselytize black children, the burgesses once again rejected the idea as "impracticable," but now the judgment was written in lower case and prefaced with the auspicious disclaimer, "being at present."[16]

The clergy's role in slave proselytism was also weak, owing in part to the general lack of evangelism among Anglican ministers in Virginia in the early eighteenth century. Anglicanism was a reading religion and did not promote outreach, as did the dissenting denominations. A primary reason for such introversion was that relatively little nonconformity existed in Virginia prior to the Great Awakening in 1740. Robert Beverley II stated in 1705 that there were only five dissenting churches in Virginia, "three small Meetings of Quakers, and two of Presbyterians." Rev. John Lang observed in 1726 that the people were "generally very Zealous" for the Church of England and "that (except Some few inconsiderable Quakers) ther's Scarce any dissenting from our communion."[17]

A more fundamental reason for the clergy's indifference, however, was that they were subordinate to the great planters' domination. Because enslaved blacks were baptized only with the permission of slaveholders, an unwilling master could neutralize the enthusiasm of the clergy. The reason, then, for any increase in proselytism lay, not with the clergy's zeal, but in masters' willingness to permit their enslaved to receive the sacrament of baptism. An analysis of the twenty-eight ministers' replies in 1724 to the bishop of London's query about Christianizing blacks reveals that slaveowners generally opposed conversion, although all the ministers said that they welcomed blacks. Rev. George Robertson of Bristol Parish wrote: "I have several times exhorted their Masters to send such of them [blacks] as could speak English to Church to be catechiz'd but they would not. Some Masters instruct their slaves at home and so bring them to baptism, but not many such." "There are many Negro slaves and but very few are

16. *JHB, 1712–1714, 1715, 1718, 1720–1722, 1723–1726,* 253, 269, 368, 370.

17. Lyon G. Tyler, "Maj. Edmund Chisman, Jr.," *WMQ*, 1st Ser., I (1892–1893), 92–93; Robert Beverley, *The History and Present State of Virginia* (1705, 1722), ed. Louis B. Wright (Chapel Hill, N.C., 1947), 261; Lang to the bishop of London, Feb. 7, 1725/6, FPP/15, 68, VCRP; Rhys Isaac, "Religion and Authority: Problems of the Anglican Establishment in Virginia in the Era of the Great Awakening and the Parsons' Cause," *WMQ*, 3d Ser., XXX (1973), 3–36.

baptiz'd, nor any means used for their Conversion," observed Rev. John Bagg of St. Anne's Parish, Essex County, "the owners Generally not approving thereof, being led away by the notion of their being and becoming worse Slaves when Christians." "The Negroes . . . cannot . . . be said to be of any Religion," surmised John Brunskill of Wilmington Parish, James City County, "for as there is no law of the Colony obliging their Masters or Owners to instruct them in the principle of Christianity and so they are hardly to be persuaded by the Minister to take so much pains with them, by which means the poor Creatures generally live and die without it." Slave proselytism, observed Rev. Hugh Jones in 1724, depended on "the power of their masters."[18]

Indeed, the clergy's influence in proselytism was severely diminished by the vestry's tremendous strength in parish affairs. At the parish level, the vestry, a self-perpetuating body consisting of both great and middling planters who served for life, managed all local ecclesiastical and some local civil affairs. The unwillingness of the vestry to give the ministry security of tenure in the form of induction led to the clergy's dependence upon the local leaders. The ministry toed the line on slavery, even if it was in practice difficult to remove a minister. Morgan Godwyn recognized that the vestry's influence made apostolic work among blacks difficult, complaining to Governor Berkeley: "The ministers are most miserably handled by their plebeian Juntos, the vesteries, to whom the living (that is the usual

18. Robertson to the bishop of London, July 8, 1724, FPP/15, 11, VCRP; John Brunskill to the bishop of London, June 18, 1724, FPP/15, 17, VCRP; John Bagg to the bishop of London, 1724, FPP/15, 68, VCRP; Hugh Jones, *The Present State of Virginia: From Whence Is Inferred a Short View of Maryland and North Carolina* (1724), ed. Richard L. Morton (Chapel Hill, N.C., 1956), 99. In one instance, however, in 1724 in North Farnham Parish, Richmond County, the zeal of a minister and the willingness of masters combined. During his first year in the colony, the Spanish-born minister John Garzia instructed and baptized fifteen blacks belonging to Colonel John Tayloe and one hundred blacks belonging to Colonel Robert "King" Carter. Born a Catholic, Garzia proved the old saw, there is no greater evangelist than a convert. See "A List of Negroes Instructed and Baptized by Mr. John Garzia Minister of the Parish of North Farnham in Richmond County Virginia [under] the Instructions of the Society by [Authority of] Doctor Thomas Bray," March 1723/4, FPP/14, 42, VCRP. The efforts of the Reverend William Black of Accomac Parish on the Eastern Shore also dovetailed with the masters' willingness to allow the enslaved instruction. He wrote to the bishop of London in 1724 that he instructed blacks at their masters' homes of which he had baptized two hundred in fifteen years, and "a great many . . . come to church" (William Black to the bishop of London, June 9, 1724, FPP/14, 21, VCRP).

word there) and admission of ministers is solely left." Rev. Hugh Jones reported in 1724 that not more than four ministers are "collated, or instituted and inducted in the whole Colony." Jones described the standing of the ministry as not only inconvenient but dangerous. "Upon any small difference with the vestry, they may pretend to assume authority to turn out such ministers as thus come in by agreement with the vestry, who have often had the church doors shut against them, and their salaries stopped, by the order and protection of such vestry-men." Undoubtedly, ministers did not stray far from the position held by the vestry on an issue as sensitive as the baptism of the enslaved.[19]

The character of the clergy also helps to explain why there was little missionary zeal toward the enslaved. Poor salaries, job insecurity, and rural living did not attract the best men to Virginia. Blair noted that "the precarious circumstances upon which they hold their livings" contribute to the "meanness and badness of the Clergy" and "discourages worthy clergymen to adventure themselves among us." The first minister to the Codrington Plantation in Barbados, Rev. Joseph Holt, the bishop of London's nominee, was removed from his post in 1714, after less than a year of service, when the SPG learned of his "lurid" history in Virginia. He had been deprived of his pastorate in Virginia because of his doctrinaire attitude, drunkenness, idleness, and immorality. Mr. Lang wrote a scathing attack on the character of the clergy in 1726. "The sober part being Slothful and negligent; and others so debaucht that they are the foremost and most bent in all Manner of Vices. Drunkenness is the common Vice, and

19. Morgan Godwyn to Governor William Berkeley, ca. 1680, in William Stevens Perry, *The History of the American Episcopal Church, 1587–1883,* 2 vols. (Boston, 1885), I, 204; Jones, *The Present State of Virginia,* ed. Morton, 25, 123; Blair to the bishop of London, July 17, 1724, in Perry, ed., *Historical Collections,* I, 259; Rutman and Rutman, *A Place in Time,* 143, 246–247, 267 n. 55; Joan R. Gundersen, *The Anglican Ministry in Virginia, 1723–1766: A Study of a Social Class* (New York, 1989), 26, 108–109; C. G. Chamberlayne, ed., *The Vestry Book and Register of St. Peter's Parish, New Kent and James City Counties, Virginia, 1684–1786* (Richmond, Va., 1937), 37, 629. See also William H. Seiler, "The Anglican Parish in Virginia," in James Morton Smith, ed., *Seventeenth-Century America: Essays in Colonial History* (Chapel Hill, N.C., 1959), 119–142; Thomas J. Wertenbaker, "The Attempt to Reform the Church of Colonial Virginia," *Sewanee Review,* XXV (1917), 257; George Maclaren Brydon, *Virginia's Mother Church and the Political Conditions under Which It Grew: An Interpretation of the Records of the Colony of Virginia and of the Anglican Church of That Colony, 1607–1727,* II (Richmond, Va., 1947), 361–407; Wesley Frank Craven, *The Southern Colonies in the Seventeenth Century, 1607–1689* (Baton Rouge, La., 1970), 181.

brings with it other indecencies which among the ignorant creates disrespect to the Character, and indifference in Matters of Religion."[20]

The clergy understood that their maintenance was tied to slaveholding. Commissary Blair, for example, submitted a companion proposal to the one on baptizing children that concerned the public support of the clergy. He wrote that Virginia law already allowed for the maintenance of the clergy by providing each minister with a glebe, or a parcel of land from which he could draw a living. He proposed that "the quantity of Land be determined . . . so that it may be sufficient to make a good plantation for 5 or 6 hands to work upon." The minister should have at his disposal "4 or 5 Negroes under an Overseer . . . and keeping the Negroes in the full number between the age of 15 and 45." Like the proposal for child baptism, Blair's suggestion never became law in Virginia, highlighting the slaveholders' authority over the clergy. Even without the subsidy in the enslaved, however, the clergy depended upon slave labor to build their glebes and churches, tend their gardens, clean their homes, and prepare their meals. If the ministry invested its living in the institution of slavery, clergymen had to engage in the correction of recalcitrant enslaved laborers. In one of the most outrageous incidents, the Rev. Samuel Gray was forced to leave his ministry at Christ Church, Middlesex County, in 1699 for whipping an enslaved black to death.[21]

Thwarting the efforts of the diligent ministers that did exist was the enormity of the task of proselytism: the great number of the enslaved, the largeness and remoteness of the parishes, and the unwillingness of masters to allow enslaved blacks time off to travel the great distances to church. James Marye wrote to the bishop of London that he had just arrived safely at St. James Parish, finding the "abundance" of blacks needing instruction a "burden." The Reverend Mr. Alexander Forbes of Upper Parish,

20. Blair to the bishop of London, July 17, 1724, in Perry, *Historical Collections,* I, 257–260; J. Harry Bennett, Jr., *Bondsmen and Bishops: Slavery and Apprenticeship on the Codrington Plantations of Barbados, 1710–1838* (Berkeley, Calif., 1958), 75–77; Lang to the bishop of London, Feb. 7, 1725/6, FPP/15, 68, VCRP. See also Lawrence De Butts's condemnation of the Virginia clergy in his letter to the Reverend Mr. Berriman, July 1, 1722, FPP/13, 133, VCRP; Joan R. Gundersen, "The Search for Good Men: Recruiting Ministers in Colonial Virginia," *Historical Magazine of the Protestant Episcopal Church,* XLVIII (1979), 453–464.

21. Blair to the SPG, Sept. 6, 1699, SPG, Package I, BV 13, Frank J. Klingberg Collection, Charles E. Young Research Library, UCLA; "Papers Relating to the Administration of Governor Nicholson and to the Founding of William and Mary College," *VMHB,* VIII (1900–1901), 60.

Isle of Wight County, estimated the size of his parish to be sixty miles in length and eleven in breadth. His parish was so "extensive" that, despite his best efforts, he had not been able "to serve it as it ought to be." The "capable" blacks are "taught and baptized by . . . some Masters, but too much neglected by many." The planters were unwilling to give blacks "time from their worldly service" for instruction and baptism, lamented Rev. Thomas Dell. Blacks and Indians went without Christian succor, except those who "had horses lent, or their Zeal would carry them on foot, because of the remote distances." Although Dell baptized some and ministered to the needs of others at his church, the majority, he wrote, "still grope in darkness at noon day."[22]

By the 1720s, however, a sea change would occur with regard to the elites' attitudes on conversion, resulting from the confluence of a charged clergy, fearful slaveholders, and a greater number of enslaved Creoles. The decisive year would be 1727, when church, crown, and colony settled on Christianity as a method of controlling an increasingly restless black population. The clergy, with their bishop's blessing and the permission of slaveholders, thus began to baptize Virginia-born blacks. The insurrection of 1730, which was inspired by Christianity, would, however, give the authorities pause before they would commit to the wholesale proselytism of the enslaved.

For Political Reasons

Rev. Hugh Jones fired the first salvo for social control through proselytism in 1724. He encouraged baptism of American-born slaves if they "be sensible, good, and understand English, and have been taught (or are willing to learn) the principles of Christianity." "The children of Negroes and Indians, that are to live among Christians," he reasoned, "undoubtedly they ought all to be baptized." Since the African-born "obstinately" persisted in practicing the religious rituals of their culture, Jones contemplated whether their baptism might not be "a prostitution of a thing so sacred." Christianity would pacify the American-born enslaved, on the other hand, making them better workers, as it had the English poor. Yet, allowing the enslaved to read the catechism, the Bible, and the Book

22. [James] Marye to the bishop of London, July 22, 1730, FPP/13, 53, VCRP; Alex[ande]r Forbes to the bishop of London, [1724], FPP/15, 2, VCRP; Thomas Dell to the bishop of London, June 1, 1724, in Perry, *Historical Collections,* I, 255–256.

of Common Prayer, encouraged in traditional Anglican pedagogy, could prove disastrous for the slaveholders. Jones, conscious of the dangers, warned that literacy should not be extended to the oppressed blacks. "Christianity encourages and orders them to become more humble and better servants." It discourages lying, swearing, and stealing in the same manner that it modifies the behavior of the "poorer sort in England." But one should not go as far as to teach them to read and write like the English poor, for this is "dangerous upon several political accounts, especially self-preservation."[23]

Jones was not the only voice promoting the conversion of the American-born enslaved as a mechanism of control. In 1727 in Westover, where William Byrd II had his home plantation, Rev. Peter Fontaine used a government-declared fast day as an opportunity to lament the planters' failure to carry out their Christian duty to baptize the enslaved. A Jeremiah among slaveholders, he exhorted his listeners to make amends in their lives, preaching that his countrymen's vices had brought pestilence and destruction to Virginia just as the Egyptians' "Inveterate Obstinacy" led to their doom. All of the suffering "comes round and is retorted" to us, who, much like the Egyptians of the Scriptures, have "come to have very Slender regards for Religion ourselves." And, like the Egyptians, the slaveholders' chief sin was their negligence of their enslaved. Such biblical imagery must have resonated among the enslaved as, later, African Americans embraced exodus motifs. But Fontaine made no radical statement about emancipation or exodus; after all, blacks were the "most valuable parts" of the planters' estates. Instead, he sought to persuade his parishioners to include blacks, "especially those who are born in [our] (family)," in the Christian community and thus make them "more faithfull serv[an]ts."[24]

23. Jones, *Present State of Virginia,* ed. Morton, 99. Slaveholders used illiteracy as a tool of domination, believing that ignorance was one way of keeping the enslaved down. They also believed that literacy would encourage the enslaved to think that their condition was not appropriate and could be used by them to help end their oppression. They could forge passes and other documents, keep up with events in the newspapers, and write to one another. Their heightened sensibility and communication could contribute to more conspiracies and insurrections. See John C. Van Horne, ed., *Religious Philanthropy and Colonial Slavery: The American Correspondence of the Associates of Dr. Bray, 1717–1777* (Urbana, Ill., 1985), 31–32, 124; David Waldstreicher, "Reading the Runaways: Self-Fashioning, Print Culture, and Confidence in Slavery in the Eighteenth-Century Mid-Atlantic," *WMQ,* 3d Ser., LVI (1999), 262–271.

24. "Sermon of Peter Fontaine," May 10, 1727, typescript, CWF. Fontaine's biblical

Policymakers in England also weighed in on the issue of slave baptism. In 1727, an unidentified ideologue in England alluded to Pharaoh and the Jews, as did Fontaine, to encourage religious instruction as a means of social control. The rulers of Egypt tried to control the Jews through ignorance and suffered the wrath of God. If savageness were allowed to remain in the plantations, a standing army would be necessary to contain the blacks. Christianity could avert rebelliousness and turn hostile blacks into obedient workers. Moreover, Edmund Gibson, the bishop of London, published two letters in 1727 exhorting slaveholders and ministers to instruct and baptize blacks. He advised them that Christianity would not cause the "least Alteration" in slave propertyholdings but would make blacks behave better and work harder.[25]

The British discussion of slave baptism found its way to Virginia. The Board of Trade understood from past experience that slave conversion could only happen with the slaveholders' blessing. For this reason, the board instructed Governor William Gooch, "with the Assistance of the Council and Assembly, to find out the best Means to facilitate and encourage the Conversion of Negroes and Indians to the Christian Religion." In response, Gooch stressed the importance of religion to Virginia society at his first meeting with the General Assembly in February 1728.[26]

Jones's book, Fontaine's sermon, a bureaucrat's opinion, Gibson's letters, the crown's instructions, and Gooch's speech probably did not change slaveholders' minds about the religious lives of their enslaved. But it is fairly clear that these lamentations and arguments for religious instruction as a method of social control did not fall upon deaf ears. By the late 1720s into the 1730s, the great planters began to realize the advan-

---

allusion must have given Byrd pause, considering what Byrd had written that year: England as reprobate Egypt and Virginia as a Canaan respite (see Chapter 7).

25. "An Examination of a Late Opinion That the Encouragement of Learning, and Religion, and Episcopal Church Government in the English Plantations, Are Inconsistent with the Interest of England," ca. 1727, FPP/14, 43, VCRP; Edmund Gibson, *Two Letters of the Lord Bishop of London: The First, to the Masters and Mistresses of Families in the English Plantations Abroad; Exhorting Them to Encourage and Promote the Instruction of Their Negroes in the Christian Faith; the Second, to the Missionaries There; Directing Them to Distribute the Said Letter, and Exhorting Them to Give Their Assistance towards the Instruction of the Negroes within Their Several Parishes* (London, 1727), 11; David Dabydeen, *Hogarth's Blacks: Images of Blacks in Eighteenth Century English Art* (Athens, Ga., 1987), 119–120.

26. BT to Gooch, March 1727, CO 5/1365, 24–25, VCRP; Gooch Address to the Council, Feb. 12, 1728, CO 5/1321, 26–27, VCRP.

tages of using Christianity to indoctrinate both enslaved and free blacks in the values of the dominant society. Slaveholders had expended little effort to convert Africans, citing their intractable disposition and foreign tongues; but they now saw blacks born in Virginia as more familiar, if not similar to themselves. Creoles, picking up their masters' ways and mannerisms, were better able to participate in the dialectic of patriarchism. Concessions such as baptism, instruction, and benefit of clergy became at once easier and more compelling to extend. With this extension — or inclusion — came the concomitant wish to have docile, tractable, and obedient slaves. Rev. Adam Dickie observed, "It is a very easy matter to Read the life of the Master or overseer in the knowledge of the Slave." William Johnson, an Anglican missionary who traveled throughout the British colonies, found the intimacy between whites and blacks on the continent made "each slave . . . a Proselyte to his own master's way of thinking."[27]

No longer viewing proselytism as impractical, the burgesses in May 1730 encouraged black conversion. The slaveholders hoped that Christianity would transform their enslaved into obedient workers by changing the way they thought about themselves, resigning themselves to their status and their master's power. If violence had been the mechanism to force blacks to obey, conversion to Christianity was meant to endow them with a sense of obedience. Dickie reported in 1732 that white people were "sensible of the advantage of having their Slaves made Christians for they who formerly were theives, lyars, Swearers, prophaners of the Sabbath, and neglecters of their business, from a Sense of Religion and of their Duty have left off all these things and make Conscience of every thing they do." Of his own enslaved, Dickie wrote that they "stand more in Awe of a Reprimand from me than formerly they did of a whipping and think it below them to do anything unworthy [of] the Christian name."[28] Indeed, Christianity idealized obedience as a virtue in an enslaved laborer. In 1736, the *Virginia Gazette* captured the essence of the docile enslaved black Christian in the epitaph of George Pompey:

27. William Byrd, *Histories of the Dividing Line betwixt Virginia and North Carolina* (ca. 1728–1736), ed. William K. Boyd (1929; reprint, New York, 1967), 3–4; Rev. Adam Dickie to Mr. Newman, June 27, 1732, FPP/14, 39, VCRP; William Johnson to the secretary of the SPG, Jan. 14, 1736, SPG Letter Books, SPG Archives, MS A, XXVI, 381, VCRP.

28. *JHB, 1727–1734, 1736–1740*, 63; Dickie to Newman, June 27, 1732, FPP/14, 39, VCRP.

Here lyeth enterred the Body of
George Pompey,
Late Negro Servant to
Sir Fisher Tench, of this Parish, Bart.
During upwards of 20 Years Service,
Was most diligent and faithful,
And though born a Heathen,
Lived and died truly a Christian;
Conscious of Innocence of Life,
Met Death with undaunted Courage,
And if concerned,
'Twas only to part so good a Master;
An Example worthy of all Servants to imitate.
He departed this Life, the 31st of August, 1735,
In the 32d Year of his Age.[29]

Because christening blacks was an avowal of patriarchal authority, the rate and progression of slave baptisms are important indicators of the crystallization of patriarchism. The argument for slave baptism asserted racial distinction. Blacks were unable to integrate into society because of their heathen backgrounds and cultural inferiority. They not only needed but also benefited from their masters' protection. In this sense, the baptism of blacks — increasing at this time — at once affirmed the virtue of the great planters, a mark of their class status in society, and reinforced the dependence of blacks. A speaker at the College of William and Mary took notice of an endowment to the college of forty pounds annually from a landed estate in Yorkshire for the education of Indian children, which has implications for christening blacks. He expounded in 1722 that the "Education of heathen Children in the Christian faith" presents no contradiction for the basic value system of the society. Not only did Christian education provide an ideological justification but also the expectation "that in time they may by [this means of education, be] bringing and adding [to] the Countrys Stock of wealth."[30]

By comparing the number of baptisms to the aggregate live black popu-

29. *Va. Gaz.*, Feb. 18, 1736; M. I. Finley, *Ancient Slavery and Modern Ideology* (New York, 1980), 104. See also Joseph Vogt, *Ancient Slavery and the Ideal of Man,* trans. Thomas Wiedemann (Oxford, 1974), 140–145.

30. Oration (vernacular), College of William and Mary, Williamsburg, Va., 1722, BV 13, SPG, Package II, Klingberg Collection.

Plate 16. St. Peter's Parish Church. *New Kent County, Virginia. Built from 1701–1703 with 1739–1740 tower addition. Photograph by Dell Upton*

lation in St. Peter's Parish, New Kent County, a typical tidewater community in its population and settlement, one can see the pattern of conversion. Before 1727, few blacks were baptized; after that date, more and more blacks were brought to the baptismal font. At first, those baptized were the American-born enslaved capable of reciting the catechism; then during the 1730s infant baptism became common. Only nine black baptisms were recorded in St. Peter's Parish before 1720, less than 2 percent of the enslaved. The baptizing of blacks began slowly during the first five years of the 1720s, when eight were registered. The relative number of blacks baptized, reflecting a change of attitude, had increased significantly by 1729. Slaveowners had thirty-four blacks baptized from 1725 to 1729. Only ten were baptized from 1730 to 1734, but this number is most likely the result of missing leaves in the register than a change in the social pattern. Another eighty-one blacks were baptized in the final five years of the 1730s. This sprinkling of baptisms (assuming a proportional death rate among Christians, who were younger than the non-Christian African-born slaves) left approximately 14 percent of St. Peter's blacks converted to Christianity by 1740. John Custis IV, who had ninety-five enslaved blacks in St. Peter's

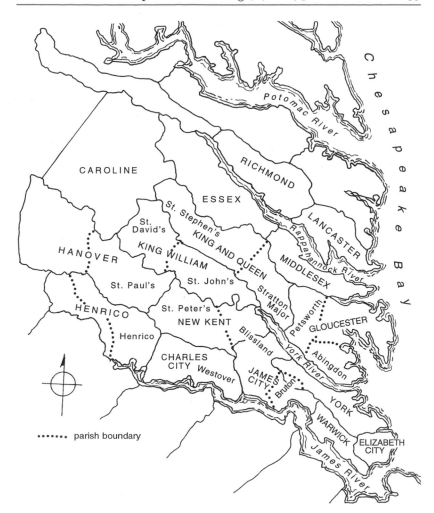

Map 3. Parish Lines of Virginia, 1720–1730. *After C. G. Chamberlayne,*
The Vestry Book of Petsworth Parish, Gloucester County, Virginia,
1677–1793 *(Richmond, Va., 1933). Drawn by Richard Stinely*

Parish in 1736, had baptized nineteen (20 percent) before 1740, slightly
better than the average.[31]

31. "A List of Negroes in Saint Peter's Parish in New Kent County, October 2, 1736,"
Custis Family Papers, 1658–1858, MS 1 C9698, VHS; Gundersen, *The Anglican Ministry
in Virginia,* 104. See also Chamberlayne, ed., *Vestry Book and Register.* These two manuscript volumes contain the earliest consecutive records of St. Peter's Parish. In its original
form, the vestry book, or volume I, contained twenty to thirty more leaves than the cur-

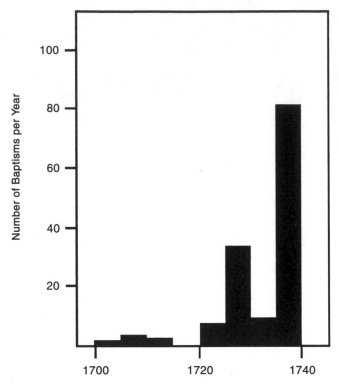

Figure 5. Black Baptisms in St. Peter's Parish, 1700–1740.
Drawn by Peter Schweighofer

The ministers in St. Peter's Parish witnessed the slaveholders' changing attitudes about slave baptism, describing them with shifting metaphors of anguish and affection. In replying to the 1723 query of the bishop of London about proselytizing blacks, Rev. Henry Collings of St. Peter's Parish indifferently summed up the extent of baptisms during the first quarter of the eighteenth century: "Some of [the blacks] are suffered by their respective masters to be baptiz'd and to attend on divine service; but others are not." Only two years later, the reluctant sufferance of blacks at the baptis-

rent edition. Chamberlayne believed these to have been torn out at random. The latter part of volume I contains registers of births, marriages, baptisms, and deaths in the parish between 1685 and 1730 or 1731. The original volume II contained at least five more leaves than the current edition. This volume was used exclusively as a parish register of births, baptisms, and deaths from 1733 to the end of the century. There are few entries for the period 1740–1756, and after 1767 the entries are again few and scattered.

mal font that Collings had observed would be described by his successor as a fondness. Rev. John Lang observed that the slaveholders "are fond of bringing their Negroe Servants to Baptism how soon [as] they are capable to rehearse the Creed Lords prayer and Com[mandmen]ts."[32]

Slave baptismal patterns also demonstrated the role white gentry women played in the emerging ethos of patriarchism in Virginia. Although women were only 20 percent of the slaveholders in St. Peter's Parish, they were 29 percent of the slaveholders who christened blacks. Alice Field and Frances Littlepage were trendsetters, each having five blacks baptized. Field's christenings counted for more than one-half of black baptisms before 1720, and Littlepage's counted for more than one-third from 1721 to 1725. Piety as sanctified submission to a superior being both ratified the hierarchy of authority and supported those in subordinate positions. Women were pivotal in the valorization of the ideals of the social order. Judith Carter Page, for example, the daughter of Robert "King" Carter, "piously" memorialized these ideals of patriarchism in the 1730 epitaph of her husband, great planter Mann Page: an honest, forthright public servant; an affectionate, good husband, father, and master. These platitudes follow his personal and public vita:

His Publick Trust he faithfully Discharged
with
Candour and Discretion
Truth and Justice
Nor was he less eminent in his private Behaviour
For he was
A tender husband and Indulgent Father
A gentle Master and a faithful Friend
Being to All
Courteous and Benevolent Kind and Affable
This Monument was piously erected to his memory
By His Mournfully Surviving Lady.[33]

Although Christian enslaved blacks remained a minority, Creole converts became more numerous in the late 1720s and 1730s. The emphasis on

32. Collings to the bishop of London, June 1, 1724, FPP/15, 10, VCRP. See also John Brunskill to the bishop of London, June 18, 1724, FPP/15, 17, VCRP; Lang to the bishop of London, Feb. 7, 1725/6, FPP/15, 68, VCRP.

33. Brown, *Good Wives, Nasty Wenches,* 313–318; "Virginia Council Journals, 1726–1753," *VMHB,* XXXII (1924), 45.

nativity and instruction indicates that these converts were born in America and regarded by their masters as capable of professing Christian principles. For example, Rev. William Le Neve of James City Parish reported to the bishop of London: "My Lord, I have examined and improved several Negroes, Natives of Virginia." What is more significant, Creoles were active seekers for themselves and their children. Commissary James Blair observed in 1729: "The Negroes themselves in our neighbourhood are very desirous to become Christians; and in order to it come and give an account of the Lords prayer, and the Creed, and ten Commandments, and so are baptized and frequent the church." Finally realizing his goal of thirty years, Blair closed with the observation, "The Negro children are now commonly baptized."[34]

The pattern of nativity and child baptism held for St. Peter's Parish. From 1725 to 1729, 85 percent of the baptisms in the register were praying blacks or those that could be educated. By the 1730s, masters were forgoing instruction as a prerequisite for christening. The advance of baptism during that decade changed from the American-born capable of professing Christian principles to black infants. Within the first five years of the 1730s, 60 percent of blacks baptized in St. Peter's Parish were infants. Between 1735 and 1739, this figure increased to 93 percent of all blacks baptized. During the latter half of the 1730s, almost half (47 percent) of blacks born in St. Peter's Parish were christened.[35]

Conversion was not a passive acceptance of an alien worldview; blacks incorporated Christian beliefs into their ethos. They took what they wanted from Christianity and fit it into an emerging slave culture, much of which was based on African religious beliefs. Almighty God was their creator god; the Trinity recalled the plurality of lesser gods. Divine anger and an afterlife where evildoers suffered were intelligible to them, but they found the doctrine of original sin, specifying man's inherent depravity, repugnant. Olaudah Equiano, a Christian convert, retained throughout his life his Igbo notion of an all-powerful spirit that was involved in his fate.

34. Perry, *Historical Collections,* I, 344; Blair to the bishop of London, June 28, 1729, FPP/15, 109, VCRP (quotation); Le Neve to the bishop of London, 1724, FPP/15, 14, VCRP. See also to the bishop of London, all in VCRP: Lang, Feb. 7, 1725/6, FPP/15, 68; Brooke, 1724, FPP/15, 1; Robertson, July 8, 1724, FPP/15, 11; Collings, June 18, 1724, FPP/15, 10; Fontaine, 1724, FPP/15, 18; Dan[ie]l Taylor, [1724], Blissland Parish, FPP/15, 5; Jones, 1724, FPP/15, 4; Forbes, 1724, FPP/15, 2; Yates, June 15, 1724, FPP/15, 3; Blair, July 15, 1724, FPP/14, 1; Black, June 8, 1724, FPP/15, 21; Falconar, May 27, 1724, FPP/15, 19.

35. Chamberlayne, ed., *Vestry Book and Register,* 341–556. See also Appendix 2, below.

Indeed, Equiano was representative of the Igbos, whose views of time and work, if not their notions of eternity and original sin, were similar to those of Calvinists.[36]

Many whites, not understanding the behavior of praying blacks, questioned their sincerity. They observed that black Christians lived much as their unconverted neighbors. Moreover, Christianity gave them status, made them proud, and encouraged them in their quest for freedom. Rev. John Lang reported to Bishop Gibson from St. Peter's Parish that, to his chagrin, black Christians often asked their unconverted friends to stand as godparents for their children at baptism. The converts also continued to hone in on Christianity's implicit message of freedom. James Blair wrote to Gibson in 1729: "I doubt not some of the Negroes are sincere Converts; but the far greater part of them little mind the serious part, only are in hopes that they shall meet with so much the more respect, and that some time or other Christianity will help them to their freedom." In another missive to the bishop in the following year, Blair conveyed the great planters' belief that Christianity was changing the character of the enslaved: "Some [slaveholders] allege it makes them prouder, and inspires them with thoughts of freedom, but I take this to be rather a common prejudice than anything else." Such convictions contrasted sharply with the competing expectation that Christianity would render the enslaved more humble and faithful.[37]

Slaveholders' fears seemed partly justified in 1730, when Christianity inspired blacks to revolt for freedom. A rumor that Governor Alexander Spotswood was returning from England with an order to free enslaved Christians—an order suppressed by local authorities—spread rapidly throughout the black community (see Chapter 5). In truth, the English at-

36. Equiano, *Interesting Narrative*, ed. Edwards, I, 28–29; Olaudah Equiano, *The Interesting Narrative and Other Writings*, ed. Vincent Carretta (New York, 1995), 241 n. 3; Frey and Wood, *Come Shouting to Zion*, 35–62; Albert J. Raboteau, *Slave Religion: The "Invisible Institution" in the Antebellum South* (New York, 1978), 127; Mechal Sobel, *Trabelin' On: The Slave Journey to an Afro-Baptist Faith* (1979; reprint, Princeton, N.J., 1988), 64–71; Sobel, *The World They Made Together: Black and White Values in Eighteenth-Century Virginia* (Princeton, N.J., 1987), 28, 172–179; Jon F. Sensbach, *A Separate Canaan: The Making of an Afro-Moravian World in North Carolina, 1763–1840* (Chapel Hill, N.C., 1998), 75, 112–113, 116; Michael A. Gomez, *Exchanging Our Country Marks: The Transformation of African Identities in the Colonial and Antebellum South* (Chapel Hill, N.C., 1998), 129–130.

37. Lang to the bishop of London, Feb. 7, 1725/6, FPP/15, 68, VCRP; Blair to the bishop of London, June 28, 1729, FPP/15, 109, July 20, 1730, FPP/13, 131, VCRP.

torney general and solicitor general had just issued the Yorke-Talbot opinion that confirmed the slavery of Christian and non-Christian blacks alike.
But, Blair observed, blacks "were willing to feed themselves with a [great]
fancy that it [the edict of emancipation] did [free them], and that the
King designed that all Christians should be made free." The rumor was
"sufficient," thought William Gooch, "to Incite them to Rebellion." The
anxiety arising from the social unrest in 1730 not only caused Gooch to
issue a proclamation ordering whites to carry their arms to church but also
caused Dr. Thomas Bray's Associates to reconsider proselytism to blacks.
Dr. Thomas Bray (1658–1730) established the Associates in 1724 and reorganized it in 1730 with a bequest from Abel Tassin, Sieur D'Allone,
for "Erecting a School or Schools for the thorough instructing in the
Christian Religion the young Children of the Negroe Slaves and such of
their parents as should show themselves inclinable and desirous of such
Instruction." After reviewing the situation in the colonies, however, the
Associates concluded that any insurrection of the enslaved "was not occasioned . . . by any Design of Instructing them in the Christian Religion."[38]

Gooch observed after the rebellion that the submission of blacks to
their masters was the result of force; but, if slaveholders had "hope" that
the enslaved would "rest contented with their condition," then masters
had to provide them with some incentives. He later wrote to William Anne
Keppel, earl of Albermarle, absentee governor of Virginia (1737–1754): "I
am persuaded . . . how absolutely necessary Rewards as well as Punishments are to maintain authority in any Government." With this remark,
Gooch was simply observing the principle of realpolitik: hegemony must
be backed by force, but to be truly effective the oppressed class had to
be persuaded to acquiesce in the constituted power. One way to achieve
that end in Virginia was to grant concessions and benefits to the enslaved.
Co-opted with concessions, blacks were less likely to rebel.[39]

One concession granted to Christian blacks consistent with the emergence of patriarchism was the benefit of clergy. In 1731, Gooch used his authority as ordinary to bring to the York County court's attention the right

38. Blair to the bishop of London, May 14, 1731, FPP/15, 110, VCRP; Gooch to the
bishop of London, May 28, 1731, FPP/15, 111, VCRP; "Virginia Council Journals, 1726–
1753: Proclamation for Suppressing the Meetings of Slaves," *VMHB,* XXXVI (1928), 345;
Minutes of Dr. Bray's Associates, Oct. 2, Nov. 10, 1730, I, SPG, London, VCRP; Dabydeen, *Hogarth's Blacks,* 119; Van Horne, ed., *Religious Philanthropy,* 5.

39. Gooch to the bishop of London, May 28, 1731, FPP/15, 111, VCRP; Gooch to
Albermarle, Sept. 3, 1739, CO 5/1337, 208–211, VCRP.

of Mary Aggie, an enslaved Christian standing trial for stealing, to benefit of clergy. Gooch remembered that Aggie had sued for her freedom and had given a "tolerable account" of "her Faith" in the General Court. The county court and General Court were divided over whether Aggie should be able to plead, although Gooch, the attorney general, and several other lawyers supported benefit of clergy for enslaved Christians. The council, recognizing that Aggie had been "convicted of Felony for which if she was a Free woman She ought to have Benefit" of the king's law, issued her a pardon on the condition that she be sold to another English colony. With the case of Aggie resolved, the Council of State referred the question to Whitehall for adjudication. (Gooch also requested and received a New-gate pardon for Sarah Williamson, "a poor Indian woman convicted for the murder of her own child," because of "her Christian behavior during the time of her Tryal and imprisonment.") Benefit of clergy should "be carried in favour of the Christian though a black one . . . [for] political reasons," wrote Gooch, for the laws "are of equal force against white as black People being Christians."[40]

Not waiting for the crown to act, the General Assembly passed an act in 1732 allowing benefit of clergy to enslaved Christians in felony cases, except when forbidden by English statute. English law excluded manslaughter, which, unlike today, comprehended "under it all manner of felonious homicide" and property crimes that occurred in dwelling places at night or that were worth more than five shillings sterling. Those convicted of these crimes could not plead and "shall suffer death." In the same act, the General Assembly took away from nonwhite Christians the right to give testimony except in the trial of enslaved persons for capital offenses, stating its reason in the preamble to the law: although these people would

40. Gooch to Secretary of State Newcastle, June 9, 1728, CO 5/1337, VCRP; Newcastle to Gooch, December 1728, CO 5/1337, 126–127, VCRP. An ordinary was a clergyman appointed under English law to attend condemned criminals. The governor served as ordinary because the commissary, the bishop's representative in Virginia, had no such authoirty under Virginia law. See Ivor Noël Hume, *Here Lies Virginia: An Archaeologist's View of Colonial Life and History* (New York, 1963), 169–170; Gooch to the bishop of London, May 28, 1731, in Rev. G. MacLaren Brydon, ed., "The Virginia Clergy," *VMHB,* XXXII (1924), 322–324; *EJCCV,* IV, 243; Gooch to BT, July 10, 1731, CO 5/1322, 201–204, July 18, 1732, CO 5/1323, 44–49, VCRP; Landon C. Bell, "Benefit of Clergy," MS, VHS; Rev. G. MacLaren Brydon to Landon C. Bell, Oct. 6, 1931, Bell to Brydon, Oct. 8, 1931, Brydon Box, folder 1, VHS. Benefit of clergy was granted to an enslaved person earlier in 1726 (Philip J. Schwarz, *Twice Condemned: Slaves and the Criminal Laws of Virginia, 1705–1865* [Baton Rouge, La., 1988], 19n).

"have professed themselves to be christians, and been able to give some account of the principles of the christian religion. . . . They are people of such base and corrupt natures, that credit of their testimony cannot be certainly depended upon." The decision further marked blacks' separate standing in civil society, inscribing racial inferiority and justifying the necessity of masters' guidance. Gooch, champion of the benefit of clergy for Christian blacks, thought the reason given in this bill "certainly a very good one."[41]

The slaveholders were willing to assent to slave baptism, hopeful that it would make blacks more manageable, but they would not allow Christianity to interfere with slavery. The callousness of this Christianity of slavery can be seen in the utter disregard for the sacraments. Rev. John Lang was appalled that, even after instruction and baptism, blacks continued living together in common-law marriages, as did non-Christian blacks. Their masters separated married couples, demonstrating contempt for the sanctity of that sacrament. Rather than condemning this clearly unchristian practice, Rev. Adam Dickie questioned his superiors about whether the church would allow these separated spouses to have new partners. With the exception of baptism, Virginia blacks were "not to be allowed to be Churched" or to be brought to church to receive its rites of communion, confirmation, and ordination because it would contribute to their sense of equality with whites. Slaveholders also forbade their Christian blacks from serving as godparents to one another's children, which would have recognized their capacity to be responsible, a clear violation of patriarchism.[42]

Indeed, white resistance to blacks' entering the church was a persistent problem. Blacks might become more tractable as a result of Christianity, yet "white People thought it a Mighty Scandal to have their Children repeat the Catechism with Negroes." Some Anglican ministers attempted to solve this problem by instructing blacks on Sunday morning before service. Robert "King" Carter included a separate black pew when he rebuilt Christ Church in Lancaster County in 1732. Great planters, using Christianity as a bulwark of slavery, were careful not to allow Christian concepts

41. *SAL*, IV, 325–327; Gooch to the BT, July 18, 1732, CO 5/1323, 44–49, VCRP; Peter Linebaugh, *The London Hanged: Crime and Civil Society in the Eighteenth Century* (New York, 1991), 53–54, 65, 79–82; *Oxford English Dictionary*, online ed., s.v. "manslaughter."

42. Lang to the bishop of London, Feb. 7, 1725/6, FPP/15, 68, VCRP; Dickie to Newman, June 27, 1732, FPP/14, 39, VCRP.

such as the Golden Rule or equality before God to interfere with the racial caste of the society.[43]

The experience of Rev. Anthony Gavin highlights the contradiction of the Christianity of slavery. After the Spanish-born minister arrived in 1735, he wrote to Dr. Bray's Associates that he had received 150 acres of good land from the vestry in Henrico Parish on the James River. He had to purchase "slaves and other Necessaries" to work it, which would put him into debt for two or three years. He recommended Virginia to any "Sober Clergyman," for there were several vacant parishes that would provide a salary of sixteen thousand pounds of tobacco along with a house, a glebe, and good society. A spokesman for the ideology of patriarchism, he wrote: "I have not heard an Oath as yet in this Colony, and we have so good Governor and so Exemplary that all Vice and Immoral Actions are almost banished out of the Colony; and it is a Pleasure for a Clergyman to live among sober, religious People." A convert from Catholicism and an enthusiast about the new evangelism, he baptized 172 blacks. After only three years in the colony, he had a change of mind. He expressed his disappointment "to see Episcopacy so little regarded in this Colony, and the cognizance of Spiritual Affairs left to Governour and Council by the Law of this Colony." He was appalled "to see the greatest Part of our Bretheren taken up in farming and buying Slaves, which in my humble Opinion is unlawfull for any Christian, and particular for a Clergyman[;] by this the Souls Committed to their Care must suffer."[44]

In spite of their best intentions, clergymen quickly learned that their ministry was severely compromised by slavery. Always mindful of their inferior status in society, Virginia's clergy fitted well into the imagery of weary old men wandering in the wilderness. Rev. Charles Bridges, lament-

43. Dickie to Newman, June 27, 1732, FPP/14, 39, VCRP (quotation); Alex White to William Dawson, July 4, 1748, St. David's Parish, Dawson Papers, 1728–1775, CWF; William Willie to Reverend Sir, Aug. 30, 1749, Miscellaneous Collection, Duke University, Durham, N.C.; Jonathan Boucher to the Reverend Mr. John Waring, ca. 1767, Dr. Bray's Associates American Papers, 1735–1774, book 2, SPG Archives, VCRP; Joseph B. Earnest, Jr., *The Religious Development of the Negro in Virginia* (Charlottesville, Va., 1914), 39; W. A. R. Goodwin, *Historical Sketch of Bruton Church, Williamsburg, Virginia* ([Williamsburg], Va., 1903), 15, 32; Dell Upton, *Holy Things and Profane: Anglican Parish Churches in Colonial Virginia* (New York, 1986), 218.

44. Rev. Anthony Gavin to Rev. Samuel Smith, Oct. 20, 1735, in Van Horne, ed., *Religious Philanthropy*, 83–84; Gavin to the bishop of London, Aug. 5, 1738, FPP/14, 51, VCRP.

ing the clergy's dismal efforts at instructing blacks and fearing that the bishop of London's new designs for proselytism would "come to nothing," apologized in 1738. "The Commissary and I grow in years, and the world hangs heavy upon us. I am rous'd sometimes and then call upon him, and then he is asleep . . . too."[45]

*   *   *

BY THE LATE 1720s, the great planters began to appreciate the advantages of Christian education for indoctrinating blacks in the values of the dominant society, values codified in the ideology of patriarchism. The great planters had gone from anxious Englishmen to whom Protestantism was crucial to their identity as free men — an identity to which they desperately clung — to provincial patriarchs whose self-worth derived from dominion over enslaved blacks. From a signifier of freedom, Christianity had become an essential tool of social control.

45. Charles Bridges to the bishop of London, 1738, in Perry, *Historical Collections,* I, 361.

Foul Means Must Do,
What Fair Will Not

According to William Byrd II, slavery had by 1736 made Virginia into New Guinea, an anxious place to live. He knew too well that the great planters' power and wealth had come about because of slavery. But he also knew that they had created a slave society that was becoming more and more difficult to control. It should not surprise us that these men were concerned about the behavior of the gentry's women, as they began to build great estates. Without question, they were troubled about their declining status in relation to English merchants backed by the crown. To be sure, they were uneasy with the agitation of parvenu planters for more and cheaper enslaved blacks and for less regulation of tobacco. But what Byrd feared most was that blacks would find a leader who could unite them in their struggle for liberty. There was sustained popular resistance to slavery from its inception. By both their behavior and demeanor, the enslaved challenged their owners' control. Byrd reckoned that, since the increasing number of blacks would only inspire rebelliousness and excite expectations of freedom, the great planters had better act to check the agency of the enslaved. If slave-produced tobacco had been the means to the formation of great family estates, then social control of blacks, despite its psychological costs, had to become the means to keeping them. Byrd's meditation, "Foul means must do, what fair will not," a confession of guilt, demonstrates that the great planters were not only aware of the moral cost of slavery, but they were willing to pay the price in the formation (one could say the deformation) of Virginia society.[1]

The choice of slavery was deliberate, odious, and foul. Census takers

---

1. William Byrd II to John Perceval, earl of Egmont, July 12, 1736, William Byrd II Letter Book, 1735–1736, VHS.

had already marked off blacks as different twenty years before the courts in the 1640s recognized them as enslaved. The Dutch had already supplied Barbados with enslaved Africans twenty years before the assembly in 1660 exempted them from duties. Lawmakers had already pressed slavery into the statute books twenty years before the depressed sugar market in the 1680s opened the slave trade. Authorities had already begun repressing Africans' culture twenty years before the opening of the trade direct from Africa in the 1700s. Slaveholders had already consolidated a slave code twenty years before they began masking slavery behind ideology and religion in the 1720s and 1730s.

Foul are the means of making slavery. Foul are the machinations leading to the landgrab: by forcing the Powhatans from their native soil ("so much easier than civilizing them by faire means"); by engrossing acreage, often fraudulently, putting poorer whites into their debt; and by securing headrights for blacks, whose slavery precluded opportunity. Foul are the vulgar abuses of law, religion, and ideology: by passing draconian statutes throwing state power behind the slaveholders' autocracy; by invoking a reactive ideology of patriarchism that endorsed slavery as the natural order; and by prostituting Anglicanism into sanctioning slavery. Foul are the vigilant methods of supervising the enslaved: by overseeing them in fields and households; by patrolling roads and quarters; by making bounty hunters of Indians; by manning batteries to prevent escape to the mountains. Foul are all the ruthless acts of repression designed to cow the enslaved into submission: by whipping them, often for the slightest infraction; by jailing them; by forcing them to wear iron collars, horses' bits, or iron muzzles. Foul are the torturous punishments inflicted on the enslaved: by selling or exiling them from loved ones, by hanging, burning, dismembering, and quartering them, their flesh left rent in public places. Foul is the rationale for the "casuall killing" of recalcitrant blacks: that murderous violence was necessary to check their obstinacy and the legal fiction that such murder was not felony homicide because slaveholders' self-interest in property precluded a propensity for malice.[2]

How foul were these means to maintaining a slave society? Byrd would

2. Edward Waterhouse, "A Declaration of the State of the Colony and Affaires in Virginia; with a Relation of the Barbarous Massacre in the Time of Peace and League, Treacherously Executed by the Native Infidels upon the English, the 22 of March Last" (1622), in W. Stitt Robinson, ed., *Virginia Treaties, 1607–1722*, vol. IV of Alden T. Vaughan, gen. ed., *Early American Indian Documents: Treaties and Laws, 1607–1789* (Frederick, Md., 1983), 37–38; *SAL*, II, 270.

equivocate: not as horrendous as those "practiced in the islands." Yet he recognized that the maintenance of slavery, which was inextricably tied to racial oppression, had compromised the ruling elite's republican virtue — so "terrible to a good natur'd Man, who must submit to be either a Fool or a Fury." Byrd's allusion to Catiline betrays his understanding that an armed insurrection by the enslaved endangered the republic. Yet, as the white Virginians constructed their republican house, they built it with the bricks and mortar of black aspirations for freedom. Thus, the architects of American freedom were not merely the founders romanticized in our national narrative but their enslaved from which they learned the desperate need for liberation.[3]

During the formative years of slavery in Virginia, 1660–1740, the great planters were less concerned with their own freedom than with the expropriation of Indian land, the production of tobacco, and the enslavement of blacks. The great planters were anxious because women, small planters, and, most important, blacks were not quiescent in their designs. The Powhatans fought two wars with the English in 1622 and 1644 before losing control of the tidewater. During the remainder of the seventeenth century, settler incursions challenged English efforts to reconcile Indian reserves with planter ambition and rebellion. Throughout the period, planters' widows jockeyed with their new husbands for wealth and property. After the great planters' engrossment of land, smaller planters and freed servants were chafed by dismal prospects of landownership. Tobacco farmers rioted and destroyed tobacco plants in 1682; a later generation burned tobacco warehouses in 1732. Indentured and enslaved laborers aligned with each other in common cause as fugitives, lovers, and rebels. Black and white laborers ran away together, muddied racial lines by consensual sexual relationships, and were comrades-in-arms in Bacon's Rebellion. The charter generation of blacks, many from Hispanic societies, resisted enslavement for themselves and their children by petitioning the assembly and bringing legal suits to court alleging that either their previous free status or Christianity precluded enslavement. Africans fought with the slave-trading crews on the outer voyage. Once in Virginia, the recently enslaved Africans tried to recreate a semblance of their cultural traditions by massing in the countryside, where they plotted rebellion.

The enslaved resisted by organizing mass breakouts. The increased number of blacks contributed to the great planters' anxiety and the debt

3. Byrd to Egmont, July 12, 1736, Byrd Letter Book, 1735–1736.

crisis. The great planters who had enslaved blacks wanted to restrict their importation and supported regulation to improve the price of tobacco and security. Mercantile reaction to the planters' attempts to control trade contributed to their loss of status. They understood this loss in terms of their enslaved, whom they had stripped of liberty. Thus, in this era, the loss that Byrd spoke of was less about independence, which would become the banner of the next generation, than about the control of Virginia society. The great planters resuscitated a nearly defunct patriarchism in order to repress the enslaved further rather than extend republicanism to include them. The slaveholders prostituted religion as a method of social control rather than include blacks in the Christian community. Of course, this repression extended to the society as a whole. And it is this legacy that we still live with today.

Black Headright Patents

Table 1. Frequency of Black Headright Patents, 1635–1699

Blacks per Patent (No.)	Landowners (No./Cumulative)	Landowners (%/Cumulative %)
1	198/198	24.7/ 24.7
2	170/368	21.2/ 45.9
3	120/488	15.0/ 60.4
4	63/551	7.9/ 68.8
5	46/597	5.7/ 74.5
6	47/644	5.9/ 80.4
7	23/667	2.9/ 83.3
8	27/694	3.4/ 86.6
9	19/713	2.4/ 89.0
10	14/727	1.7/ 90.8
11	5/732	0.6/ 91.4
12	8/740	1.0/ 92.4
13	5/745	0.6/ 93.0
14	5/750	0.6/ 93.6
15	6/756	0.7/ 94.4
16	9/765	1.1/ 95.5
17	4/769	0.5/ 96.0
18	3/772	0.4/ 96.4
19	1/773	0.1/ 96.5
20	3/776	0.4/ 96.9
21	1/777	0.1/ 97.0
23	4/781	0.5/ 97.5
25	2/783	0.2/ 97.7
26	2/785	0.2/ 98.0
28	1/786	0.1/ 98.1
29	1/787	0.1/ 98.2
32	1/788	0.1/ 98.4
35	1/789	0.1/ 98.5
38	1/790	0.1/ 98.6
41	1/791	0.1/ 98.7

Table 1. Continued

Blacks per Patent (No.)	Landowners (No./Cumulative)	Landowners (%/Cumulative %)
47	1/792	0.1/ 98.9
53	1/793	0.1/ 99.0
57	1/794	0.1/ 99.1
70	1/795	0.1/ 99.2
72	1/796	0.1/ 99.4
80	1/797	0.1/ 99.5
90	1/798	0.1/ 99.6
100	2/800	0.2/ 99.9
114	1/801	0.1/100.0

Source: CP, I–III.

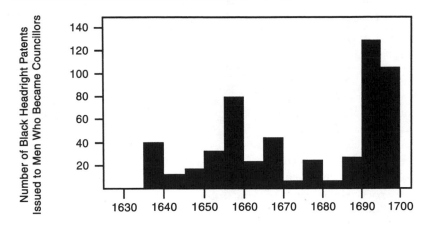

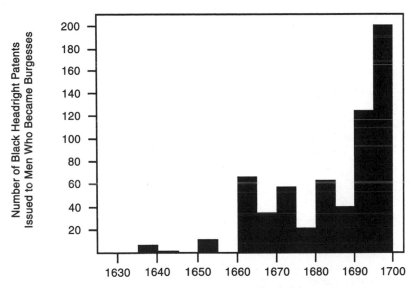

Figure A-1. Black Headrights Secured by Officeholders, 1630–1700.
Drawn by Peter Schweighofer

Table 2. Distribution of Black Headright Patents: Council of State

Landowner (First Year/Last Year in Council of State)	Year Patent Issued	No. of Blacks per Patent
Armistead, John (1688/1691)	1678	5
Bacon, Nathaniel (1656/1692)	1666	9
Ballard, Thomas (1670/1679)	1666	1
Bennett, Richard (1639/1675)	1635	1
Bennett, Richard (1639/1675)	1637	1
Bridger, Joseph (1673/1686)	1666	17
Browne, Henry (1634/1661)	1637	8
Byrd, William (1683/1704)	1676	3
Byrd, William (1683/1704)	1687	4
Bryd, William (1683/1704)	1696	100
Carter, John (1658/1689)	1665	21
Cheesman, John (1652)	1635	2
Cocke, William (1713/1720)	1698	6
Cole, William (1675/1692)	1691	1
Duke, Henry (1702/1713)	1694	2
Epes, Francis (1637/1652)	1638	5
Higginson, Humphrey (1642/1656)	1654	13
Hill, Edward, Jr. (1691/1700)	1695	3
Jenings, Edmund (1691/1726)	1689	23
Johnson, Richard (1695/1699)	1695	18
Kemp, Richard (1634/1640)	1636	2
Lee, Richard, I (1651/1664)	1660	80
Ludlow, George (1642/1655)	1651	7
Ludwell, Thomas (1661/1678)	1663	2
Menefie, George (1635/1644)	1639	15
Pate, John (1671/1672)	1669	13
Perry, Henry (1655/1661)	1642	12
Place, Rowland (1675/1678)	1676	14
Purefoy, Thomas (1632/1637)	1655	4
Reade, George (1658/1671)	1651	1
Robinson, Christopher (1692)	1678	2
Scarborough, Charles (1696/1702)	1652	3
Scarborough, Charles (1696/1702)	1674	6
Smith, John (1704/1720)	1695	5
Smith, Robert (1663/1683)	1667	2
Smith, Robert (1663/1683)	1684	6
Spencer, Nicholas (1672/1689)	1668	2
Thoroughood, Adam (1637/1638)	1637	3
Townsend, Richard (1637/1650)	1639	3

Table 2. Continued

Landowner (First Year/Last Year in Council of State)	Year Patent Issued	No. of Blacks per Patent
Warner, Augustine (1660/1671)	1652	4
Wormeley, Ralph (1650/1651)	1649	17
Wormeley, Ralph (1675/1701)	1695	100

Sources: CP, I–III; Cynthia Miller Leonard, *The General Assembly of Virginia, July 30, 1619–January 11, 1978: A Bicentennial Register of Members* (Richmond, Va., 1978).

Table 3. Distribution of Black Headright Patents: House of Burgesses

Landowners (First Year in House of Burgesses/First in Family to Hold Seat [y = yes, n = no])	Year Patent Issued	No. of Blacks per Patent
Applewaite, Henry (1684/y)	1683	4
Armistead, Anthony (1693/y)	1695	3
Armistead, John (1680/y)	1678	5
Ballard, Thomas (1666/y)	1666	1
Beverley, Robert, II (1699/y)	1692	3
Blake, John (1655/y)	1674	20
Blake, John (1655/y)	1664	7
Bland, Richard (1693/y)	1687	2
Bolling, Robert (1688/y)	1690	1
Bridger, Joseph (1657/y)	1666	17
Buckner, John (1682/y)	1691	23
Butt, Thomas (1700/y)	1697	9
Byrd, William (1677/y)	1676	3
Byrd, William (1677/y)	1687	4
Byrd, William (1677/y)	1696	100
Cary, William (1693/n)	1693	1
Clements, Francis (1693/—)	1689	6
Cocke, James (1697/—)	1697	0
Corbin, Gaw (1698/y)	1697	7
Covington, Richard (1703/y)	1698	10
Custis, John (1677/y)	1653	1
Duke, Henry (1692/y)	1694	2
Edwards, William (1693/—)	1691	7
Edwards, William (1693/—)	1678	1
Edwards, William (1693/—)	1688	1

Table 3. Continued

Landowners (First Year in House of Burgesses/First in Family to Hold Seat [y = yes, n = no])	Year Patent Issued	No. of Blacks per Patent
Field, Peter (1688/—)	1687	4
Field, Peter (1688/—)	1690	4
Giles, John (1696/y)	1698	2
Gray, Francis (1666/y)	1654	1
Gregory, Richard (1698/y)	1691	1
Hamelyn, Stephen (1654/y)	1638	1
Harmanson, Thomas (1688/y)	1667	2
Harris, John (1703/y)	1695	10
Harris, John (1703/y)	1676	4
Harris, John (1703/y)	1682	4
Harrison, Benjamin (1677/y)	1643	1
Hill, Edward (1679/—)	1695	3
Jenifer, Daniel (1684/y)	1680	1
Jenifer, Daniel (1684/y)	1675	2
Jenifer, Daniel (1684/y)	1668	6
Kendall, William (1657/y)	1666	2
Kendall, William, II (1688/n)	1674	4
Knight, Peter (1684/y)	1653	3
Lawson, Anthony (1680/y)	1673	2
Lewis, William (1692/y)	1653	2
Littlepage, Richard (1686/n)	1684	2
Mason, Lemuel (1654/y)	1693	3
Mason, Thomas (1697/n)	1697	2
Milner, Thomas (1698/y)	1696	14
Morris, George (1680/y)	1663	19
Pleasants, John (1693/y)	1690	1
Porter, John (1662/y)	1673	5
Randolph, William (1684/n)	1695	25
Read, Robert (1688/—)	1688	3
Richardson, John (1692/n)	1695	3
Robins, John (1692/y)	1672	7
Robinson, Christopher (1682/y)	1678	2
Sandford, Jon (1692/y)	1680	4
Savage, John (1665/n)	1664	25
Scarborough, Charles (1680/n)	1674	3
Scarborough, Charles (1680/n)	1674	6
Smith, John (1686/n)	1674	5
Smith, John (1686/n)	1695	5

Table 3. Continued

Landowners (First Year in House of Burgesses/First in Family to Hold Seat [y = yes, n = no])	Year Patent Issued	No. of Blacks per Patent
Smith, Lawrence (1688/n)	1673	2
Soane, William (1696/y)	1695	3
Spencer, Nicholas (1666/n)	1668	2
Stith, John (1693/y)	1692	10
Story, Joshua (1692/y)	1691	6
Taylor, James (1702/y)	1687	1
Taylor, James (1700/y)	1695	1
Thacker, Edward (1700/y)	1695	4
Thacker, Edward (1700/y)	1697	38
Thoroughgood, Adam (1664/y)	1637	3
Washbourne, John (1693/n)	1696	6
Waters, William (1680/n)	1664	1
Waters, William (1693/n)	1696	4
Weir, John (1658/n)	1664	14
West, John (1682/n)	1682	53
Whittington, William (1680/y)	1672	1
Williamson, Robert (1662/y)	1666	4
Wilson, James (1698/y)	1688	8
Wright, John (1696/y)	1678	1
Wright, John (1696/y)	1694	12
Yeo, Leonard (1644/ —)	1637	2

Sources: CP, I–III; Martin H. Quitt, *Virginia House of Burgesses, 1660–1706: The Social, Educational, and Economic Bases of Political Power* (New York, 1989), 304–364; Cynthia Miller Leonard, *The General Assembly of Virginia, July 30, 1619–January 11, 1978: A Bicentennial Register of Members* (Richmond, Va., 1978).

St. Peter's Parish

The vestry of Blissland Parish in 1678 created a new parish from its north-western sector that was called St. Peter's, a decision confirmed the following year by the General Court. St. Peter's was bounded on the northeast by the divide between the Pamunkey and the Mattaponi Rivers, on the southeast by John's, or Jack's, Creek (north of the Pamunkey), and on the southwest by the divide between the Pamunkey and the Chickahominy Rivers. No boundary lines were drawn on the northwestern frontier. In 1691 and again in 1704, St. Peter's lost a considerable amount of its territory. By an act establishing King and Queen County in 1691, the General Assembly cut off all of St. Peter's Parish lying northeast of the Pamunkey River and annexed it to St. John's Parish. In 1704, St. Peter's Parish was again divided. This time its upper, or northwestern, boundary was established as St. Paul's Parish. The Matedequin Creek became the dividing line between the two parishes, finally establishing a northwestern boundary. During the next two decades, the territorial jurisdiction of St. Peter's Parish remained the same. The Reverend Henry Collings reported to the bishop of London in 1724 that the parish was twenty miles long and contained 204 families.[1]

The transition of St. Peter's Parish from a frontier settlement to a well-established producer of the highly coveted sweet-scented tobacco was closely tied to the development of slavery. The planters of St. Peter's Parish invested heavily in enslaved blacks during the last quarter of the seventeenth century and the early decades of the eighteenth century. Virginia's

---

1. C. G. Chamberlayne, ed., *The Vestry Book and Register of St. Peter's Parish, New Kent and James City Counties, Virginia, 1684–1786* (Richmond, Va., 1937), xxxiii–xxxiv; Henry Collings to the bishop of London, June 1, 1724, FPP/15, 10, VCRP.

regional development hints at the time when the majority of the enslaved were imported into St. Peter's. Before 1713, African immigration was heaviest in the rich, sweet-scented tobacco Peninsula between the York and the James Rivers. The appearance of slave names in the parish register before 1698 suggests that blacks were laboring in the area before the lifting of the Royal African Company's exclusive charter. After that, the black population increased dramatically. One can glean St. Peter's increasing population density by dividing the aggregate number of St. Peter's tithables into the parish's total number of square miles. Tithables included white males and black persons more than sixteen years of age. From 1685 to 1699, the number of tithables per square mile almost doubled, from 1.78 to 3.34. During the first five years of the eighteenth century, the number of tithables in St. Peter's Parish increased more than 50 percent over the 1685 to 1699 average, suggesting an increase in slave importation with the opening of the slave trade. St. Paul's Parish was formed in 1704 from the northwestern sector of St. Peter's Parish "by reason of the largeness and extent of the said parish."[2] Although the number of tithables decreased by almost one-half after the partition, the reduction in total square miles was greater. On November 1, 1704, the vestry counted 502 tithables within the boundaries of St. Peter's Parish, 10.2 tithables per square mile. Over the next fifteen years, the number of tithables per square mile increased to 12.

During the 1720s and 1730s, the population steadily became denser. In 1725, the General Assembly awarded St. Peter's Parish additional acreage, which increased at once its tithables from 692 to 903, or slightly more than 30 percent. The tithables to land ratio remained steady, as the proportion of land added to St. Peter's Parish was also approximately 30 percent. During the 1720s, nearly fourteen tithables could be found for every square mile. By the 1730s, the number of tithables per square mile increased to 15.2—more than eight times the density in the late seventeenth century.

The high rate of productivity in the York River region led to the rapid settlement of that area. One means of determining how long St. Peter's remained a frontier community is to measure the spread of settlement and the formation of new counties in Virginia. If one examines the existing settlements at the turn of the century, New Kent County was indeed a frontier society, large and thinly settled, especially its northwestern sec-

2. "An Act for Dividing St. Peter's Parish in New Kent County," in Chamberlayne, ed., *Vestry Book and Register*, 626.

tor, St. Peter's Parish. To bolster the defense of the frontier against Indian attack, an act of 1705 provided that new counties should be larger to increase the size of the militia, thus rendering the expense and term of service less burdensome to each settler. Before a new county was established, the "upper," or new, division contained eight hundred tithables, a decent church, courthouse, and jail. In 1720, Hanover County was formed on the northwestern border of St. Peter's Parish, closing the frontier. Hugh Jones could easily have had St. Peter's Parish in mind in 1724 when he stated, "Most land has been long since taken up and seated except it be high up in the country."[3]

A crude estimate of the black population of St. Peter's Parish from extant birth and burial registers and tithable lists suggests that 1725 completed the influx of enslaved blacks shipped directly from Africa to St. Peter's. The black population in the parish increased naturally during the period of the expansion of the slave trade. Extant death registers from 1715 to 1739 indicate two male deaths for every female death, suggesting a sexual imbalance similar to that of the Virginia slave trade itself. Unfortunately, there are no extant death statistics in St. Peter's Parish before 1715, and black mortality rates of ten to twenty per one thousand seem too low, suggesting that deaths were underrepresented. A more accurate estimate of the mortality rate for Chesapeake blacks would be twenty to thirty per one thousand.[4]

St. Peter's enslaved population probably experienced an initial period of decline before 1715. Nonetheless, the birthrate from 1714 to 1724 was about 2.9 percent per annum. With the crude birth rate of blacks rising and its related effect of creating a more balanced population, the number of children in the slave community increased dramatically. By the 1720s, American-born blacks must have formed a significant proportion of St. Peter's population, especially in light of Hugh Jones's observation that Virginia's blacks "are very prolifick among themselves." Creolization and

3. Hugh Jones, *The Present State of Virginia: From Whence Is Inferred a Short View of Maryland and North Carolina* (1724), ed. Richard L. Morton (Chapel Hill, N.C., 1956), 92; Morgan P. Robinson, "Virginia Counties: Those Resulting from Virginia Legislation," *Bulletin of the Virginia State Library,* IX (Richmond, Va., 1916), 200.

4. Allan Kulikoff, "A 'Prolifick' People: Black Population Growth in the Chesapeake Colonies, 1700–1790," *Southern Studies,* XVI (1977), 396–403, 406–412; Russell R. Menard, "The Maryland Slave Population, 1658 to 1730: A Demographic Profile of Blacks in Four Counties," *WMQ,* 3d Ser., XXXII (1975), 32–34, 48; Edmund S. Morgan, *American Slavery, American Freedom: The Ordeal of Colonial Virginia* (New York, 1975), 420–423.

the jurisdictional development discussed above suggest that St. Peter's Parish had become a settled community by 1725.[5]

Table 4. Black Population Growth and Baptism
in St. Peter's Parish, 1685–1739

Year	Total Tithes	Black Tithes	Black Population	Black Births	Black Baptisms
1685	548	—	—	10	—
1686	542	—	—	5	—
1687	595	—	—	6	—
1688	—	—	—	3	—
1689	603	—	—	5	—
1690	609	—	—	1	—
1691	531	—	—	2	—
1692	507	—	—	4	—
1693	539	—	—	1	—
1694	534	—	—	4	—
1695	538	—	—	3	—
1696	541	—	—	1	—
1697	575	—	—	6	—
1698	618	—	—	4	—
1699	676	—	—	6	—
1700	752	—	333	15	2
1701	—	—	360	2	—
1702	895	—	387	2	—
1703	936	—	415	7	—
1704	947	—	435	9	—
1705	502	—	272	14	—
1706	533	—	299	10	—
1707	580	—	306	6	—
1708	551	—	329	9	4
1709	597	—	374	17	—
1710	555	—	394	7	1
1711	573	—	369	15	2
1712	576	—	386	9	—

5. Jones, *Present State of Virginia,* ed. Morton, 195; Chamberlayne, ed., *Vestry Book and Register;* Evarts B. Greene and Virginia D. Harrington, eds., *American Population before the Federal Census of 1790* (New York, 1932); Menard, "The Maryland Slave Population," *WMQ,* 3d Ser., XXXII (1975), 29–54; Morgan, *American Slavery, American Freedom,* 420–423; Kulikoff, "A 'Prolifick' People," *So. Studies,* XVI (1977), 391–428.

Table 4. Continued

Year	Total Tithes	Black Tithes	Black Population	Black Births	Black Baptisms
1713	587	—	414	15	—
1714	603	272	423	8	—
1715	584	284	442	14	—
1716	—	302	470	14	—
1717	605	317	493	10	—
1718	606	337	524	17	—
1719	643	360	560	18	—
1720	593	335	521	7	—
1721	655	356	554	25	4
1722	670	373	580	19	1
1723	668	374	582	6	—
1724	692	385	599	21	3
1725	902	414	644	31	3
1726	899	432	672	26	—
1727	899	470	731	33	3
1728	971	504	784	35	17
1729	971	549	854	35	11
1730	973	557	877	21	—
1731	997	559	902	6	1
1732	949	566	927	1	—
1733	967	575	951	7	5
1734	938	570	975	41	4
1735	956	578	989	24	7
1736	924	584	1,022	52	20
1737	986	584	1,038	42	20
1738	1,004	593	1,063	25	13
1739	1,024	601	1,083	29	21

Source: C. G. Chamberlayne, ed., *The Vestry Book and Register of St. Peter's Parish, New Kent and James City Counties, Virginia, 1684–1786* (Richmond, Va., 1937).

Table 5. Slave Baptisms in St. Peter's Parish, 1700–1739

Name of Baptized	Names of Owners	Year of Birth	Year of Baptism
Mary	Lightfoot, Col. John	—	1700
Agree	Lightfoot, Col. John	—	1700
Mary	Field, Alice	—	1708
Phillis	Field, Alice	—	1708
Anne	Field, Alice	—	1708
Musea-doras	Field, Alice	—	1708
John	Clopton, William	—	1710
Hannah	Lightfoot, Mary	1711	1711
Richard	Littlepage, Richard	—	1711
Dorthy	Bray, Thomas	—	1721
James	Bray, Thomas	—	1721
Tom	Lightfoot, Sherwood	—	1721
Ann	Littlepage, Frances	—	1721
Doll	Otey, John	—	1722
Joseph	Chamberlayne, William	—	1724
Mary	Chamberlayne, William	—	1724
Mary	Foster, Joseph	—	1724
Elizabeth	Littlepage, Frances	—	1725
Susanna	Poindexter, George	—	1725
Jones	Poindexter, George	1725	1725
Julius	Chamberlayne, William	—	1727
Jesse	Chamberlayne, William	1727	1727
Judith	Littlepage, Frances	1727	1727
Jane	Atkinson, William	—	1728
Susanna	Atkinson, William	—	1728
Nelly	Brown, William	—	1728
Mary	Brown, William	—	1728
Sarah	Brown, William	—	1728
Charles	Custis, John	—	1728
Guy	Custis, John	—	1728
Richard	Custis, John	—	1728
Matthew	Custis, John	—	1728
Sarah	Custis, John	—	1728
William	Littlepage, Frances	—	1728
John	Poindexter, Jacob	—	1728
Rebecca	Poindexter, Jacob	—	1728
Mars	Waddill, Joseph	—	1728
Jane	Waddill, Joseph	—	1728

Table 5. Continued

Name of Baptized	Names of Owners	Year of Birth	Year of Baptism
Mary	Winfree, Charles	—	1728
Joseph	Winfree, Charles	—	1728
James	Adams, Ebenezer	—	1729
Edward	Brown, William	—	1729
Sarah	Chamberlayne, William	—	1729
Kitt	Clopton, Walter and Mary	1729	1729
William	Hardyman, Judith	—	1729
James	Hilliard, Thomas	—	1729
Joseph	Hopkins, Sarah	—	1729
Dorothy	Nance, James	—	1729
Sarah	Sims, Frances	—	1729
Napier	Sims, James	—	1729
Rebecca	Webb, George	—	1729
Henry	Hopkins, Sarah	1731	1731
Jane	Chamberlayne, William	1733	1733
Temperance	Lightfoot, John	—	1733
Frances	Marsten, Benjamin	—	1733
Sarah	Moss, Alexander	—	1733
Judith	Poindexter, George	—	1733
Julius	Foster, Joseph	1734	1734
Moll	Foster, Joseph	1734	1734
Charles	Hopkins, Sarah	1734	1734
Frank	Poindexter, George	1734	1734
Mary Holt	[Free Black]	1734	1735
Esther	Foster, Joseph	1735	1735
Elizabeth	Jones, Lane	1735	1735
Tom	Lightfoot, Mrs.	1734	1735
William	Massie, William	1735	1735
Jacob	Moore, Sarah	1735	1735
Sarah	Pinchback, Thomas	1735	1735
George	Adams, Tabitha	1736	1736
Susanna	Brown, William	—	1736
Jeremy	Brown, William	1736	1736
Hannah	Brown, William	1736	1736
William	Butts, Thomas	1736	1736
Matthew	Butts, Thomas	1736	1736
Thomas	Careless, John	1736	1736
Agnes	Chamberlayne, William	1736	1736

Table 5. Continued

Name of Baptized	Names of Owners	Year of Birth	Year of Baptism
Squire	Custis, John	1736	1736
Bella	Custis, John	1736	1736
Moses	Custis, John	1736	1736
Grace	Custis, John	1736	1736
James	Lacy, Henry and Angelica	—	1736
Thomas	Lacy, Henry and Angelica	1736	1736
Matt	Lightfoot, John	1735	1736
Julius	Massie, William	1736	1736
Daniel	Nance, James	1736	1736
William	Page, Madam	—	1736
Peter	Poindexter, George	1735	1736
John	Poindexter, George	1736	1736
Robert	Bayley, Ann	1734	1737
Sarah	Bolton, Charles	1737	1737
James	Chamberlayne, Elizabeth	1736	1737
Dinah	Custis, John	1737	1737
Philip	Custis, John	1737	1737
Lucy	Custis, John	1737	1737
Michael	Custis, John	1737	1737
Matthew	Foster, Joseph	1737	1737
George	Foster, Joseph	1737	1737
Peter	Lightfoot, Sherwood	1737	1737
Richard	Littlepage, Richard	1737	1737
Cloe	Littlepage, Richard	1737	1737
Esther	Littlepage, Richard	1737	1737
Jack	Meux, Richard	1736	1737
Matthew	Moore, Sarah	1737	1737
Phebe	Mossom, David	1736	1737
Thomas	Pinchback, Thomas	1737	1737
Davy	Vaidem, Jaco	1737	1737
Watlington	Whitlock, John	1737	1737
Doll	Winfree, Charles	1736	1737
George Holt	[Free Black]	1737	1737
Elizabeth	Arnott, Thomas	—	1738
George	Atkinson, William	1737	1738
Isham	Brown, William	—	1738
Steven	Brown, William	1738	1738
Lucy	Brown, William	1738	1738

Table 5. Continued

Name of Baptized	Names of Owners	Year of Birth	Year of Baptism
Laney	Custis, John	1738	1738
Moses	Farell, Elizabeth	—	1738
Rachel	Farell, Elizabeth	1738	1738
Abraham	Meredith, Alice	1737	1738
Benjamin	Poindexter, George	1738	1738
Elizabeth	Turner, Mary	1738	1738
Spy	Winfree, Charles	1738	1738
Thomas	Adams, Tabitha	1738	1739
Edward	Adams, Tabitha	1738	1739
Chloe	Adams, Tabitha	1739	1739
Elizabeth	Bailey, Ann	1739	1739
Richard	Clopton, Robert	1739	1739
Toney	Custis, John	1739	1739
Nisom	Custis, John	1739	1739
Joseph	Custis, John	1739	1739
Elizabeth	Custis, John	1739	1739
Frank	Darricott, John	1739	1739
Prudence	Foster, Joseph	1739	1739
Rebecca	Gray, William	1739	1739
Randal	Hilliard, Thomas	1737	1739
George	Meux, Richard	1739	1739
Esther	Mossom, David	1739	1739
Lucy	Ussory, John	1739	1739
Frances	Vaidem, Jacob	1739	1739
Matthew	Whitlock, John	1739	1739
William	Winch, William	1739	1739
Judith	Winfree, Charles	1738	1739
Richard	Winfree, Charles	1739	1739

Source: C. G. Chamberlayne, ed., *The Vestry Book and Register of St. Peter's Parish, New Kent and James City Counties, Virginia, 1684–1786* (Richmond, Va., 1937).

Index